volume
2

ASADORA!

NAOKI URASAWA

Chapter 9 ◎ That Thing

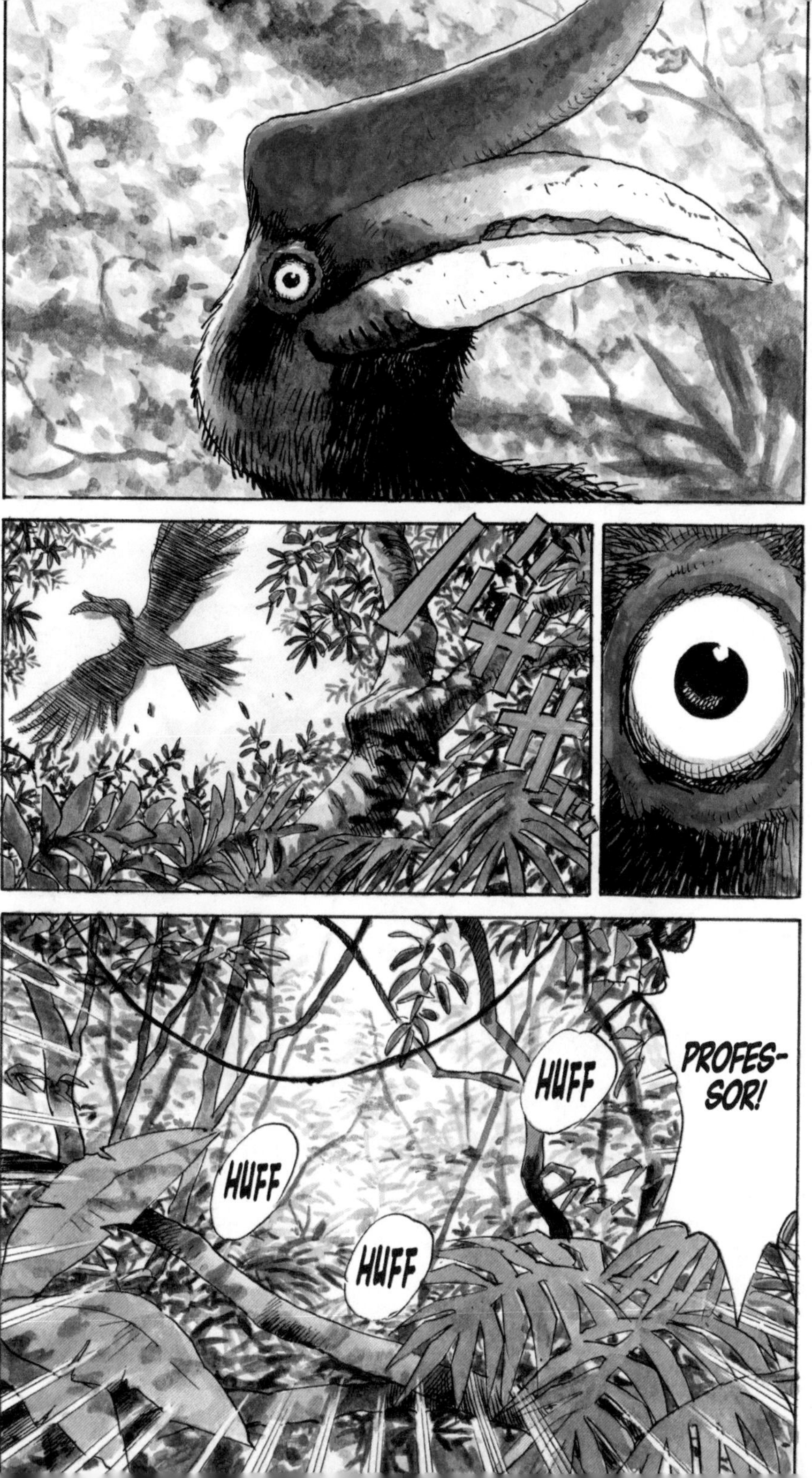
PROFES-
SOR!
HUFF
HUFF
HUFF

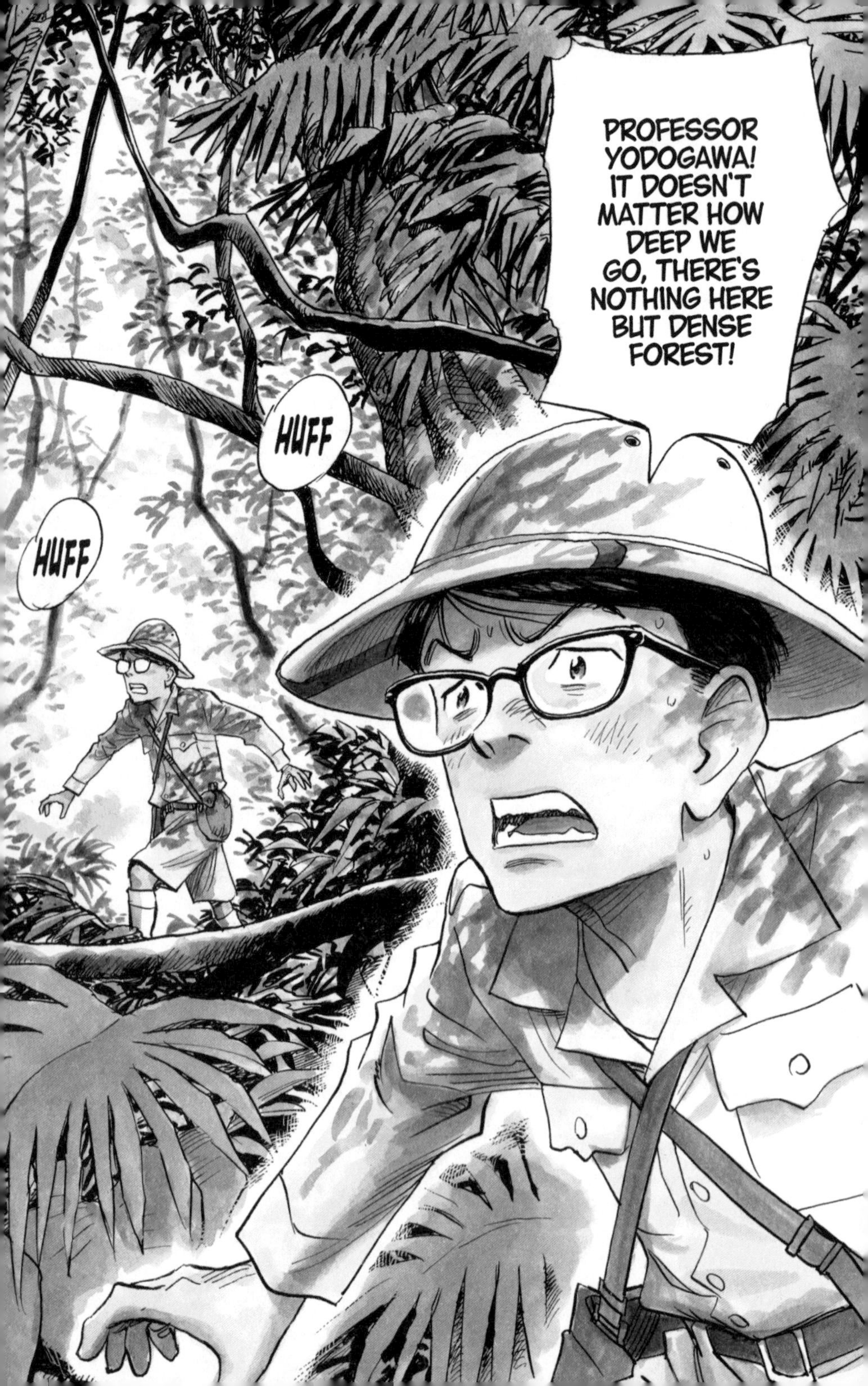
PROFESSOR YODOGAWA! IT DOESN'T MATTER HOW DEEP WE GO, THERE'S NOTHING HERE BUT DENSE FOREST!
HUFF
HUFF

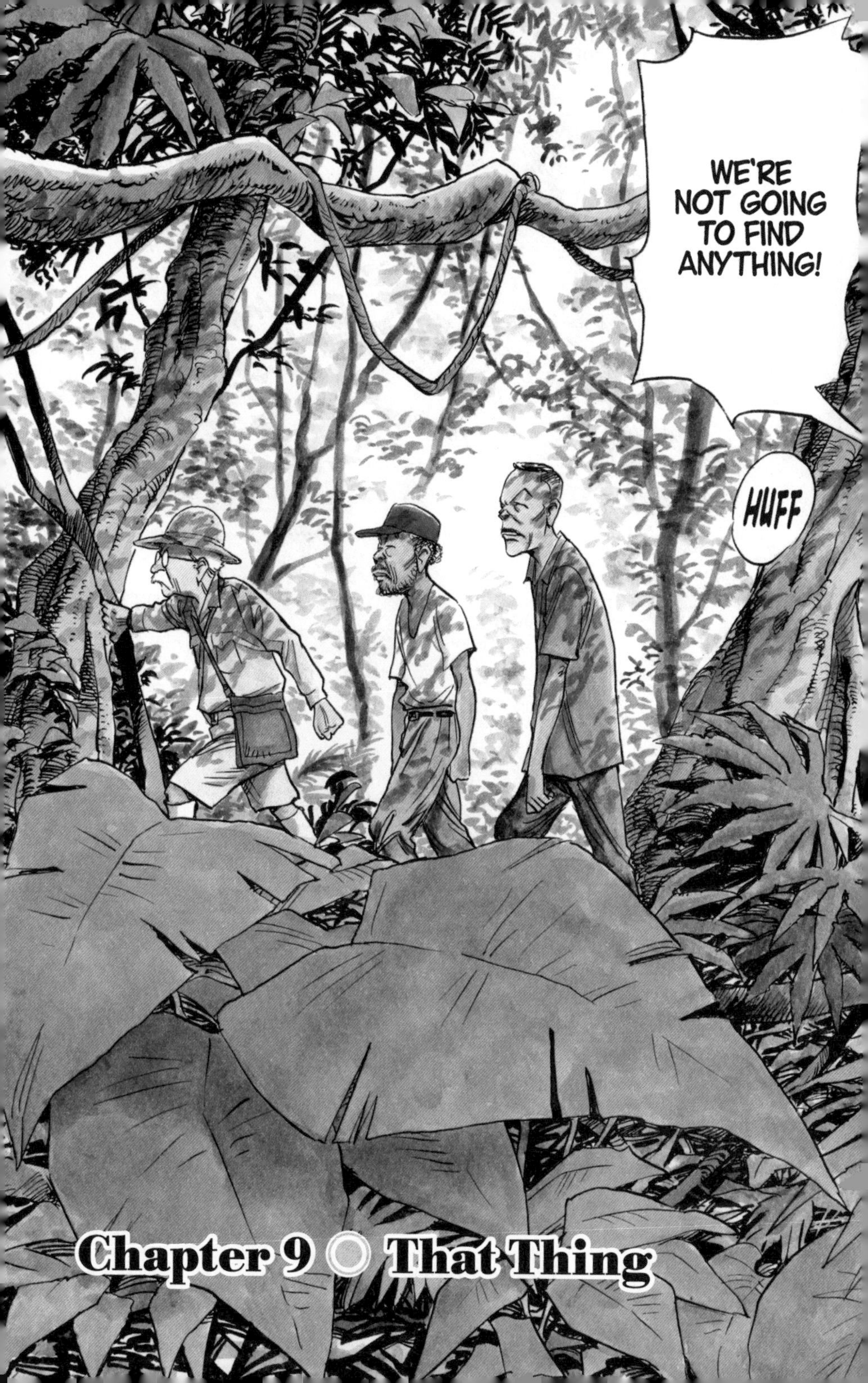
WE'RE NOT GOING TO FIND ANYTHING!
HUFF
Chapter 9 That Thing

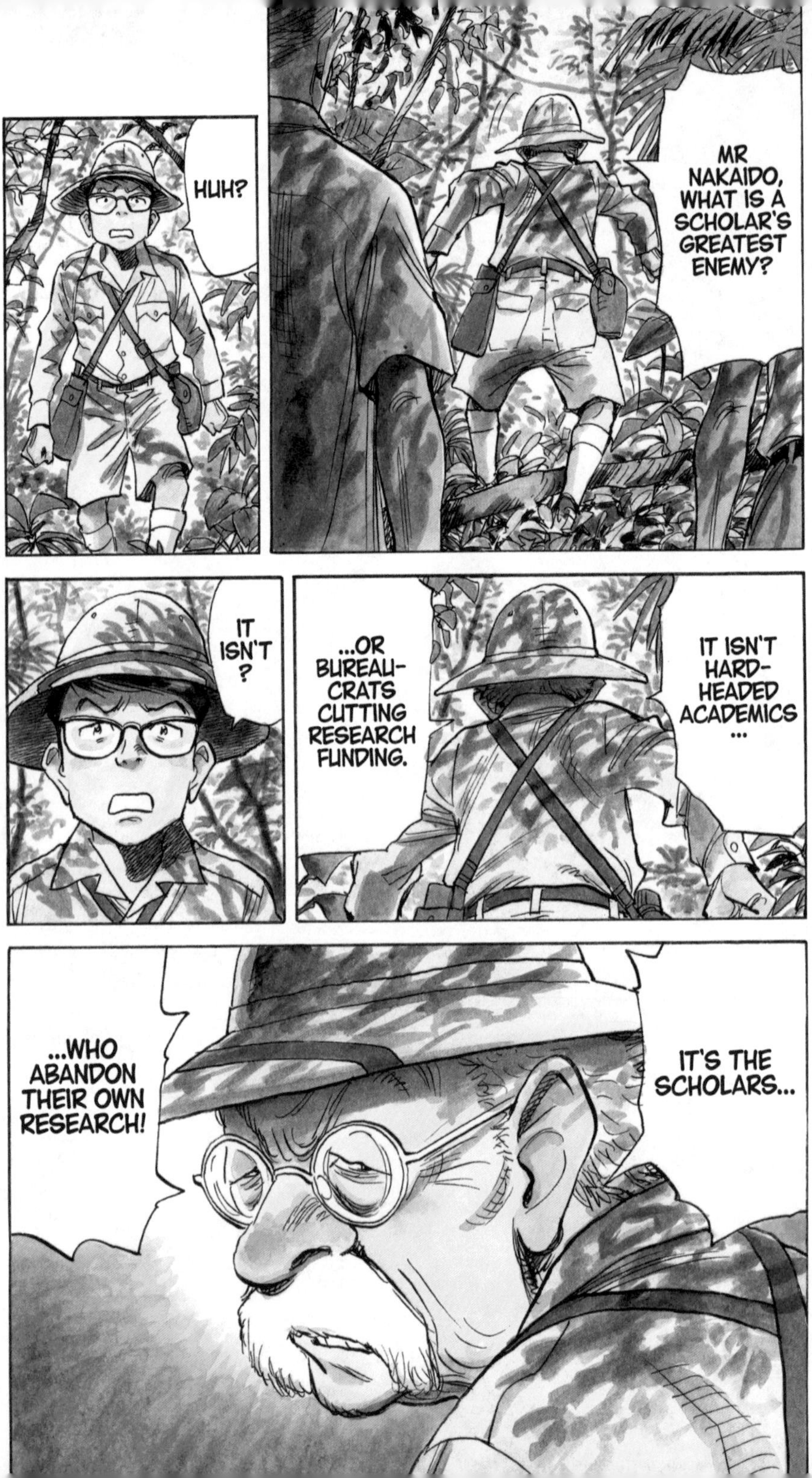
MR NAKAIDO, WHAT IS A SCHOLAR'S GREATEST ENEMY?
HUH?
IT ISN'T HARD-HEADED ACADEMICS ...
...OR BUREAU-CRATS CUTTING RESEARCH FUNDING.
IT ISN'T ?
IT'S THE SCHOLARS...
...WHO ABANDON THEIR OWN RESEARCH!

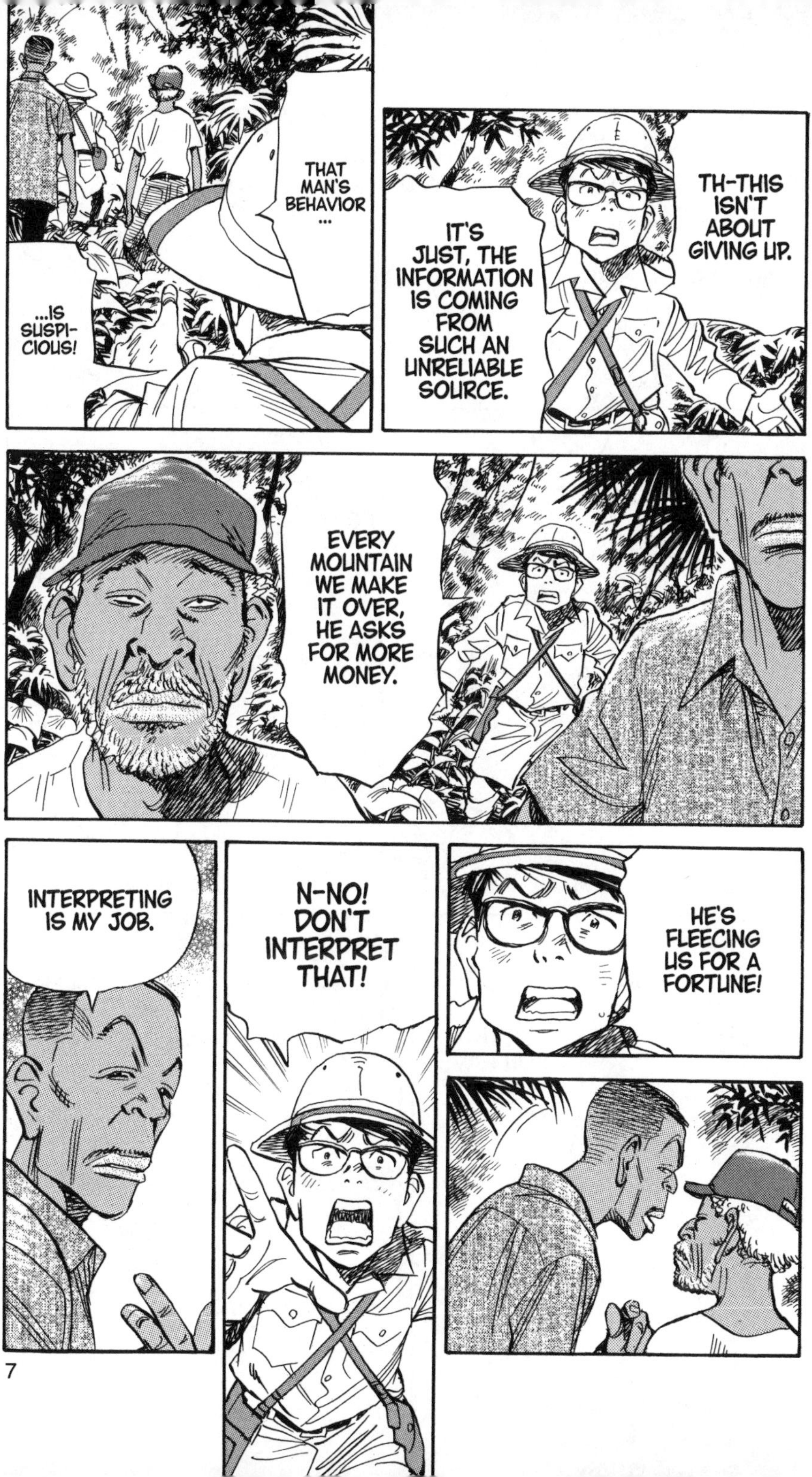
TH-THIS ISN'T ABOUT GIVING UP.
IT'S JUST, THE INFORMATION IS COMING FROM SUCH AN UNRELIABLE SOURCE.
THAT MAN'S BEHAVIOR ...
...IS SUSPICIOUS!
EVERY MOUNTAIN WE MAKE IT OVER, HE ASKS FOR MORE MONEY.
HE'S FLEECING US FOR A FORTUNE!
N-NO! DON'T INTERPRET THAT!
INTERPRETING IS MY JOB.

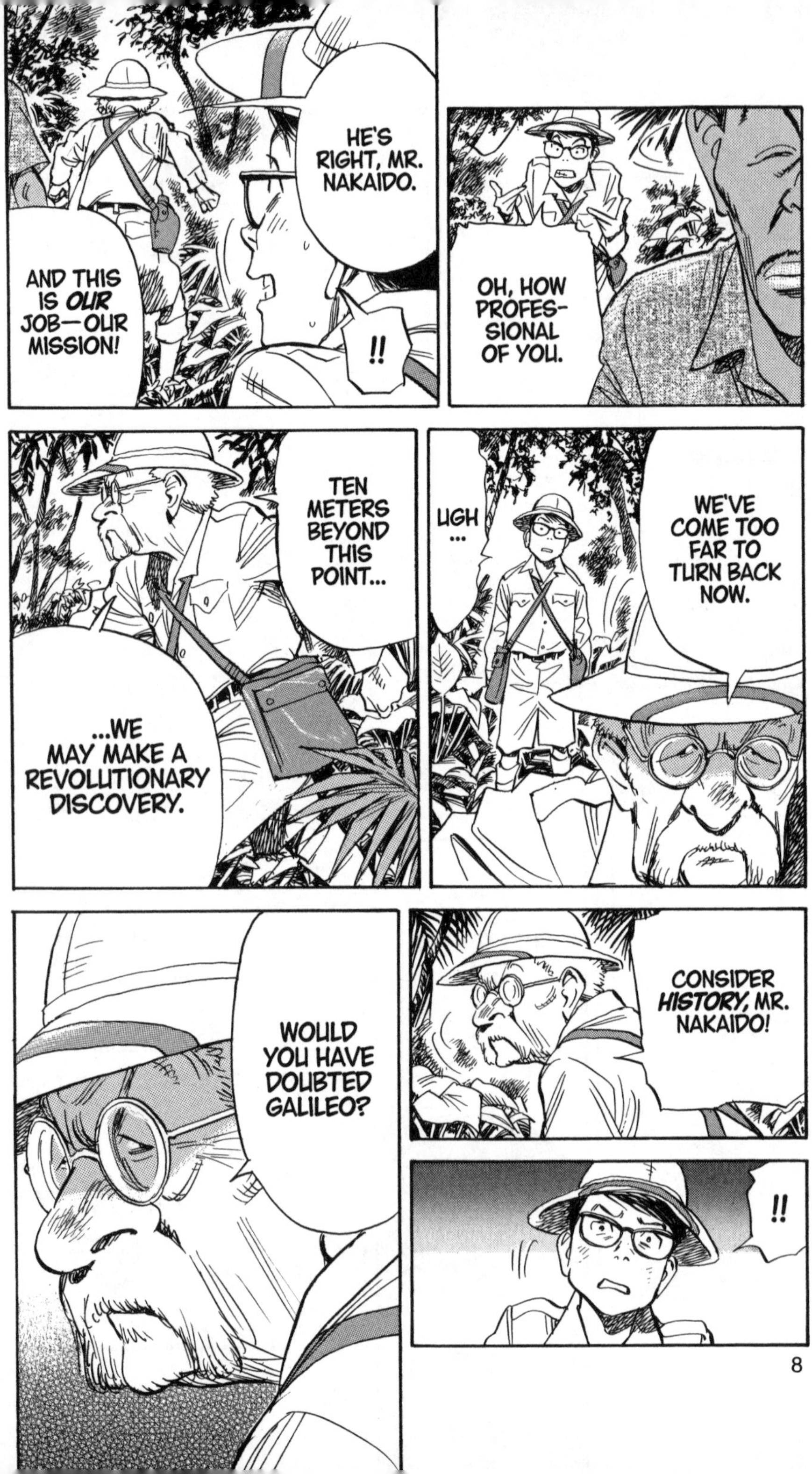
OH, HOW PROFESSIONAL OF YOU.
HE'S RIGHT, MR. NAKAIDO.
!!
AND THIS IS *OUR* JOB—OUR MISSION!
WE'VE COME TOO FAR TO TURN BACK NOW.
UGH ...
TEN METERS BEYOND THIS POINT...
...WE MAY MAKE A REVOLUTIONARY DISCOVERY.
CONSIDER *HISTORY,* MR. NAKAIDO!
!!
WOULD YOU HAVE DOUBTED GALILEO?

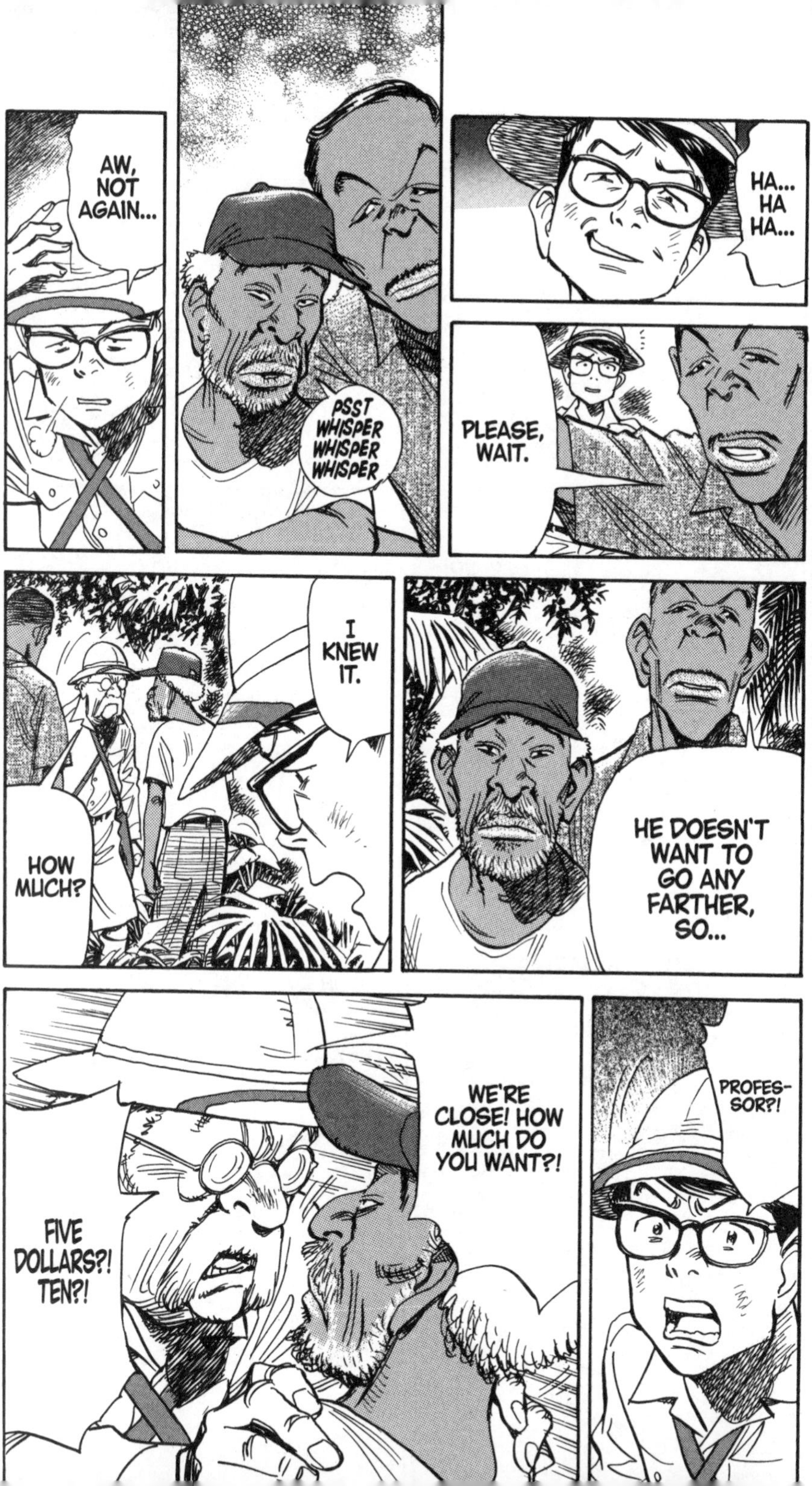
HA... HA HA...
PLEASE, WAIT.
PSST WHISPER WHISPER WHISPER
AW, NOT AGAIN...
HE DOESN'T WANT TO GO ANY FARTHER, SO...
I KNEW IT.
HOW MUCH?
PROFESSOR?!
WE'RE CLOSE! HOW MUCH DO YOU WANT?!
FIVE DOLLARS?! TEN?!

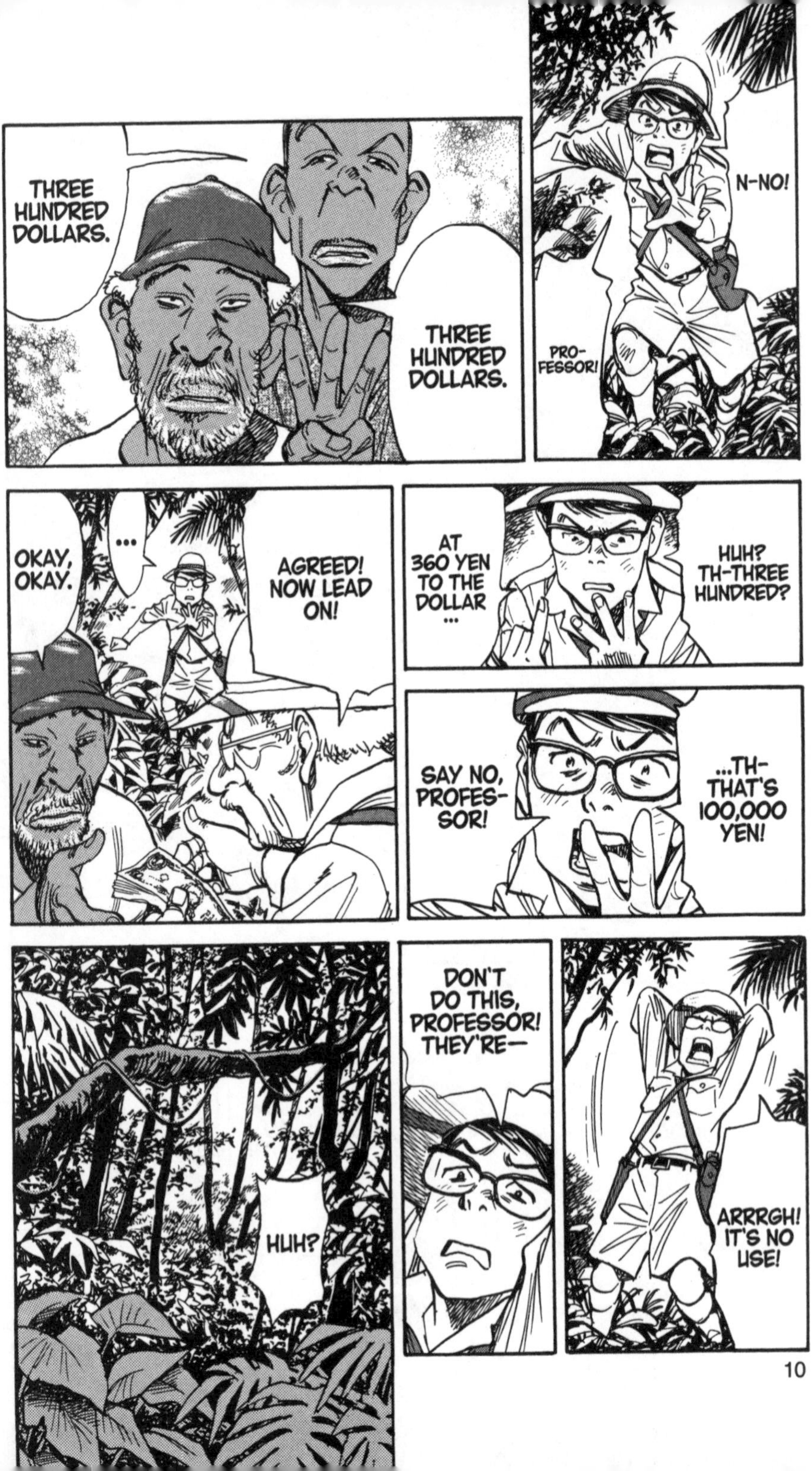
N-NO!
PRO-FESSOR!
THREE HUNDRED DOLLARS.
THREE HUNDRED DOLLARS.
HUH? TH-THREE HUNDRED?
AT 360 YEN TO THE DOLLAR ...
...TH-THAT'S 100,000 YEN!
SAY NO, PROFES-SOR!
AGREED! NOW LEAD ON!
...
OKAY, OKAY.
ARRRGH! IT'S NO USE!
DON'T DO THIS, PROFESSOR! THEY'RE—
HUH?

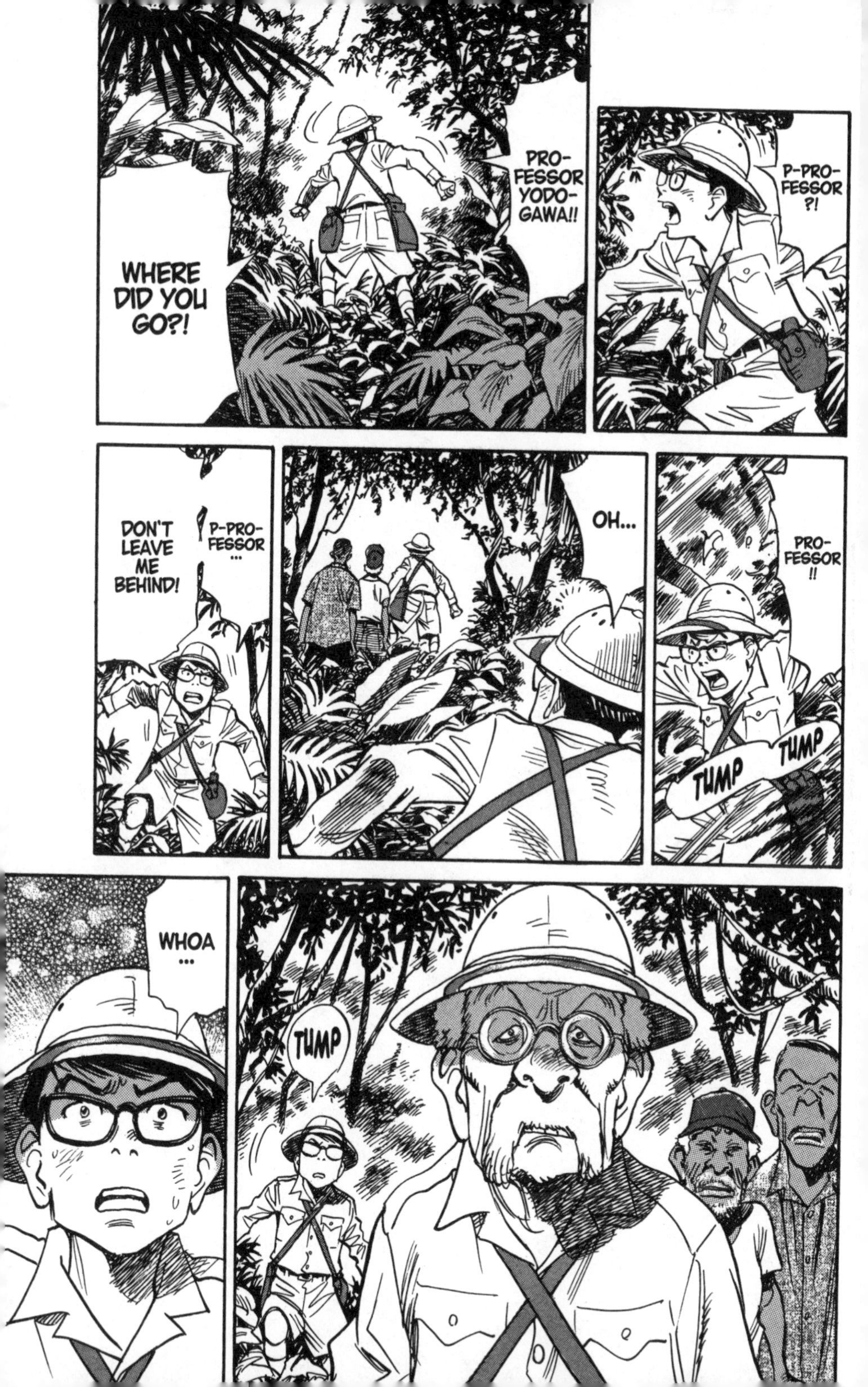
P-PRO-FESSOR ?!
PRO-FESSOR YODO-GAWA!!
WHERE DID YOU GO?!
PRO-FESSOR !!
TUMP TUMP
OH...
P-PRO-FESSOR ...
DON'T LEAVE ME BEHIND!
TUMP
WHOA ...

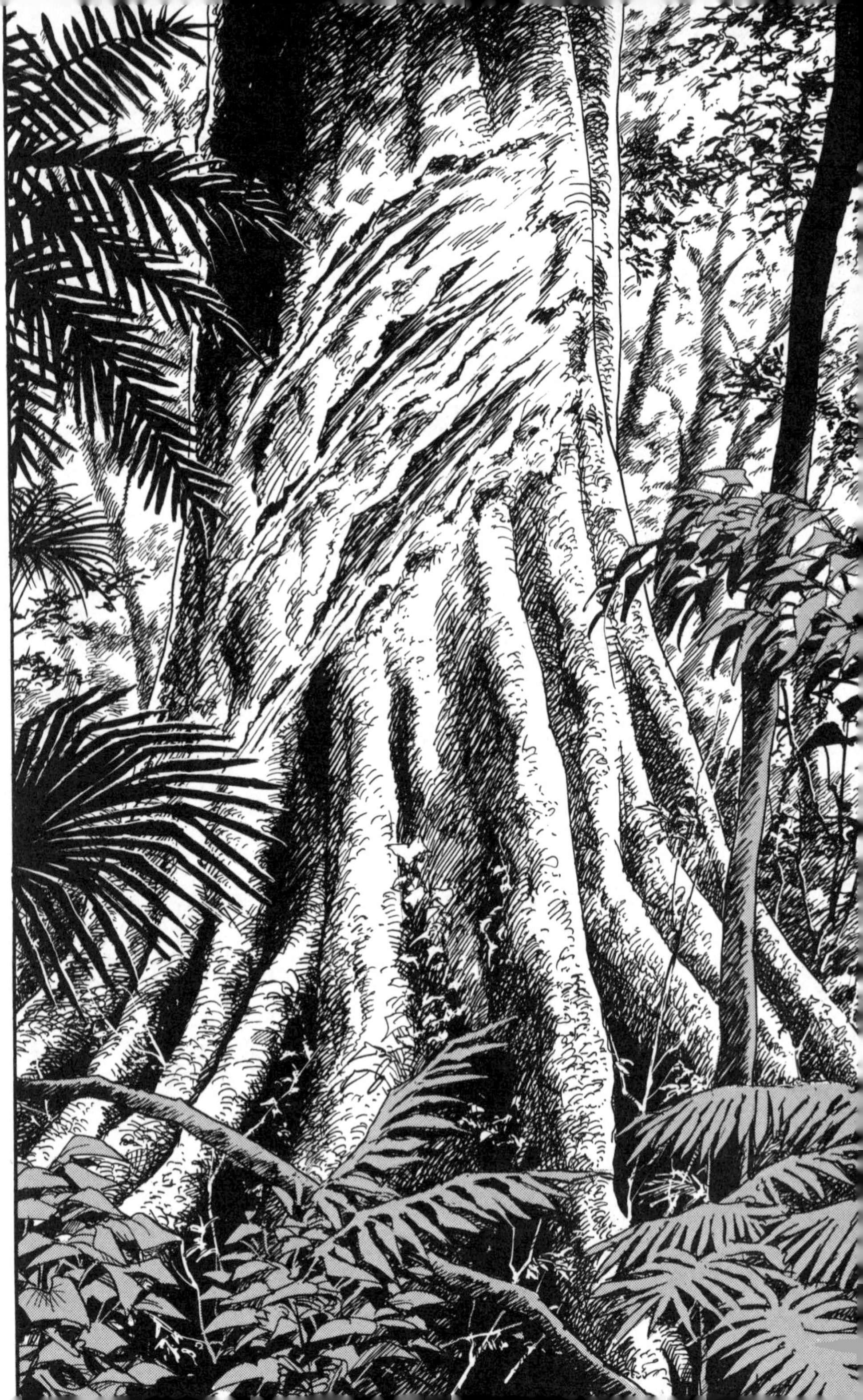

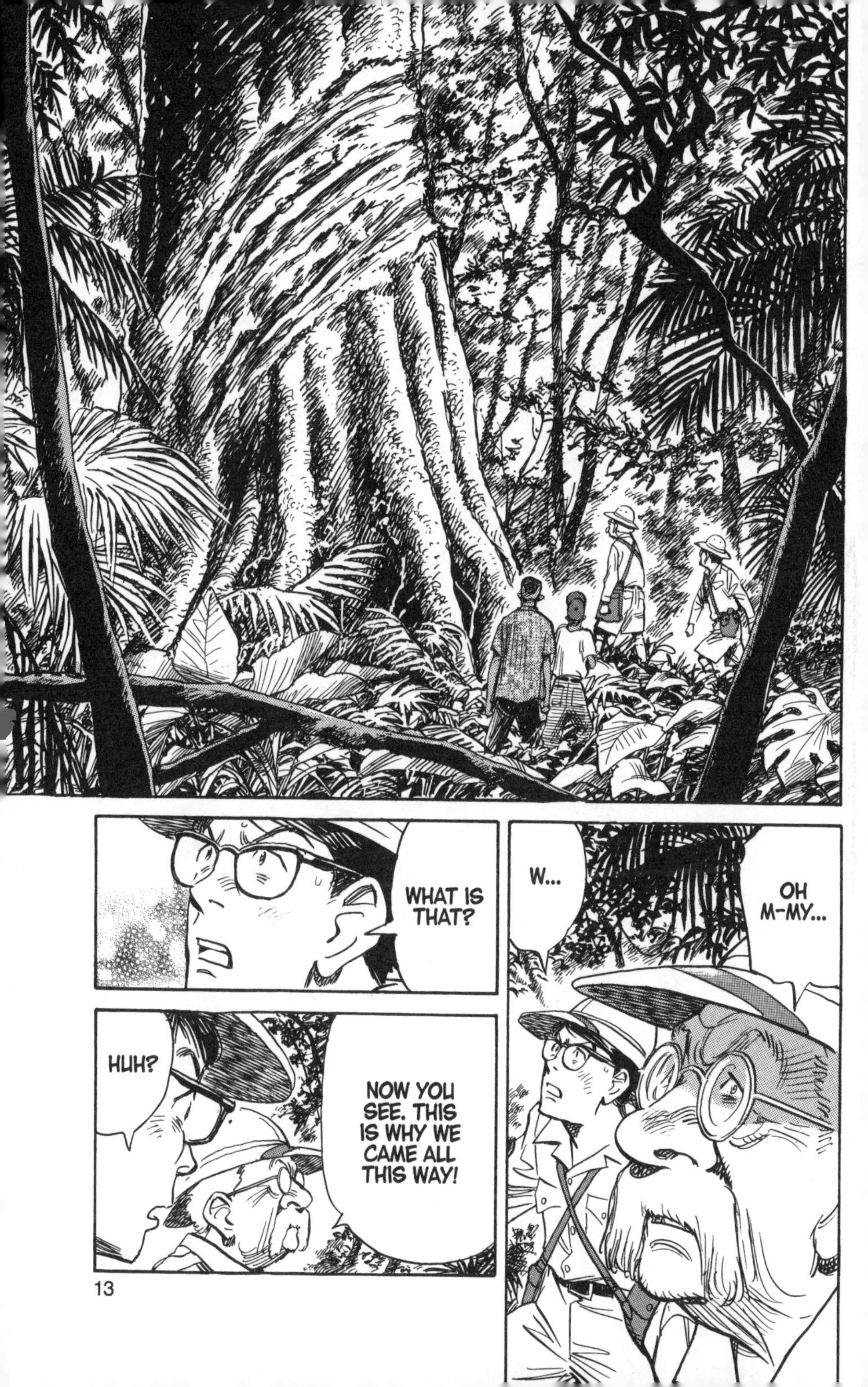
OH M-MY...
W...
WHAT IS THAT?
NOW YOU SEE. THIS IS WHY WE CAME ALL THIS WAY!
HUH?

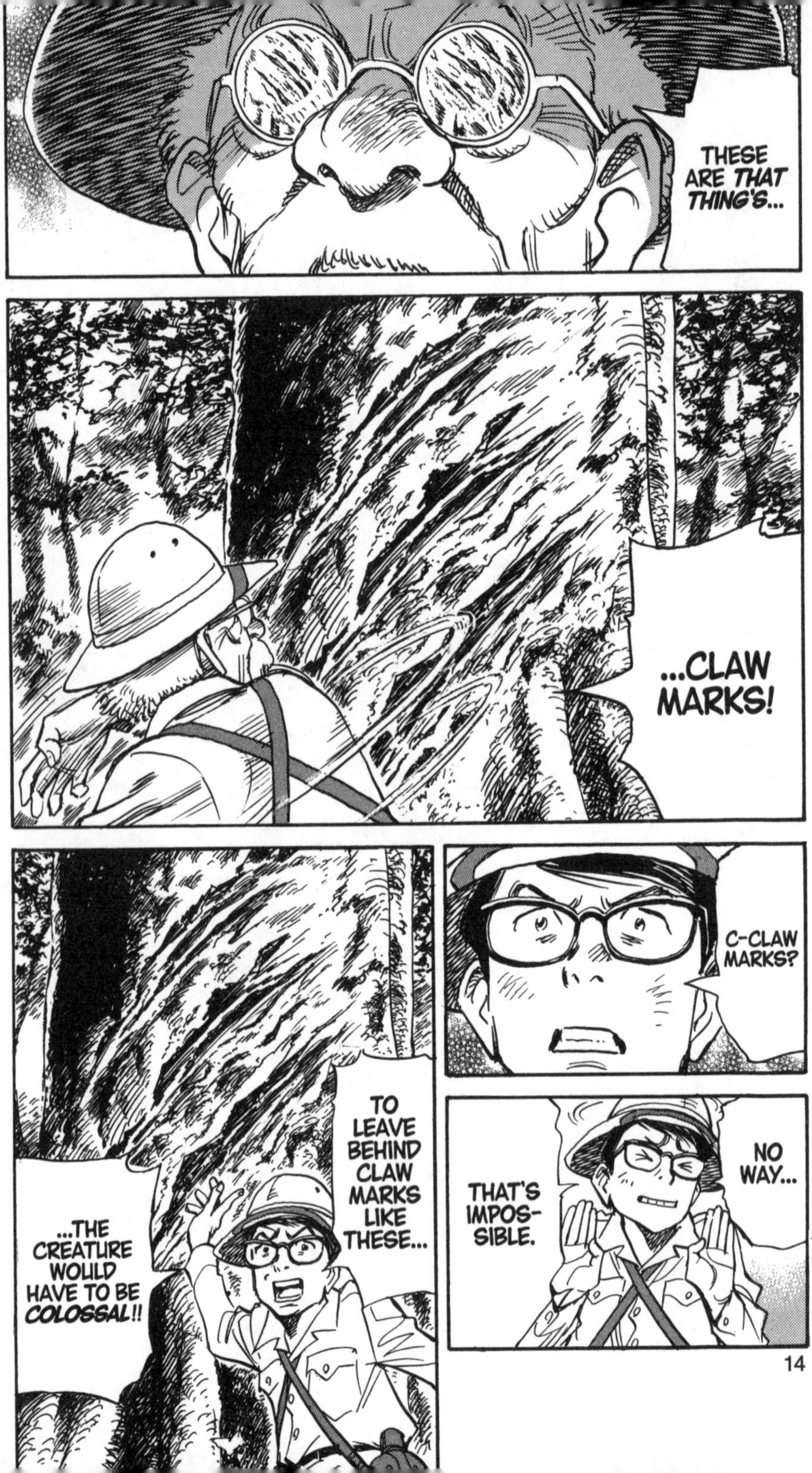
THESE ARE *THAT THING'S*...
...CLAW MARKS!
C-CLAW MARKS?
NO WAY...
THAT'S IMPOSSIBLE.
TO LEAVE BEHIND CLAW MARKS LIKE THESE...
...THE CREATURE WOULD HAVE TO BE *COLOSSAL*!!

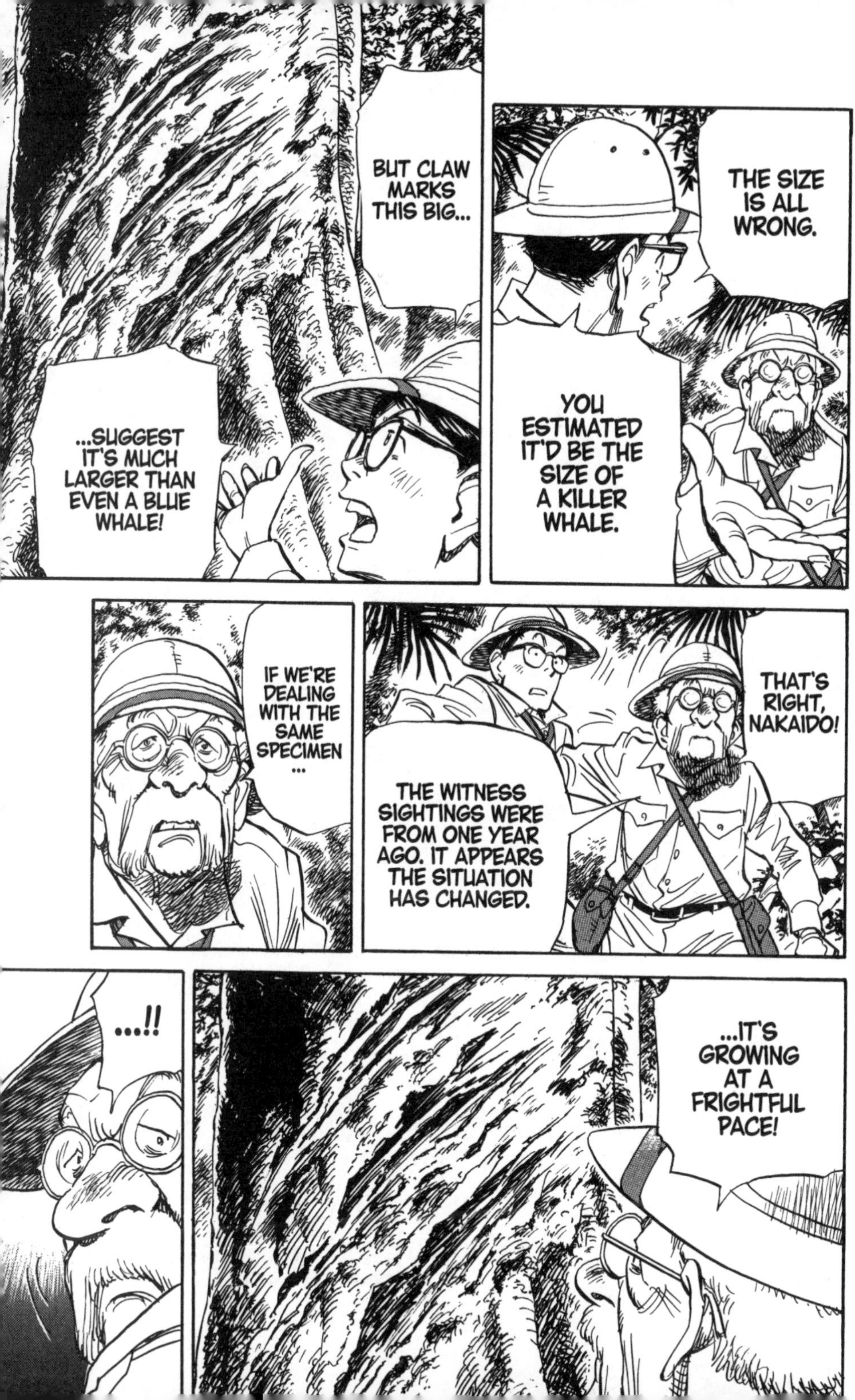
THE SIZE IS ALL WRONG.
YOU ESTIMATED IT'D BE THE SIZE OF A KILLER WHALE.
BUT CLAW MARKS THIS BIG...
...SUGGEST IT'S MUCH LARGER THAN EVEN A BLUE WHALE!
THAT'S RIGHT, NAKAIDO!
THE WITNESS SIGHTINGS WERE FROM ONE YEAR AGO. IT APPEARS THE SITUATION HAS CHANGED.
IF WE'RE DEALING WITH THE SAME SPECIMEN ...
...IT'S GROWING AT A FRIGHTFUL PACE!
...!!

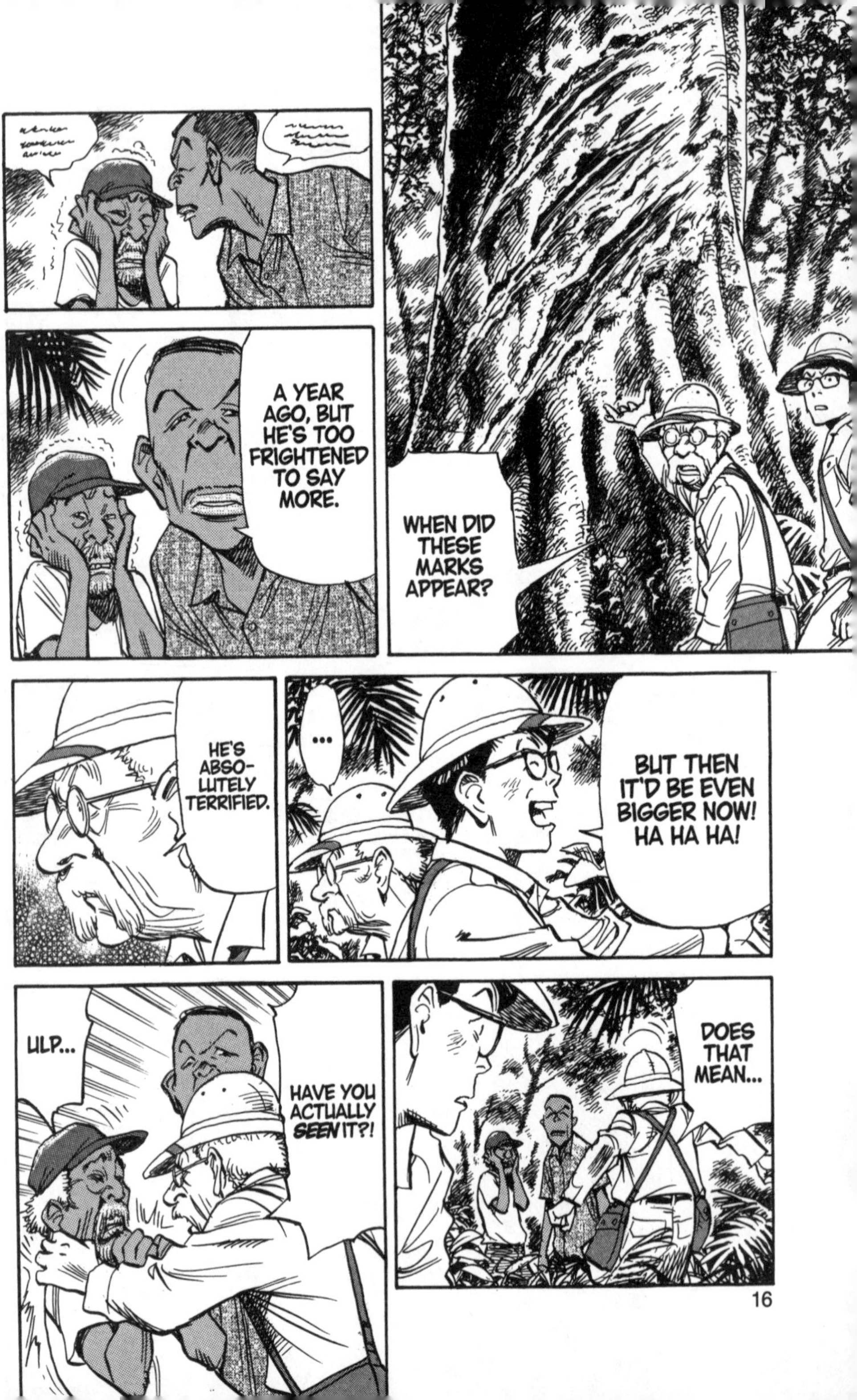
WHEN DID THESE MARKS APPEAR?
A YEAR AGO, BUT HE'S TOO FRIGHTENED TO SAY MORE.
BUT THEN IT'D BE EVEN BIGGER NOW! HA HA HA!
...
HE'S ABSO-LUTELY TERRIFIED.
DOES THAT MEAN...
HAVE YOU ACTUALLY SEEN IT?!
ULP...

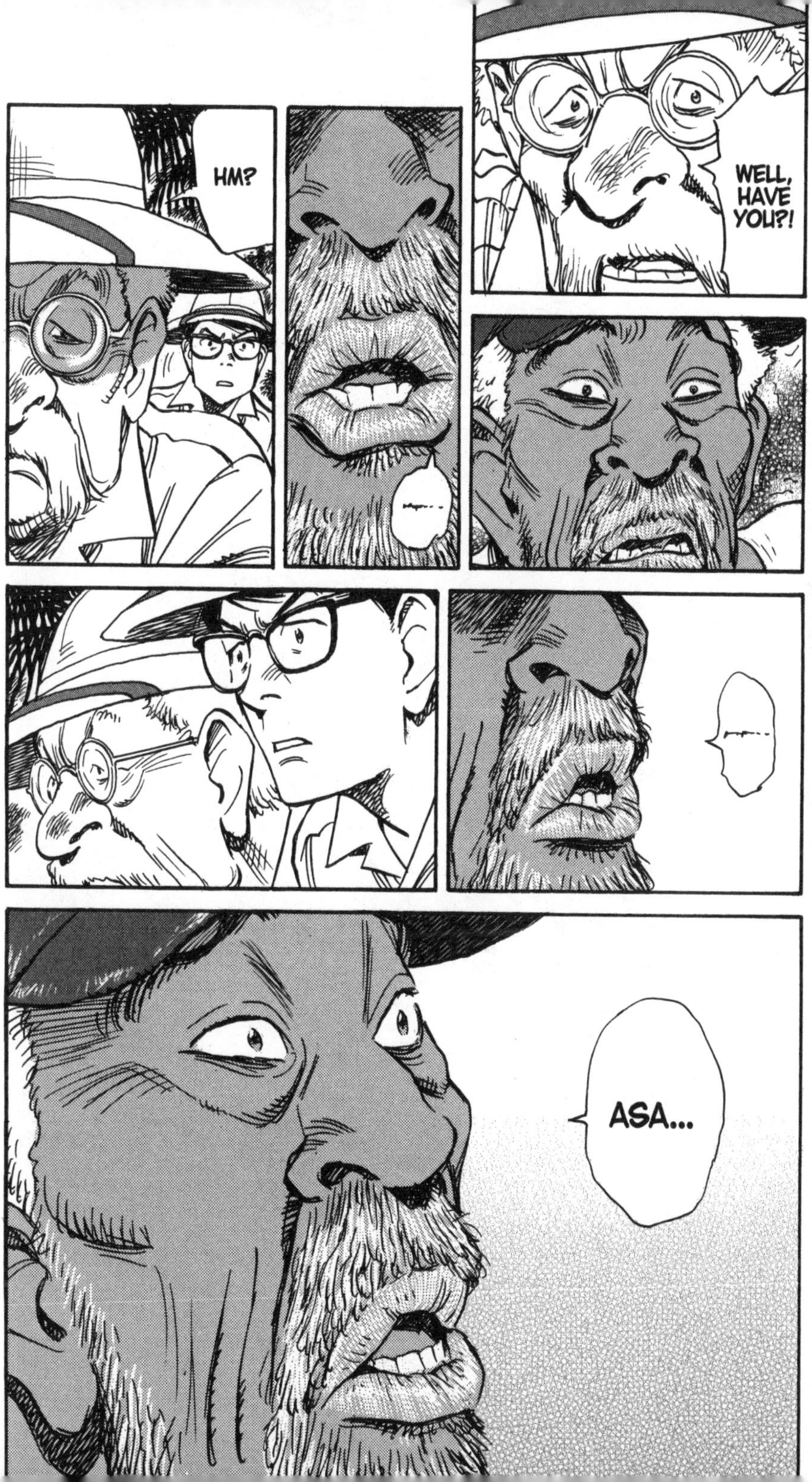

WELL, HAVE YOU?!
......
HM?
......
ASA...

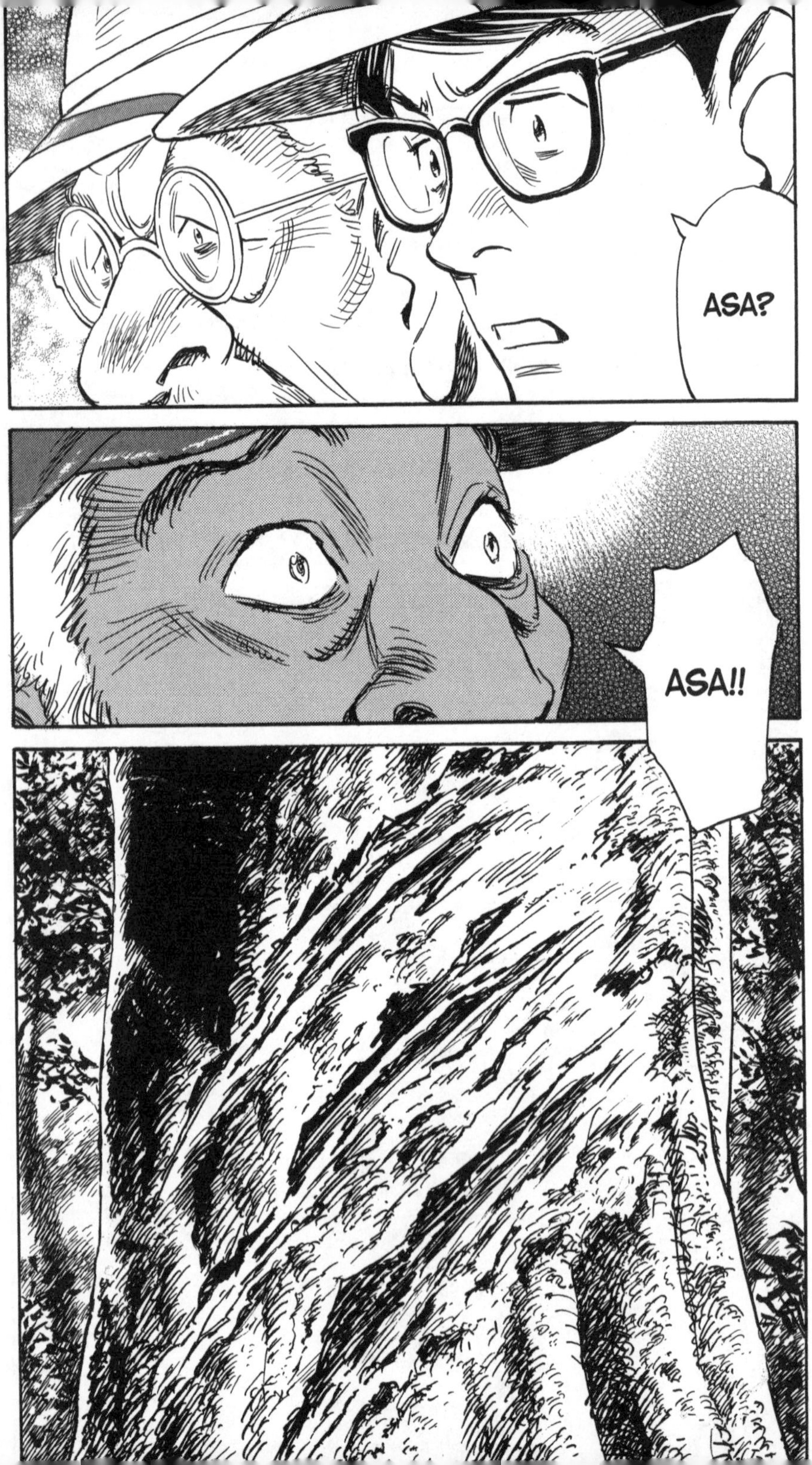
ASA?
ASA!!

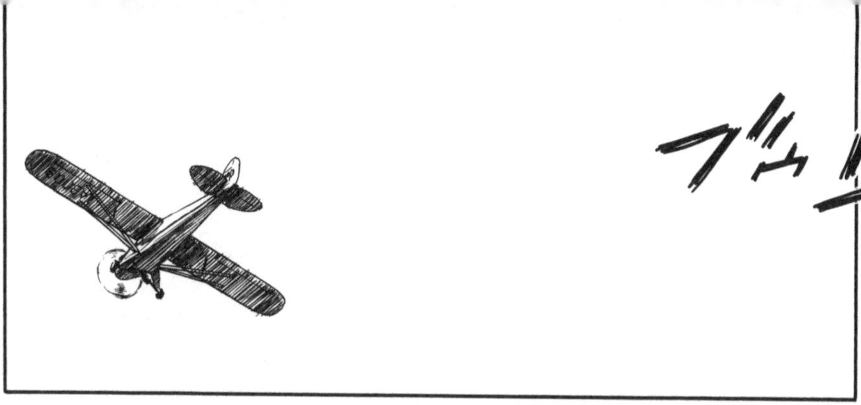
ブゥ!!
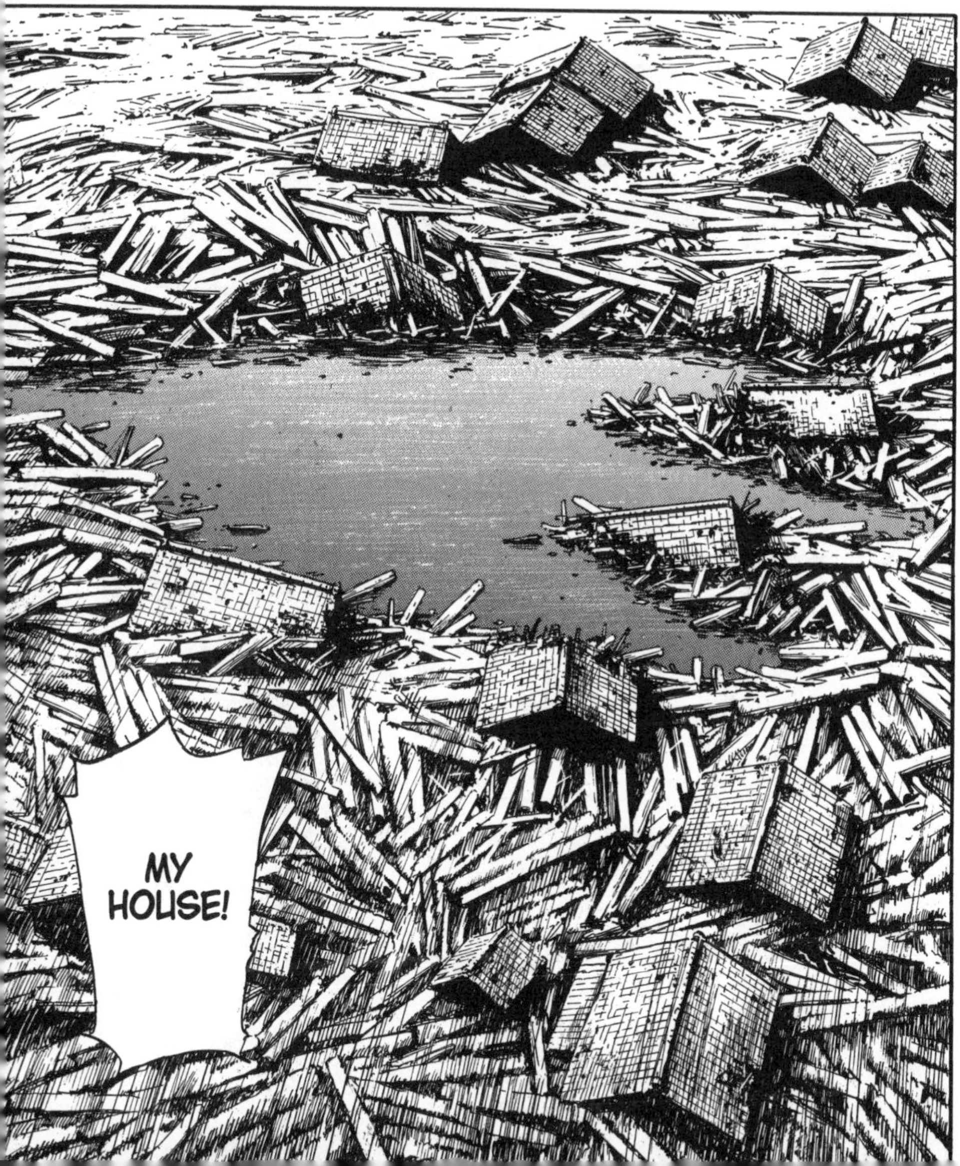
MY HOUSE!

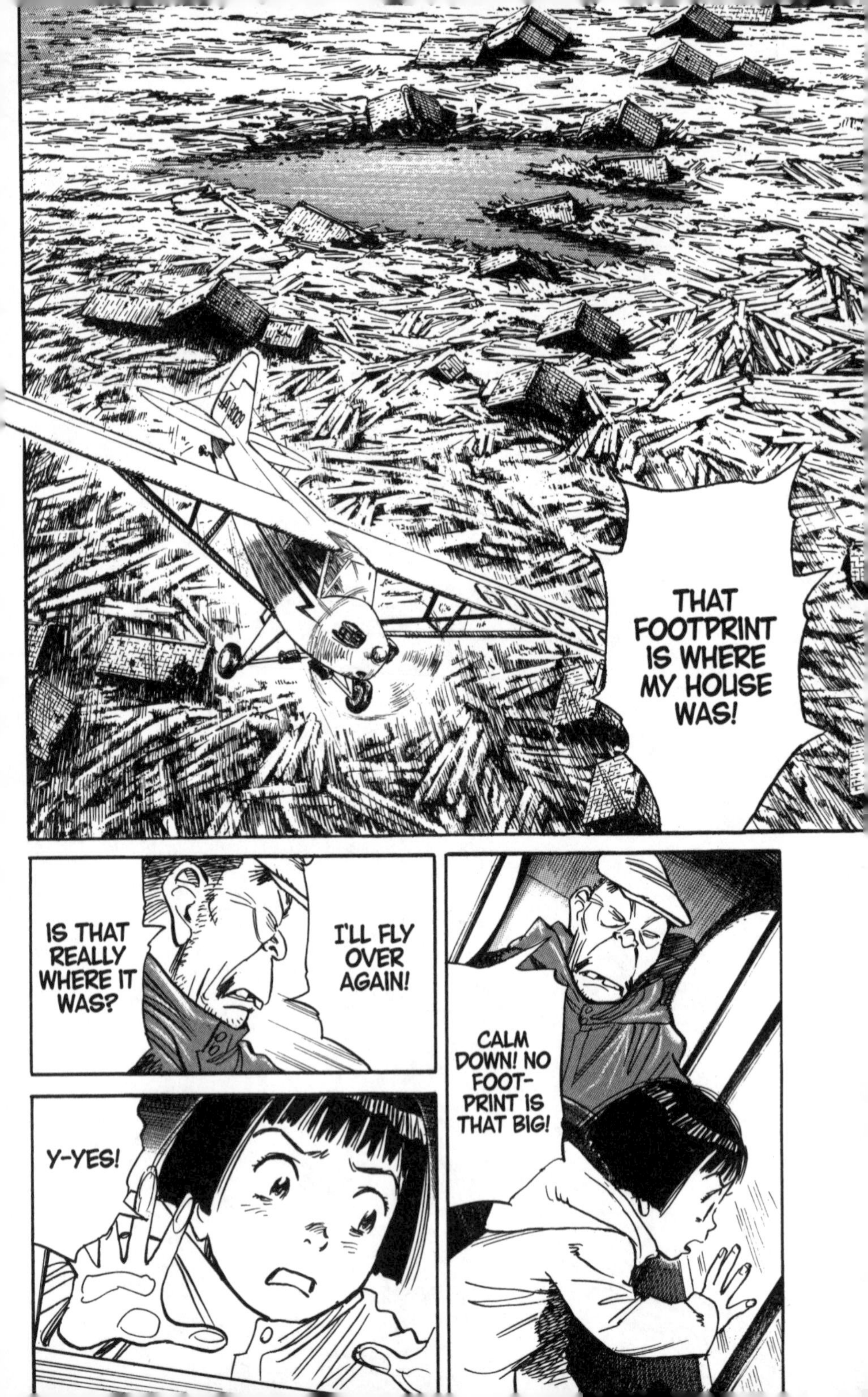
THAT FOOTPRINT IS WHERE MY HOUSE WAS!
CALM DOWN! NO FOOT-PRINT IS THAT BIG!
I'LL FLY OVER AGAIN!
IS THAT REALLY WHERE IT WAS?
Y-YES!

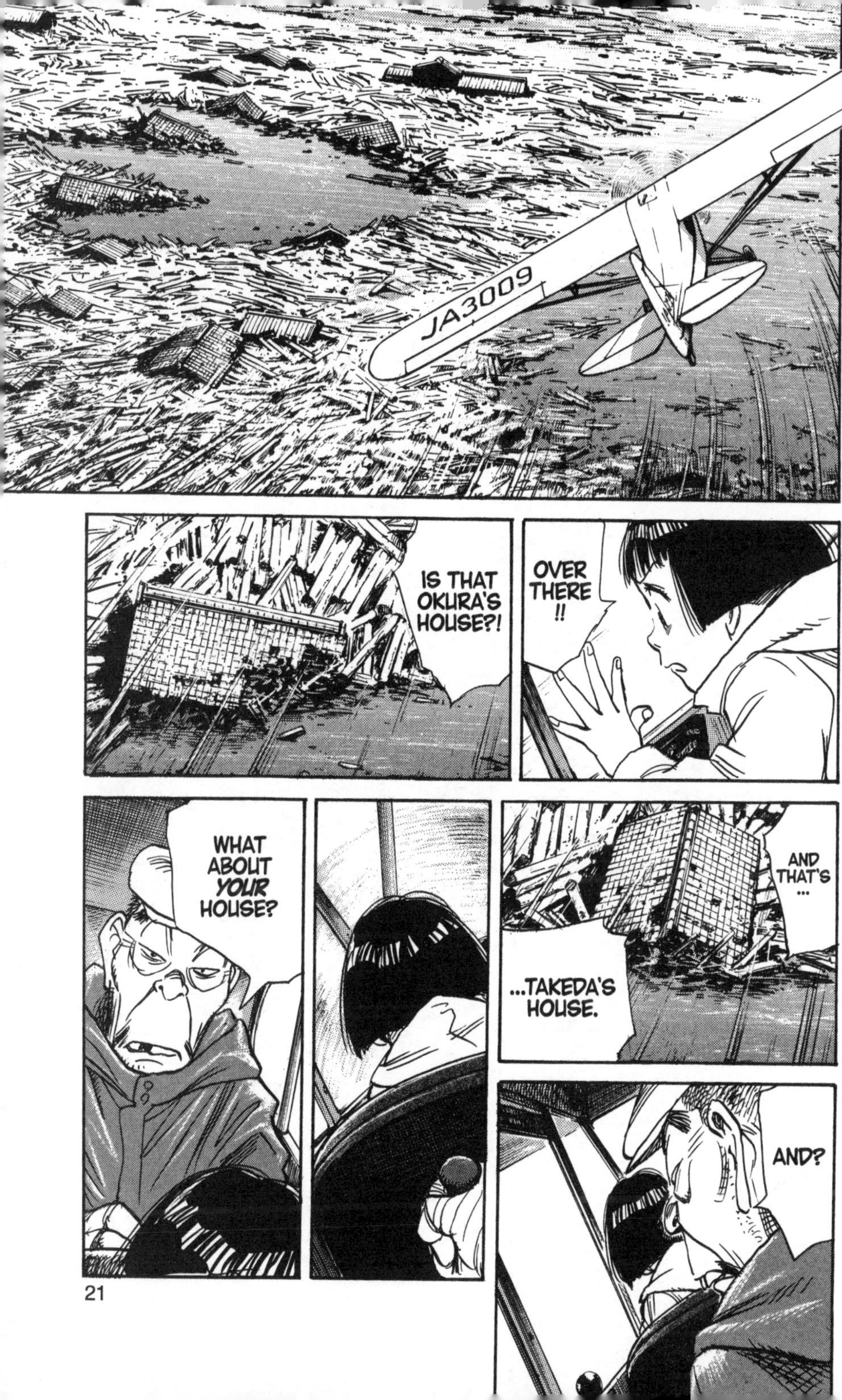
JA3009
OVER THERE !!
IS THAT OKURA'S HOUSE?!
AND THAT'S ...
...TAKEDA'S HOUSE.
AND?
WHAT ABOUT *YOUR* HOUSE?

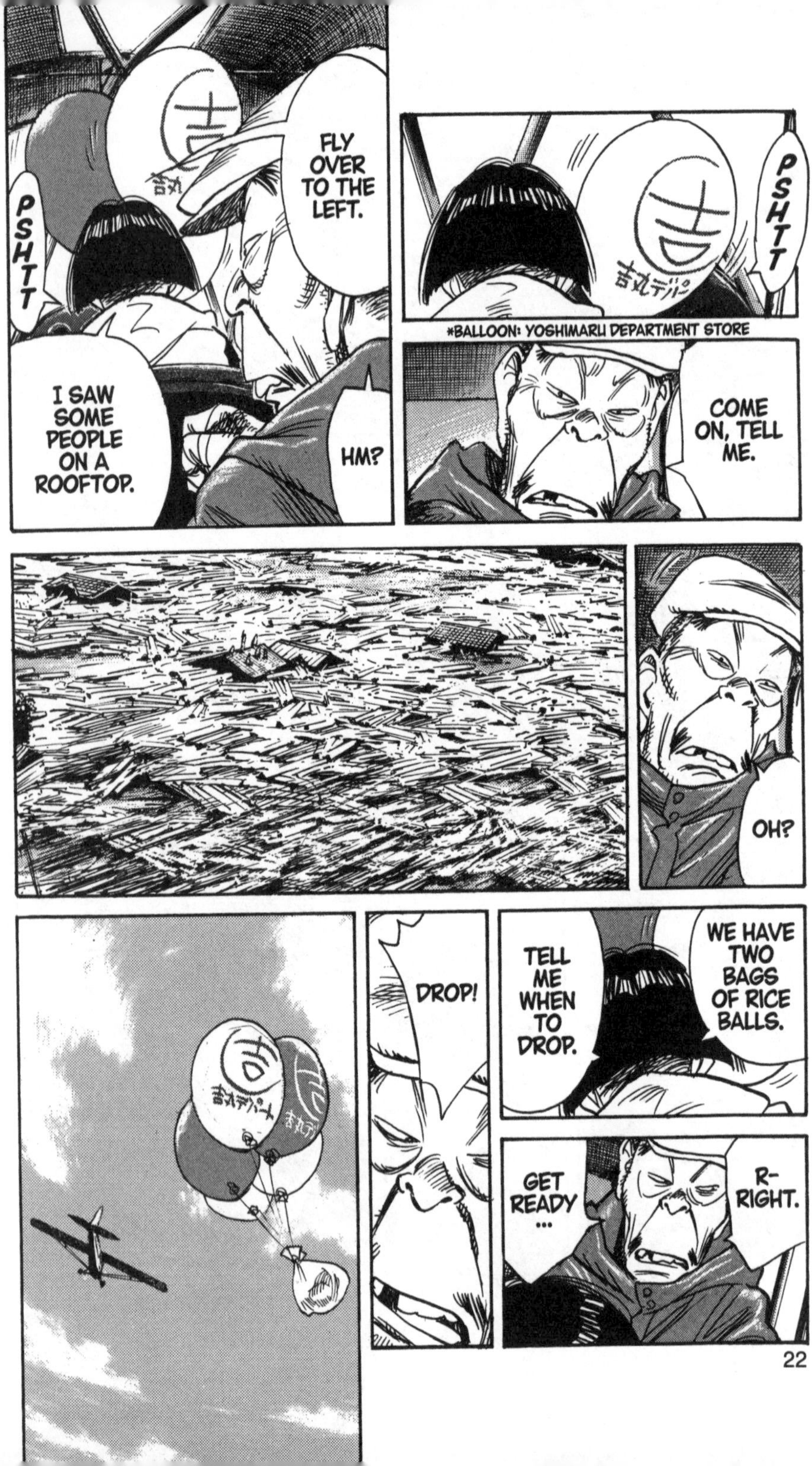
PSHTT
*BALLOON: YOSHIMARU DEPARTMENT STORE
COME ON, TELL ME.
FLY OVER TO THE LEFT.
PSHTT
HM?
I SAW SOME PEOPLE ON A ROOFTOP.
OH?
WE HAVE TWO BAGS OF RICE BALLS.
TELL ME WHEN TO DROP.
R-RIGHT.
GET READY ...
DROP!

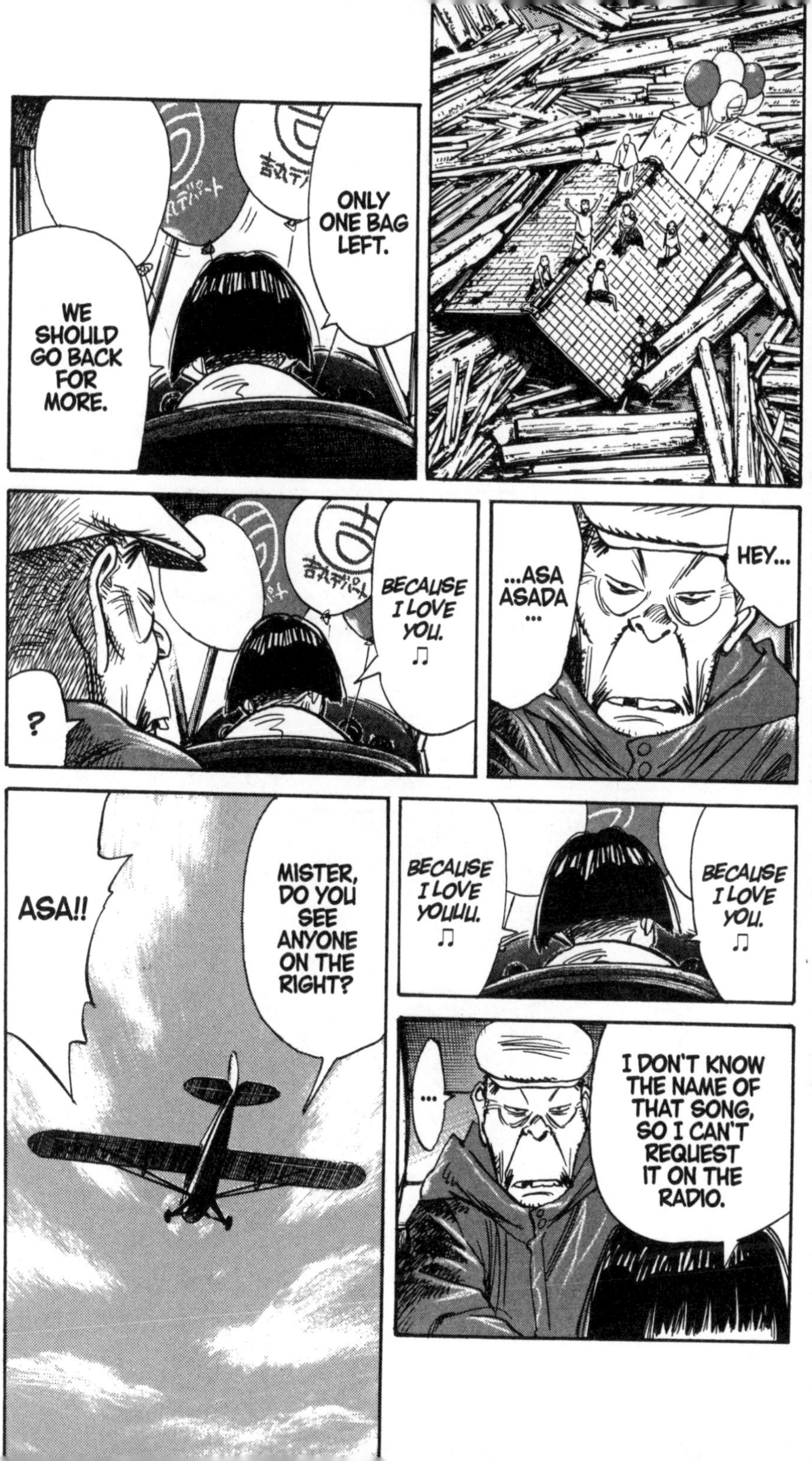
ONLY ONE BAG LEFT.
WE SHOULD GO BACK FOR MORE.
HEY...
...ASA ASADA ...
BECAUSE I LOVE YOU. ♫
?
BECAUSE I LOVE YOU. ♫
BECAUSE I LOVE YOUUU. ♫
I DON'T KNOW THE NAME OF THAT SONG, SO I CAN'T REQUEST IT ON THE RADIO.
...
MISTER, DO YOU SEE ANYONE ON THE RIGHT?
ASA!!

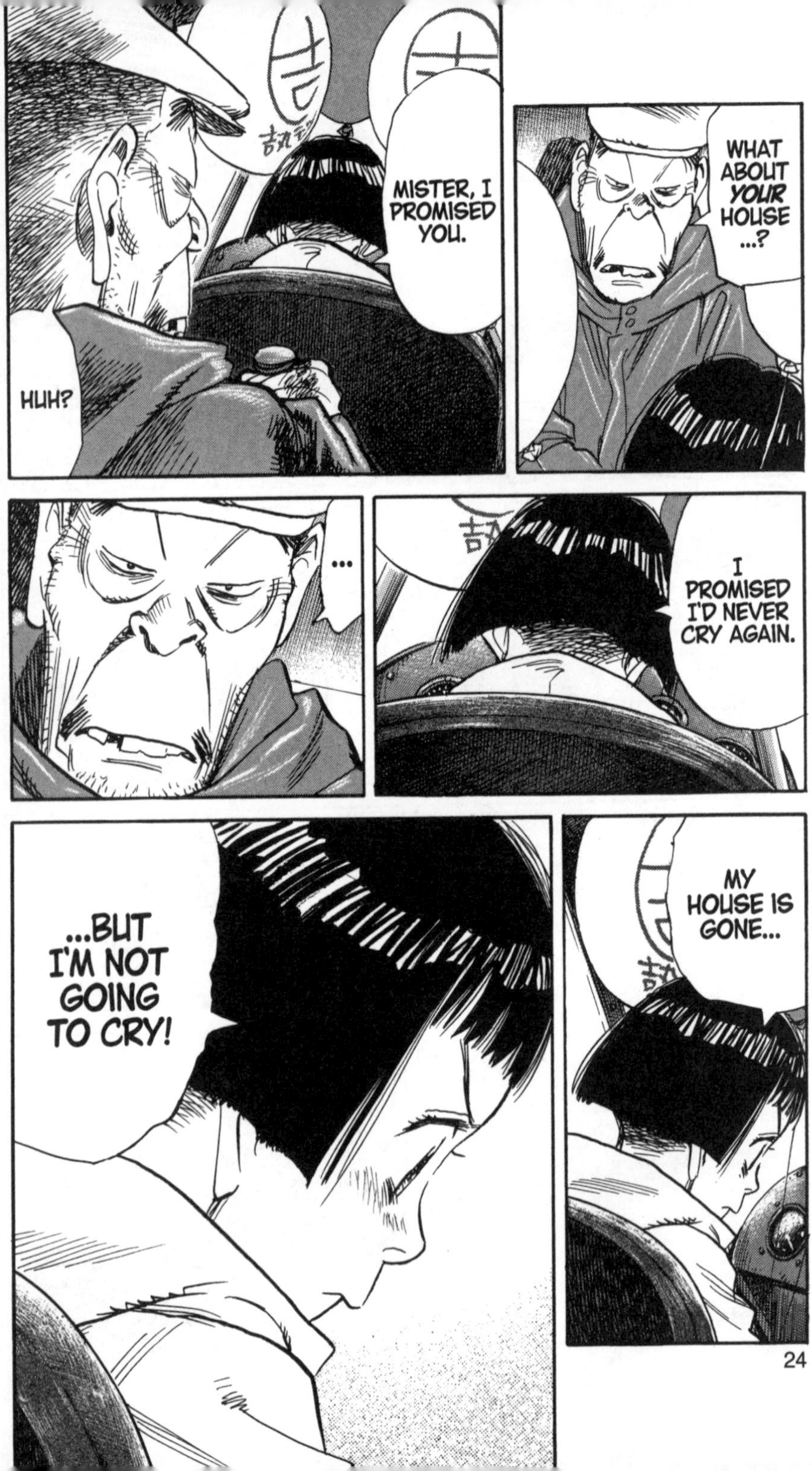
WHAT ABOUT *YOUR* HOUSE ...?
MISTER, I PROMISED YOU.
HUH?
I PROMISED I'D NEVER CRY AGAIN.
...
MY HOUSE IS GONE...
...BUT I'M NOT GOING TO CRY!

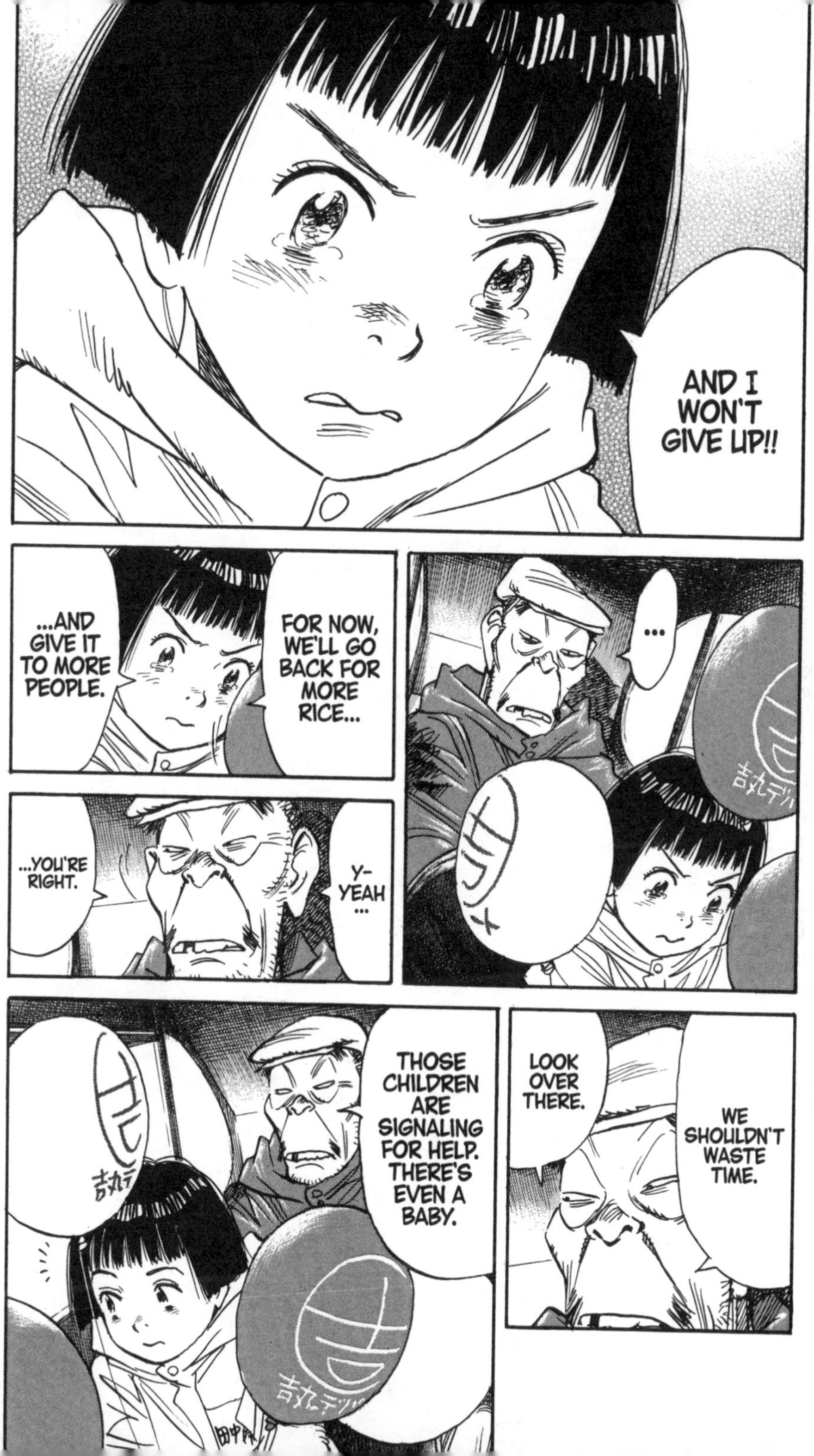
AND I WON'T GIVE UP!!
...
FOR NOW, WE'LL GO BACK FOR MORE RICE...
...AND GIVE IT TO MORE PEOPLE.
Y-YEAH...
...YOU'RE RIGHT.
WE SHOULDN'T WASTE TIME.
LOOK OVER THERE.
THOSE CHILDREN ARE SIGNALING FOR HELP. THERE'S EVEN A BABY.

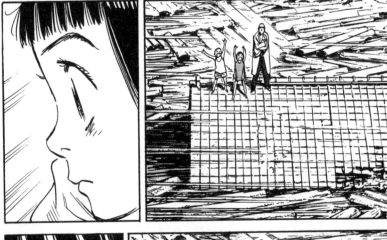

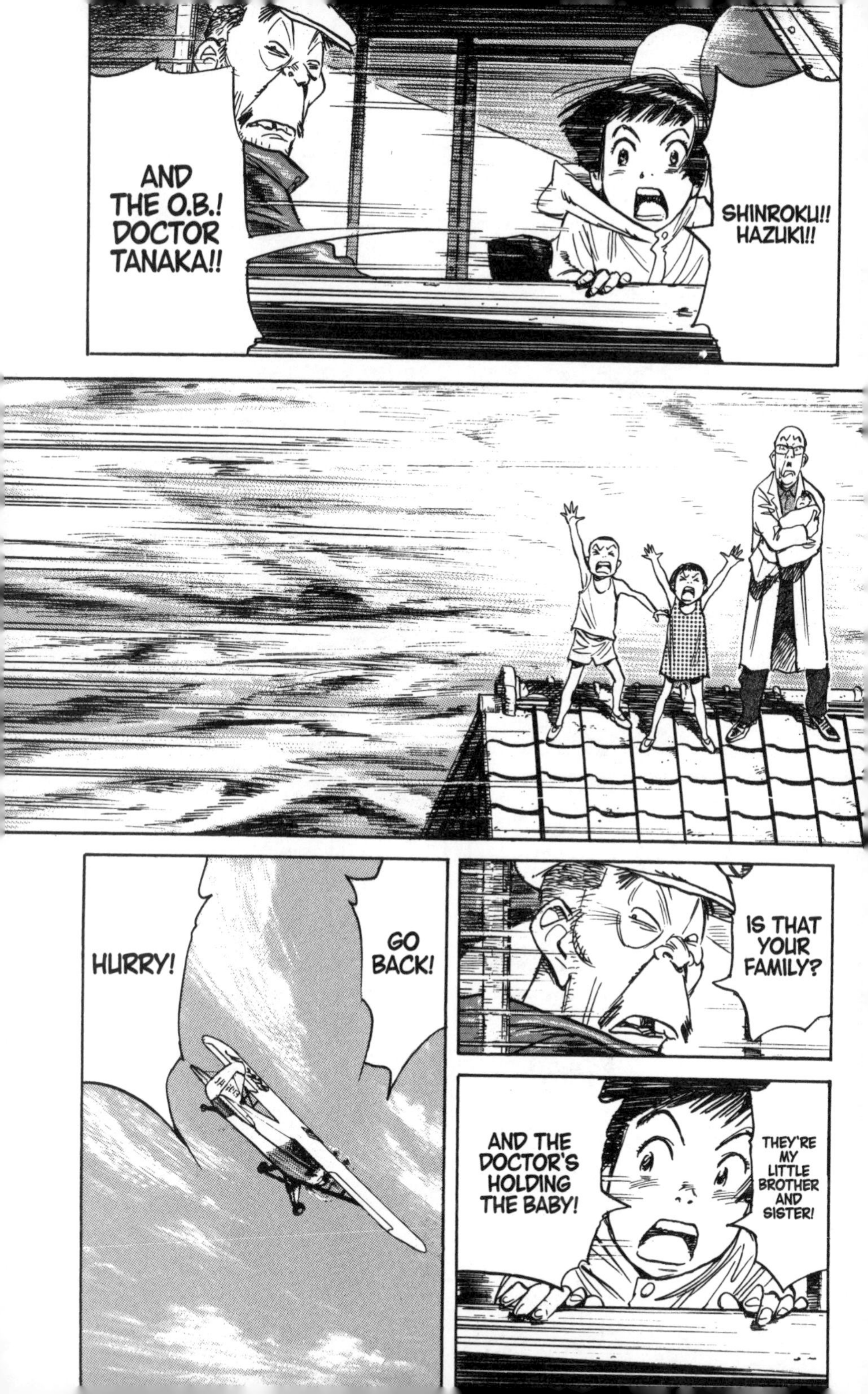
SHINROKU!! HAZUKI!!
AND THE O.B.! DOCTOR TANAKA!!
IS THAT YOUR FAMILY?
THEY'RE MY LITTLE BROTHER AND SISTER!
AND THE DOCTOR'S HOLDING THE BABY!
GO BACK!
HURRY!

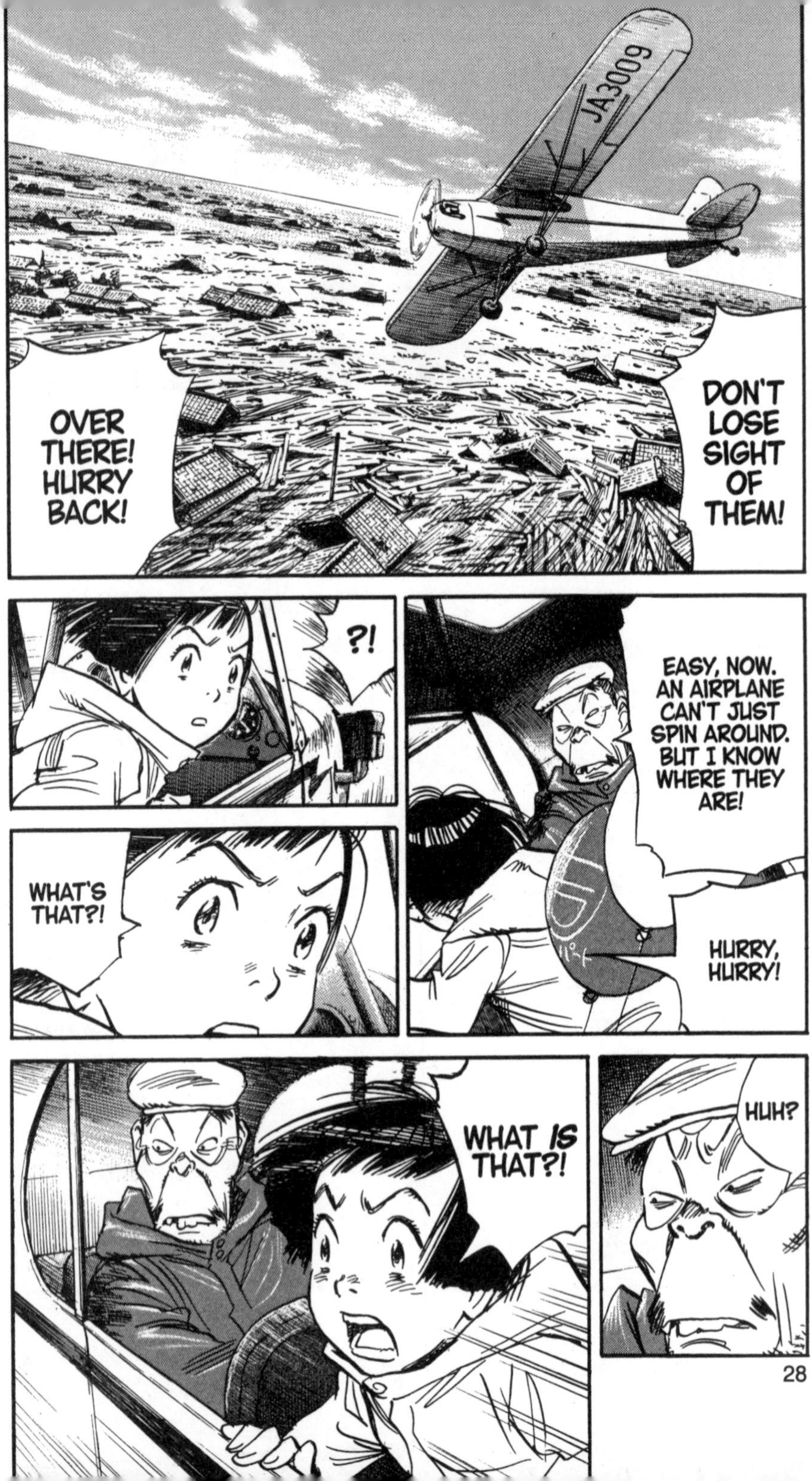
JA3009
DON'T LOSE SIGHT OF THEM!
OVER THERE! HURRY BACK!
EASY, NOW. AN AIRPLANE CAN'T JUST SPIN AROUND. BUT I KNOW WHERE THEY ARE!
HURRY, HURRY!
?!
WHAT'S THAT?!
HUH?
WHAT *IS* THAT?!

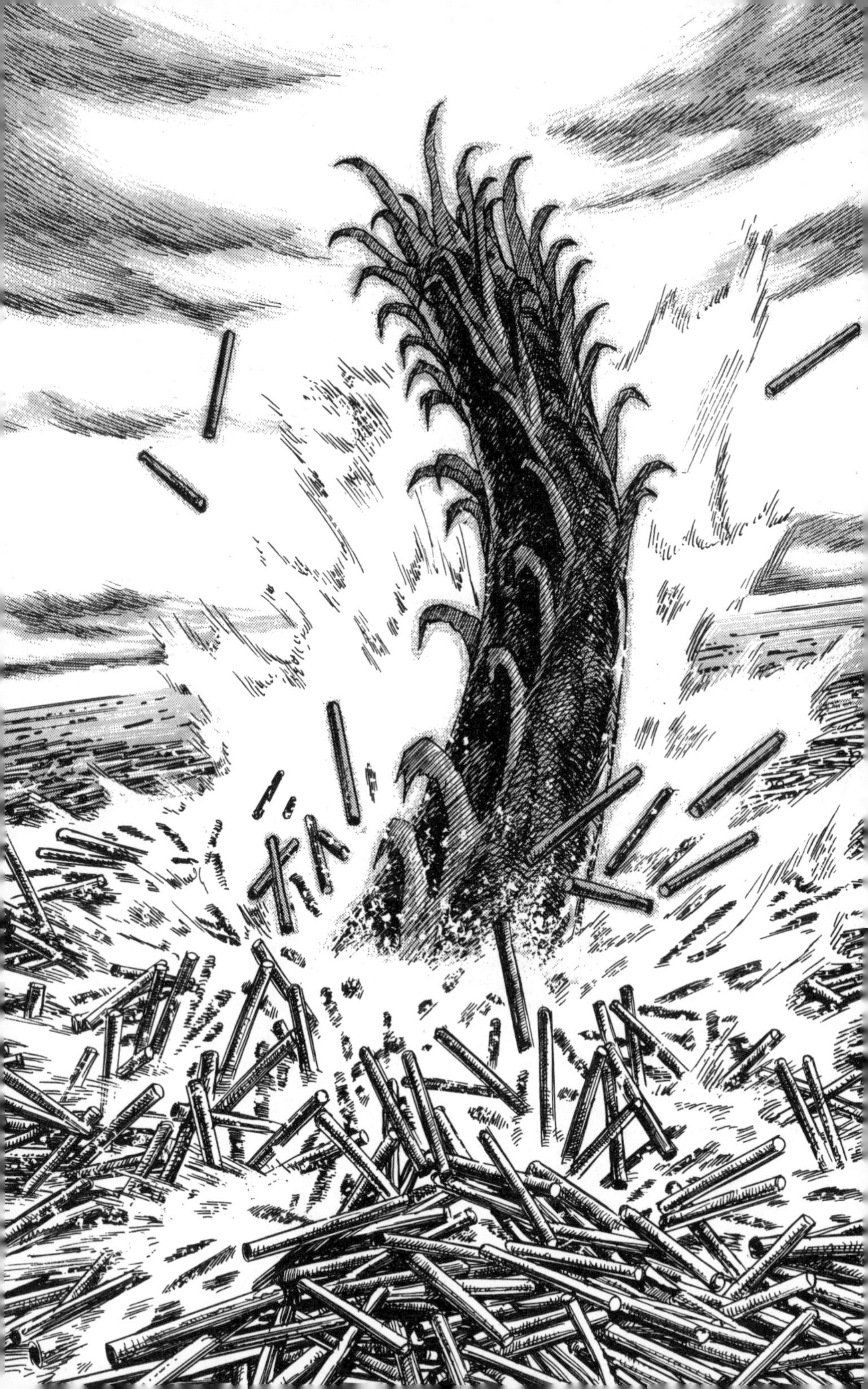

THEY HAVEN'T NOTICED IT!

!!

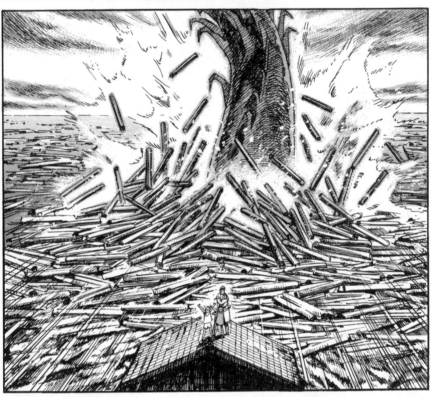

RUUUN!!

Chapter 10 ● Close Encounter

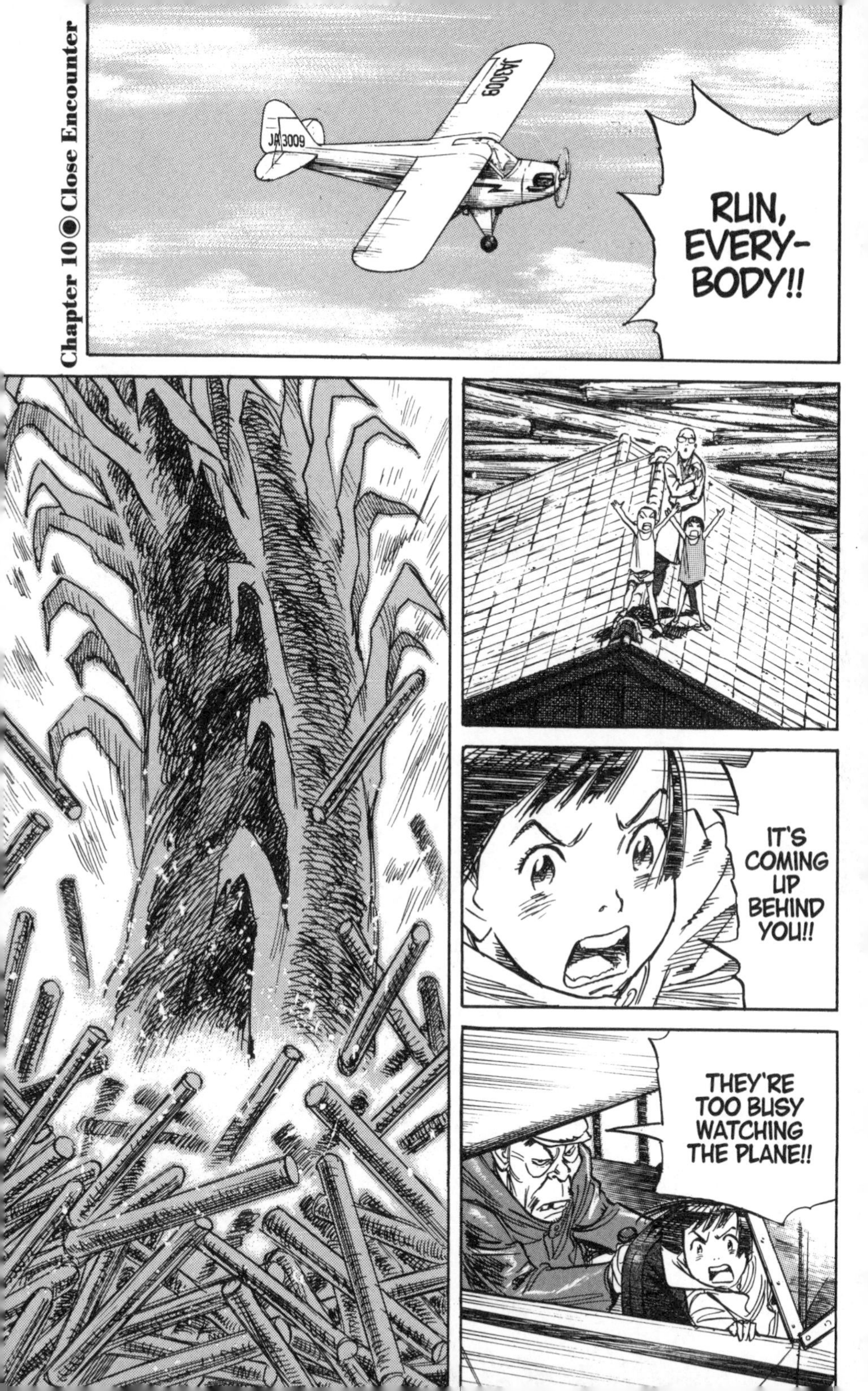

JA3009
RUN, EVERY-BODY!!
IT'S COMING UP BEHIND YOU!!
THEY'RE TOO BUSY WATCHING THE PLANE!!

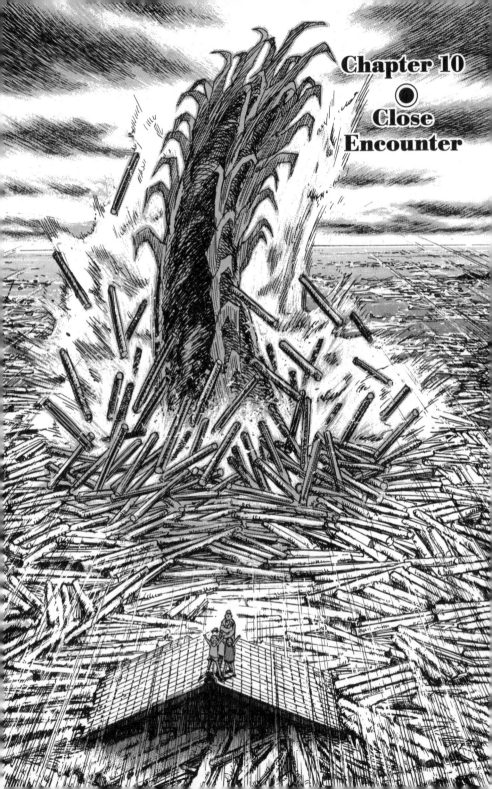

Chapter 10
● Close Encounter

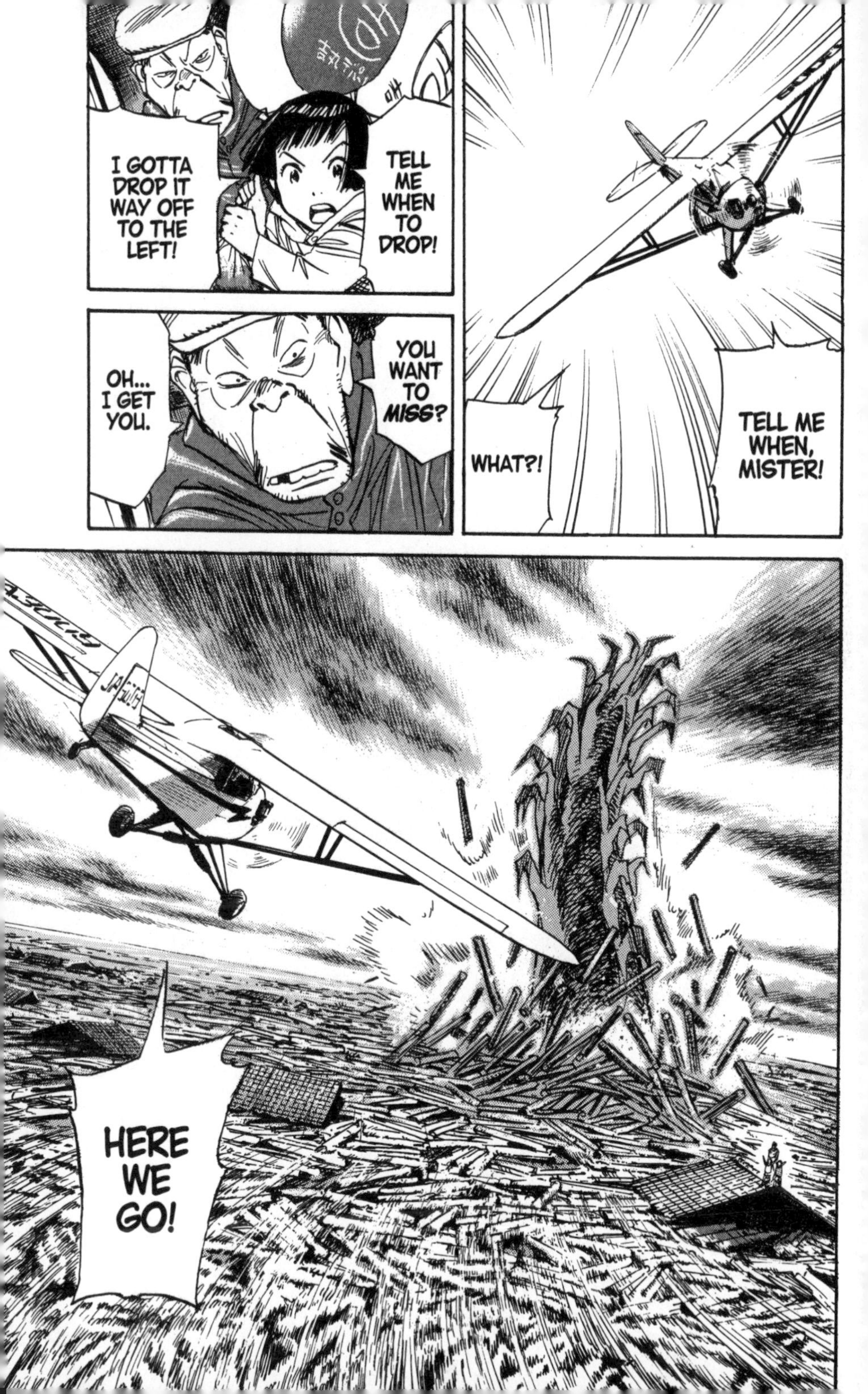
TELL ME WHEN, MISTER!
WHAT?!
TELL ME WHEN TO DROP!
I GOTTA DROP IT WAY OFF TO THE LEFT!
YOU WANT TO *MISS?*
OH... I GET YOU.
HERE WE GO!

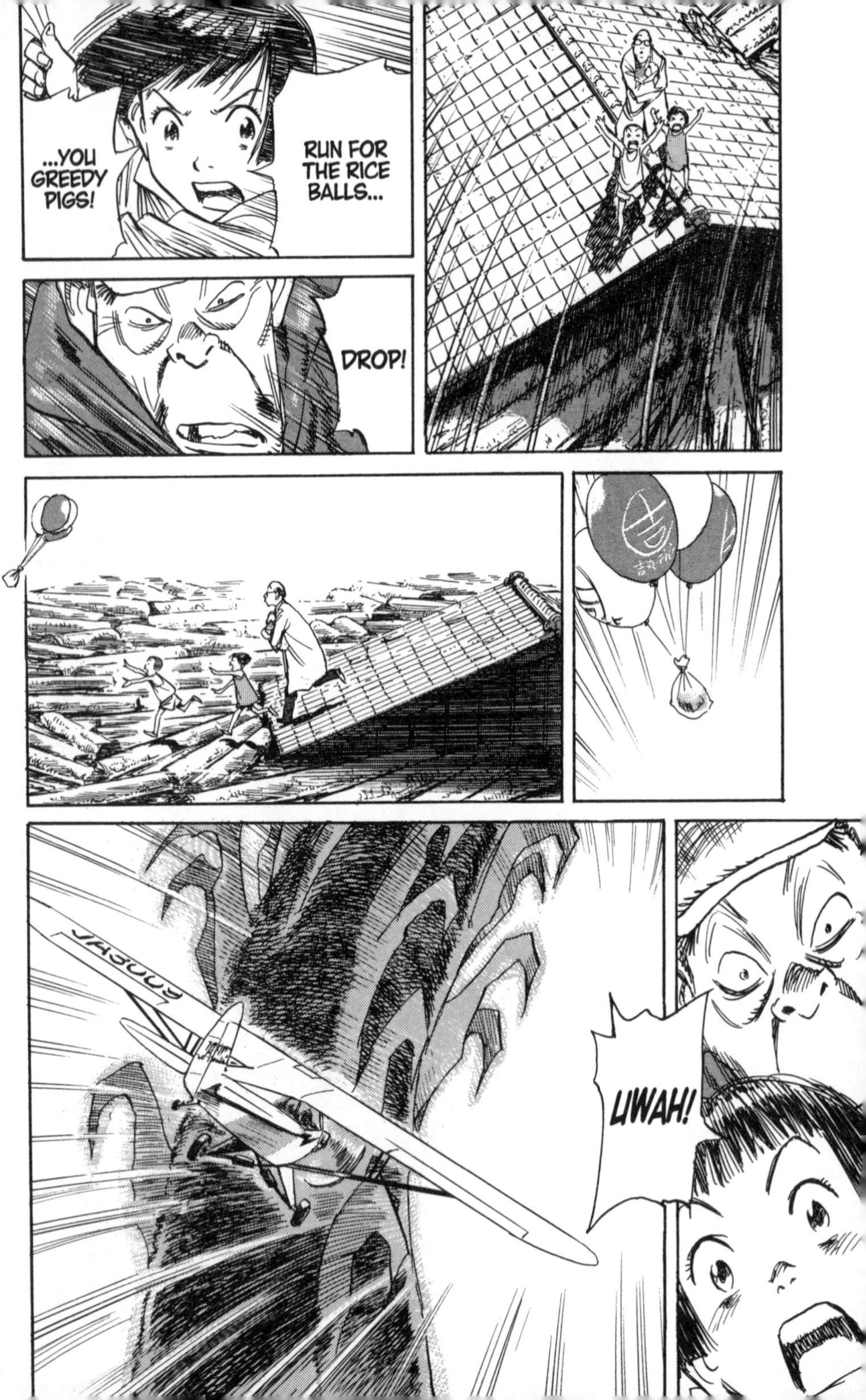
RUN FOR THE RICE BALLS...
...YOU GREEDY PIGS!
DROP!
UWAH!

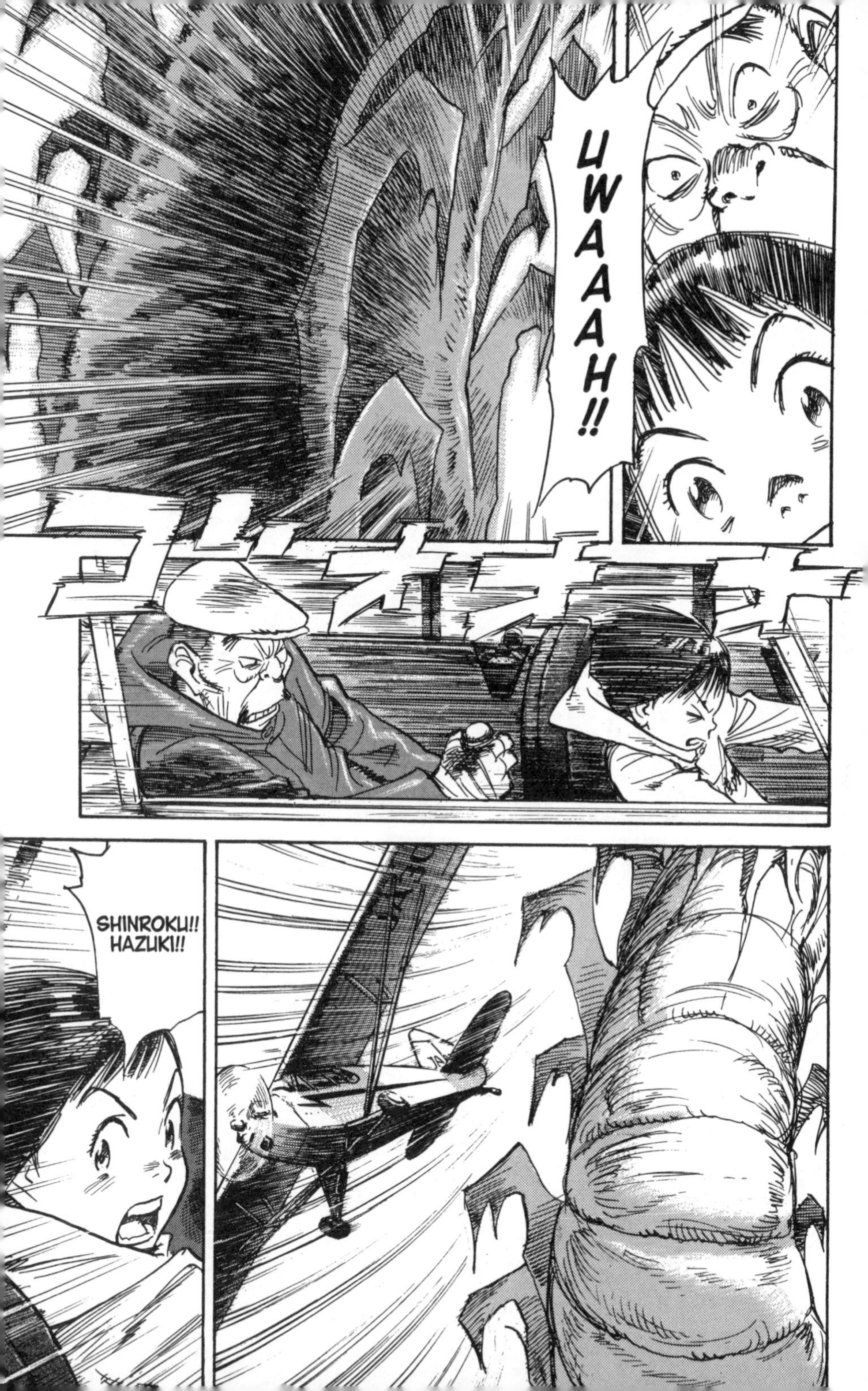
UWAAAAH!!
SHINROKU!! HAZUKI!!

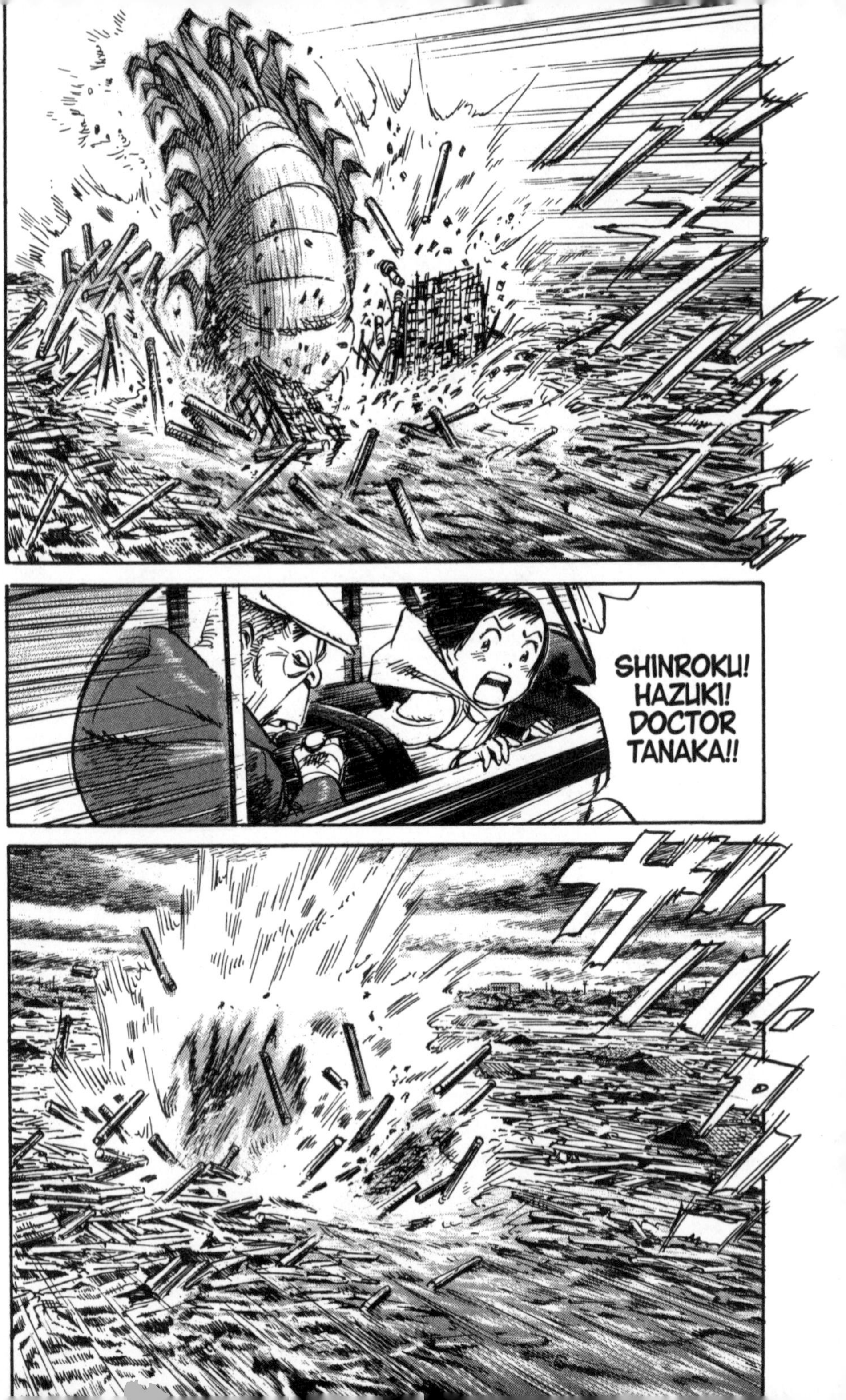
SHINROKU! HAZUKI! DOCTOR TANAKA!!

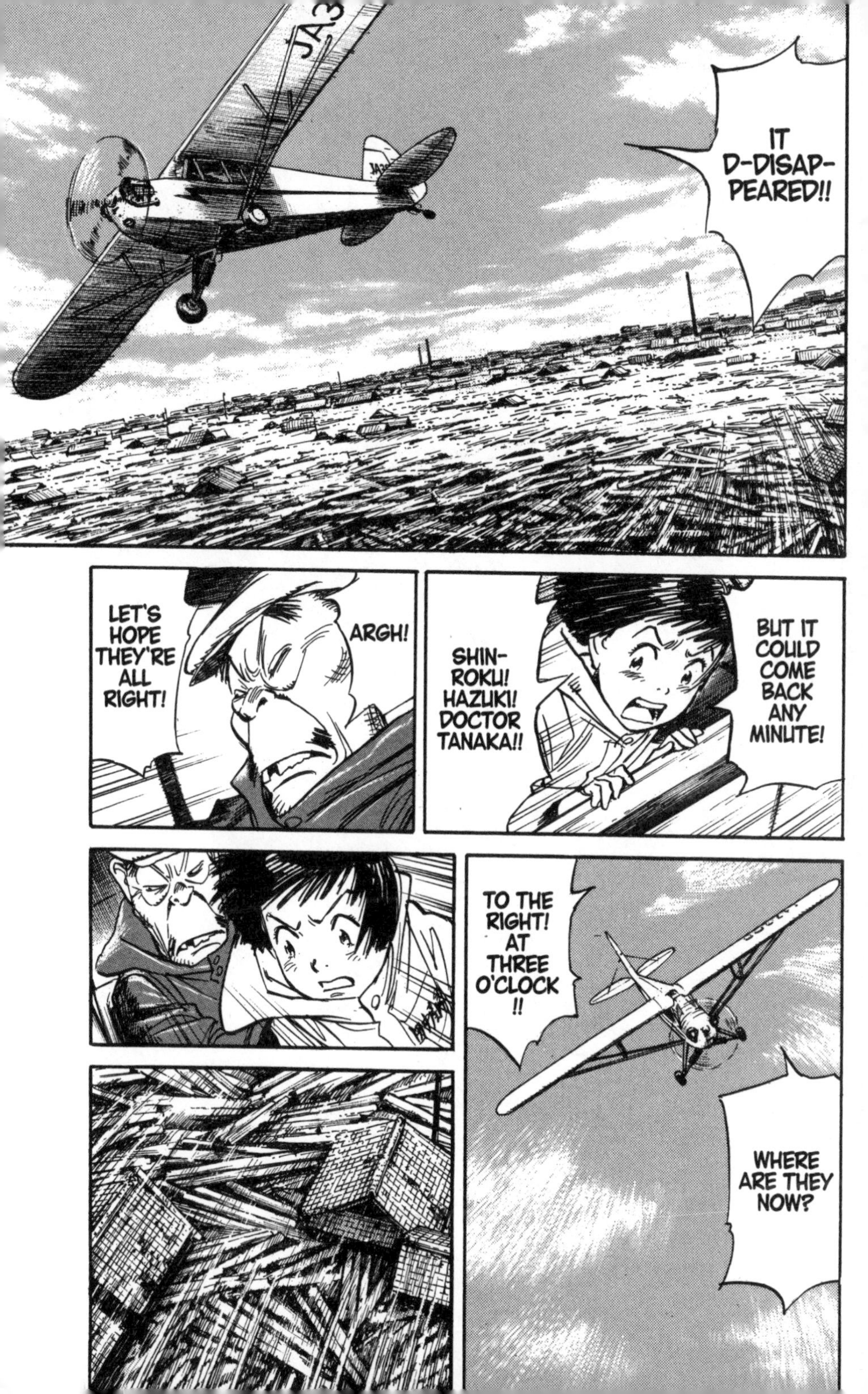
IT D-DISAP-PEARED!!
BUT IT COULD COME BACK ANY MINUTE!
SHIN-ROKU! HAZUKI! DOCTOR TANAKA!!
ARGH!
LET'S HOPE THEY'RE ALL RIGHT!
TO THE RIGHT! AT THREE O'CLOCK!!
WHERE ARE THEY NOW?

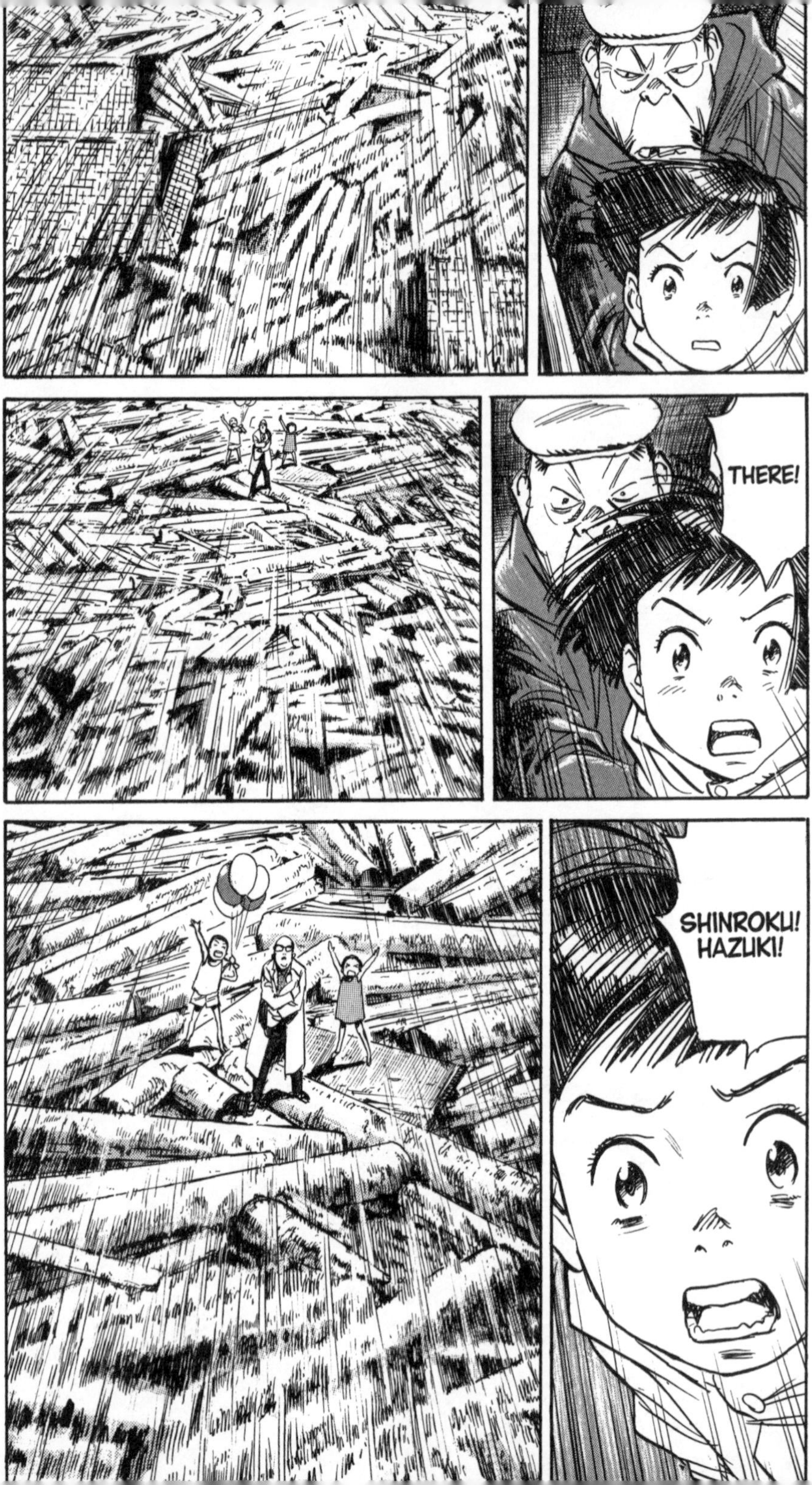
THERE!
SHINROKU!
HAZUKI!

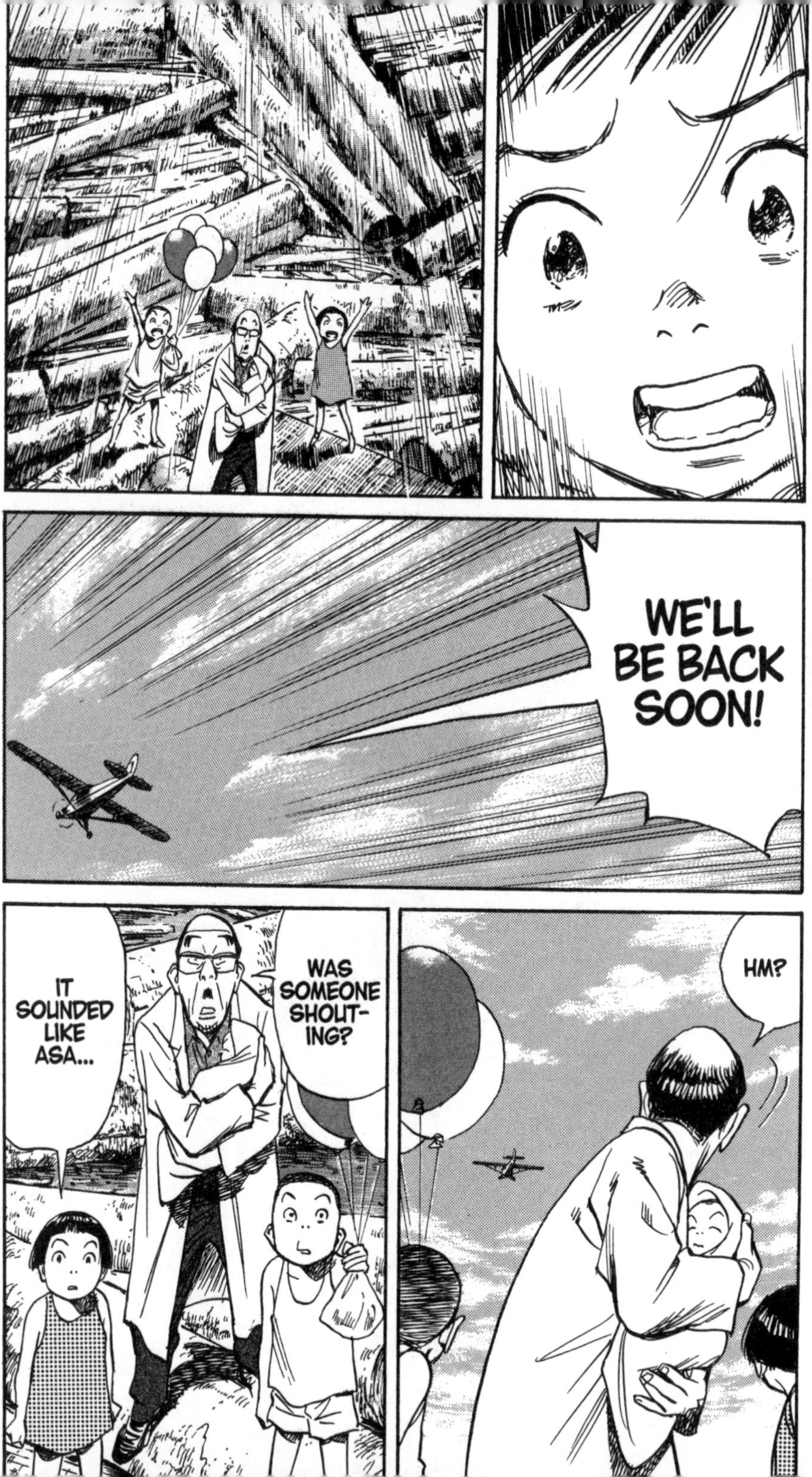
WE'LL BE BACK SOON!
HM?
WAS SOMEONE SHOUT-ING?
IT SOUNDED LIKE ASA...

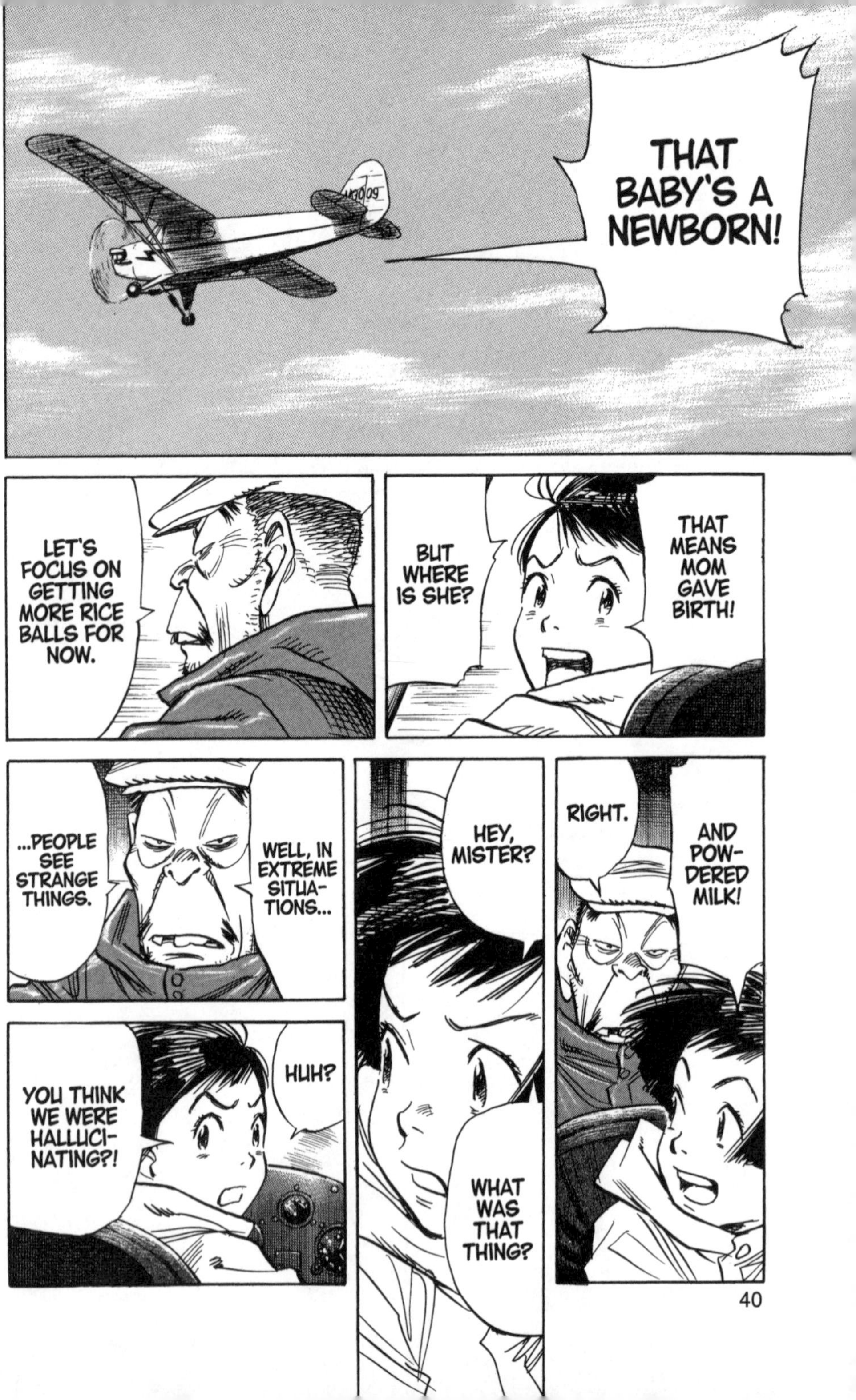
THAT BABY'S A NEWBORN!
THAT MEANS MOM GAVE BIRTH!
BUT WHERE IS SHE?
LET'S FOCUS ON GETTING MORE RICE BALLS FOR NOW.
AND POW-DERED MILK!
RIGHT.
HEY, MISTER?
WHAT WAS THAT THING?
WELL, IN EXTREME SITUA-TIONS...
...PEOPLE SEE STRANGE THINGS.
HUH?
YOU THINK WE WERE HALLUCI-NATING?!

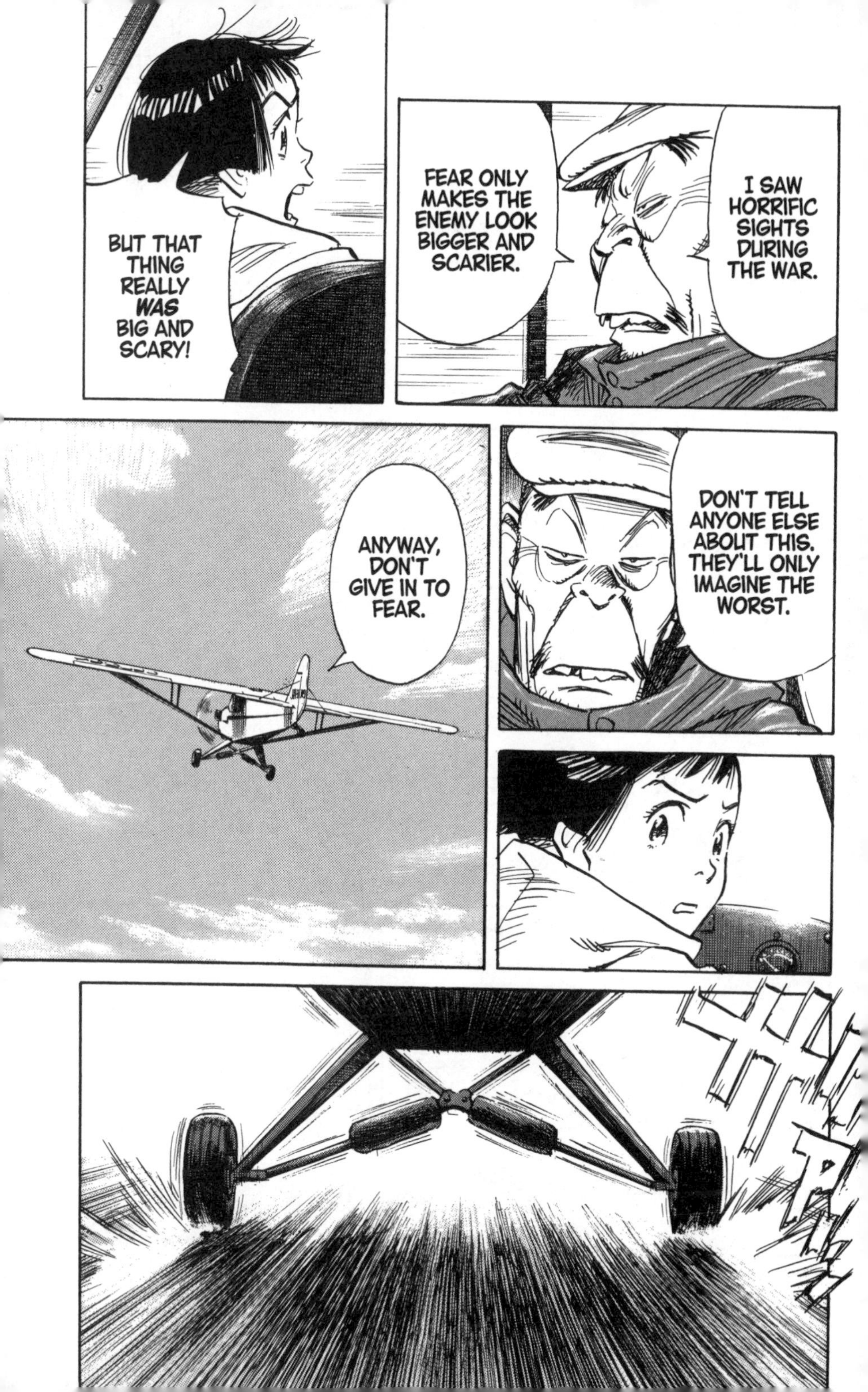
I SAW HORRIFIC SIGHTS DURING THE WAR.
FEAR ONLY MAKES THE ENEMY LOOK BIGGER AND SCARIER.
BUT THAT THING REALLY *WAS* BIG AND SCARY!
DON'T TELL ANYONE ELSE ABOUT THIS. THEY'LL ONLY IMAGINE THE WORST.
ANYWAY, DON'T GIVE IN TO FEAR.

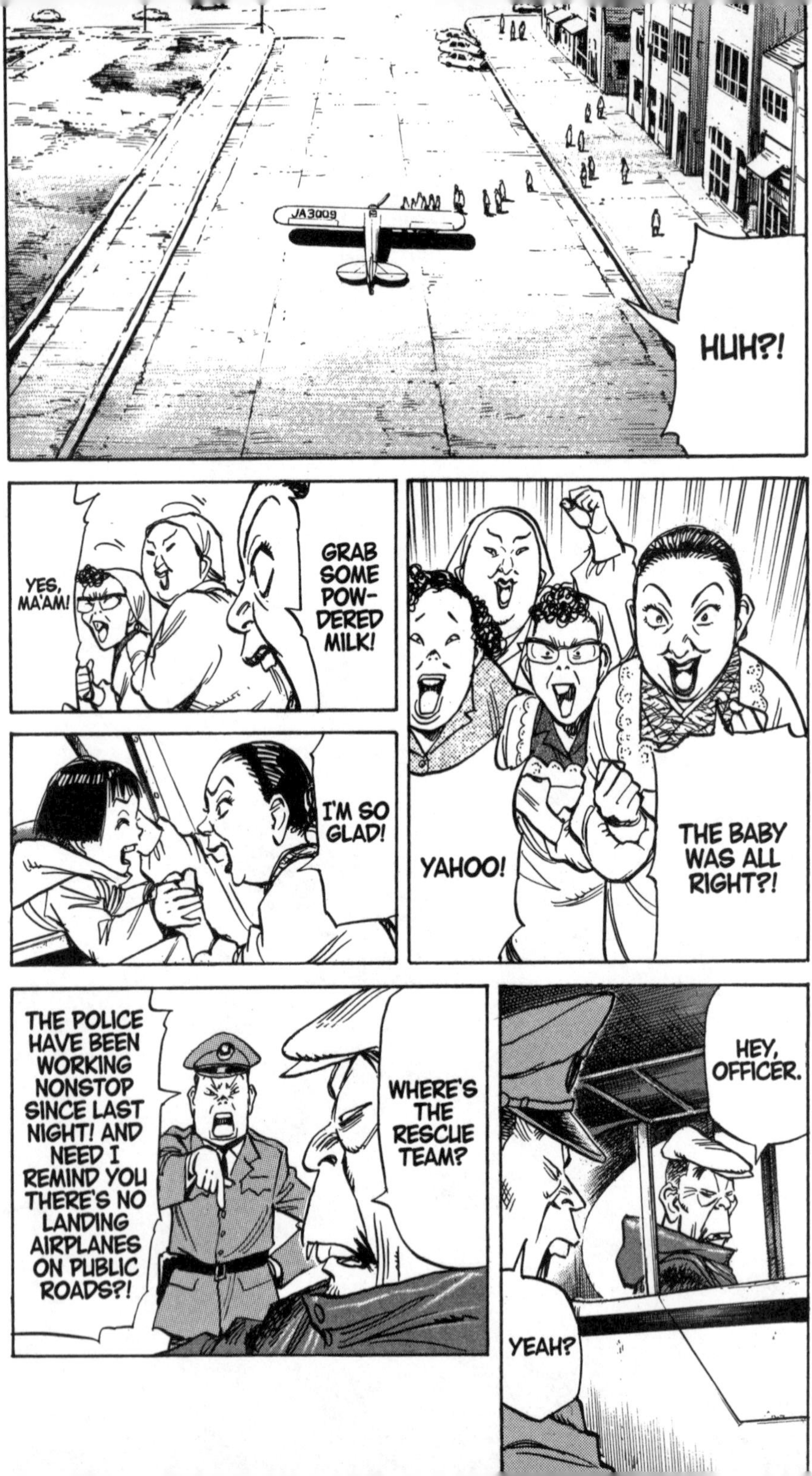
JA3009
HUH?!
THE BABY WAS ALL RIGHT?!
YAHOO!
GRAB SOME POW-DERED MILK!
YES, MA'AM!
I'M SO GLAD!
HEY, OFFICER.
YEAH?
WHERE'S THE RESCUE TEAM?
THE POLICE HAVE BEEN WORKING NONSTOP SINCE LAST NIGHT! AND NEED I REMIND YOU THERE'S NO LANDING AIRPLANES ON PUBLIC ROADS?!

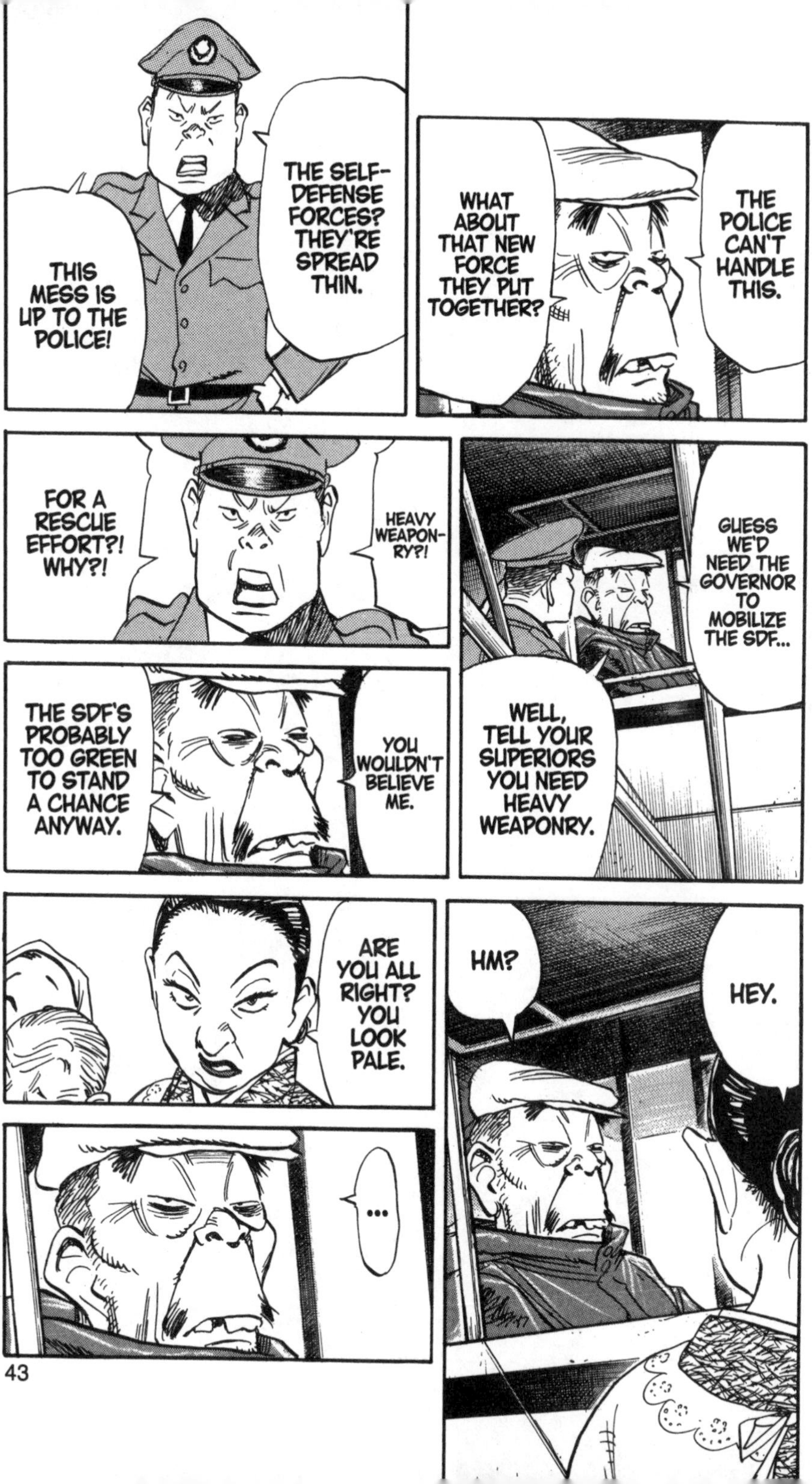
THE POLICE CAN'T HANDLE THIS.
WHAT ABOUT THAT NEW FORCE THEY PUT TOGETHER?
THE SELF-DEFENSE FORCES? THEY'RE SPREAD THIN.
THIS MESS IS UP TO THE POLICE!
GUESS WE'D NEED THE GOVERNOR TO MOBILIZE THE SDF...
WELL, TELL YOUR SUPERIORS YOU NEED HEAVY WEAPONRY.
HEAVY WEAPON-RY?!
FOR A RESCUE EFFORT?! WHY?!
YOU WOULDN'T BELIEVE ME.
THE SDF'S PROBABLY TOO GREEN TO STAND A CHANCE ANYWAY.
HEY.
HM?
ARE YOU ALL RIGHT? YOU LOOK PALE.
...

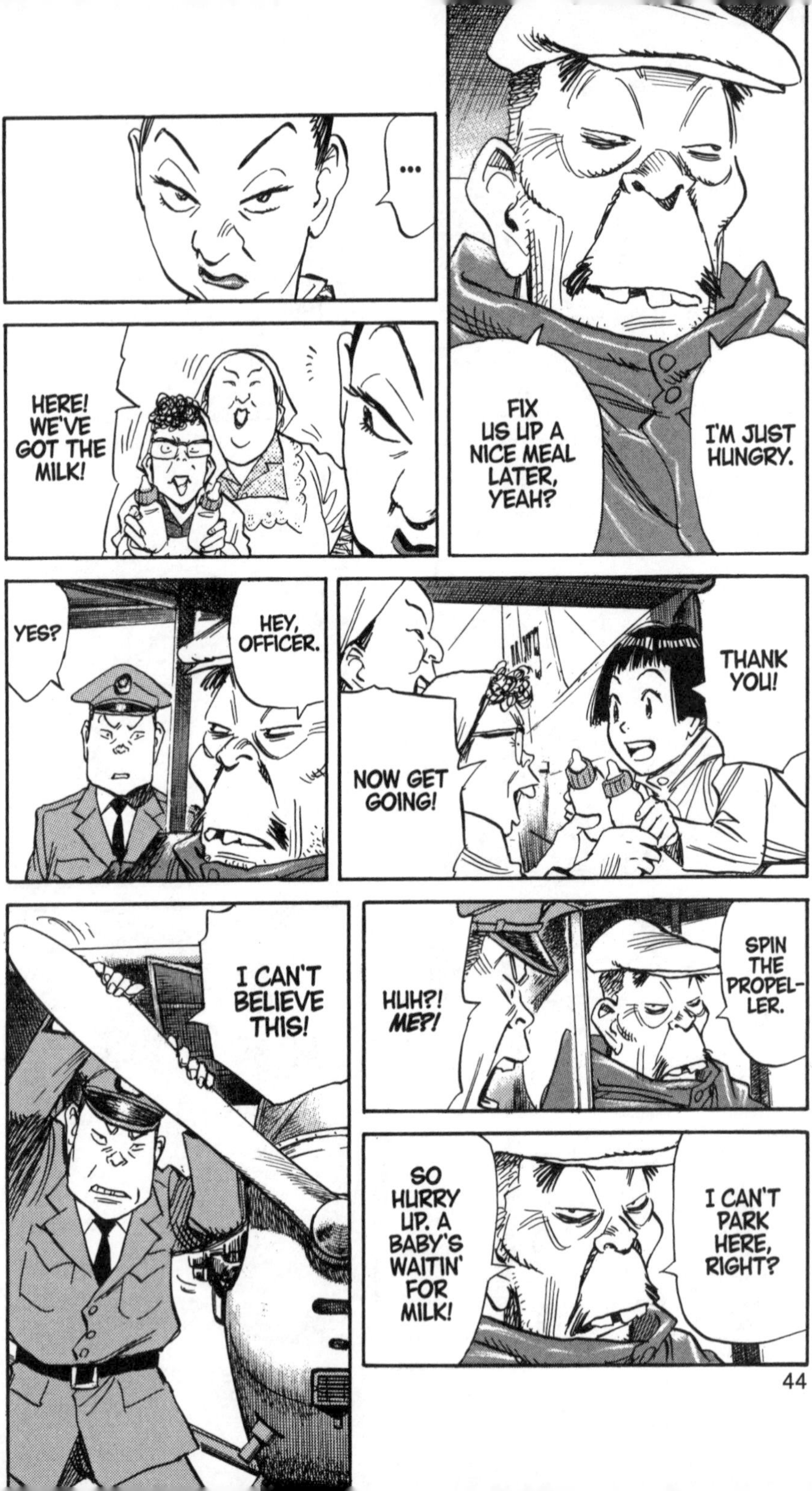
I'M JUST HUNGRY.
FIX US UP A NICE MEAL LATER, YEAH?
...
HERE! WE'VE GOT THE MILK!
THANK YOU!
NOW GET GOING!
HEY, OFFICER.
YES?
SPIN THE PROPEL-LER.
HUH?! *ME?!*
I CAN'T PARK HERE, RIGHT?
SO HURRY UP. A BABY'S WAITIN' FOR MILK!
I CAN'T BELIEVE THIS!

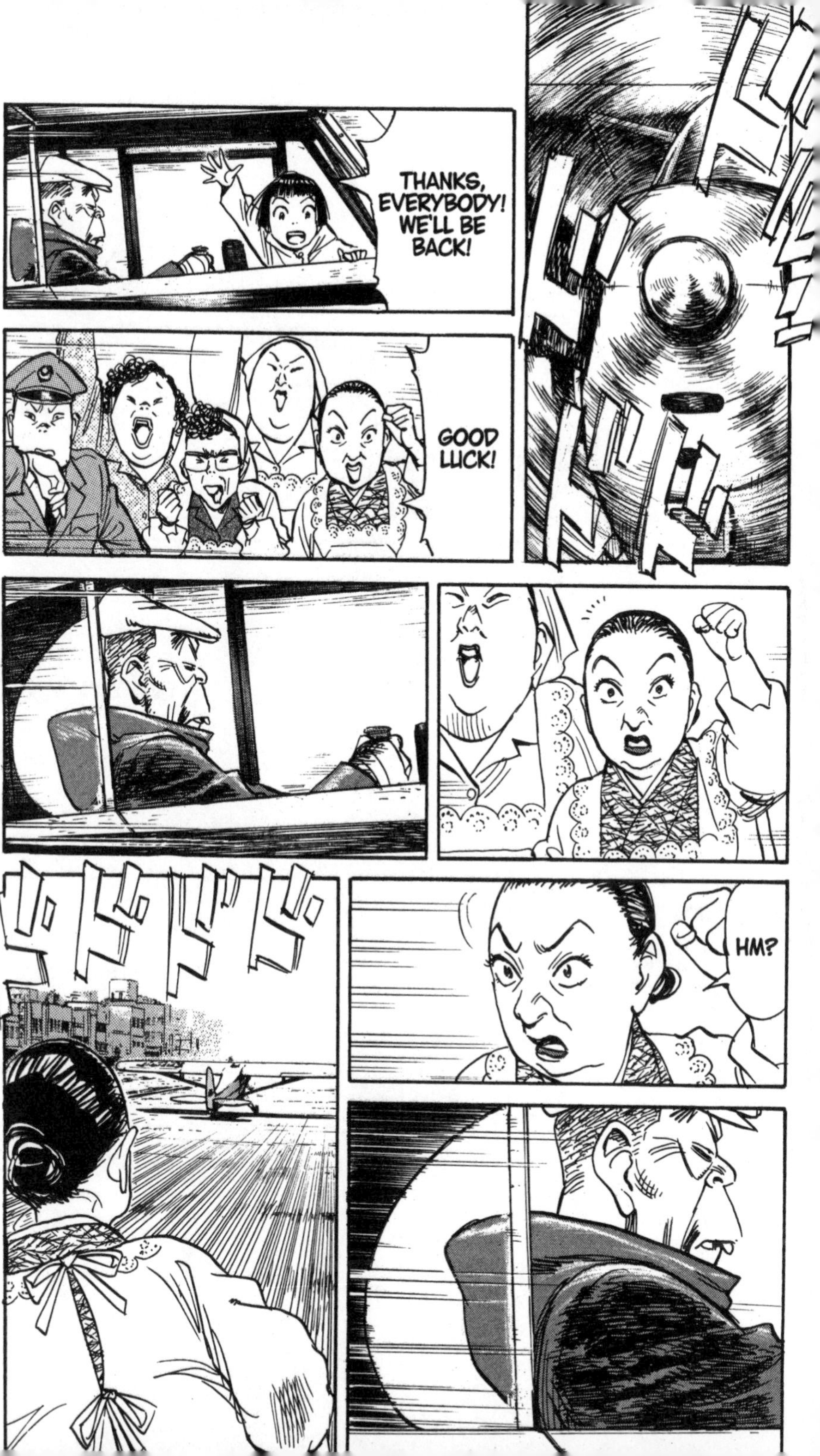
THANKS, EVERYBODY! WE'LL BE BACK!
GOOD LUCK!
HM?

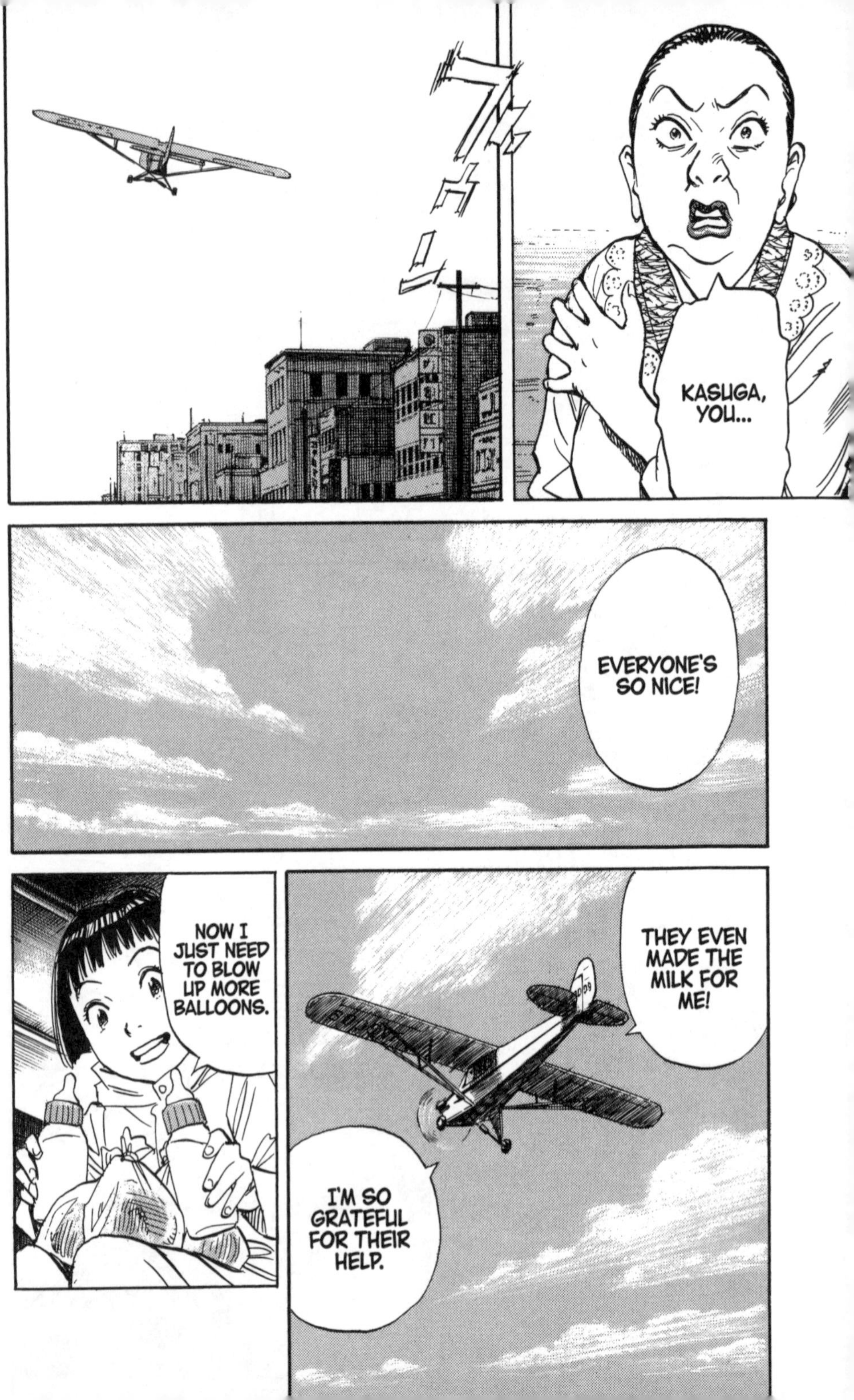
KASUGA, YOU...
EVERYONE'S SO NICE!
THEY EVEN MADE THE MILK FOR ME!
I'M SO GRATEFUL FOR THEIR HELP.
NOW I JUST NEED TO BLOW UP MORE BALLOONS.

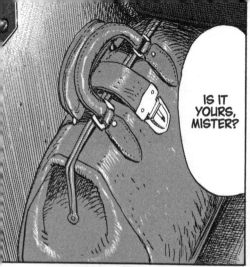

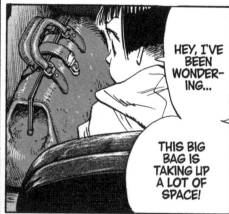

HEY, I'VE BEEN WONDERING...
THIS BIG BAG IS TAKING UP A LOT OF SPACE!
IS IT YOURS, MISTER?
WHAT'S INSIDE?
CAN I LOOK?
PCHAK
HM?
WHAT IS THIS?
OH! MORE POWDERED MILK!
YOU'RE SO NICE, MISTER!
YOU HAD POWDERED MILK FOR THE BABY ALL ALONG!

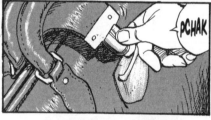

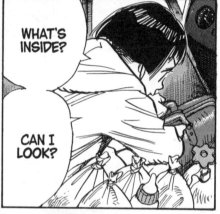

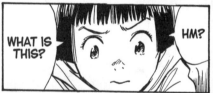

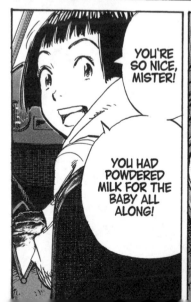

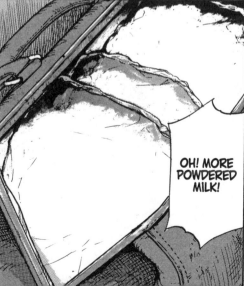

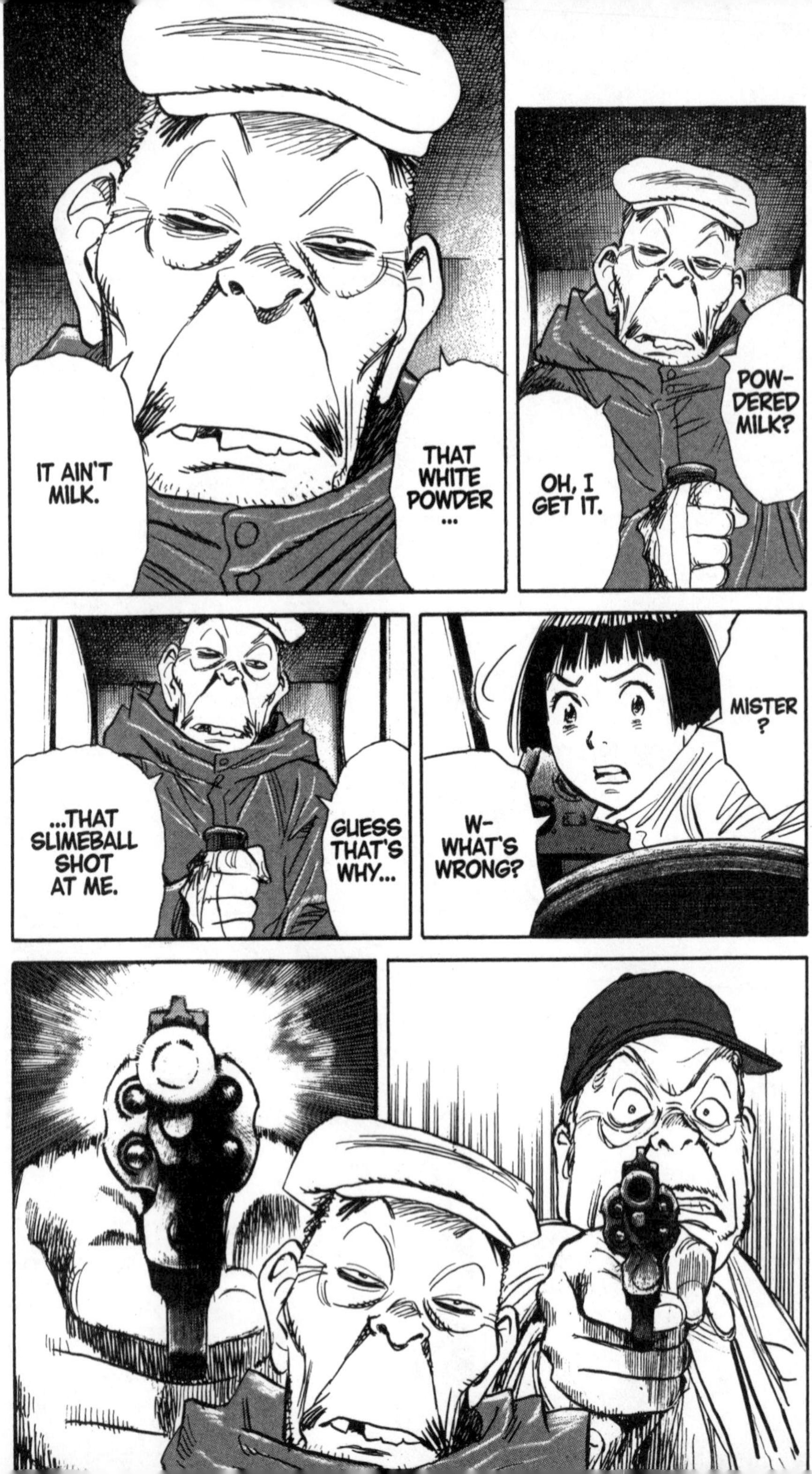
POW-DERED MILK?
OH, I GET IT.
THAT WHITE POWDER ...
IT AIN'T MILK.
MISTER ?
W-WHAT'S WRONG?
GUESS THAT'S WHY...
...THAT SLIMEBALL SHOT AT ME.

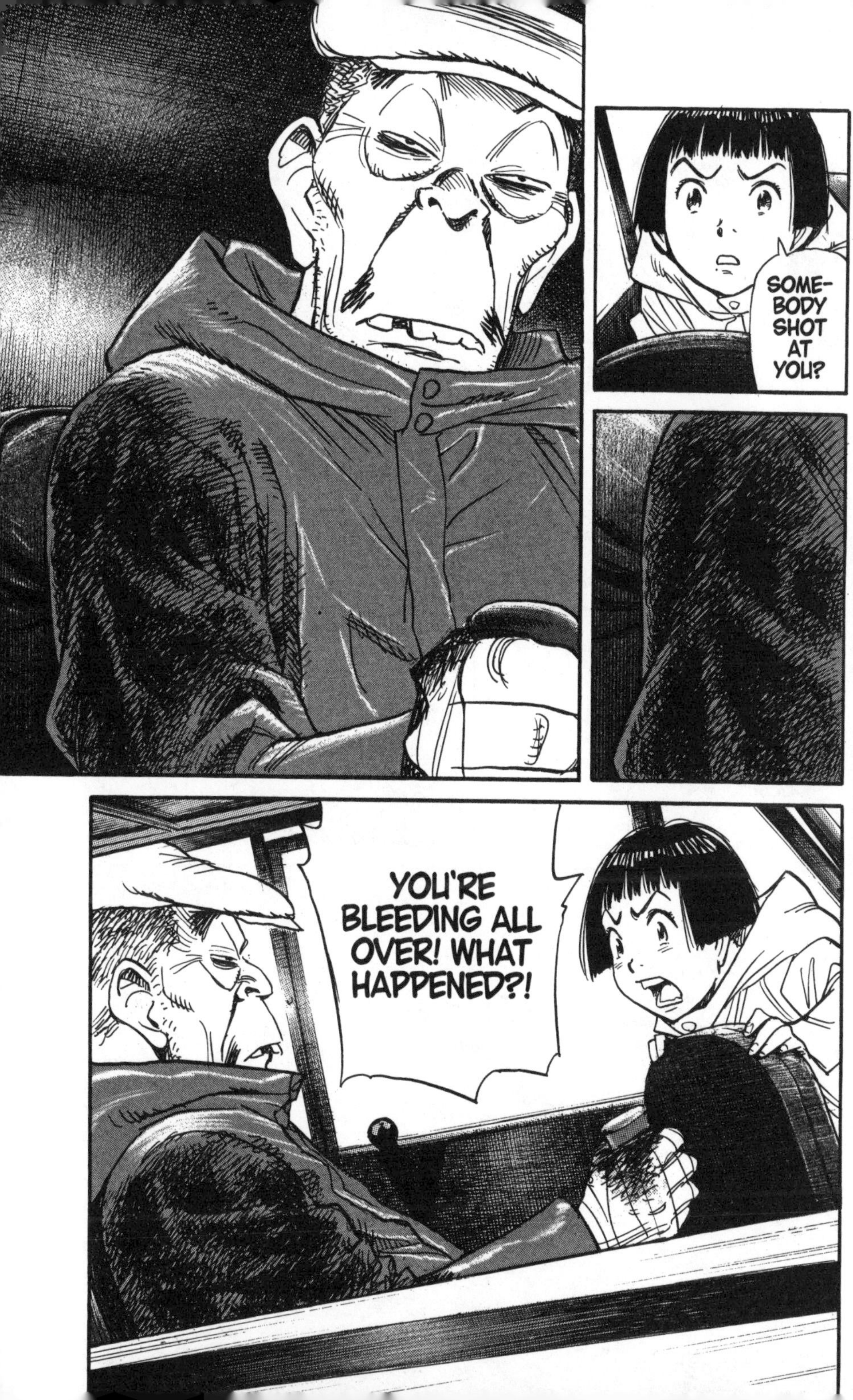
SOME-BODY SHOT AT YOU?
YOU'RE BLEEDING ALL OVER! WHAT HAPPENED?!

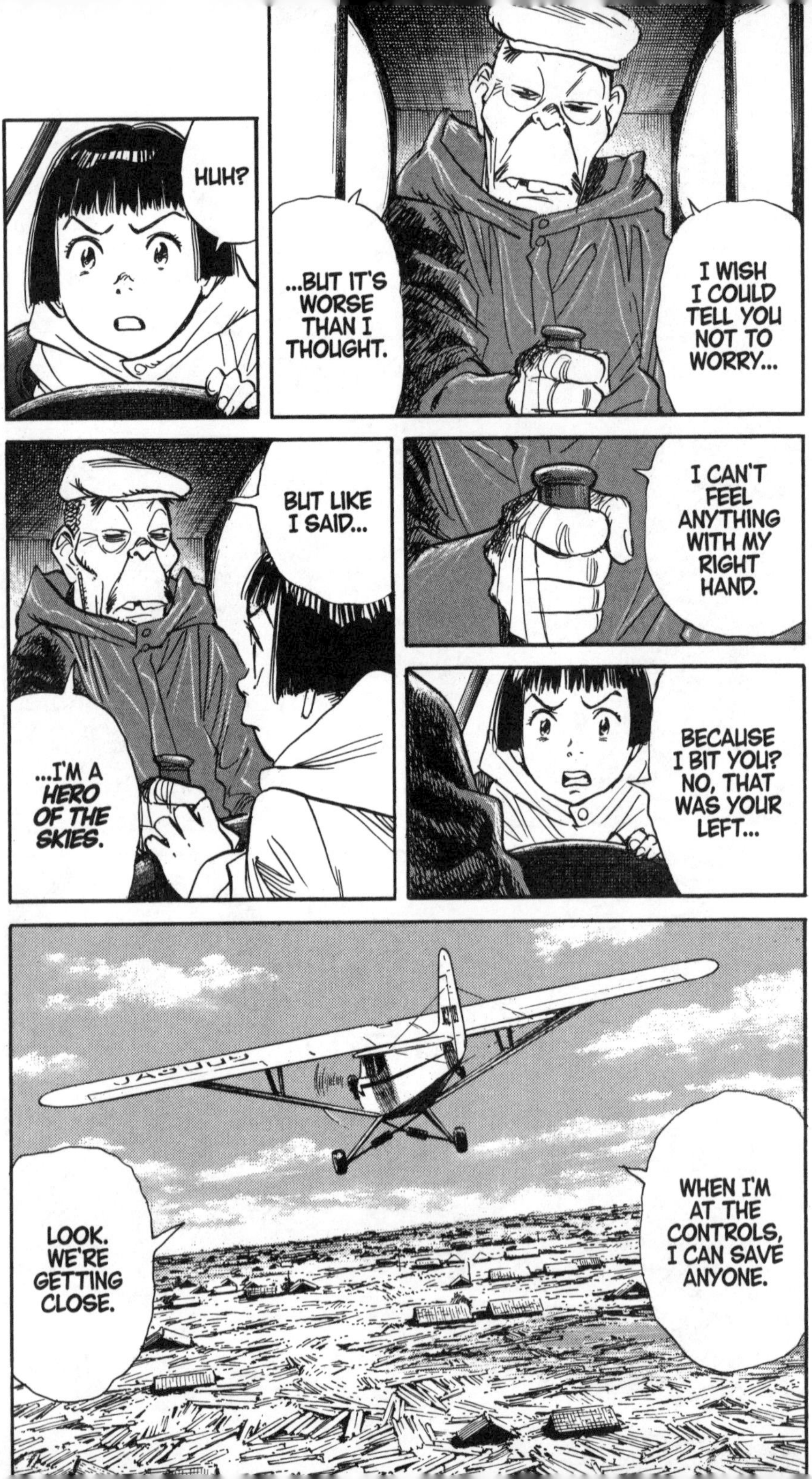
I WISH I COULD TELL YOU NOT TO WORRY...
...BUT IT'S WORSE THAN I THOUGHT.
HUH?
I CAN'T FEEL ANYTHING WITH MY RIGHT HAND.
BECAUSE I BIT YOU? NO, THAT WAS YOUR LEFT...
BUT LIKE I SAID...
...I'M A *HERO OF THE SKIES.*
WHEN I'M AT THE CONTROLS, I CAN SAVE ANYONE.
LOOK. WE'RE GETTING CLOSE.

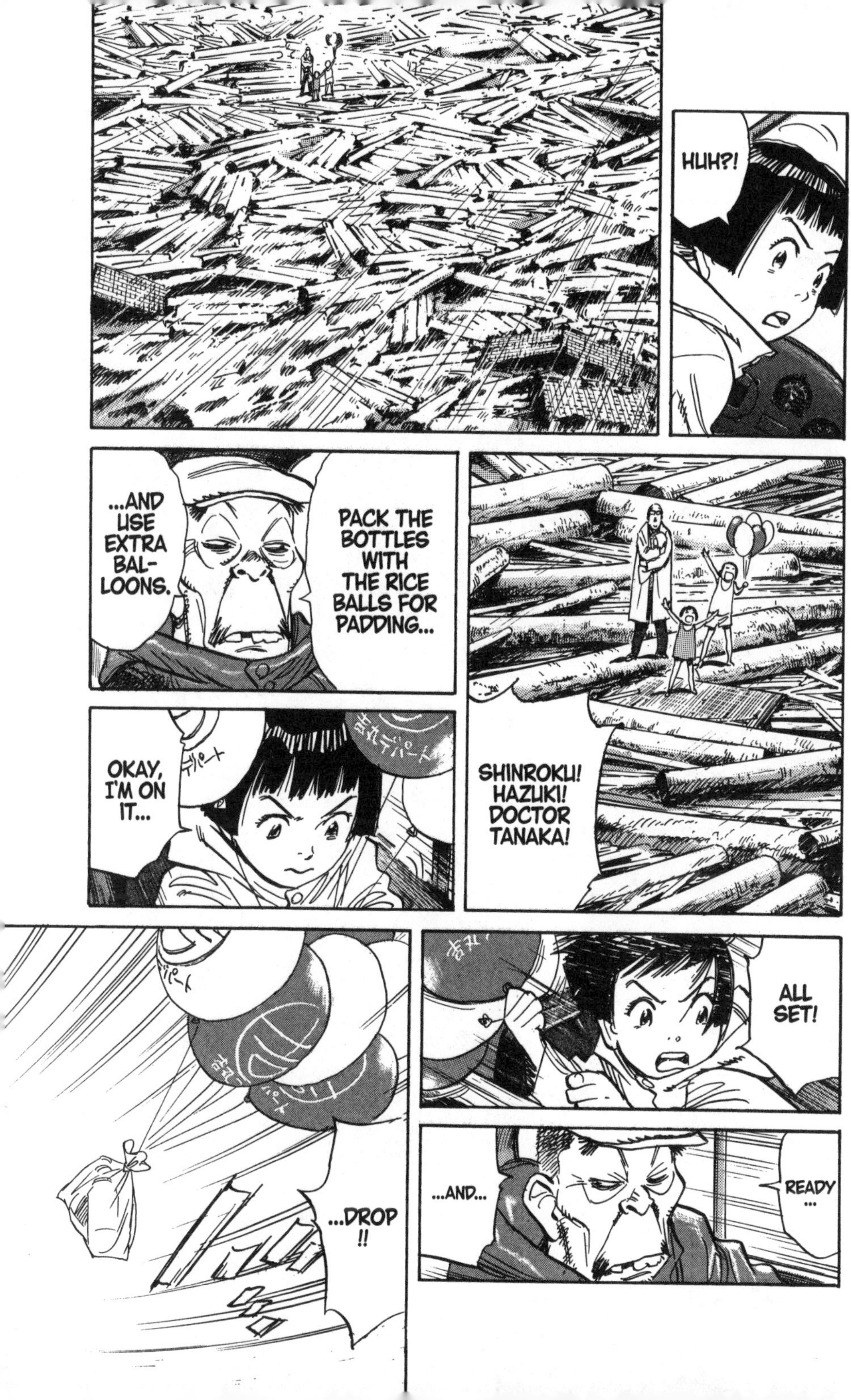
HUH?!
SHINROKU! HAZUKI! DOCTOR TANAKA!
PACK THE BOTTLES WITH THE RICE BALLS FOR PADDING...
...AND USE EXTRA BAL-LOONS.
OKAY, I'M ON IT...
ALL SET!
READY...
...AND...
...DROP!!

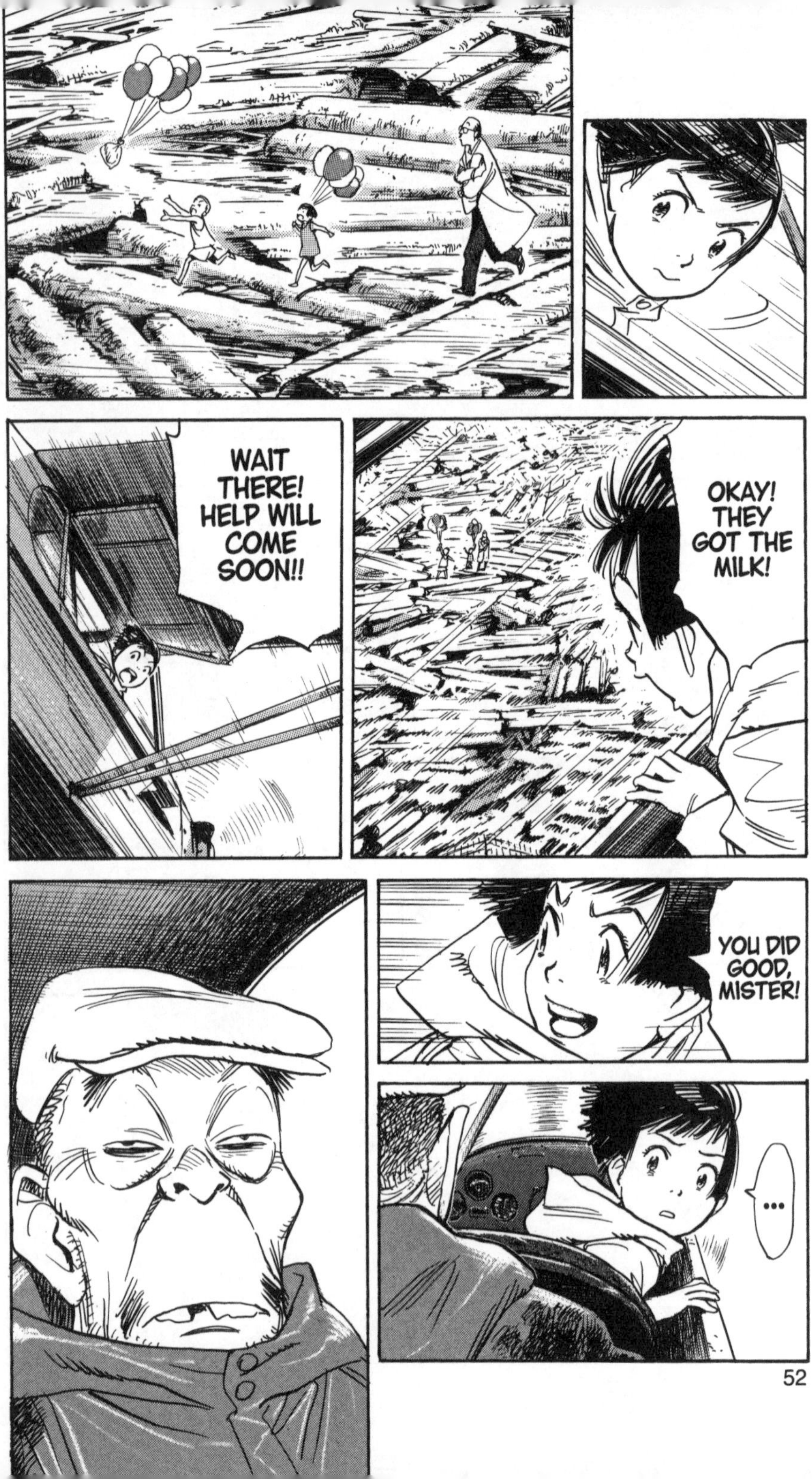
OKAY! THEY GOT THE MILK!
WAIT THERE! HELP WILL COME SOON!!
YOU DID GOOD, MISTER!
...

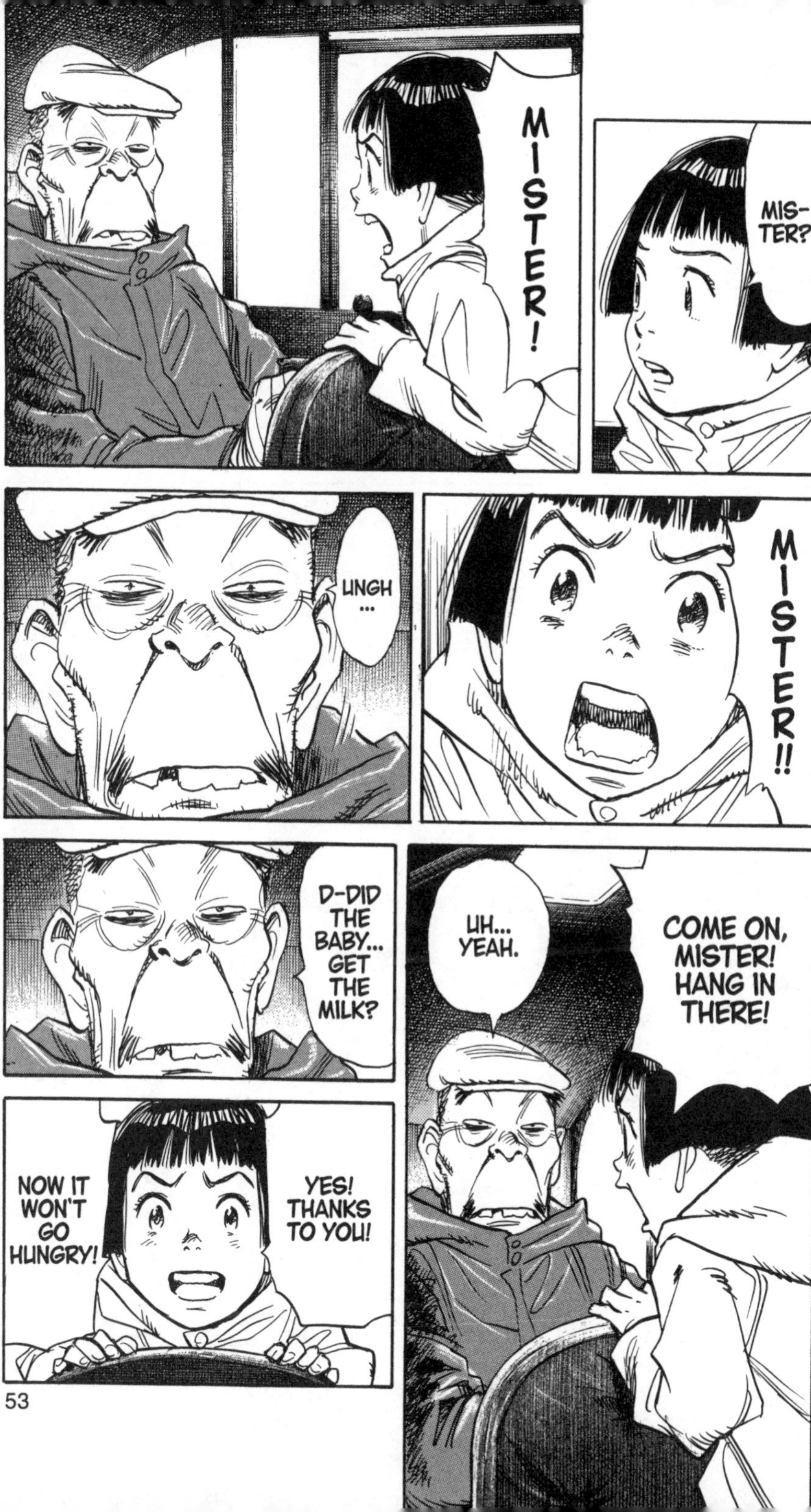
MIS-TER?
MISTER!
MISTER!!
UNGH ...
COME ON, MISTER! HANG IN THERE!
UH... YEAH.
D-DID THE BABY... GET THE MILK?
YES! THANKS TO YOU!
NOW IT WON'T GO HUNGRY!

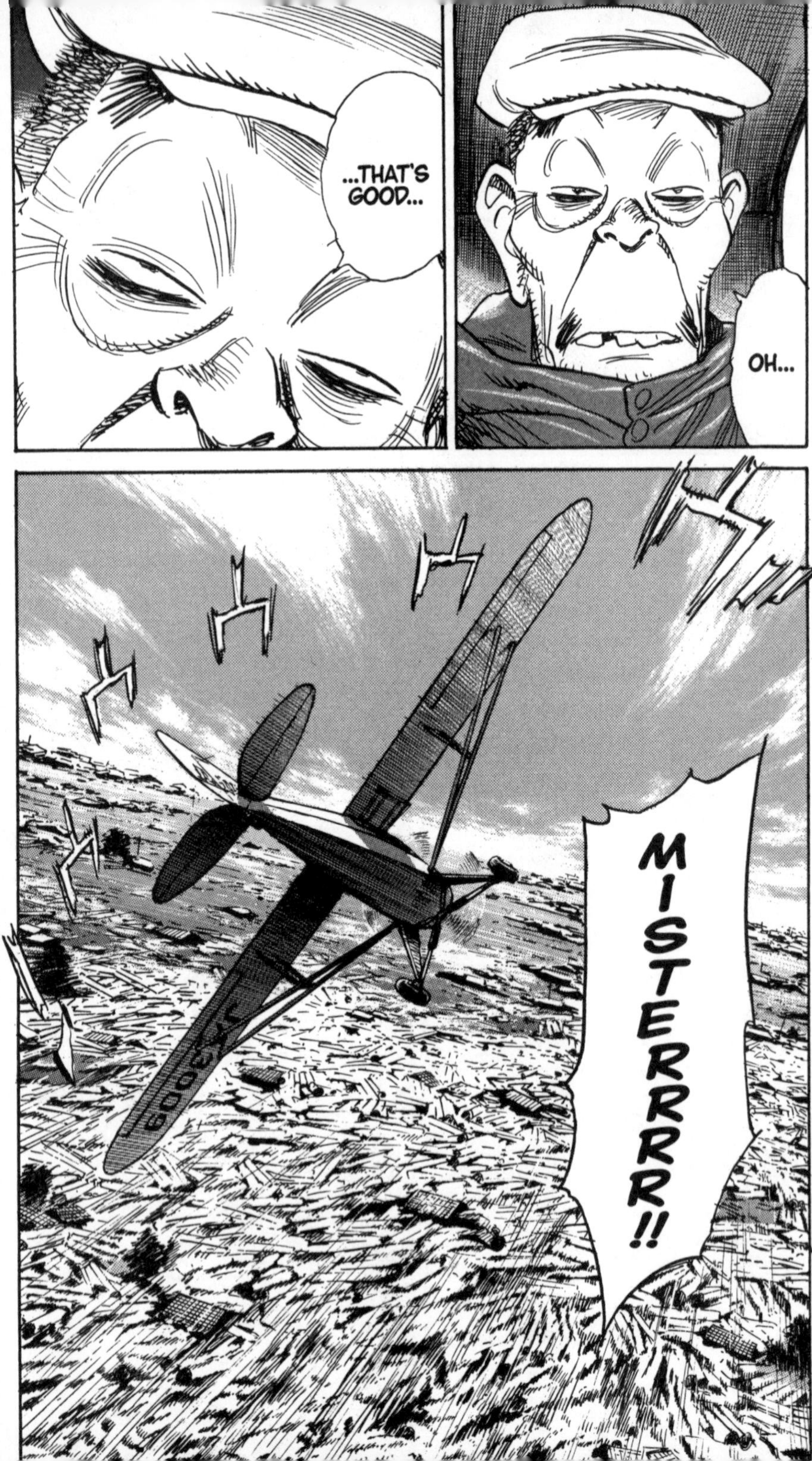
OH...
...THAT'S GOOD...
MISTERRRR!!

ASADORA!

ASADORA!

Chapter 11 ● At the Controls

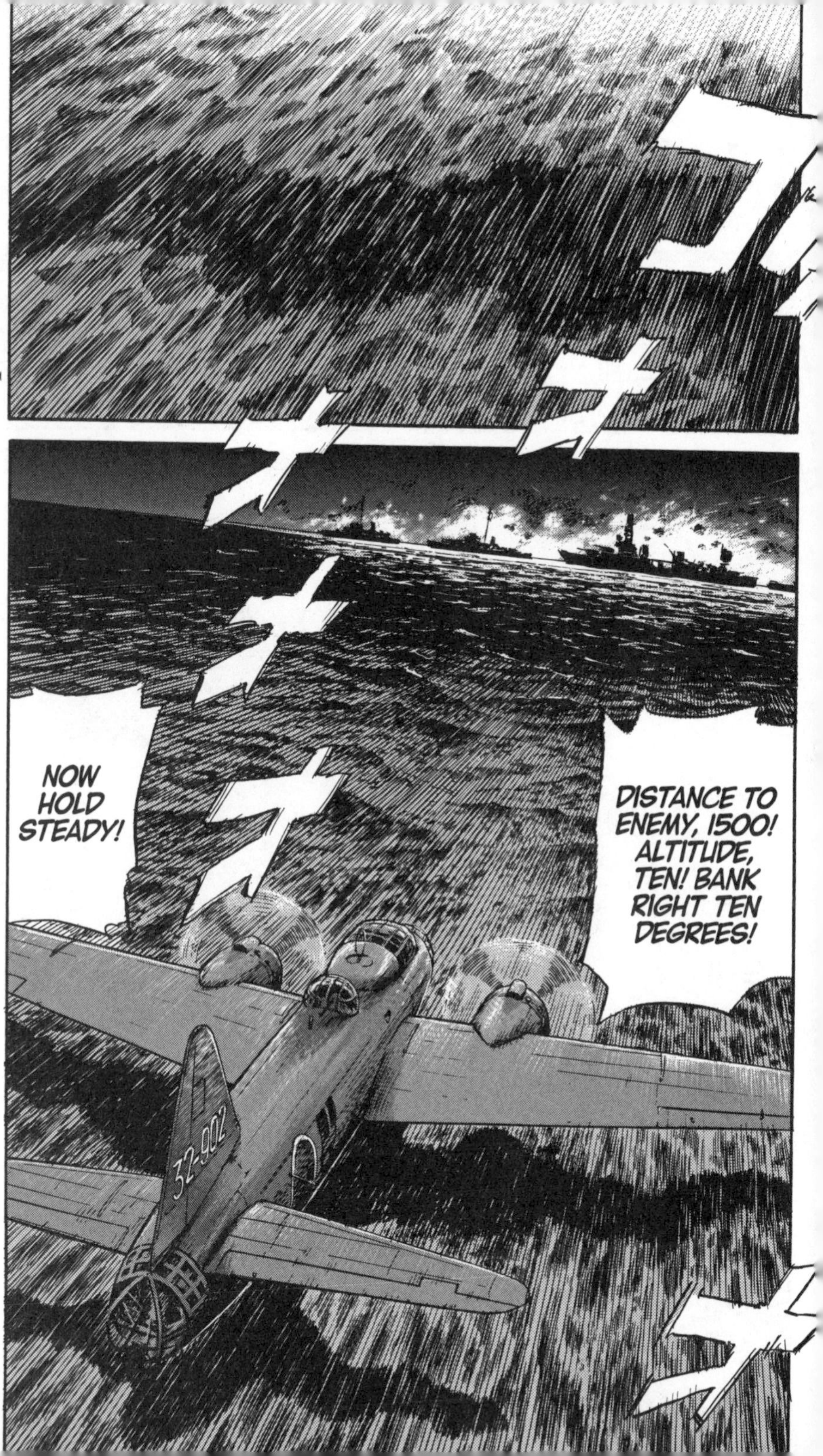

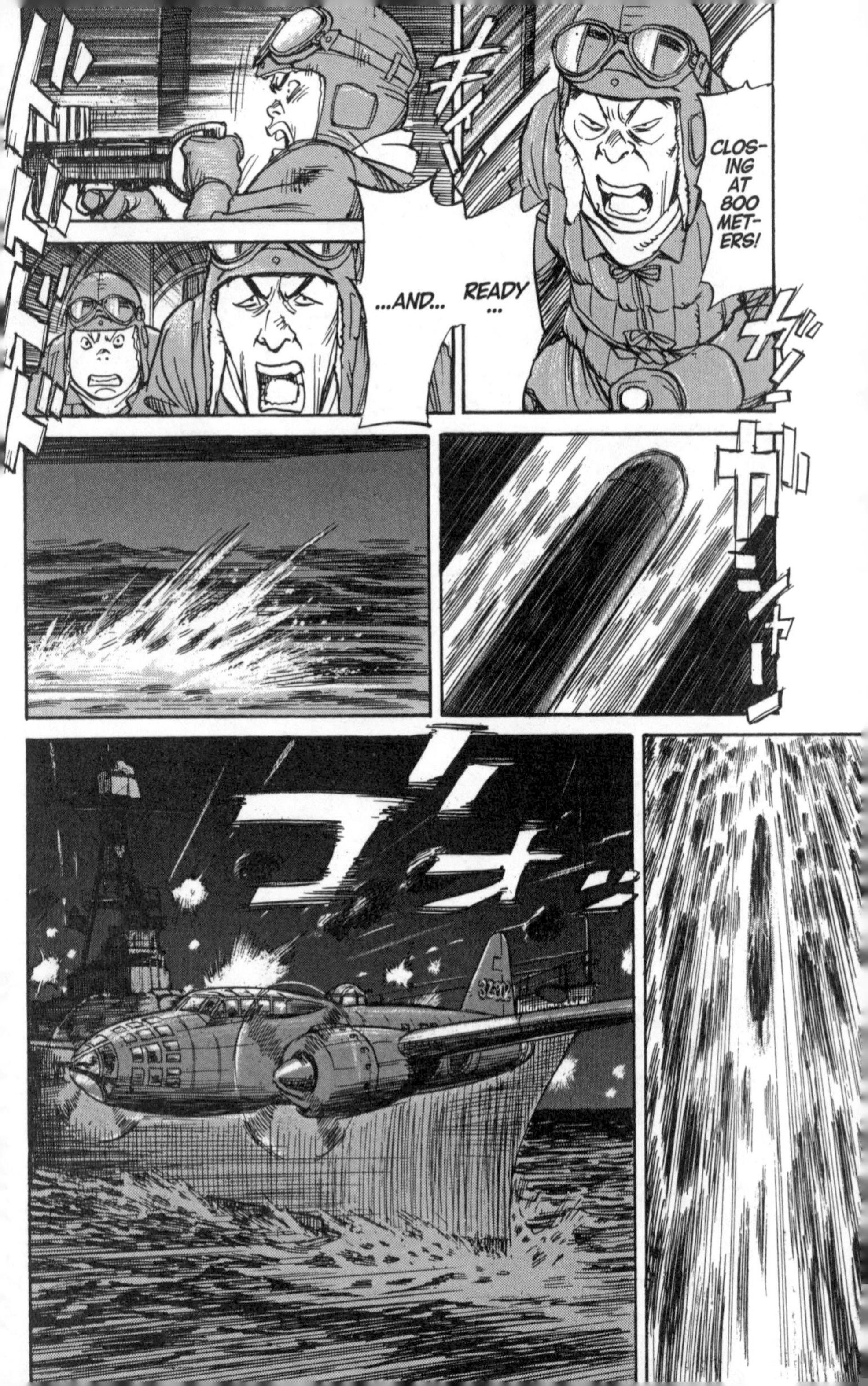

CLOSING AT 800 METERS!
READY...
...AND...

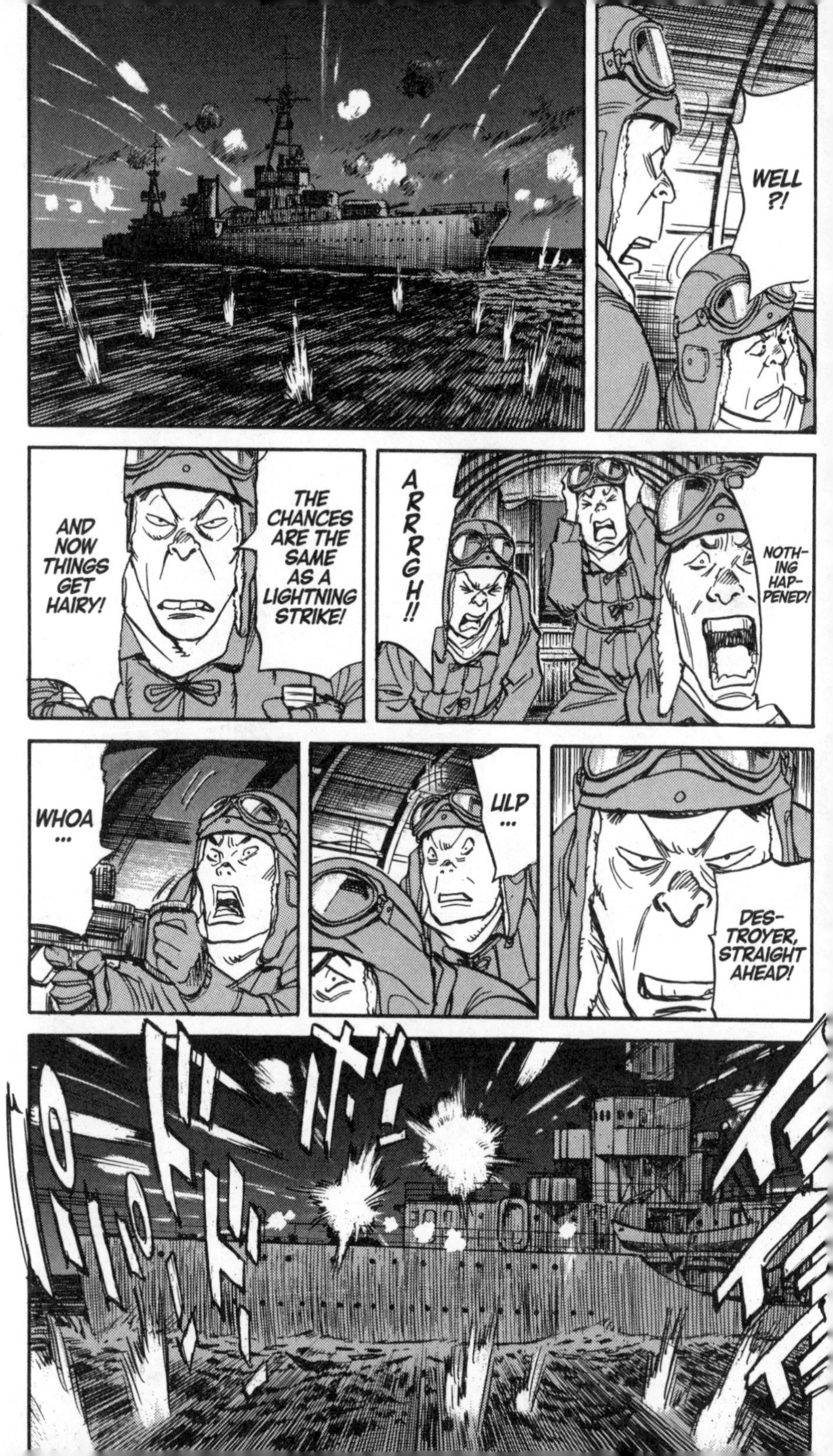
WELL ?!
ARRRGH!!
NOTHING HAPPENED!
THE CHANCES ARE THE SAME AS A LIGHTNING STRIKE!
AND NOW THINGS GET HAIRY!
DESTROYER, STRAIGHT AHEAD!
ULP ...
WHOA ...

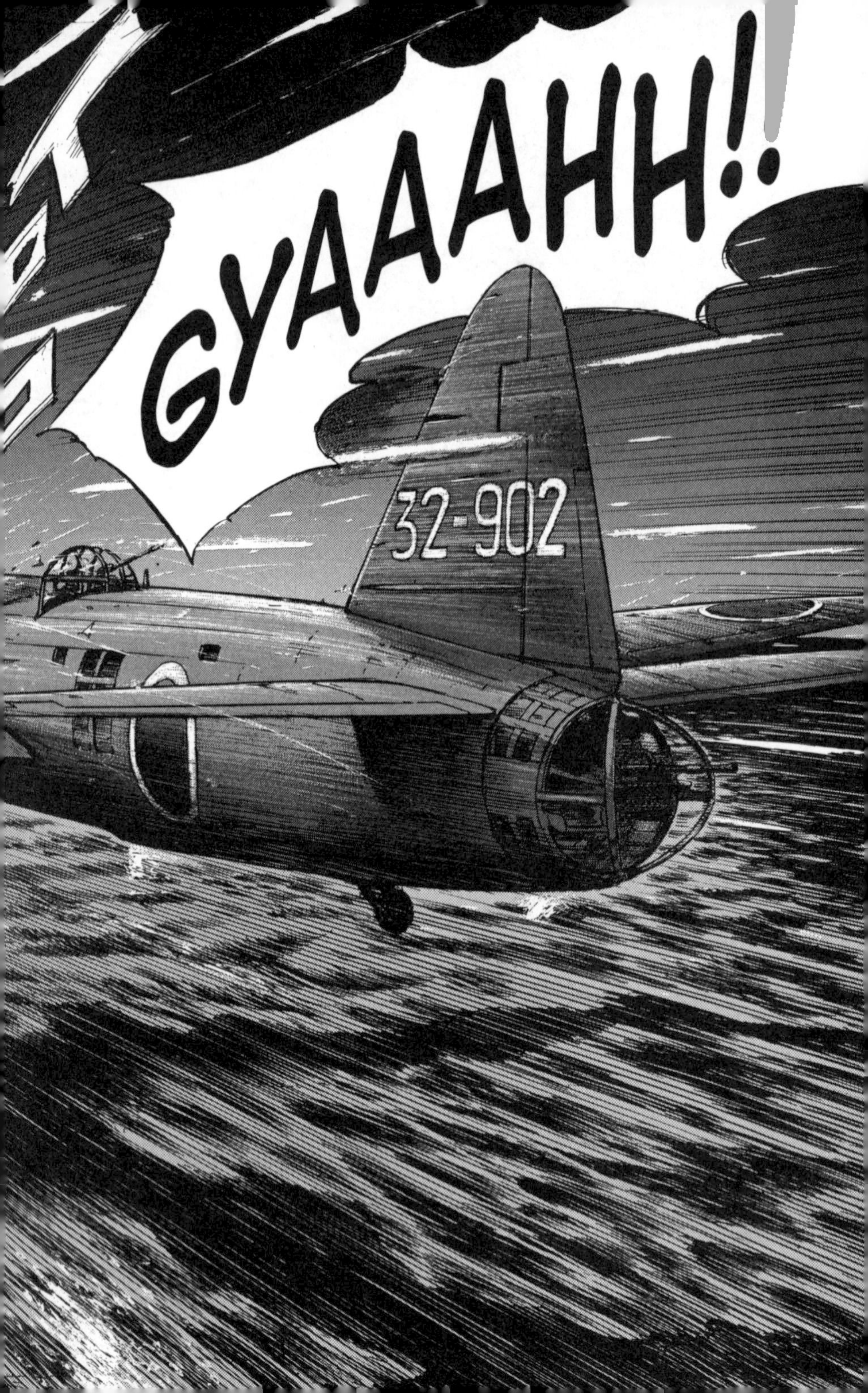
GYAAAHH!!
32-902

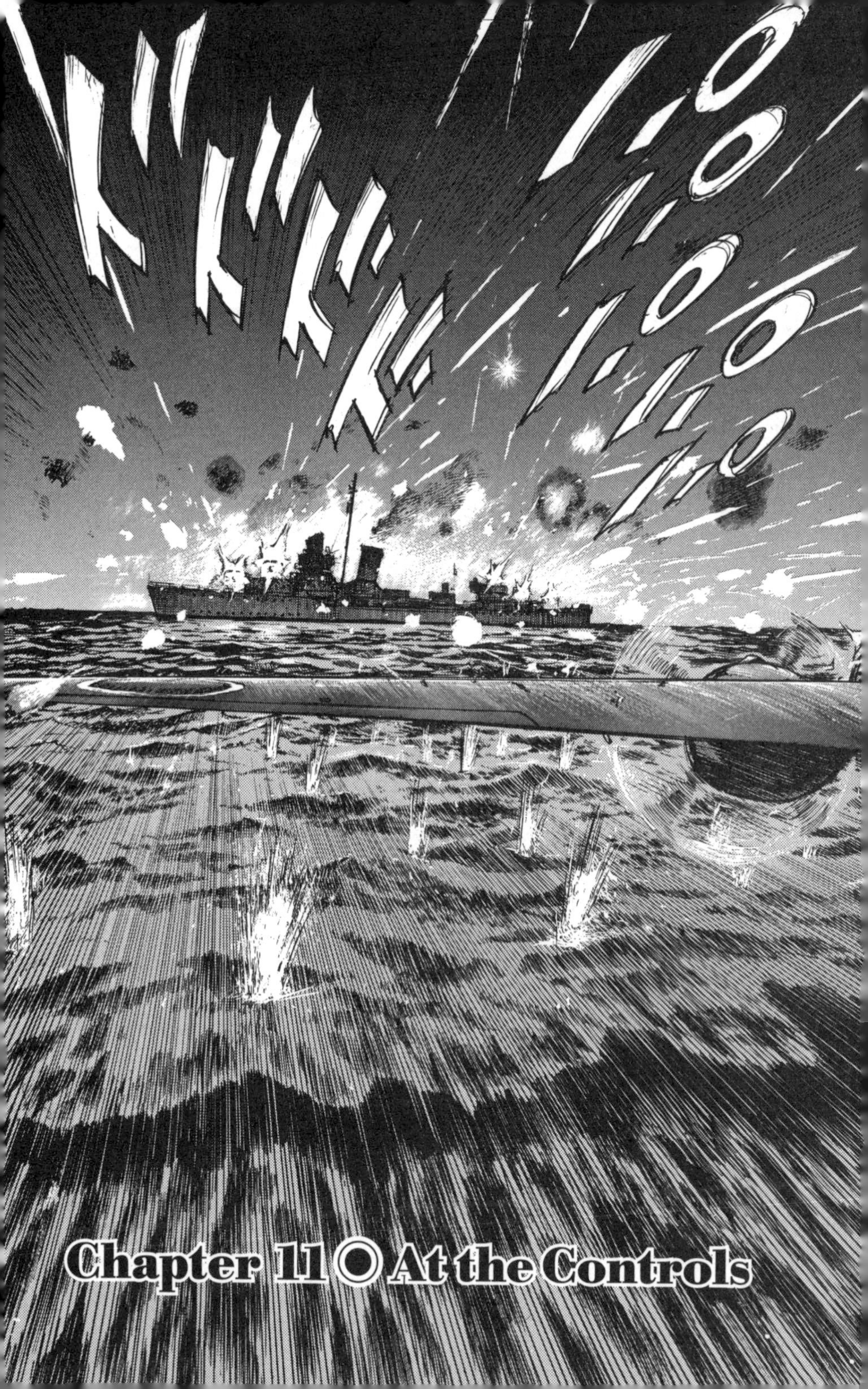
Chapter 11 ○ At the Controls

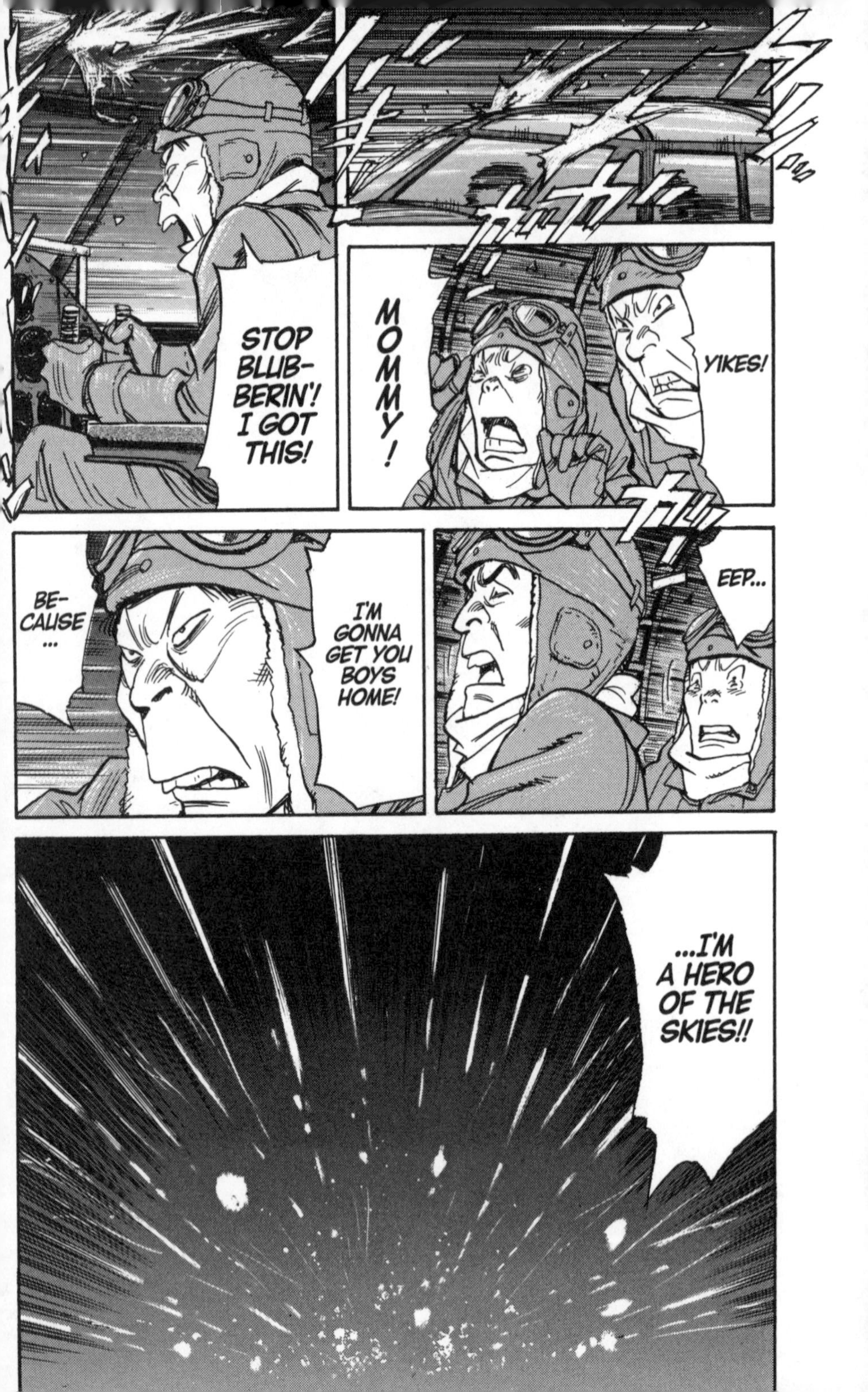
YIKES!
MOMMY!
STOP BLUB-BERIN'! I GOT THIS!
EEP...
I'M GONNA GET YOU BOYS HOME!
BE-CAUSE ...
...I'M A HERO OF THE SKIES!!

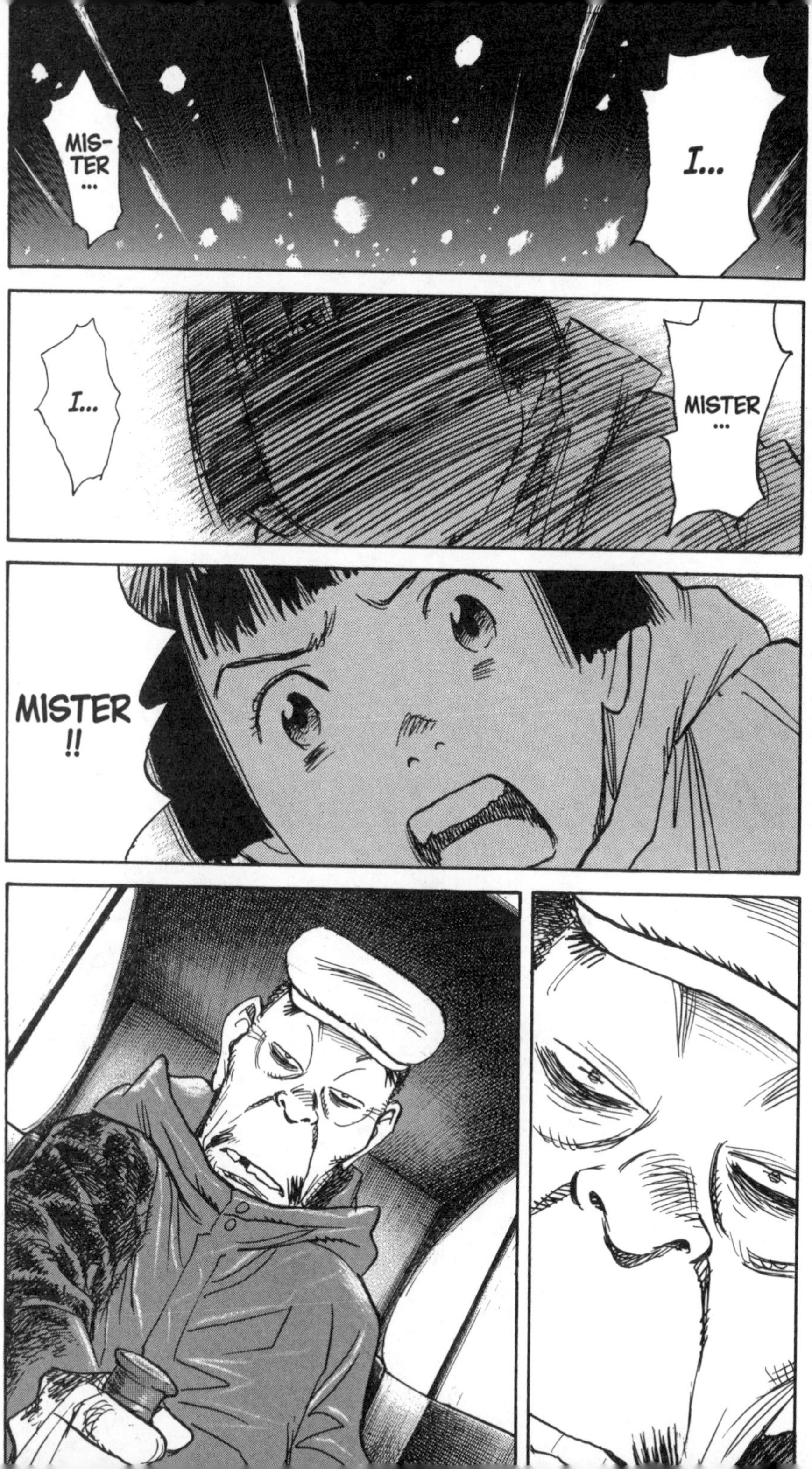
I...
MIS-TER...
MISTER...
I...
MISTER!!

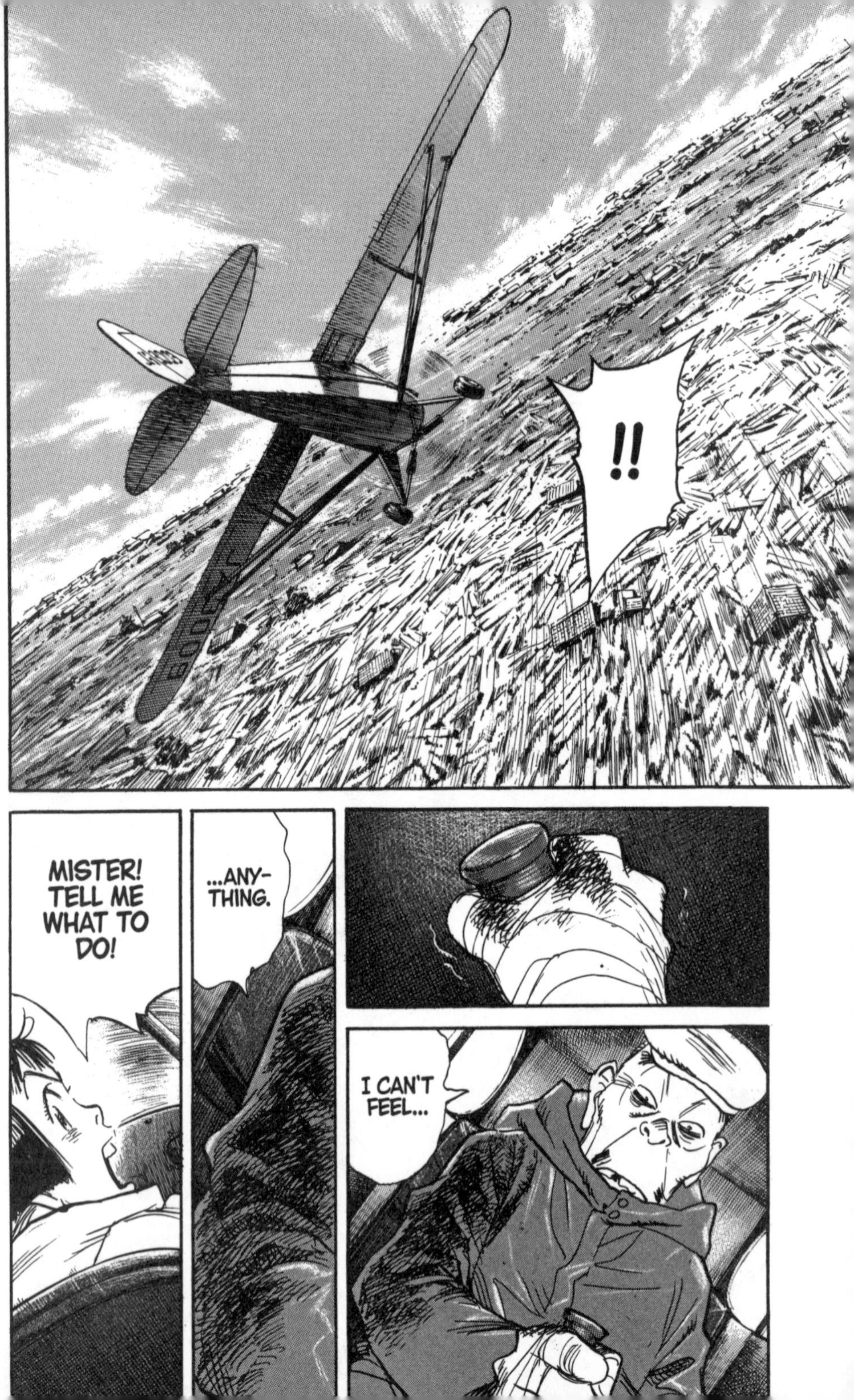
!!
I CAN'T FEEL...
...ANY-THING.
MISTER! TELL ME WHAT TO DO!

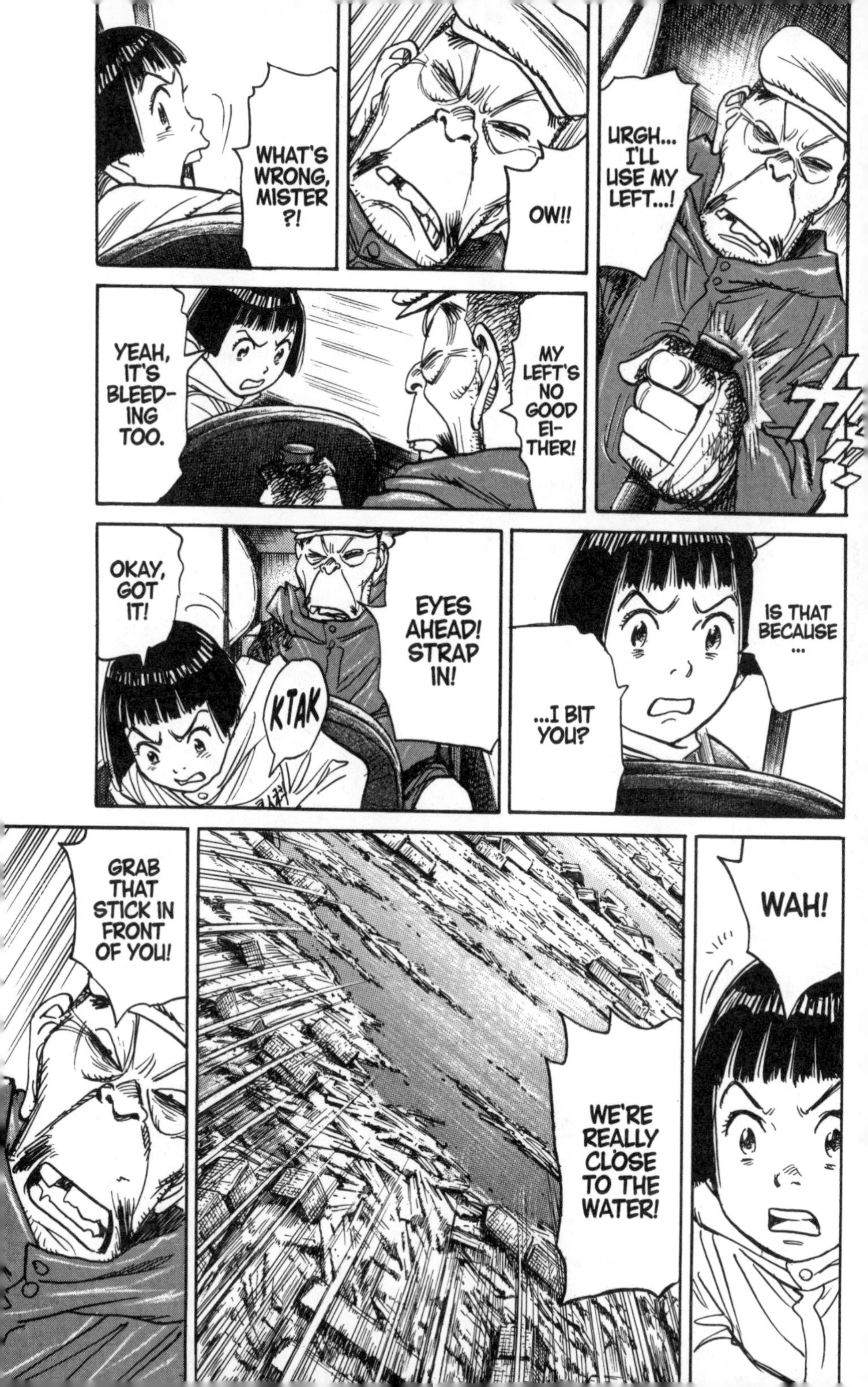
URGH... I'LL USE MY LEFT...!
OW!!
WHAT'S WRONG, MISTER ?!
MY LEFT'S NO GOOD EI- THER!
YEAH, IT'S BLEED- ING TOO.
IS THAT BECAUSE ...
...I BIT YOU?
EYES AHEAD! STRAP IN!
KTAK
OKAY, GOT IT!
WAH!
WE'RE REALLY CLOSE TO THE WATER!
GRAB THAT STICK IN FRONT OF YOU!

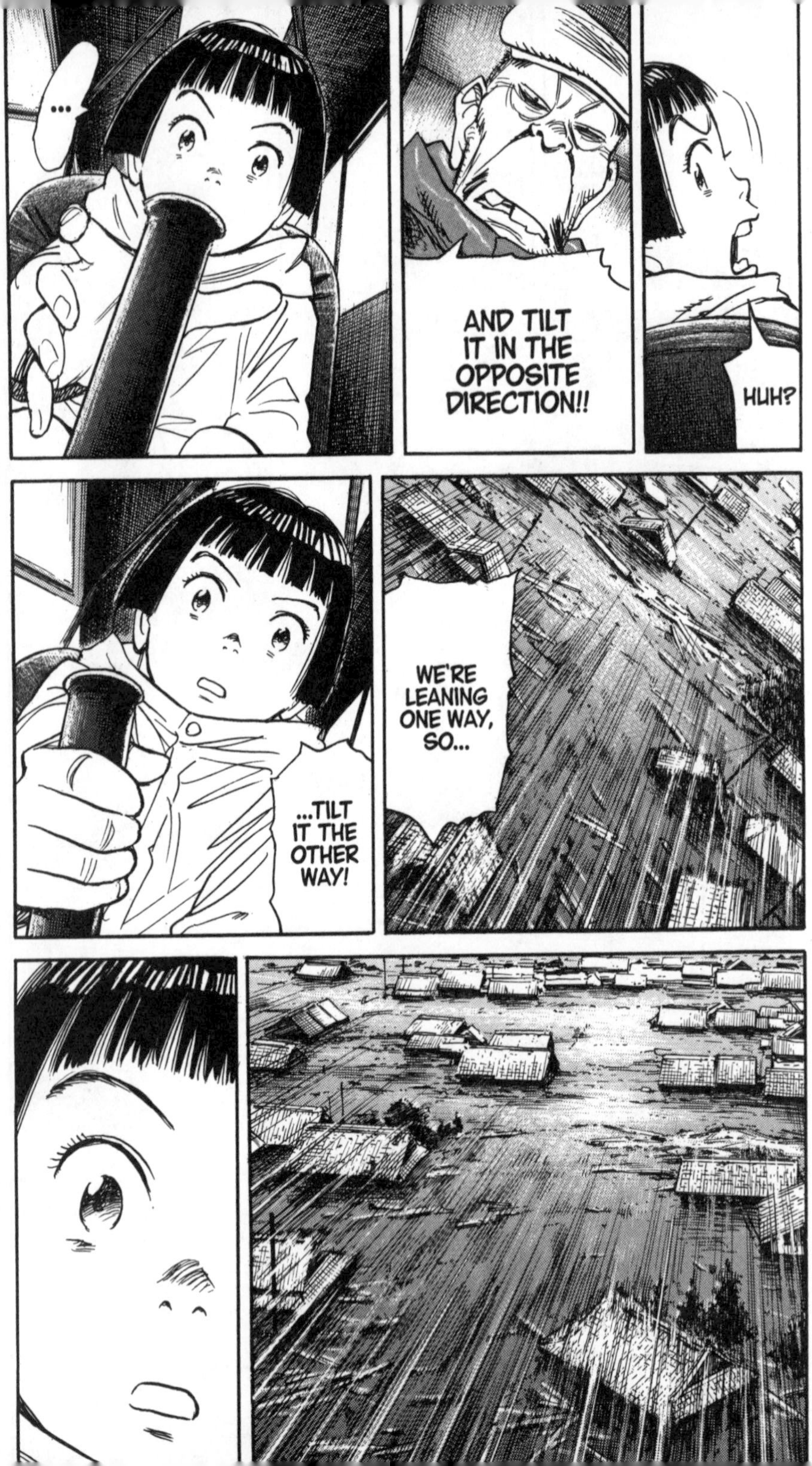
HUH?
AND TILT IT IN THE OPPOSITE DIRECTION!!
...
WE'RE LEANING ONE WAY, SO...
...TILT IT THE OTHER WAY!

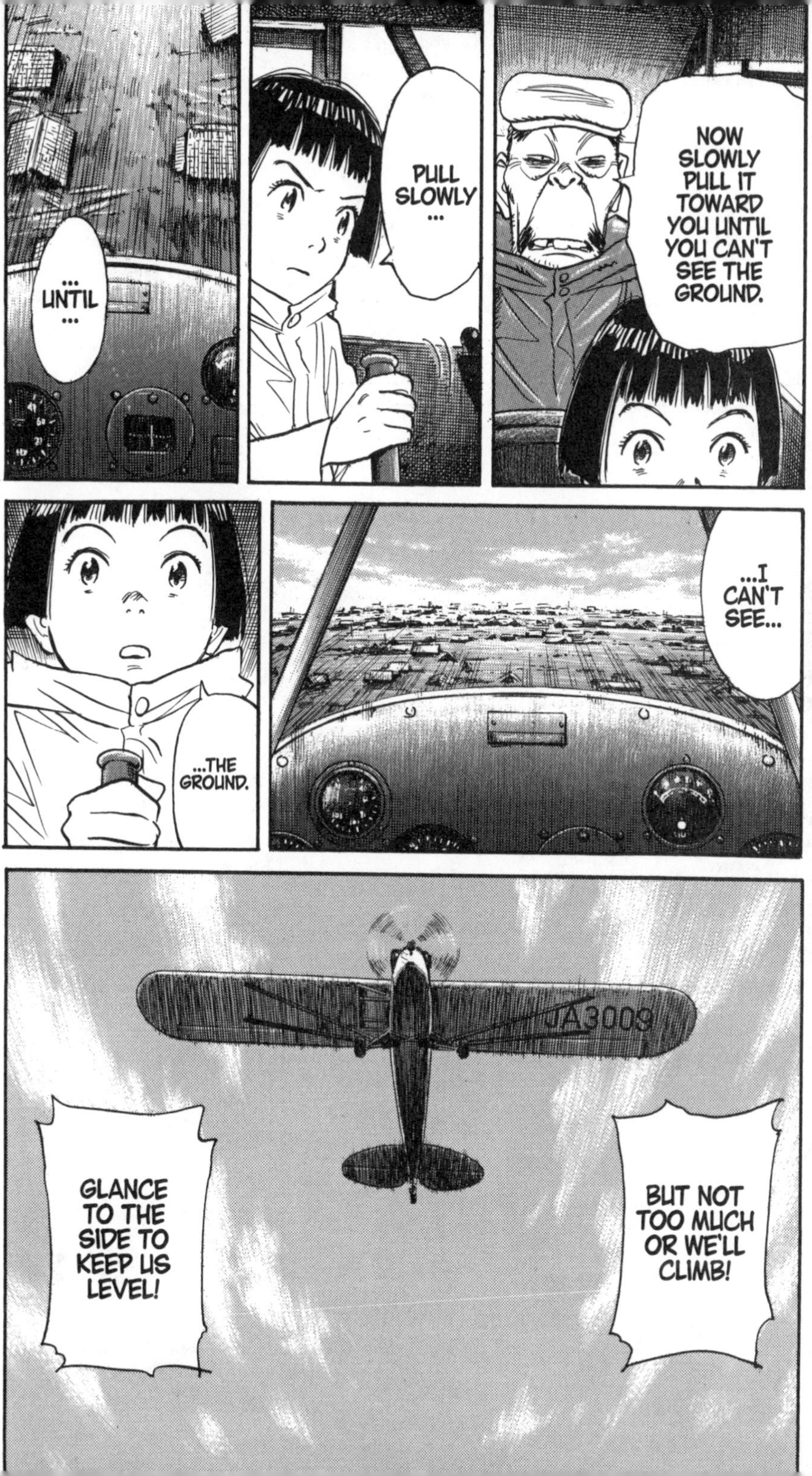
NOW SLOWLY PULL IT TOWARD YOU UNTIL YOU CAN'T SEE THE GROUND.
PULL SLOWLY ...
... UNTIL ...
...I CAN'T SEE...
...THE GROUND.
BUT NOT TOO MUCH OR WE'LL CLIMB!
JA3009
GLANCE TO THE SIDE TO KEEP US LEVEL!

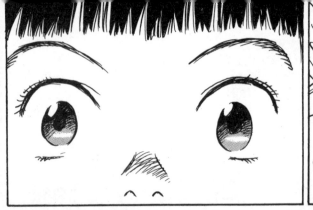

...THE GROUND...

LEVEL WITH...

MISTER, I—

I'M REALLY DOING IT!

MISTER!

I'M FLYING!

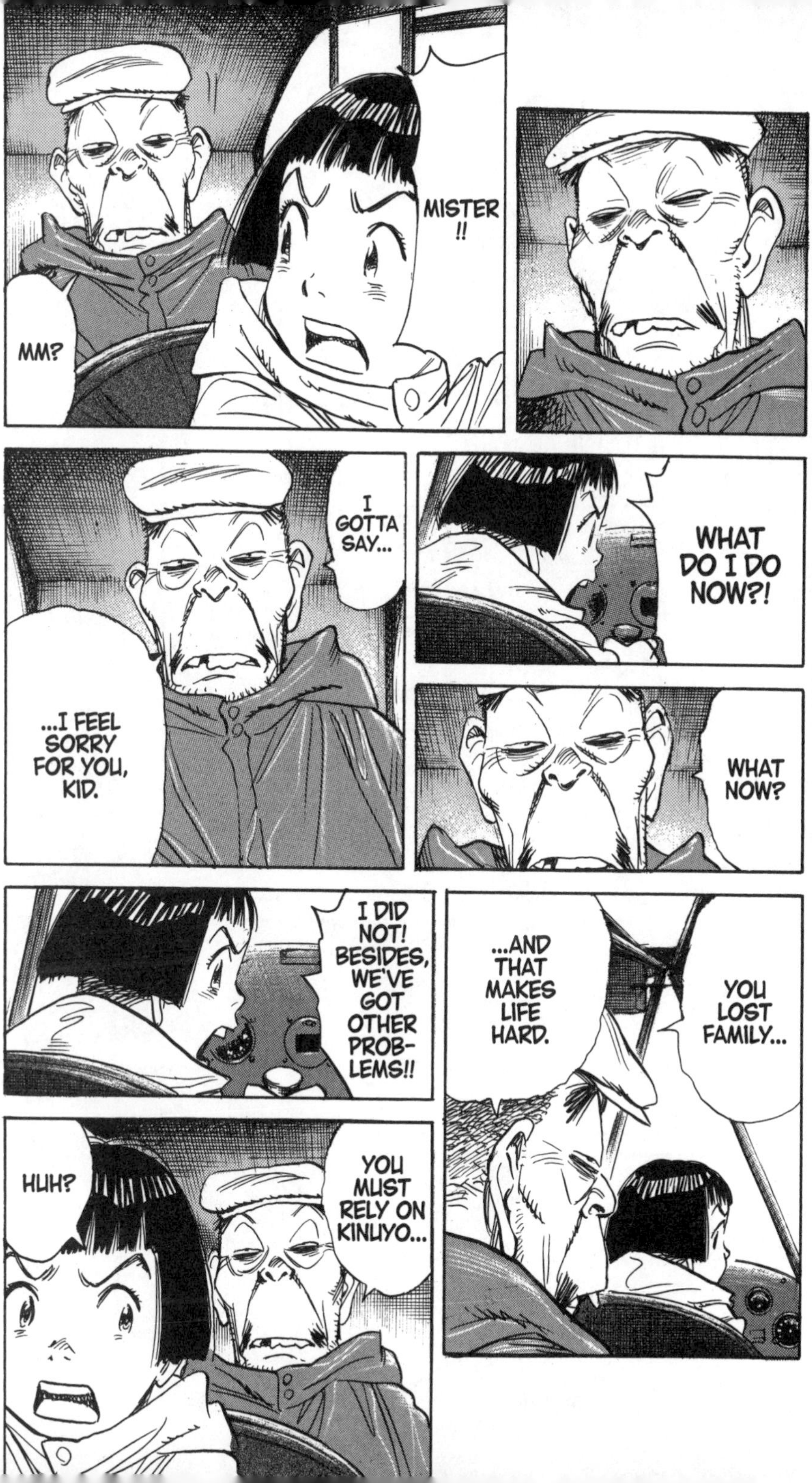
MISTER !!
MM?
WHAT DO I DO NOW?!
WHAT NOW?
I GOTTA SAY...
...I FEEL SORRY FOR YOU, KID.
YOU LOST FAMILY...
...AND THAT MAKES LIFE HARD.
I DID NOT! BESIDES, WE'VE GOT OTHER PROB-LEMS!!
YOU MUST RELY ON KINUYO...
HUH?

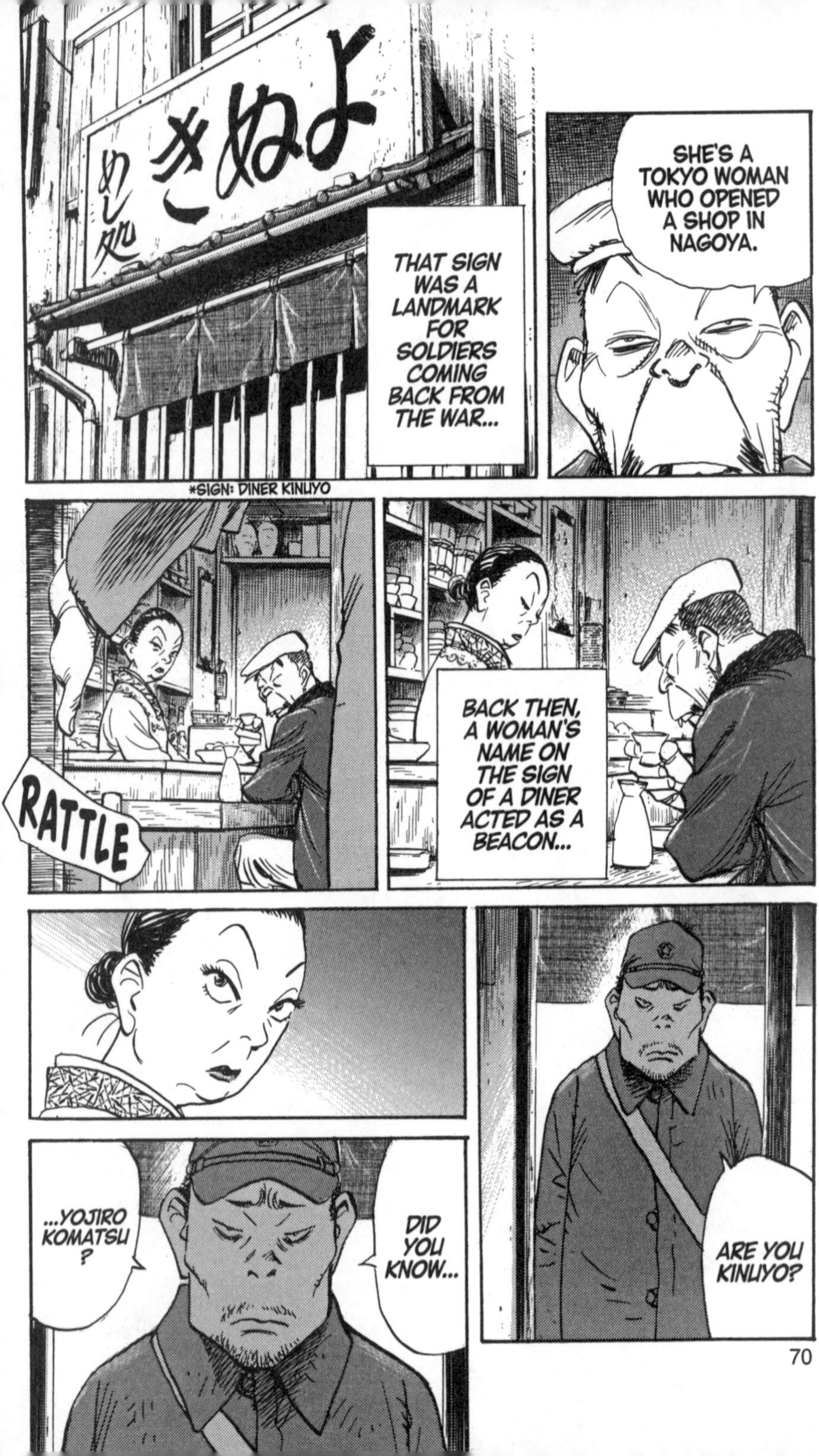
SHE'S A TOKYO WOMAN WHO OPENED A SHOP IN NAGOYA.
きぬよ
めし処
THAT SIGN WAS A LANDMARK FOR SOLDIERS COMING BACK FROM THE WAR...
*SIGN: DINER KINUYO
BACK THEN, A WOMAN'S NAME ON THE SIGN OF A DINER ACTED AS A BEACON...
RATTLE
ARE YOU KINUYO?
DID YOU KNOW...
...YOJIRO KOMATSU?

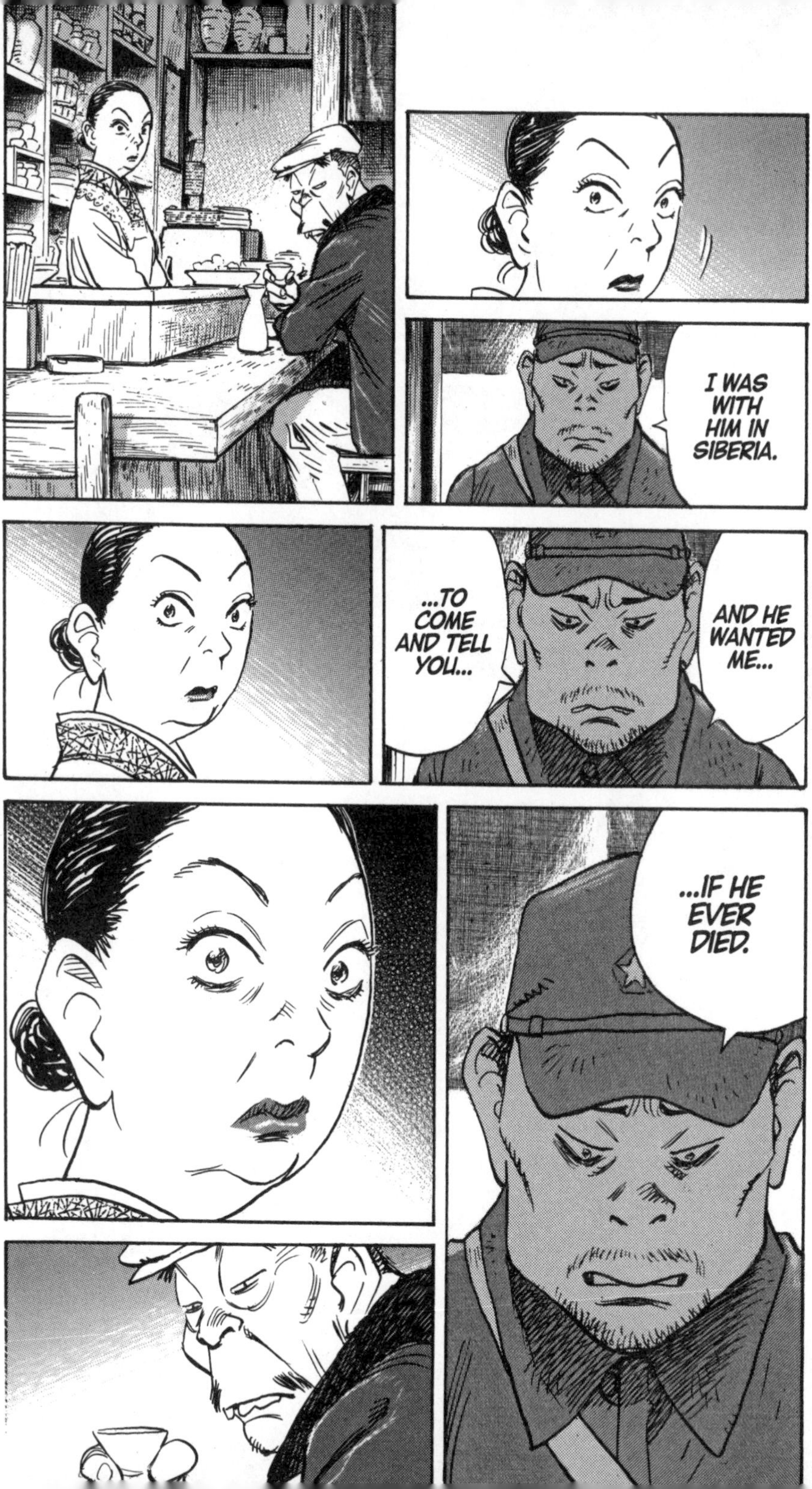
I WAS WITH HIM IN SIBERIA.
AND HE WANTED ME...
...TO COME AND TELL YOU...
...IF HE EVER DIED.

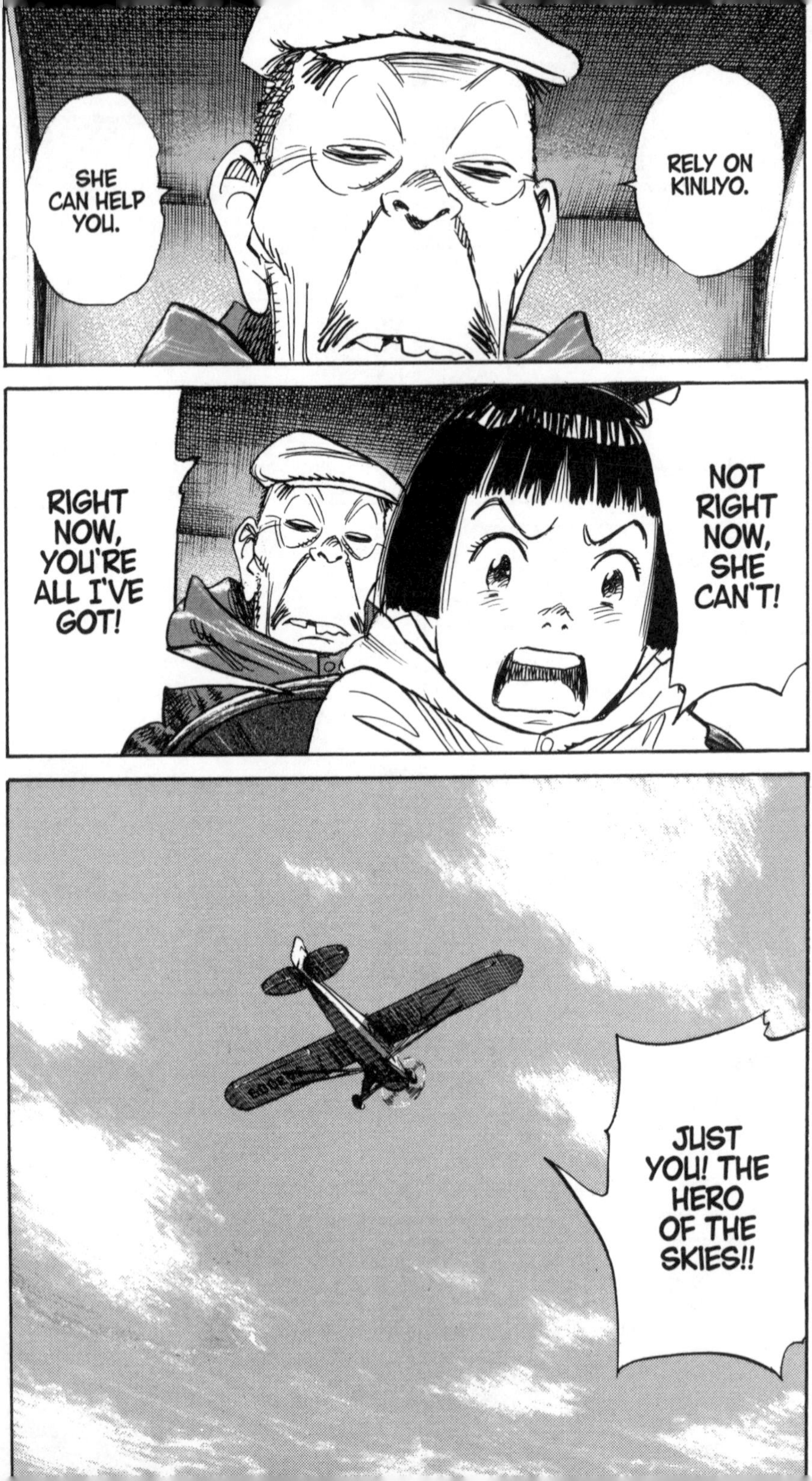
RELY ON KINUYO.
SHE CAN HELP YOU.
NOT RIGHT NOW, SHE CAN'T!
RIGHT NOW, YOU'RE ALL I'VE GOT!
JUST YOU! THE HERO OF THE SKIES!!

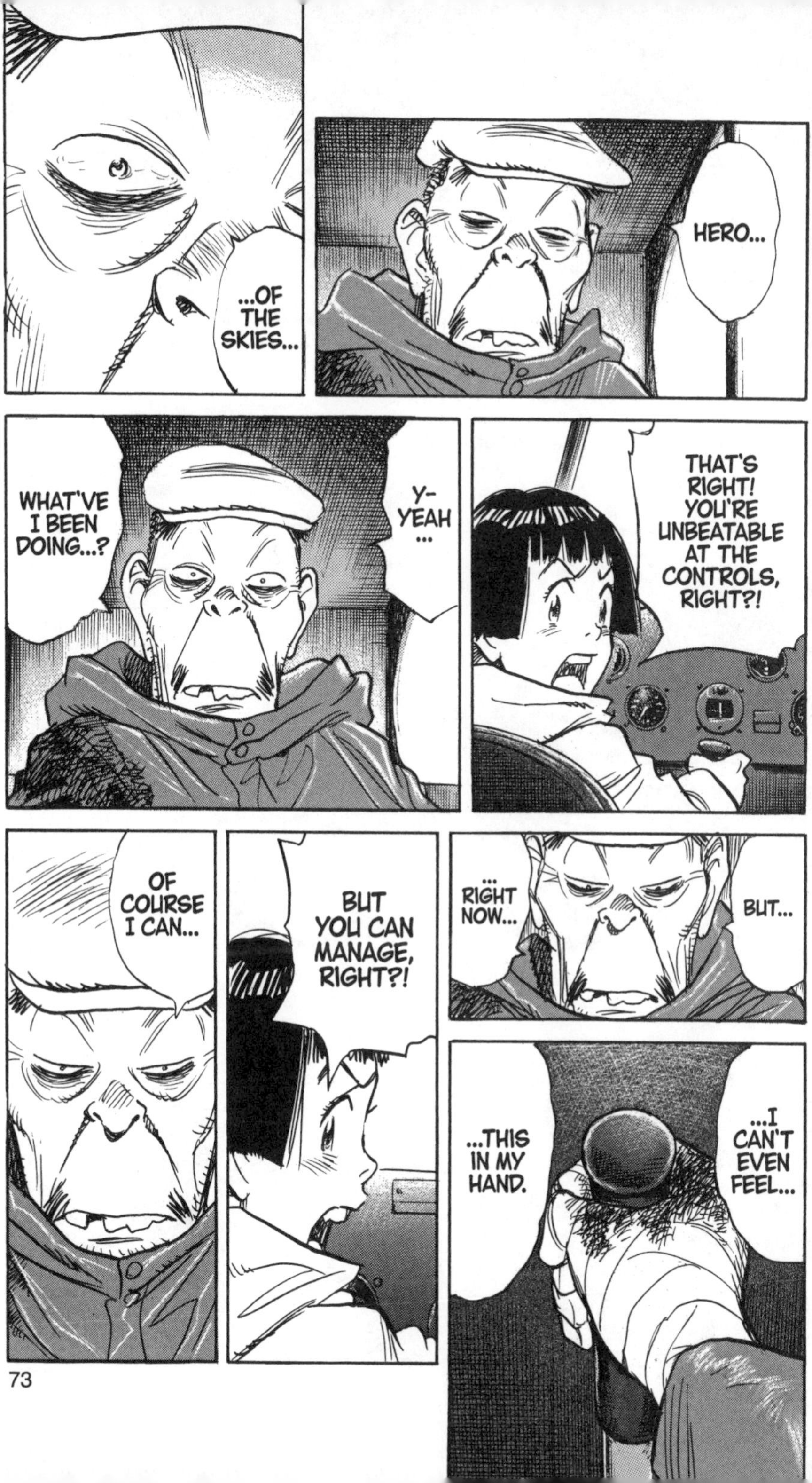
HERO...
...OF THE SKIES...
THAT'S RIGHT! YOU'RE UNBEATABLE AT THE CONTROLS, RIGHT?!
Y-YEAH...
WHAT'VE I BEEN DOING...?
BUT...
...RIGHT NOW...
...I CAN'T EVEN FEEL...
...THIS IN MY HAND.
BUT YOU CAN MANAGE, RIGHT?!
OF COURSE I CAN...

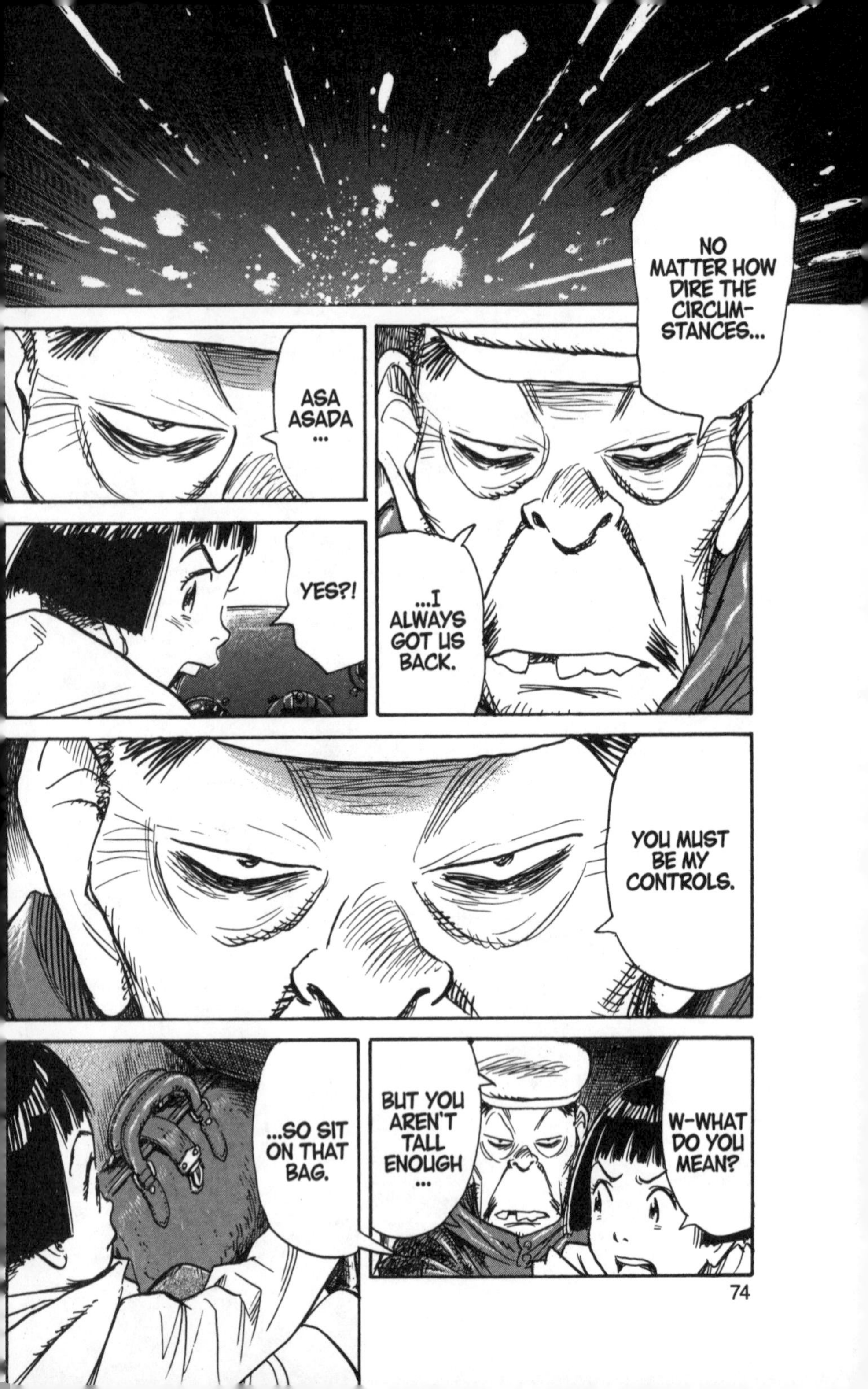

NO MATTER HOW DIRE THE CIRCUM-STANCES...
...I ALWAYS GOT US BACK.
ASA ASADA ...
YES?!
YOU MUST BE MY CONTROLS.
W-WHAT DO YOU MEAN?
BUT YOU AREN'T TALL ENOUGH ...
...SO SIT ON THAT BAG.

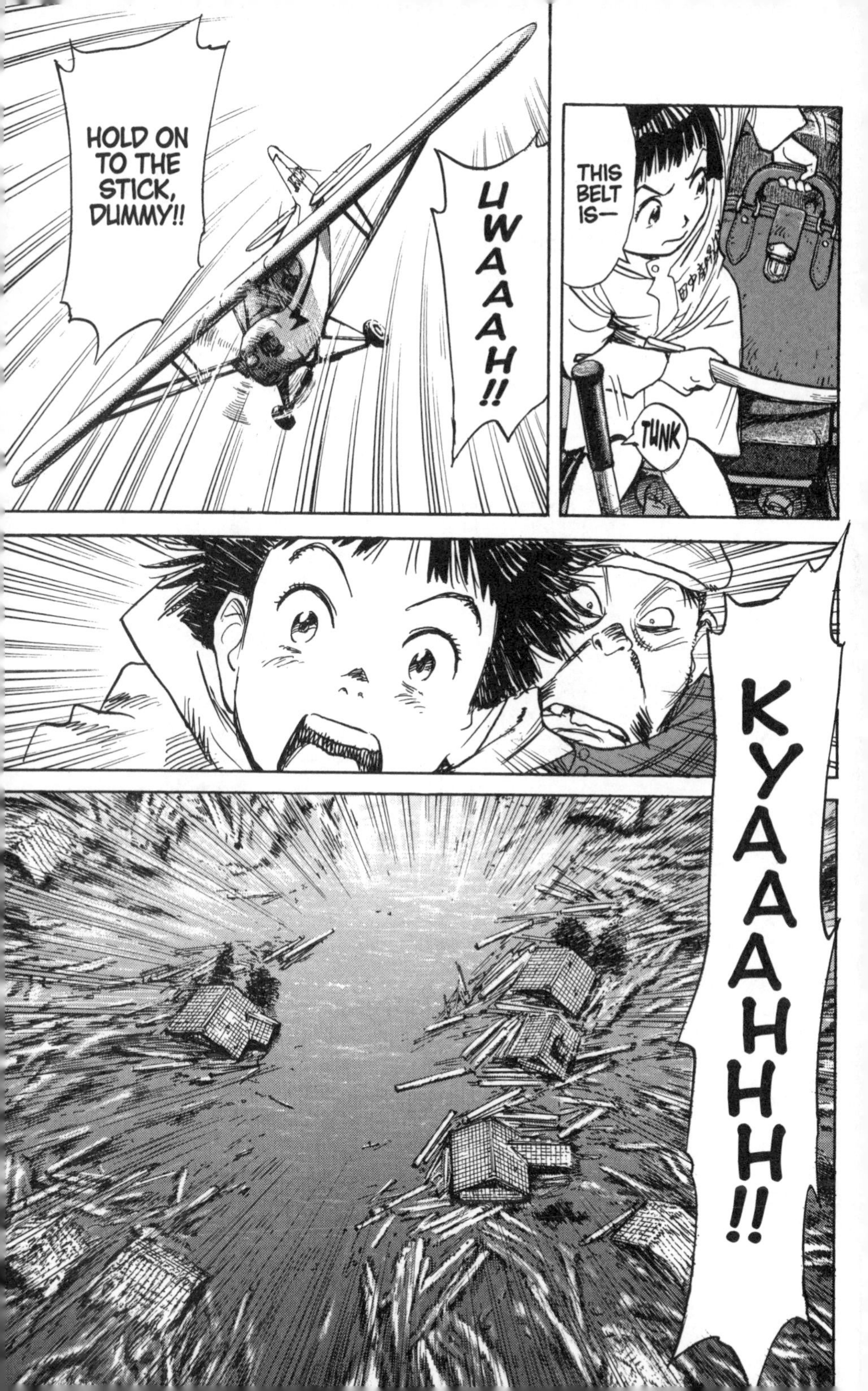
THIS BELT IS—
TUNK
UWAAAAH!!
HOLD ON TO THE STICK, DUMMY!!
KYAAAHHH!!

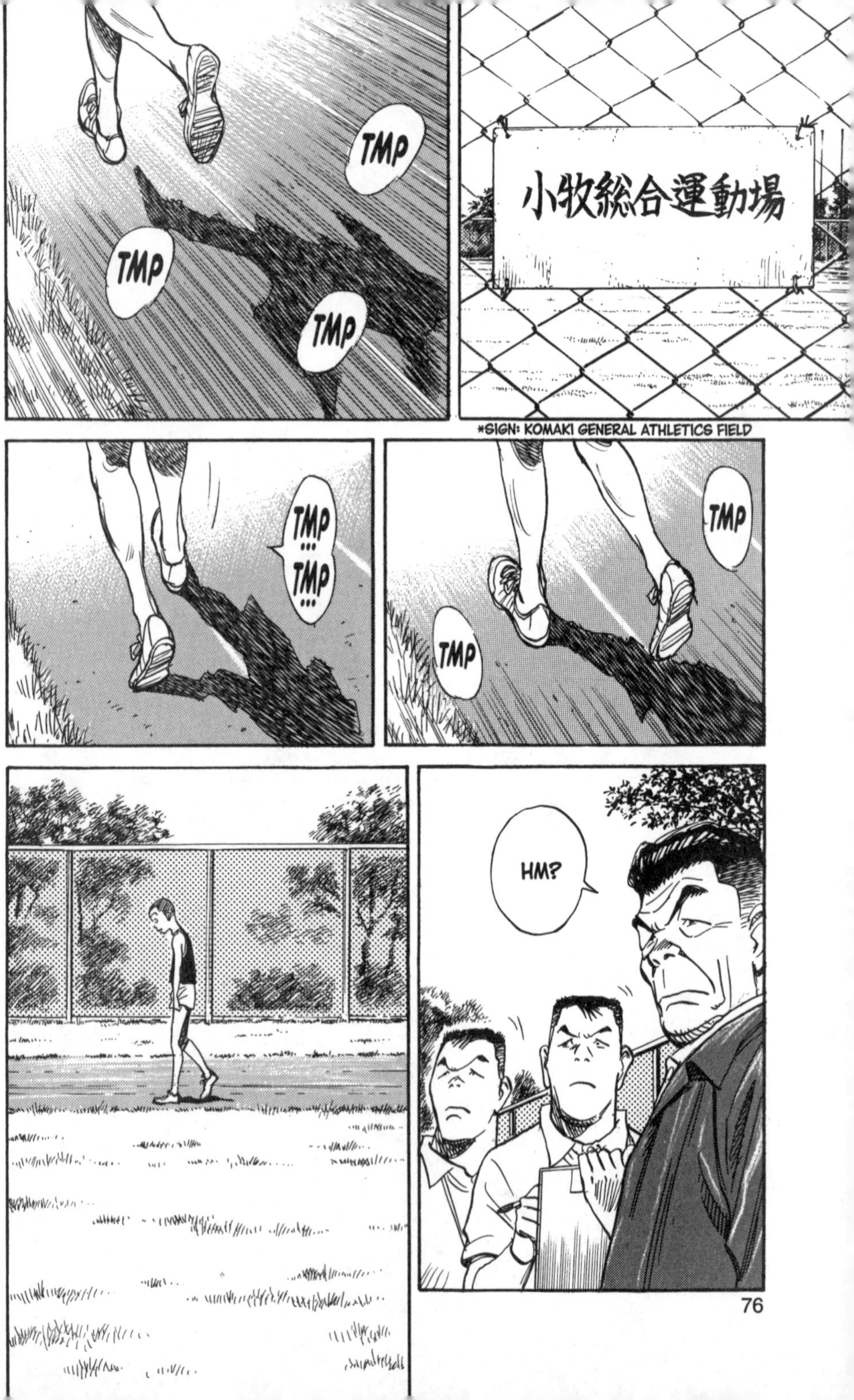
小牧総合運動場
*SIGN: KOMAKI GENERAL ATHLETICS FIELD
TMP
TMP
TMP
TMP
TMP
TMP... TMP...
HM?

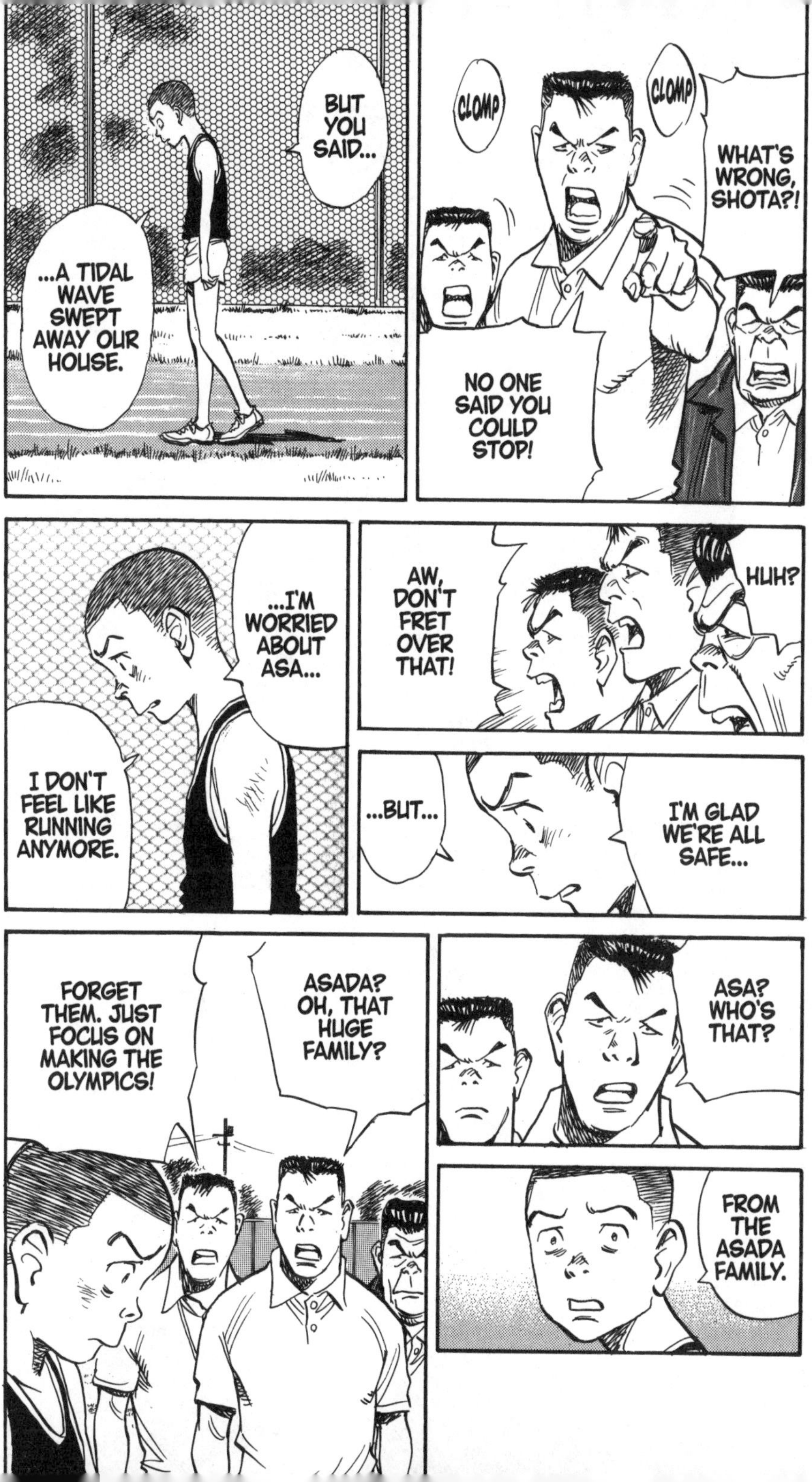
CLOMP
CLOMP
WHAT'S WRONG, SHOTA?!
NO ONE SAID YOU COULD STOP!
BUT YOU SAID...
...A TIDAL WAVE SWEPT AWAY OUR HOUSE.
HUH?
AW, DON'T FRET OVER THAT!
I'M GLAD WE'RE ALL SAFE...
...BUT...
...I'M WORRIED ABOUT ASA...
I DON'T FEEL LIKE RUNNING ANYMORE.
ASA? WHO'S THAT?
FROM THE ASADA FAMILY.
ASADA? OH, THAT HUGE FAMILY?
FORGET THEM. JUST FOCUS ON MAKING THE OLYMPICS!

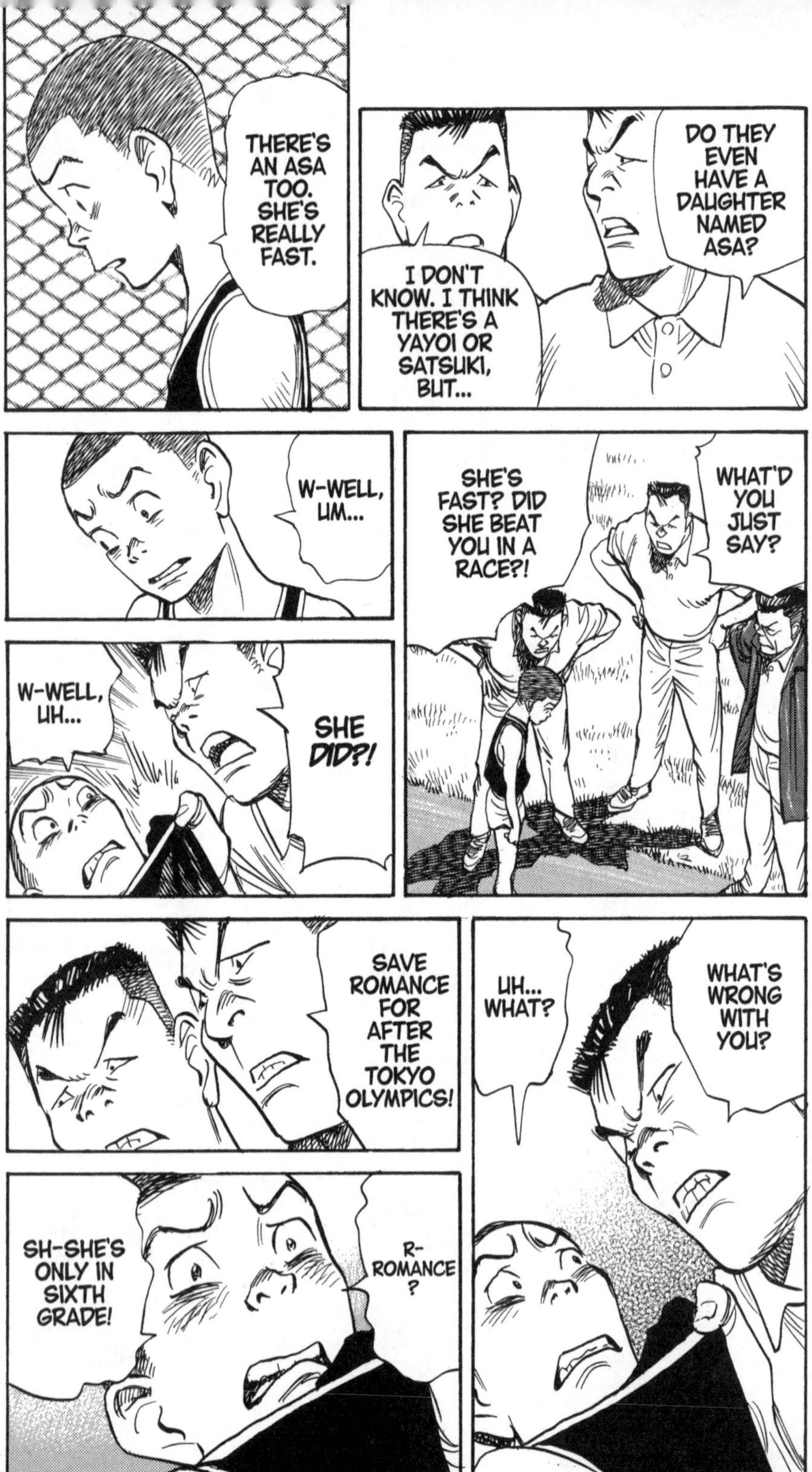
DO THEY EVEN HAVE A DAUGHTER NAMED ASA?
I DON'T KNOW. I THINK THERE'S A YAYOI OR SATSUKI, BUT...
THERE'S AN ASA TOO. SHE'S REALLY FAST.
WHAT'D YOU JUST SAY?
SHE'S FAST? DID SHE BEAT YOU IN A RACE?!
W-WELL, UM...
SHE DID?!
W-WELL, UH...
WHAT'S WRONG WITH YOU?
UH... WHAT?
SAVE ROMANCE FOR AFTER THE TOKYO OLYMPICS!
R-ROMANCE?
SH-SHE'S ONLY IN SIXTH GRADE!

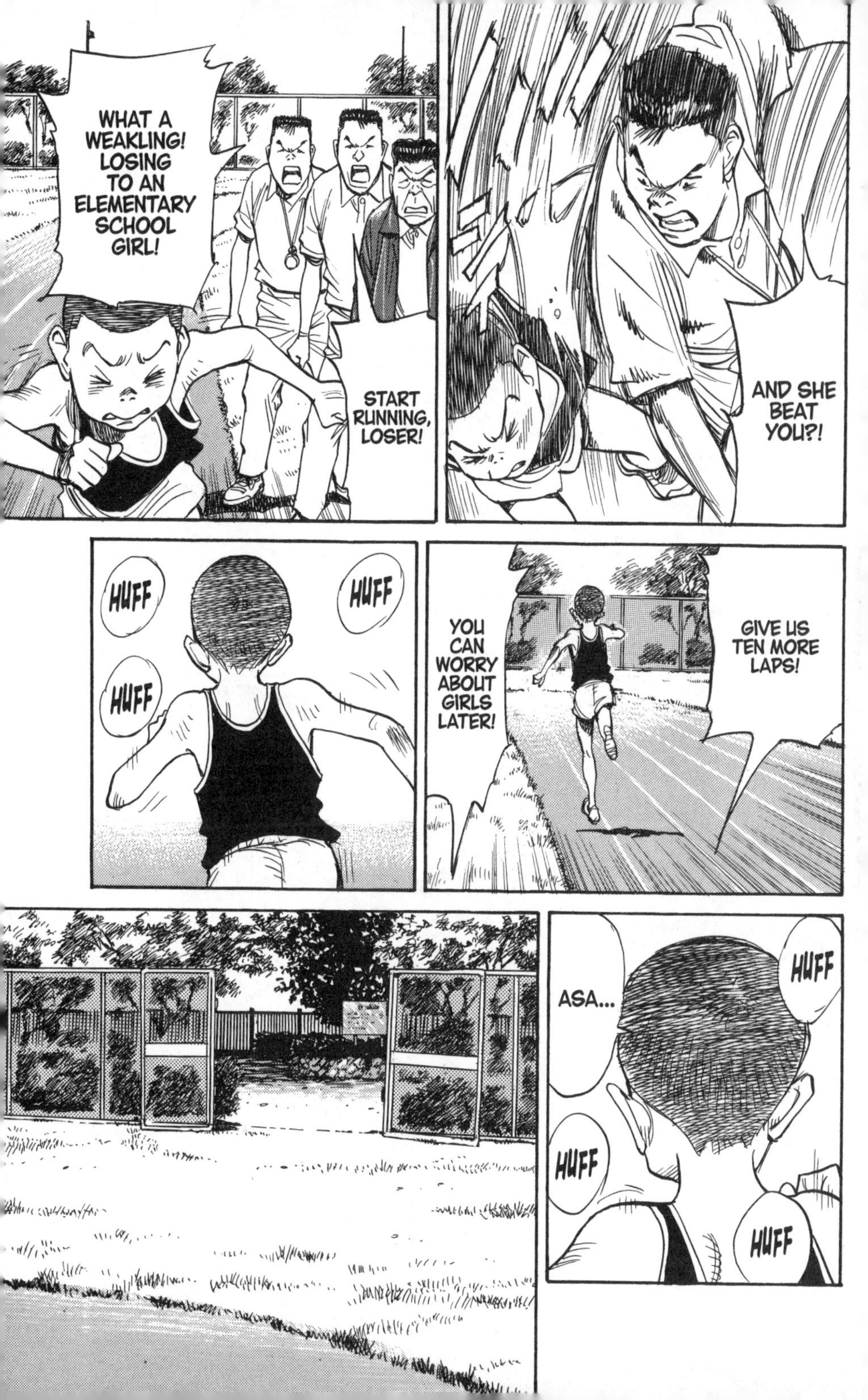
AND SHE BEAT YOU?!
WHAT A WEAKLING! LOSING TO AN ELEMENTARY SCHOOL GIRL!
START RUNNING, LOSER!
GIVE US TEN MORE LAPS!
YOU CAN WORRY ABOUT GIRLS LATER!
HUFF
HUFF
HUFF
HUFF
ASA...
HUFF
HUFF

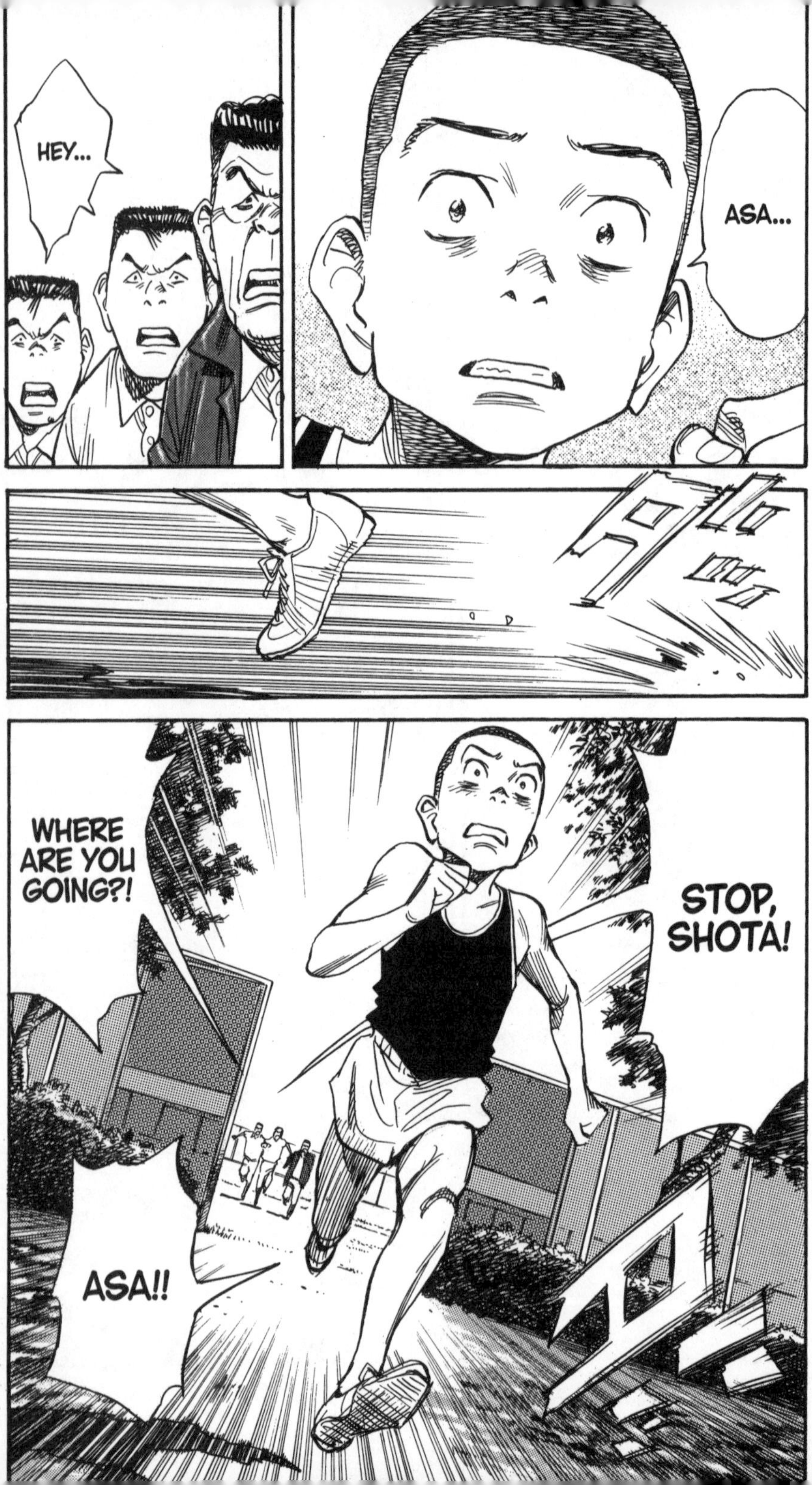
ASA...
HEY...
STOP, SHOTA!
WHERE ARE YOU GOING?!
ASA!!

ASADORA!

ASADORA!

Chapter 12 ● Truly Flying

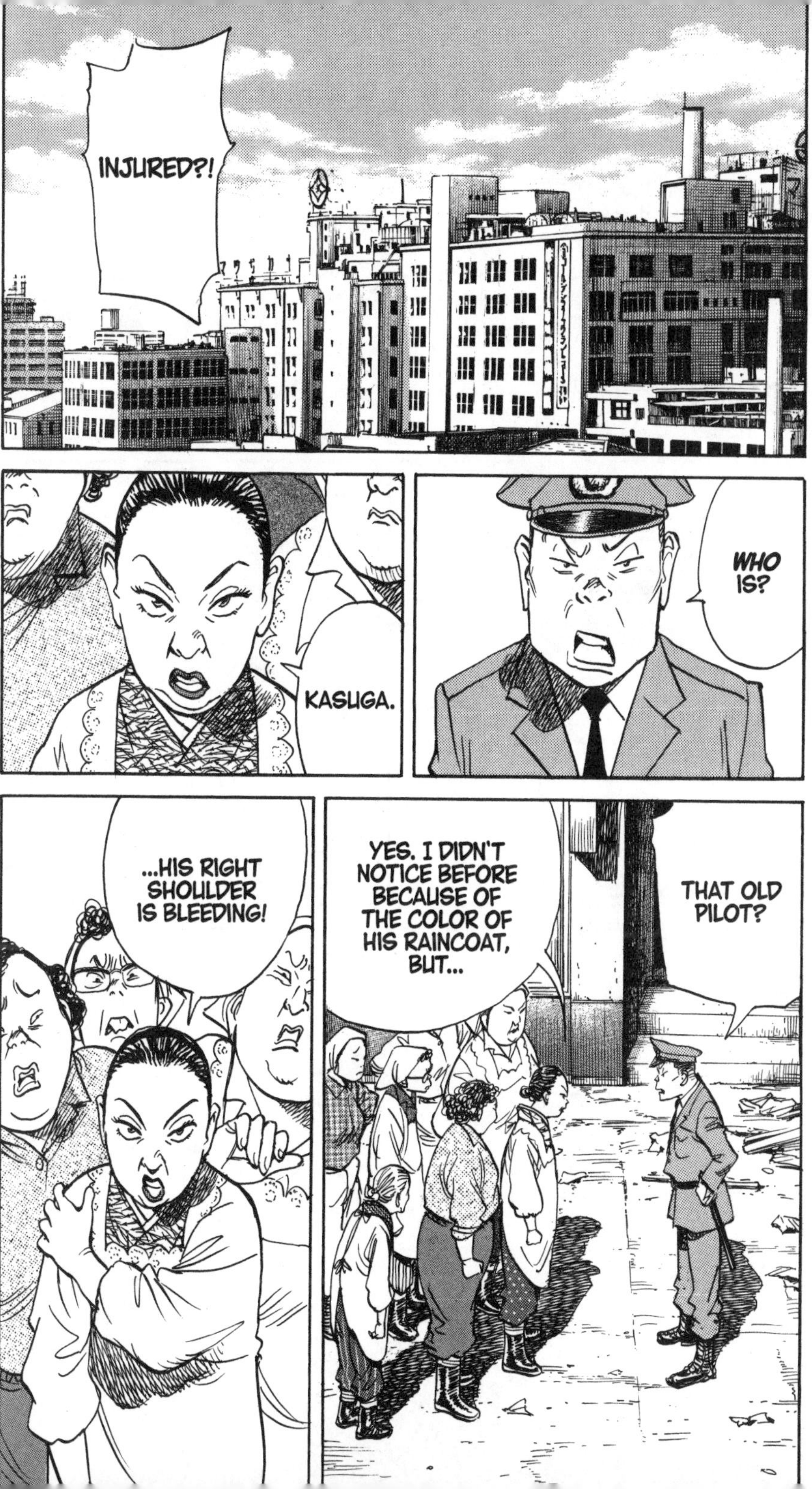
INJURED?!
WHO IS?
KASUGA.
THAT OLD PILOT?
YES. I DIDN'T NOTICE BEFORE BECAUSE OF THE COLOR OF HIS RAINCOAT, BUT...
...HIS RIGHT SHOULDER IS BLEEDING!

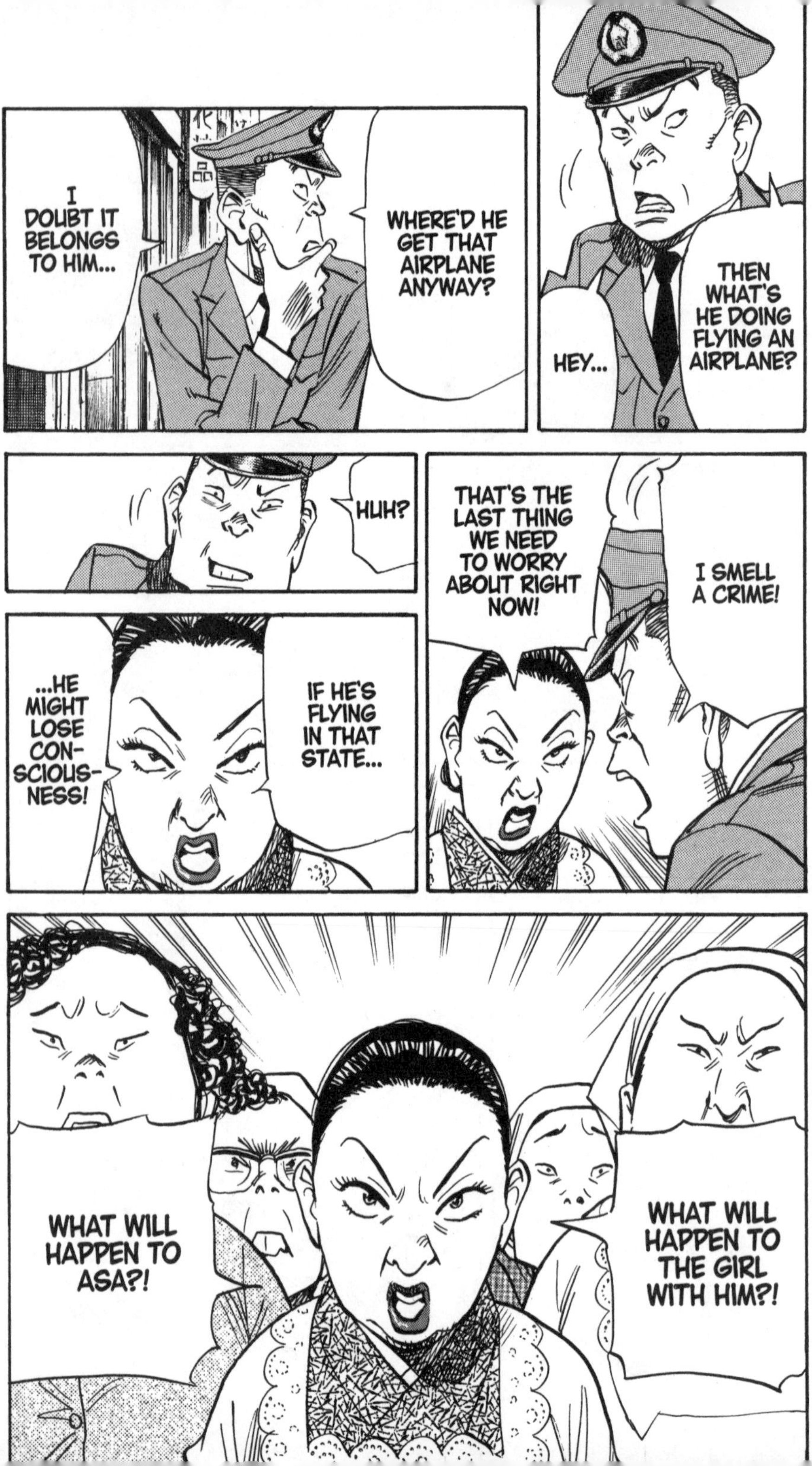
THEN WHAT'S HE DOING FLYING AN AIRPLANE?
HEY...
WHERE'D HE GET THAT AIRPLANE ANYWAY?
I DOUBT IT BELONGS TO HIM...
I SMELL A CRIME!
THAT'S THE LAST THING WE NEED TO WORRY ABOUT RIGHT NOW!
HUH?
IF HE'S FLYING IN THAT STATE...
...HE MIGHT LOSE CON-SCIOUS-NESS!
WHAT WILL HAPPEN TO THE GIRL WITH HIM?!
WHAT WILL HAPPEN TO ASA?!

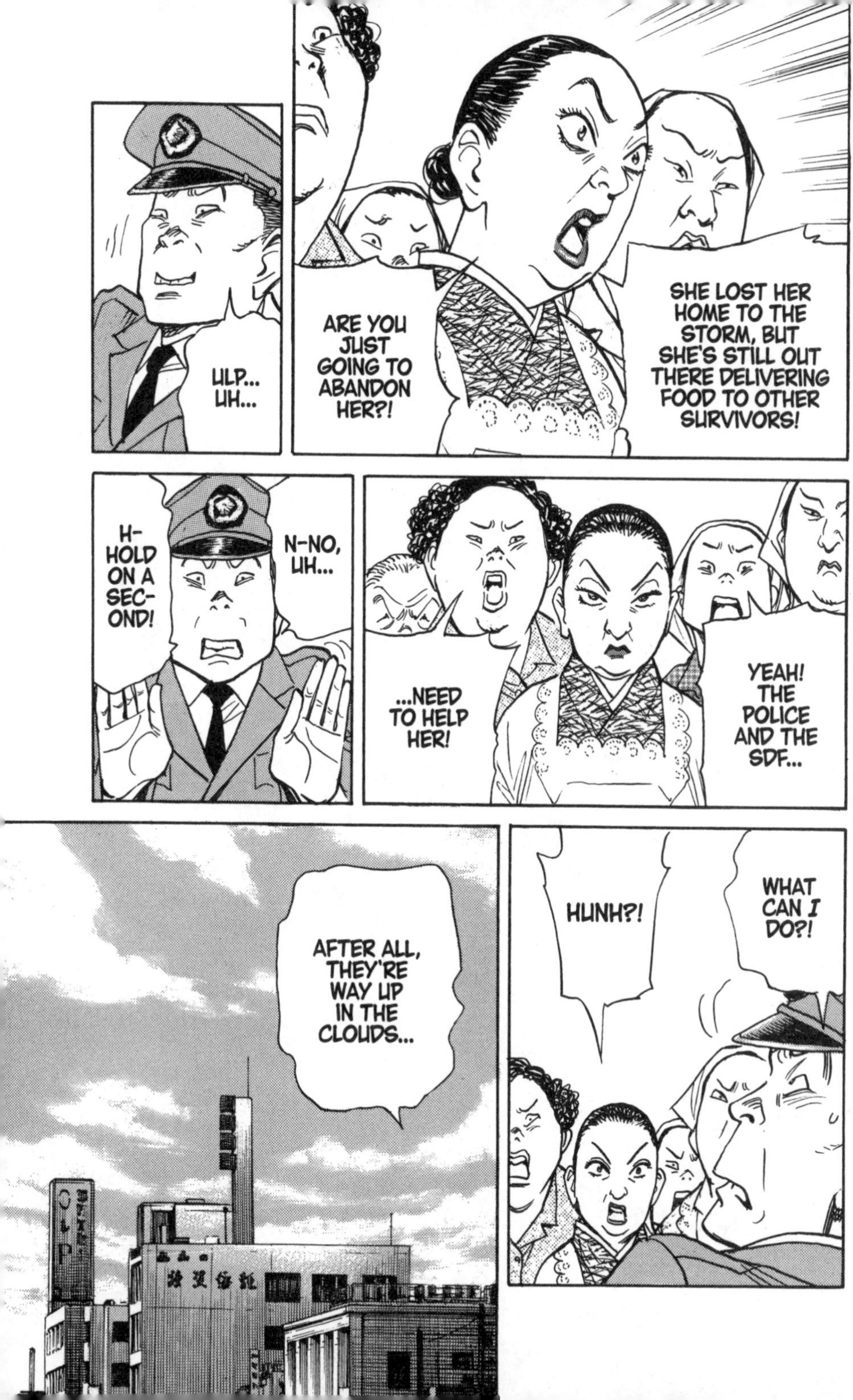
SHE LOST HER HOME TO THE STORM, BUT SHE'S STILL OUT THERE DELIVERING FOOD TO OTHER SURVIVORS!
ARE YOU JUST GOING TO ABANDON HER?!
ULP... UH...
YEAH! THE POLICE AND THE SDF...
...NEED TO HELP HER!
N-NO, UH...
H-HOLD ON A SEC-OND!
WHAT CAN *I* DO?!
HUNH?!
AFTER ALL, THEY'RE WAY UP IN THE CLOUDS...

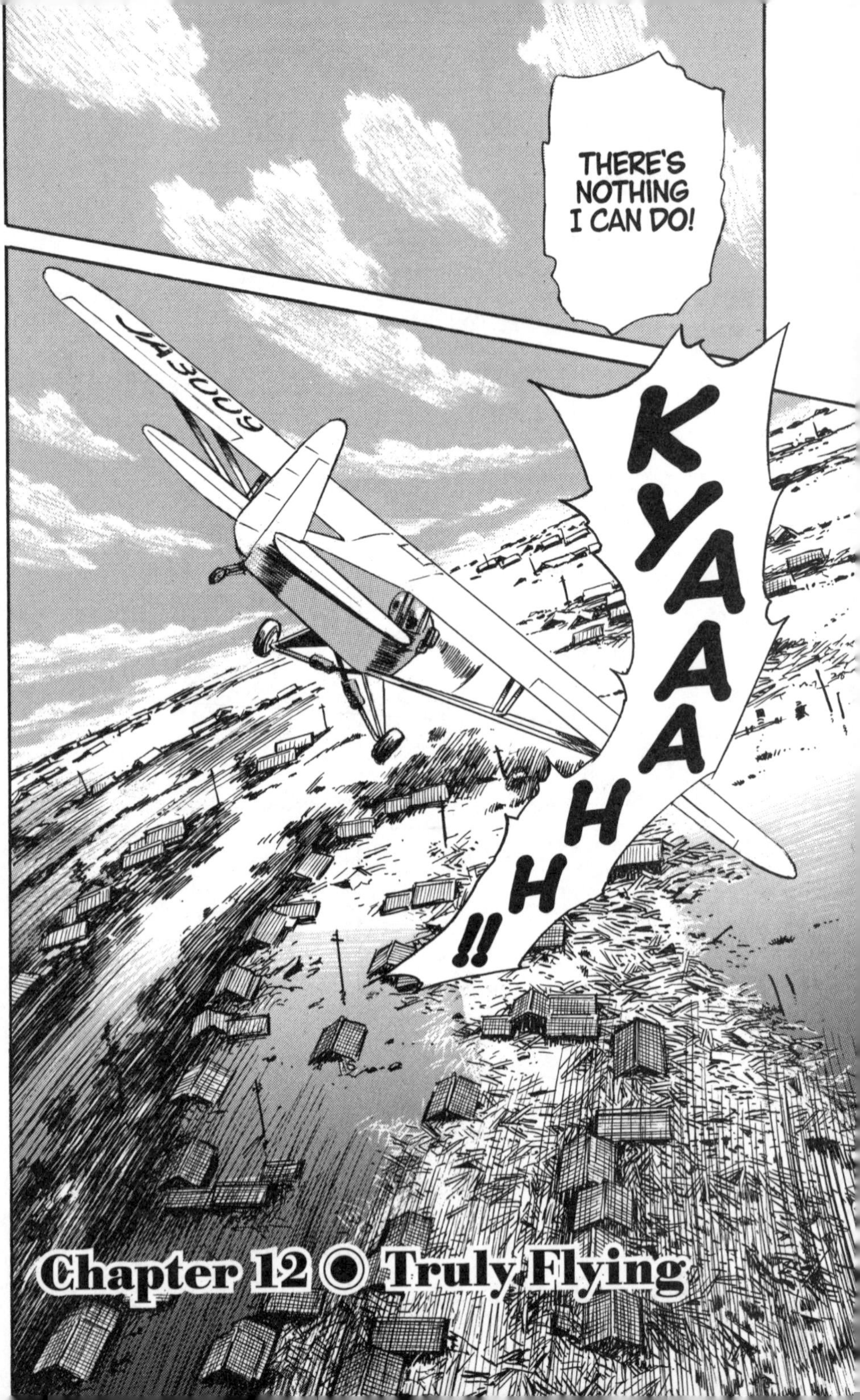

Chapter 12 ◯ Truly Flying

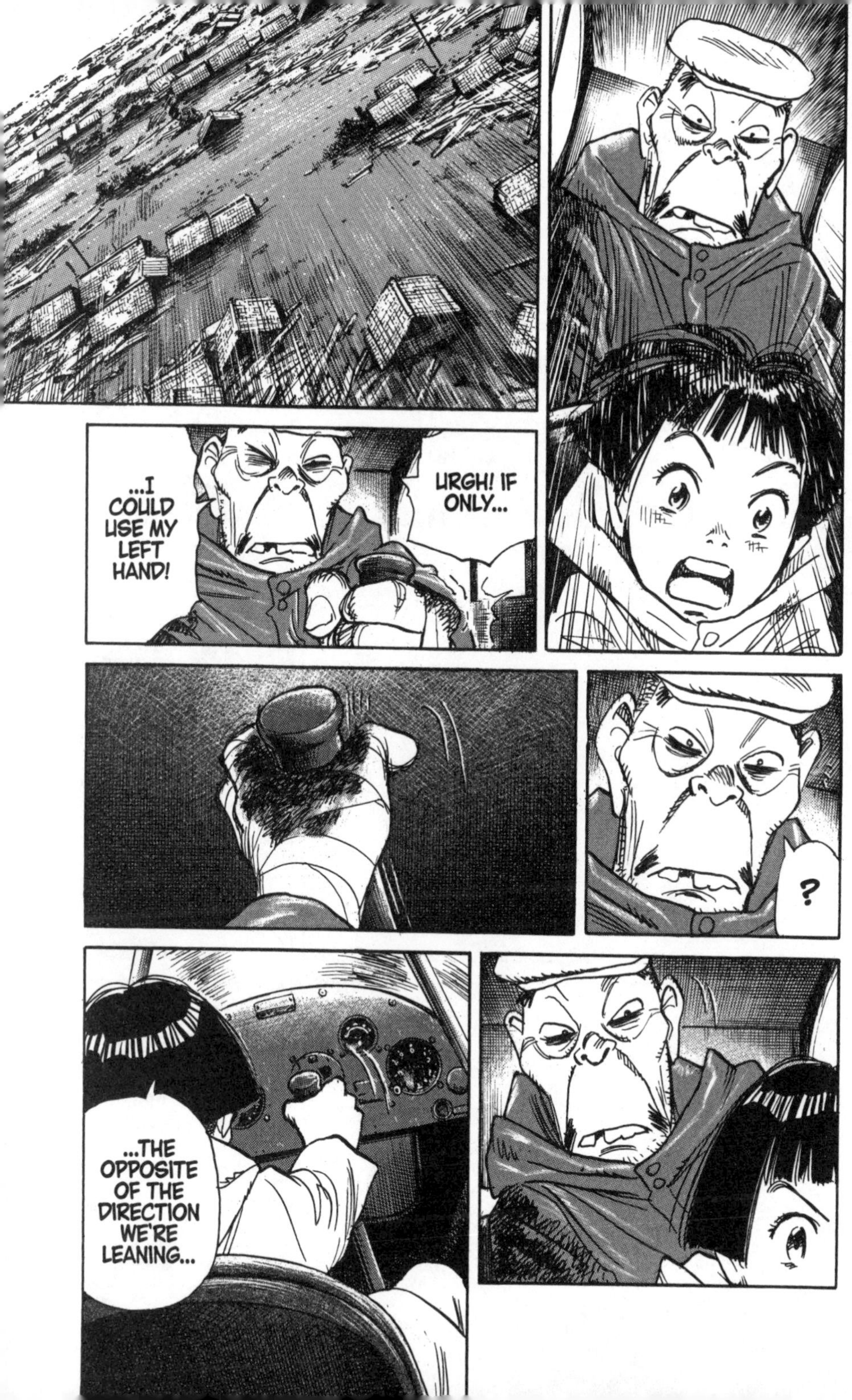
URGH! IF ONLY...
...I COULD USE MY LEFT HAND!
?
...THE OPPOSITE OF THE DIRECTION WE'RE LEANING...

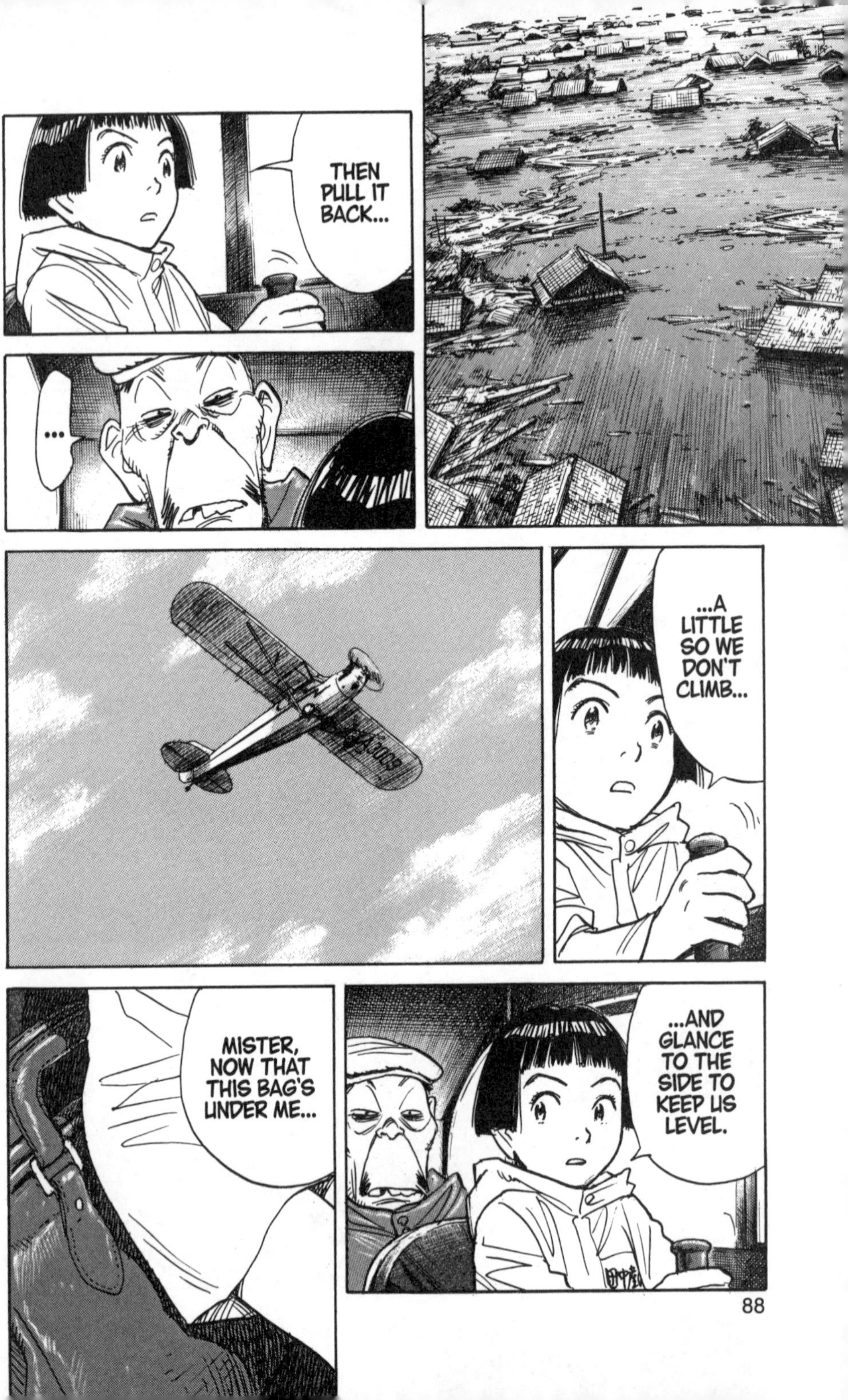
THEN PULL IT BACK...
...
...A LITTLE SO WE DON'T CLIMB...
...AND GLANCE TO THE SIDE TO KEEP US LEVEL.
MISTER, NOW THAT THIS BAG'S UNDER ME...

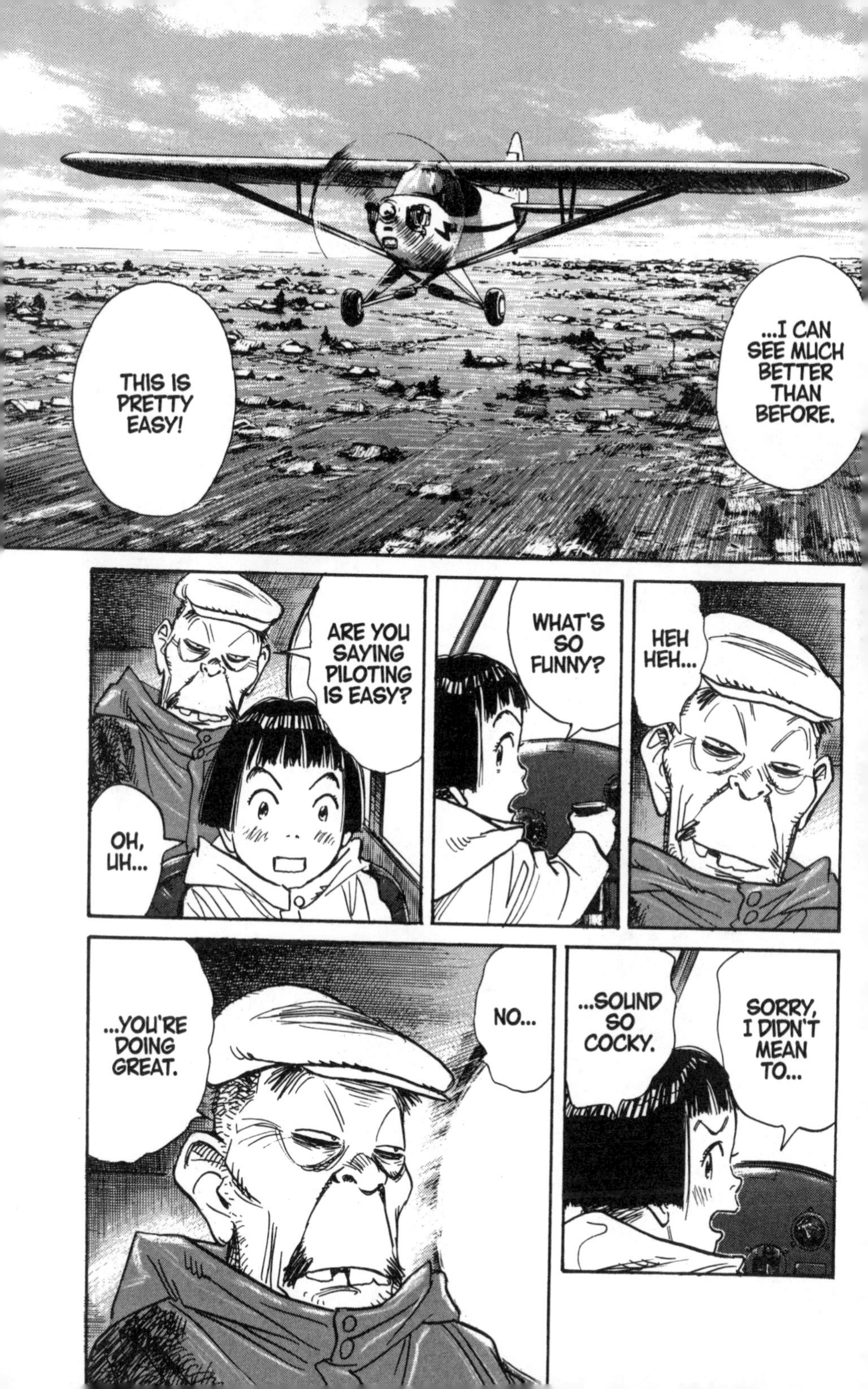
...I CAN SEE MUCH BETTER THAN BEFORE.
THIS IS PRETTY EASY!
HEH HEH...
WHAT'S SO FUNNY?
ARE YOU SAYING PILOTING IS EASY?
OH, UH...
SORRY, I DIDN'T MEAN TO...
...SOUND SO COCKY.
NO...
...YOU'RE DOING GREAT.

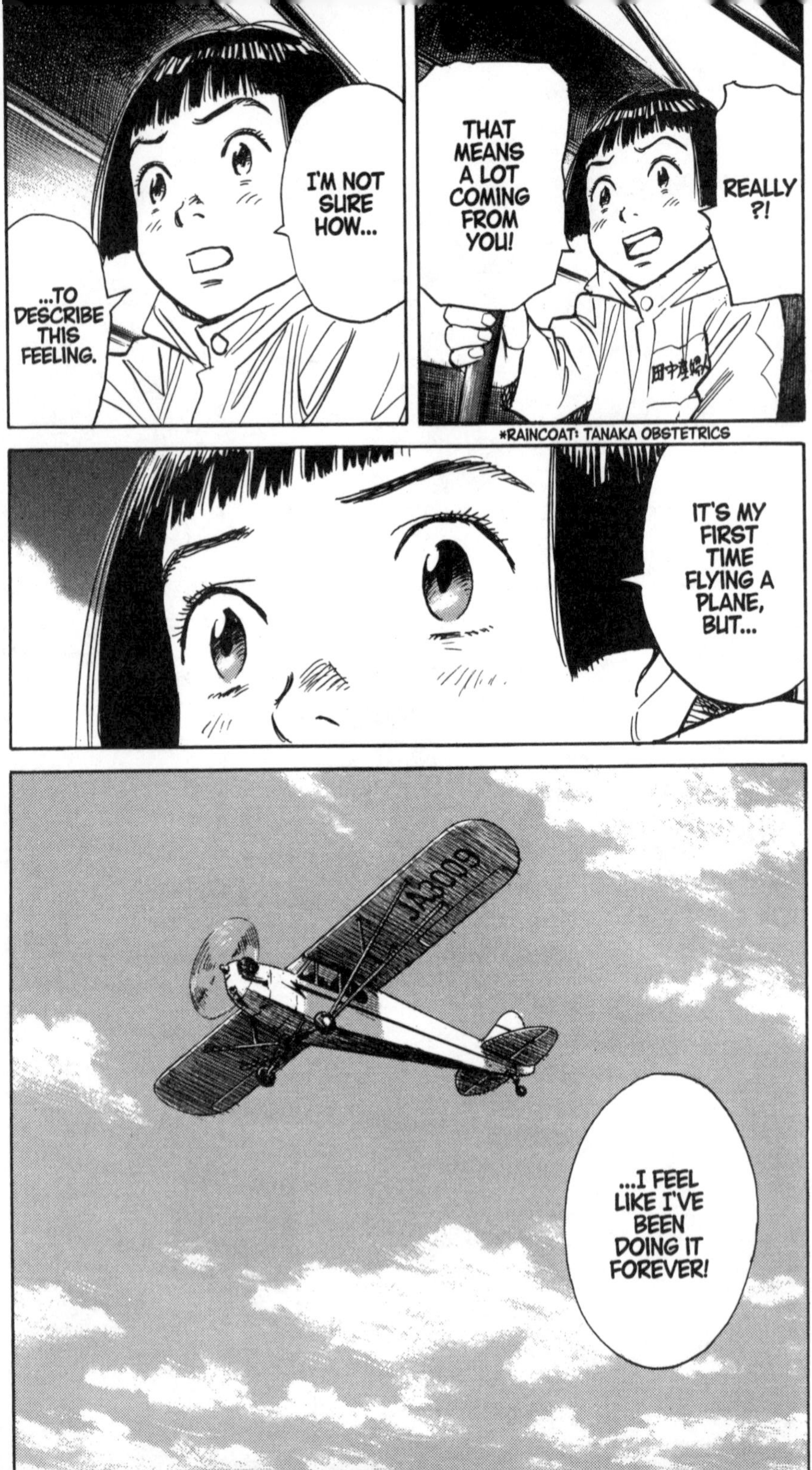
REALLY ?!
THAT MEANS A LOT COMING FROM YOU!
I'M NOT SURE HOW...
...TO DESCRIBE THIS FEELING.
*RAINCOAT: TANAKA OBSTETRICS
IT'S MY FIRST TIME FLYING A PLANE, BUT...
JA3009
...I FEEL LIKE I'VE BEEN DOING IT FOREVER!

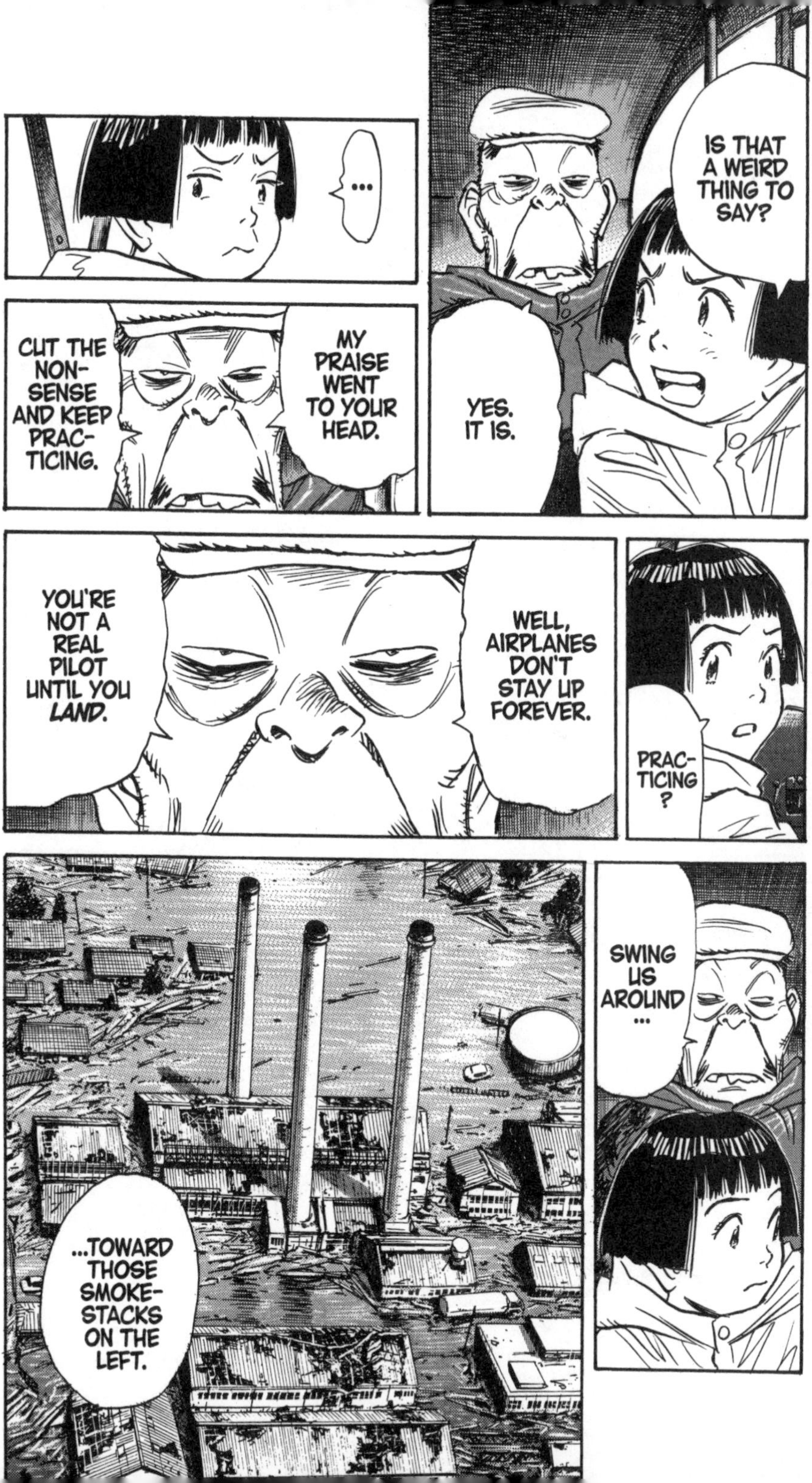
IS THAT A WEIRD THING TO SAY?
YES. IT IS.
...
MY PRAISE WENT TO YOUR HEAD.
CUT THE NON-SENSE AND KEEP PRAC-TICING.
PRAC-TICING?
WELL, AIRPLANES DON'T STAY UP FOREVER.
YOU'RE NOT A REAL PILOT UNTIL YOU *LAND*.
SWING US AROUND...
...TOWARD THOSE SMOKE-STACKS ON THE LEFT.

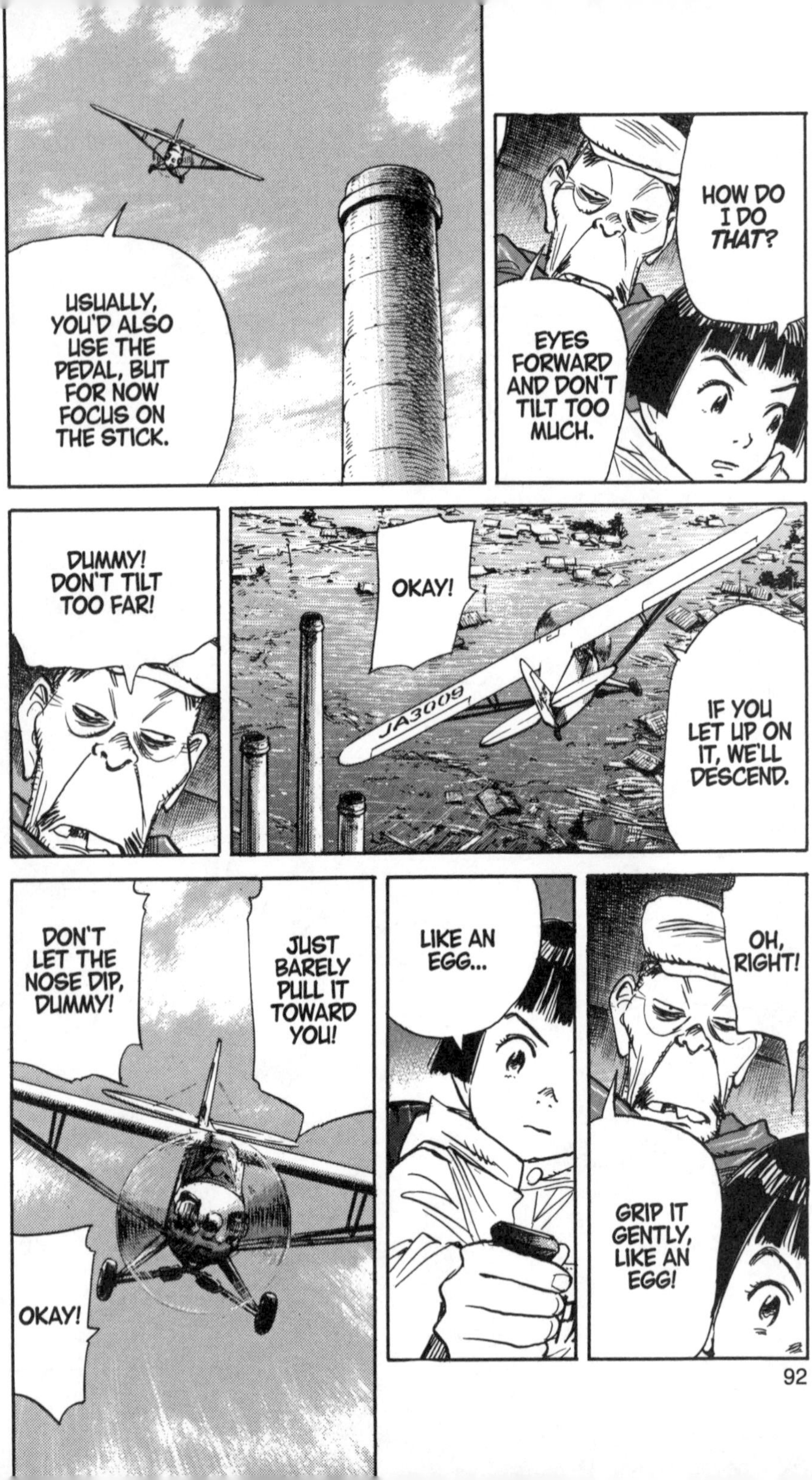
HOW DO I DO *THAT*?
EYES FORWARD AND DON'T TILT TOO MUCH.
USUALLY, YOU'D ALSO USE THE PEDAL, BUT FOR NOW FOCUS ON THE STICK.
IF YOU LET UP ON IT, WE'LL DESCEND.
OKAY!
JA3009
DUMMY! DON'T TILT TOO FAR!
OH, RIGHT!
GRIP IT GENTLY, LIKE AN EGG!
LIKE AN EGG...
JUST BARELY PULL IT TOWARD YOU!
DON'T LET THE NOSE DIP, DUMMY!
OKAY!

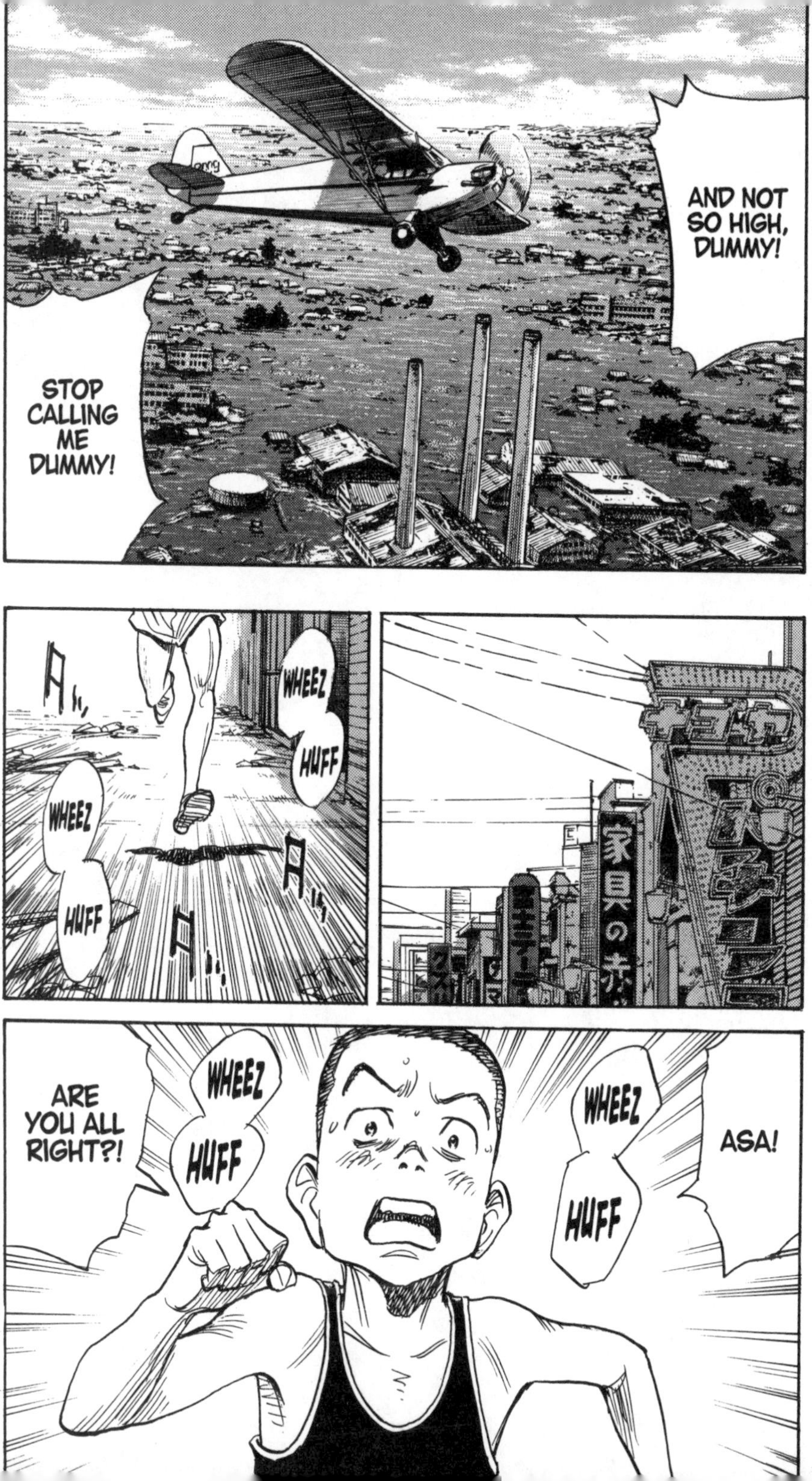
AND NOT SO HIGH, DUMMY!
STOP CALLING ME DUMMY!
家具の
WHEEZ
HUFF
WHEEZ
HUFF
ASA!
WHEEZ
HUFF
WHEEZ
HUFF
ARE YOU ALL RIGHT?!

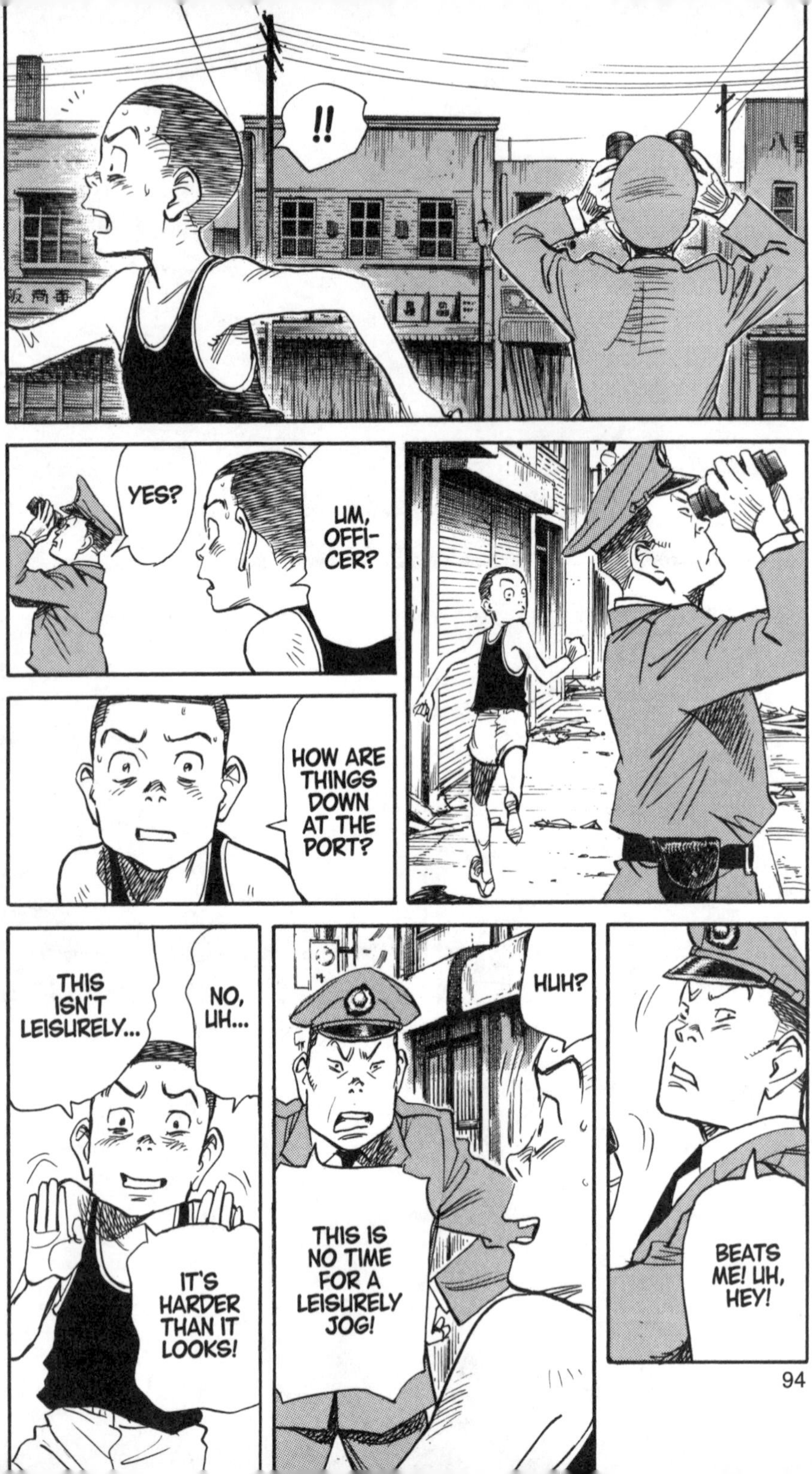
!!
UM, OFFI-CER?
YES?
HOW ARE THINGS DOWN AT THE PORT?
BEATS ME! UH, HEY!
HUH?
THIS IS NO TIME FOR A LEISURELY JOG!
NO, UH...
THIS ISN'T LEISURELY...
IT'S HARDER THAN IT LOOKS!

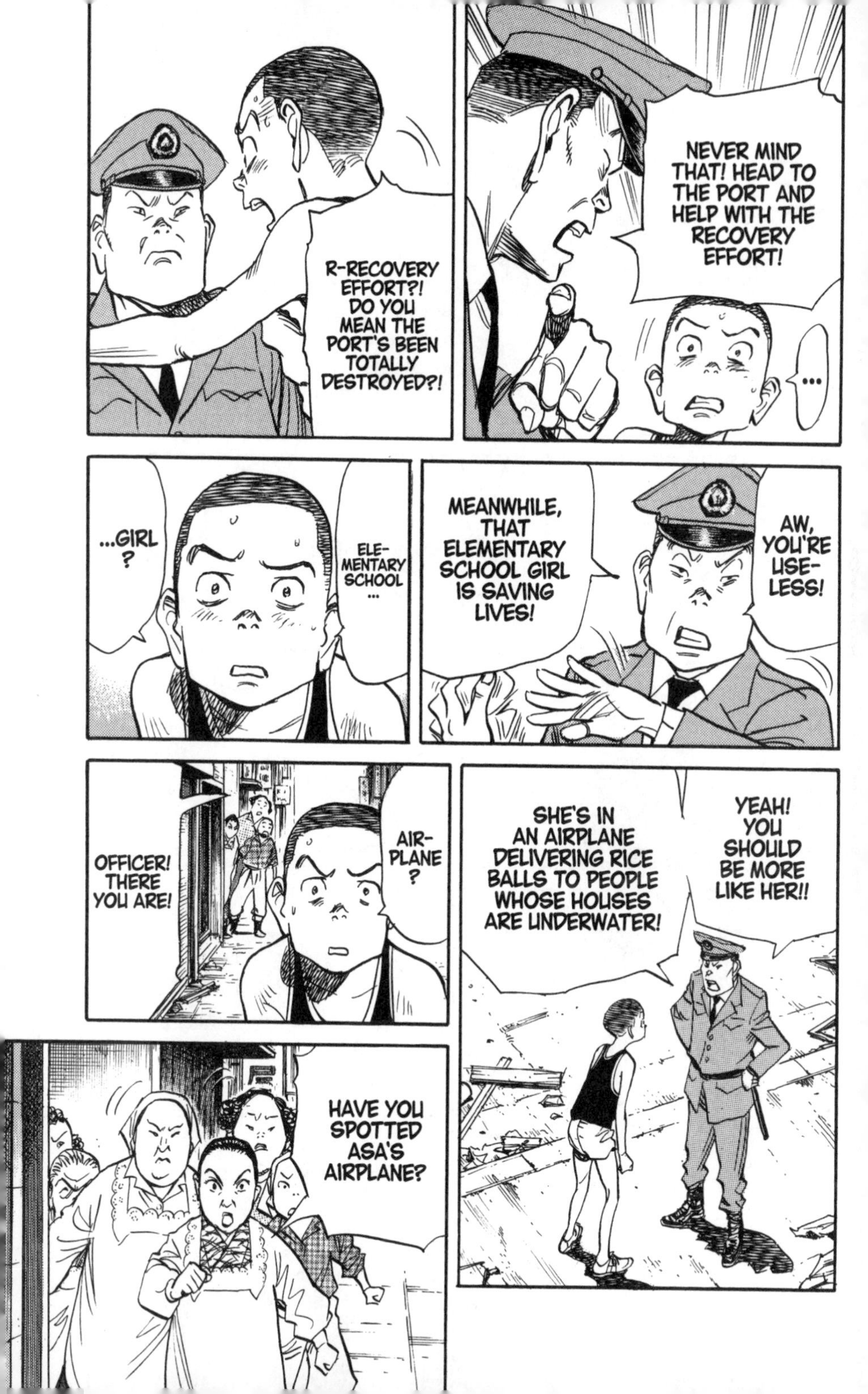
NEVER MIND THAT! HEAD TO THE PORT AND HELP WITH THE RECOVERY EFFORT!
...
R-RECOVERY EFFORT?! DO YOU MEAN THE PORT'S BEEN TOTALLY DESTROYED?!
AW, YOU'RE USE-LESS!
MEANWHILE, THAT ELEMENTARY SCHOOL GIRL IS SAVING LIVES!
ELE-MENTARY SCHOOL ...
...GIRL ?
YEAH! YOU SHOULD BE MORE LIKE HER!!
SHE'S IN AN AIRPLANE DELIVERING RICE BALLS TO PEOPLE WHOSE HOUSES ARE UNDERWATER!
AIR-PLANE ?
OFFICER! THERE YOU ARE!
HAVE YOU SPOTTED ASA'S AIRPLANE?

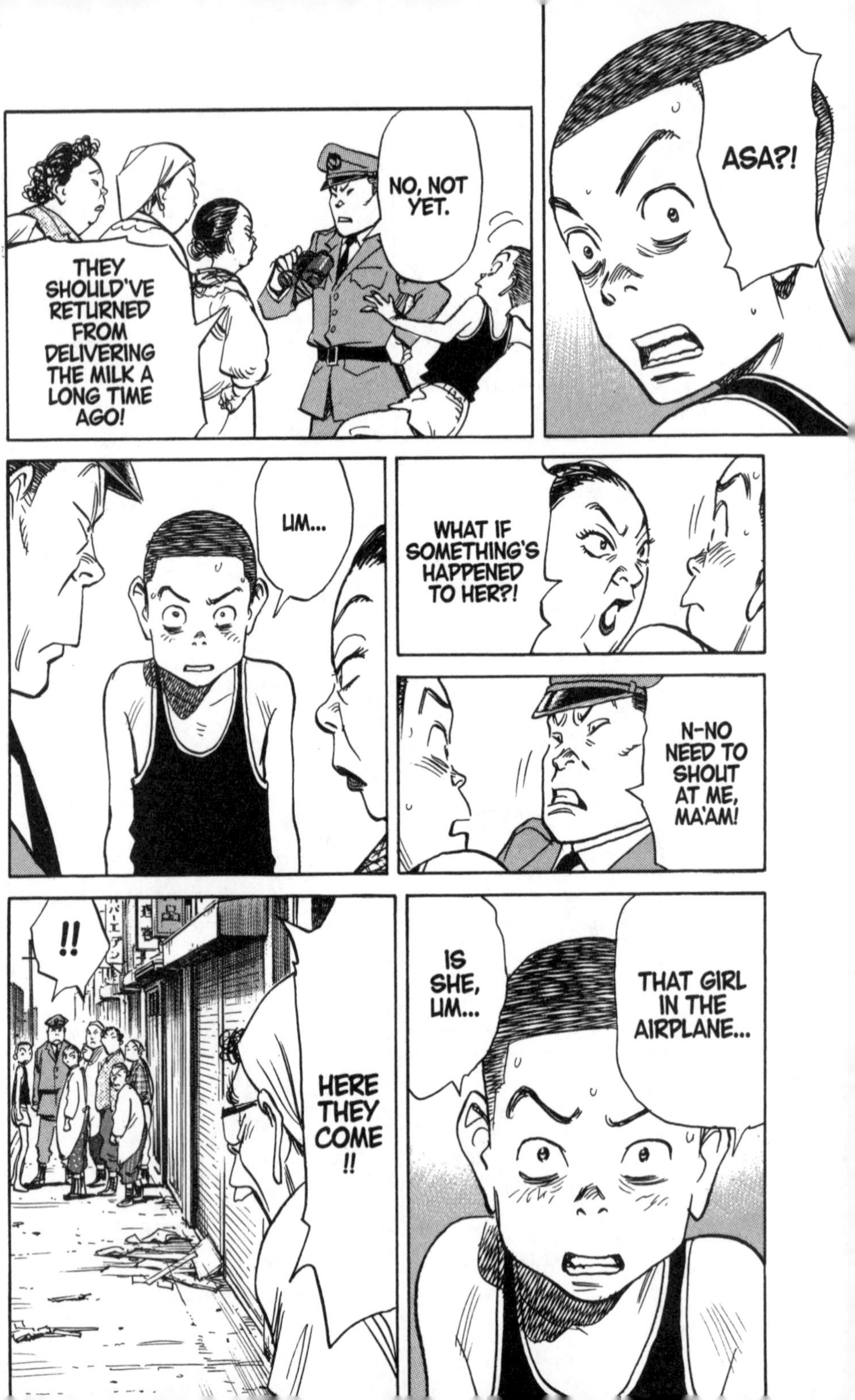
ASA?!
NO, NOT YET.
THEY SHOULD'VE RETURNED FROM DELIVERING THE MILK A LONG TIME AGO!
WHAT IF SOMETHING'S HAPPENED TO HER?!
N-NO NEED TO SHOUT AT ME, MA'AM!
UM...
THAT GIRL IN THE AIRPLANE...
IS SHE, UM...
!!
HERE THEY COME !!

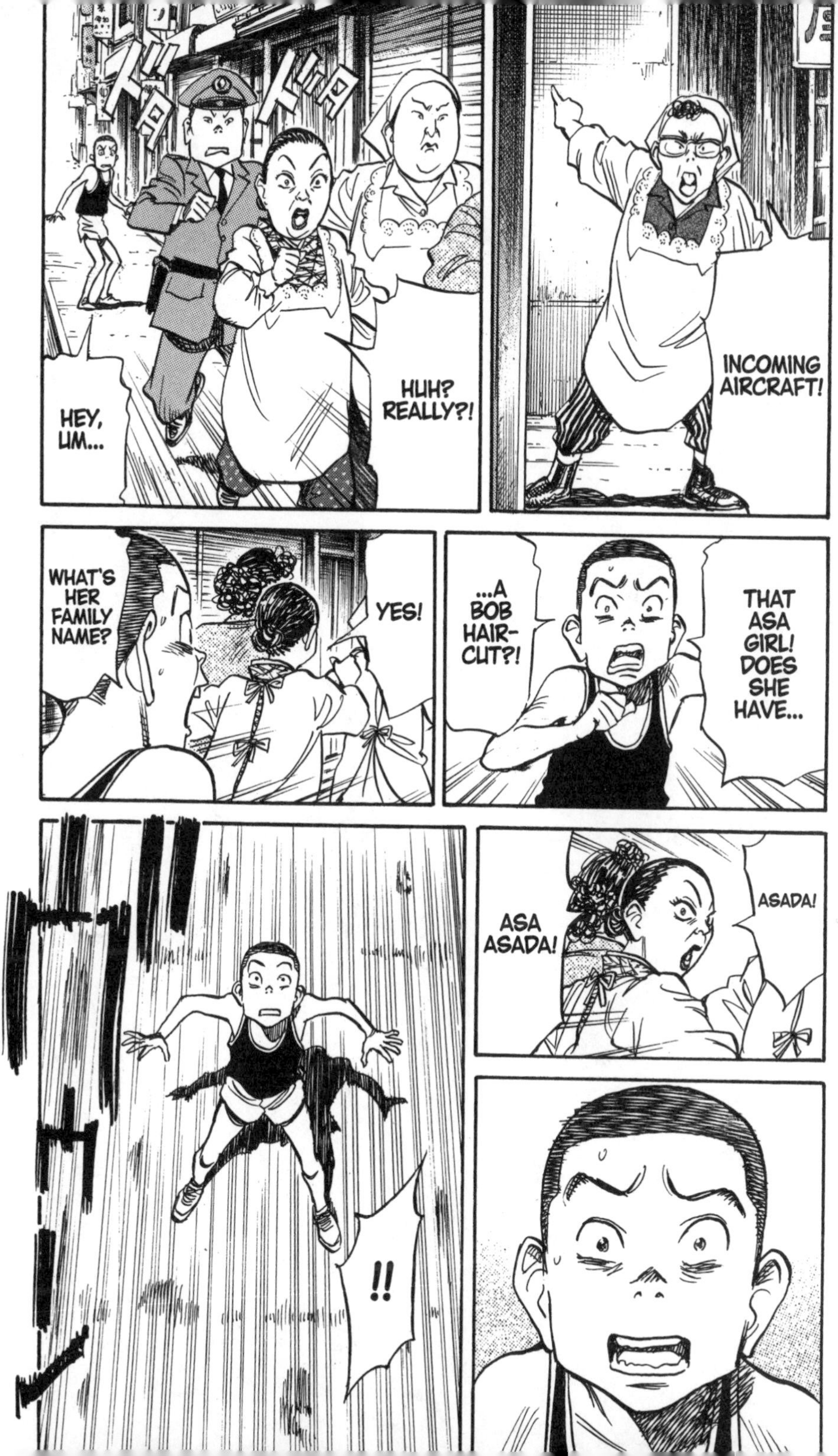
INCOMING AIRCRAFT!
ドタドタ
HUH? REALLY?!
HEY, UM...
THAT ASA GIRL! DOES SHE HAVE...
...A BOB HAIR-CUT?!
YES!
WHAT'S HER FAMILY NAME?
ASADA!
ASA ASADA!
!!

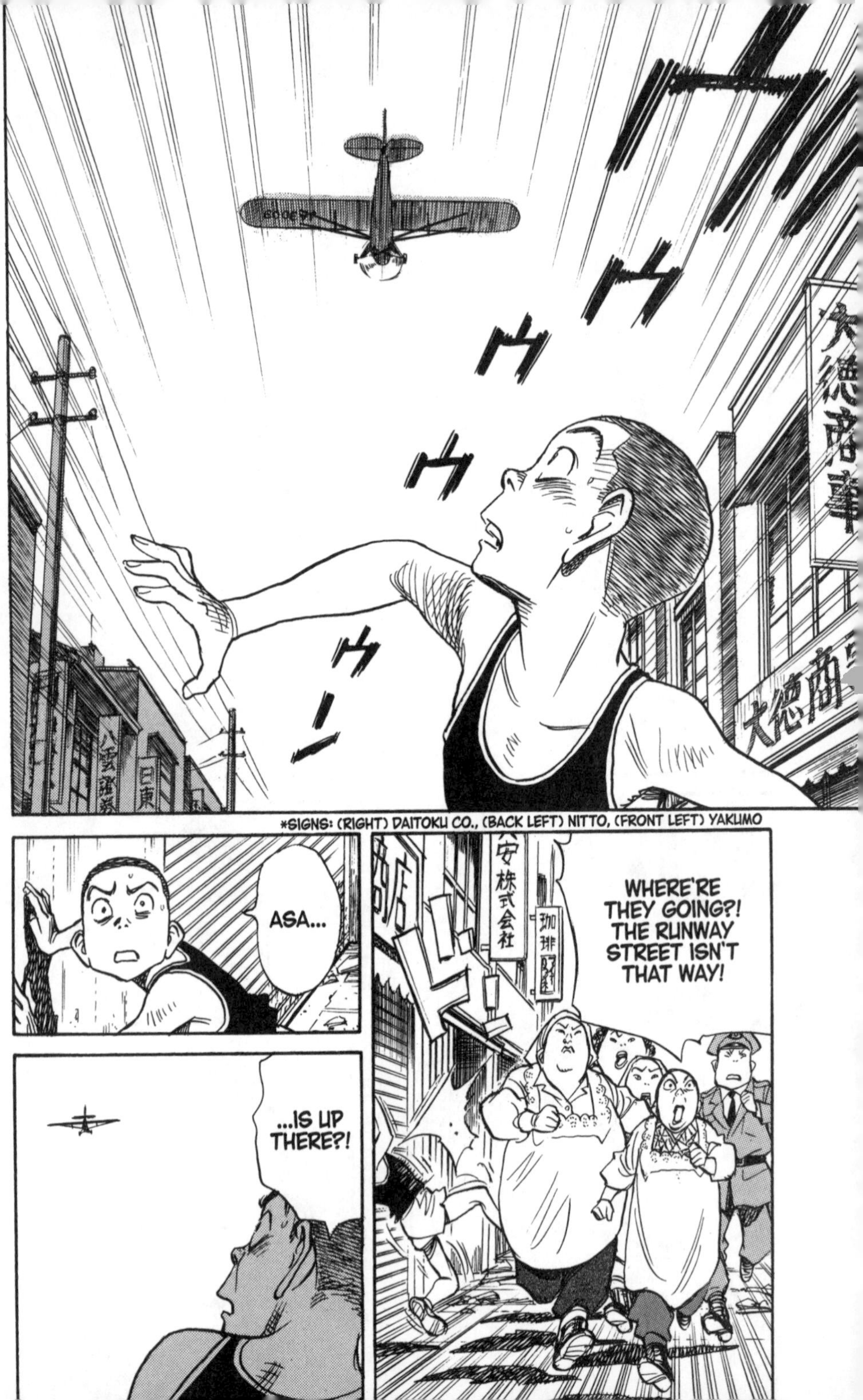
ウウウウウウーン
大徳商事
大徳商
日東
八雲證券
*SIGNS: (RIGHT) DAITOKU CO., (BACK LEFT) NITTO, (FRONT LEFT) YAKUMO
WHERE'RE THEY GOING?! THE RUNWAY STREET ISN'T THAT WAY!
株式会社
珈琲
ASA...
...IS UP THERE?!

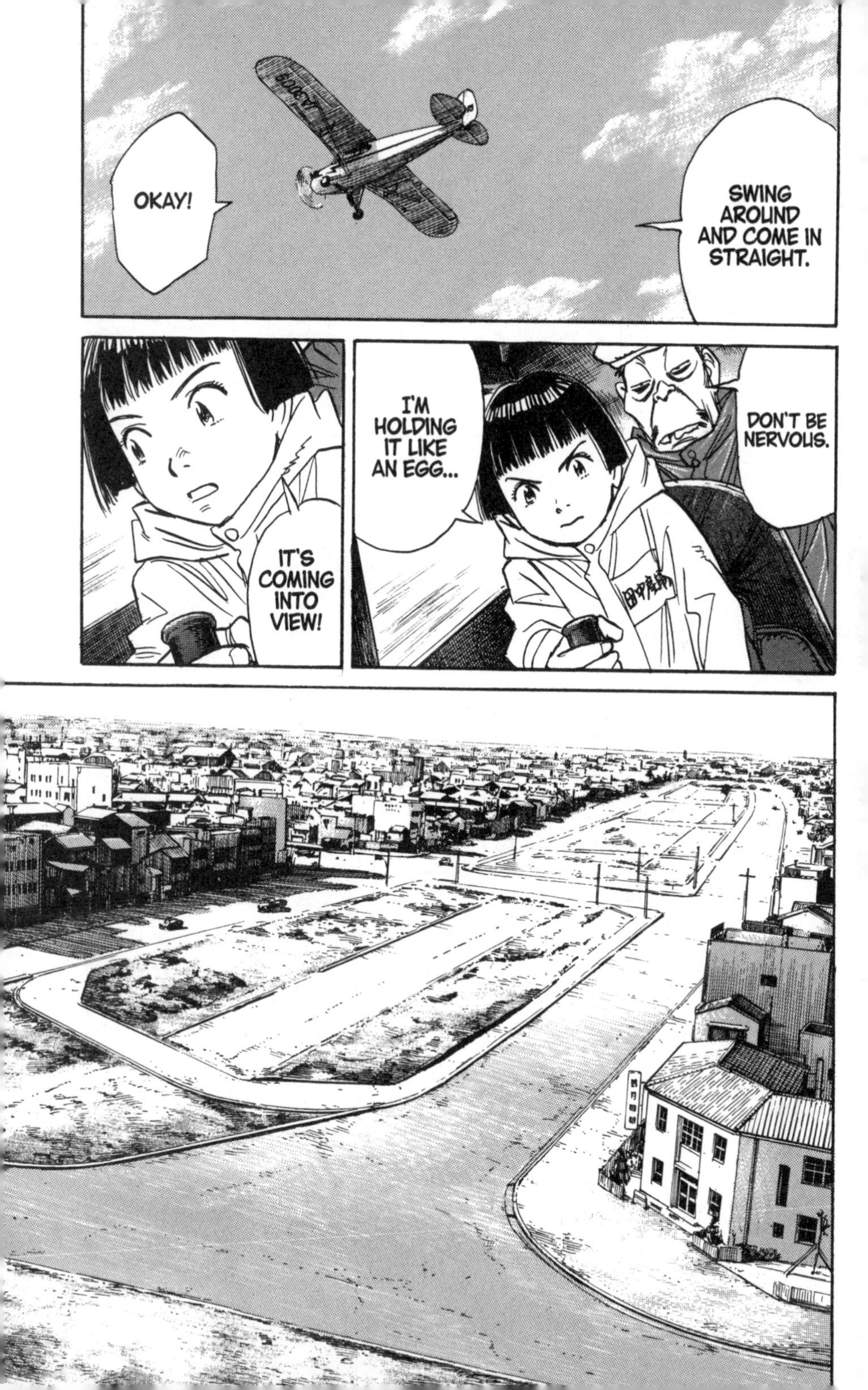
SWING AROUND AND COME IN STRAIGHT.
OKAY!
DON'T BE NERVOUS.
I'M HOLDING IT LIKE AN EGG...
IT'S COMING INTO VIEW!

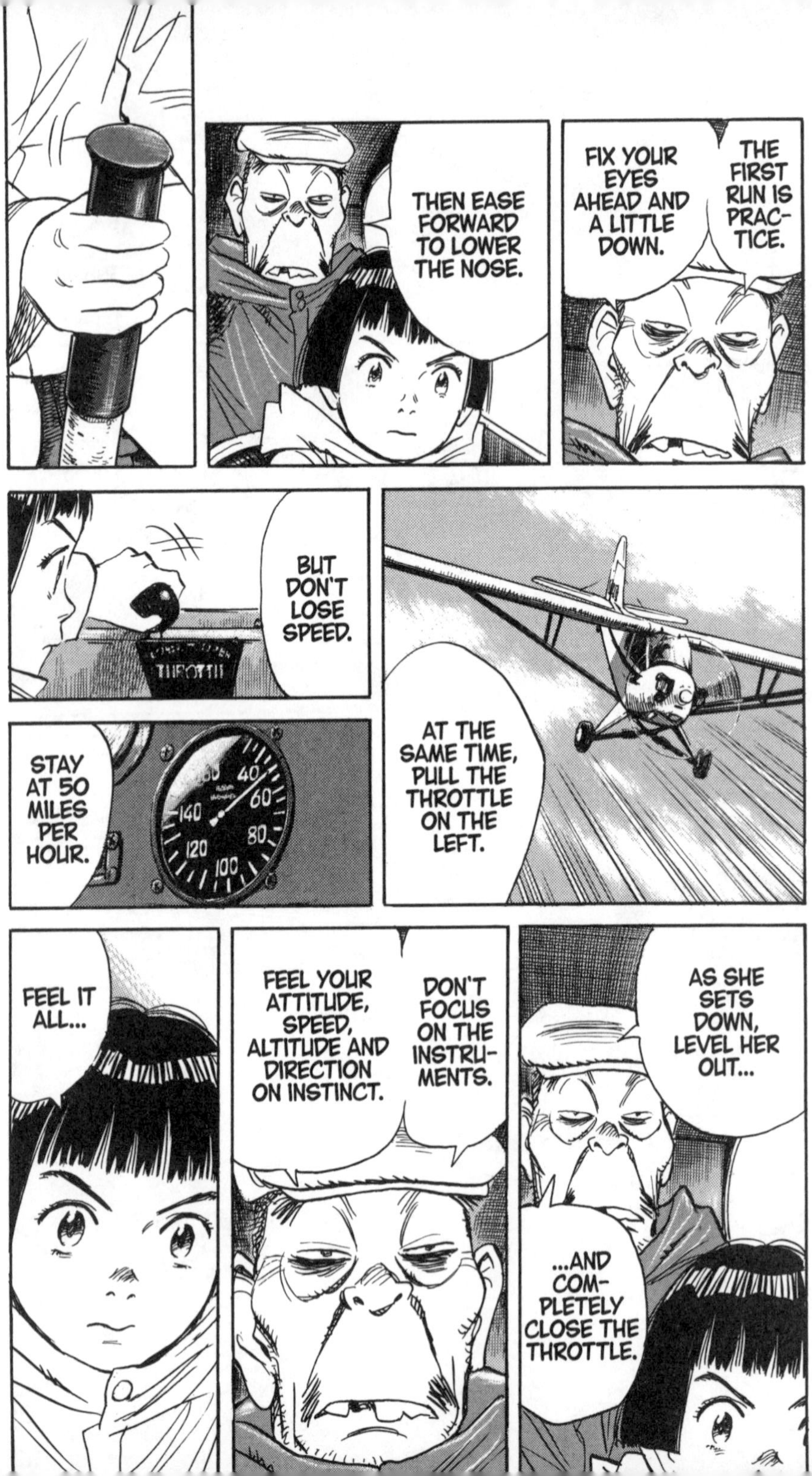
THE FIRST RUN IS PRACTICE.
FIX YOUR EYES AHEAD AND A LITTLE DOWN.
THEN EASE FORWARD TO LOWER THE NOSE.
AT THE SAME TIME, PULL THE THROTTLE ON THE LEFT.
BUT DON'T LOSE SPEED.
STAY AT 50 MILES PER HOUR.
AS SHE SETS DOWN, LEVEL HER OUT...
...AND COMPLETELY CLOSE THE THROTTLE.
DON'T FOCUS ON THE INSTRUMENTS.
FEEL YOUR ATTITUDE, SPEED, ALTITUDE AND DIRECTION ON INSTINCT.
FEEL IT ALL...

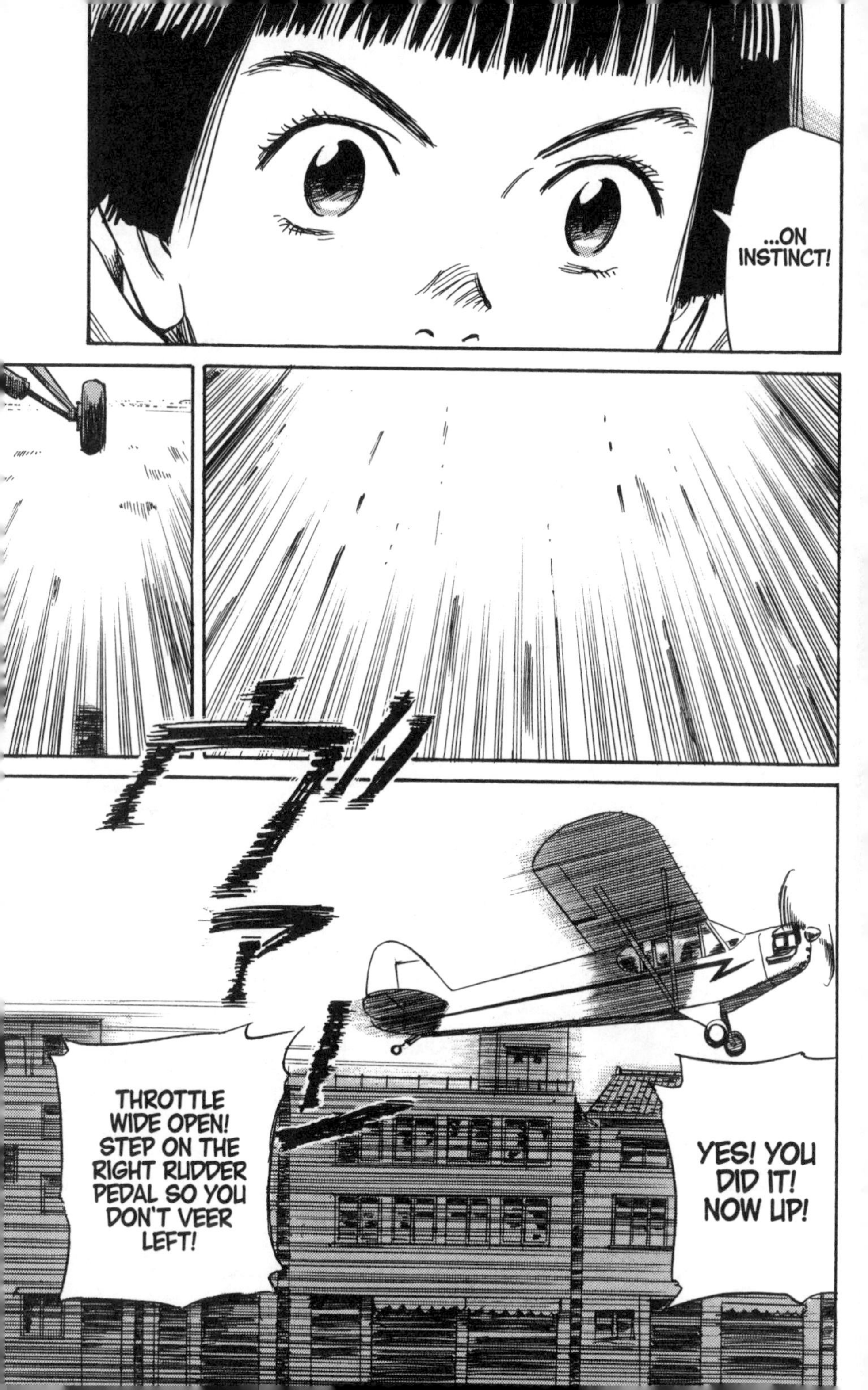
...ON INSTINCT!
YES! YOU DID IT! NOW UP!
THROTTLE WIDE OPEN! STEP ON THE RIGHT RUDDER PEDAL SO YOU DON'T VEER LEFT!

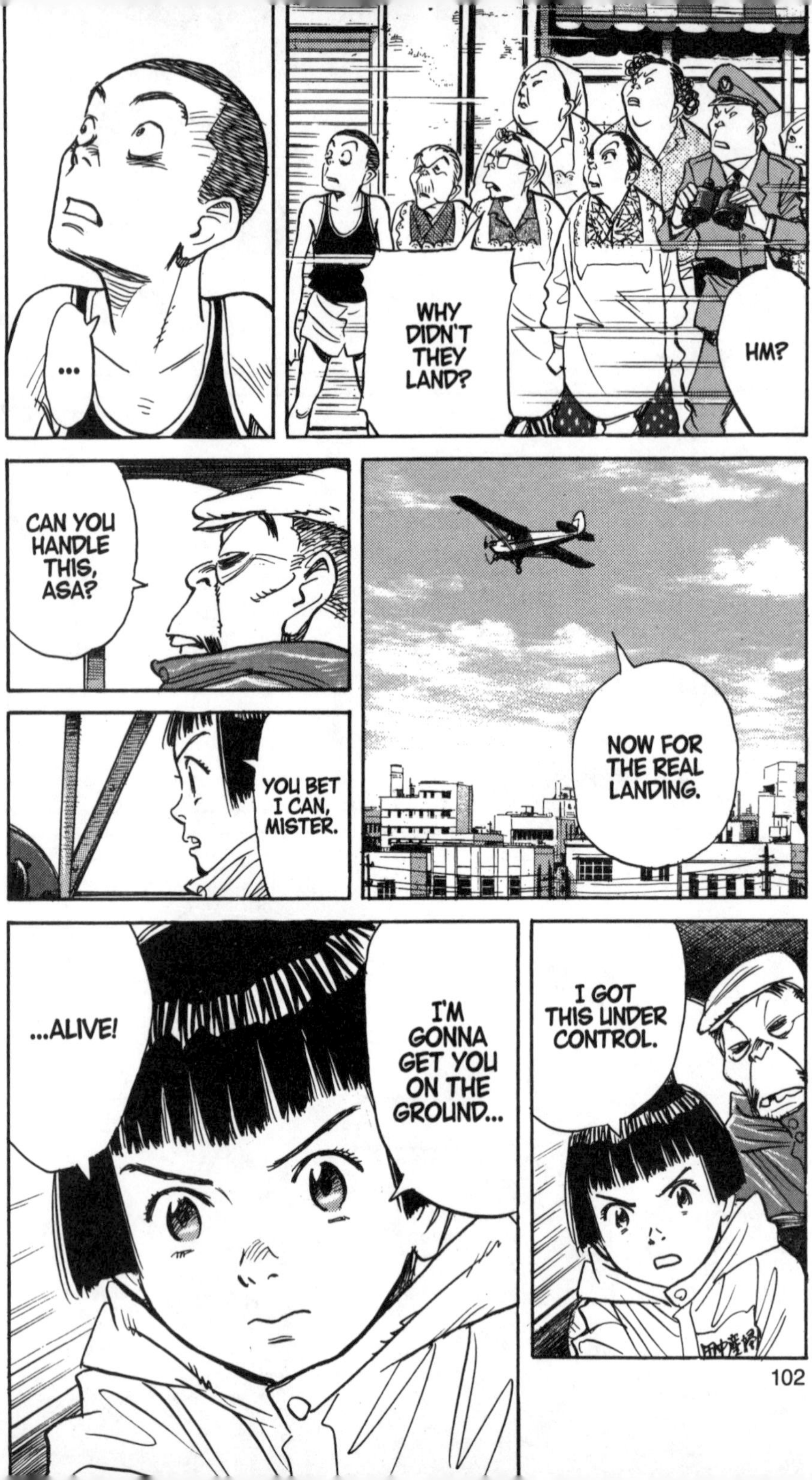
HM?
WHY DIDN'T THEY LAND?
...
NOW FOR THE REAL LANDING.
CAN YOU HANDLE THIS, ASA?
YOU BET I CAN, MISTER.
I GOT THIS UNDER CONTROL.
I'M GONNA GET YOU ON THE GROUND...
...ALIVE!

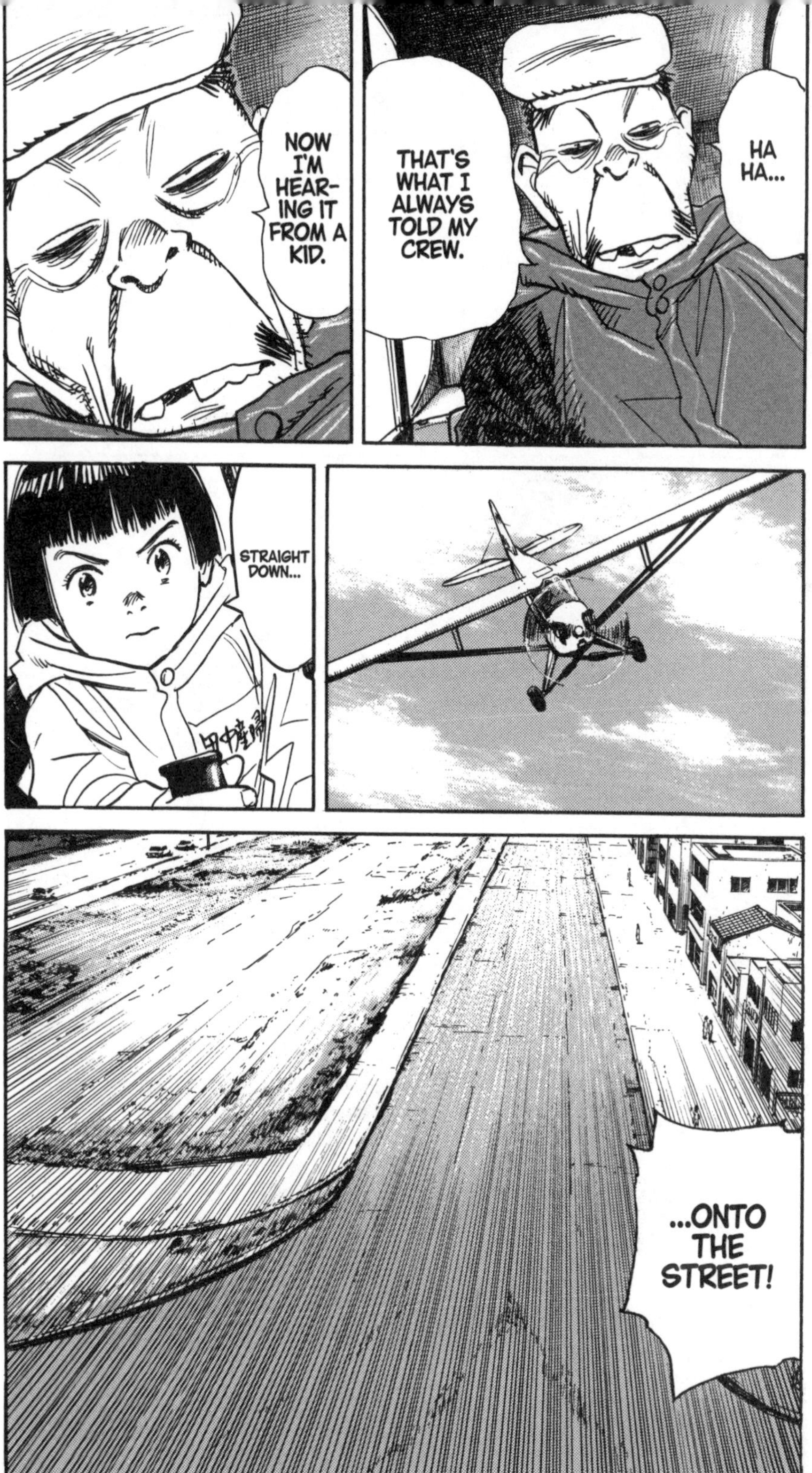
HA HA...
THAT'S WHAT I ALWAYS TOLD MY CREW.
NOW I'M HEARING IT FROM A KID.
STRAIGHT DOWN...
...ONTO THE STREET!

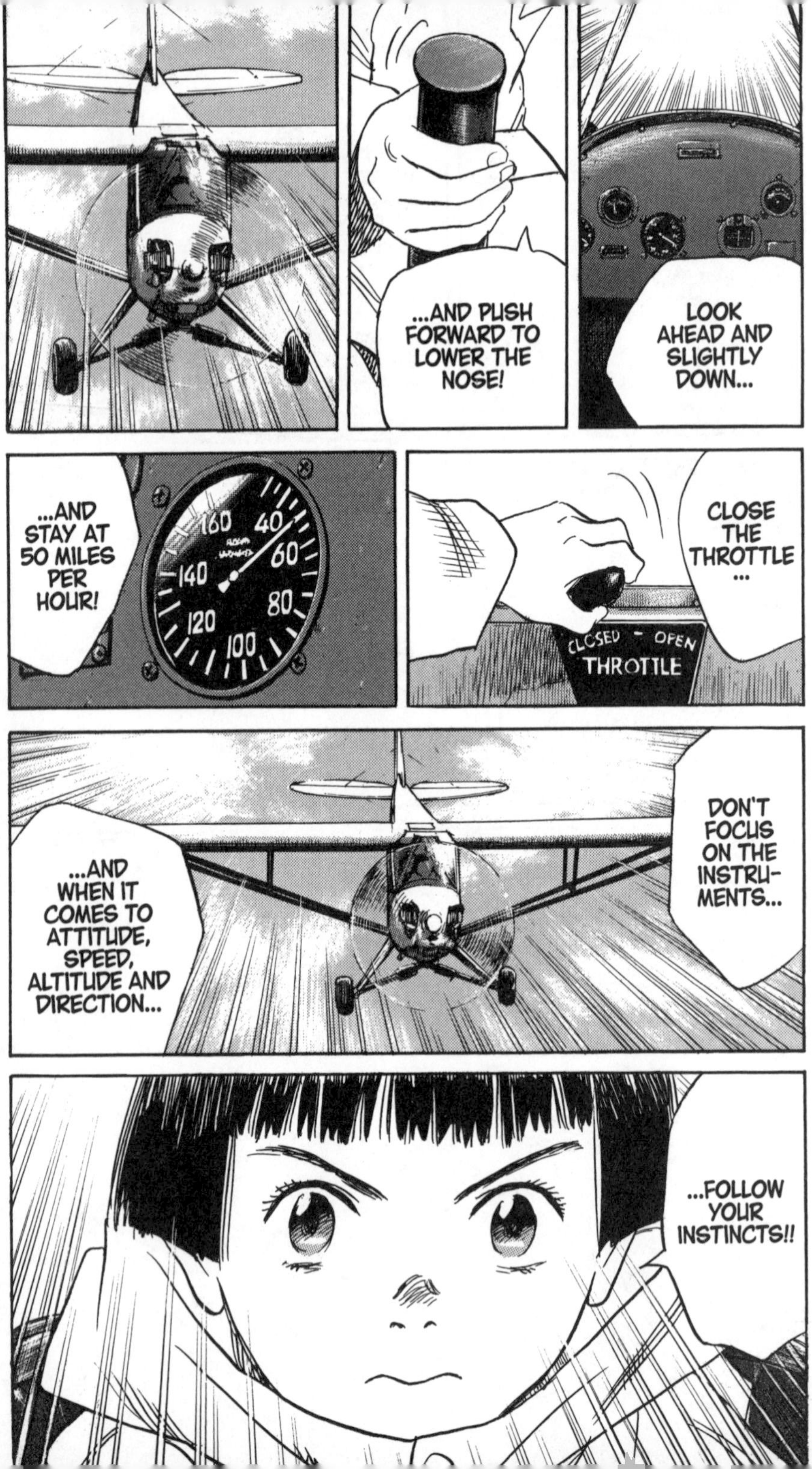

LOOK AHEAD AND SLIGHTLY DOWN...
...AND PUSH FORWARD TO LOWER THE NOSE!
CLOSE THE THROTTLE ...
CLOSED - OPEN
THROTTLE
...AND STAY AT 50 MILES PER HOUR!
DON'T FOCUS ON THE INSTRU-MENTS...
...AND WHEN IT COMES TO ATTITUDE, SPEED, ALTITUDE AND DIRECTION...
...FOLLOW YOUR INSTINCTS!!

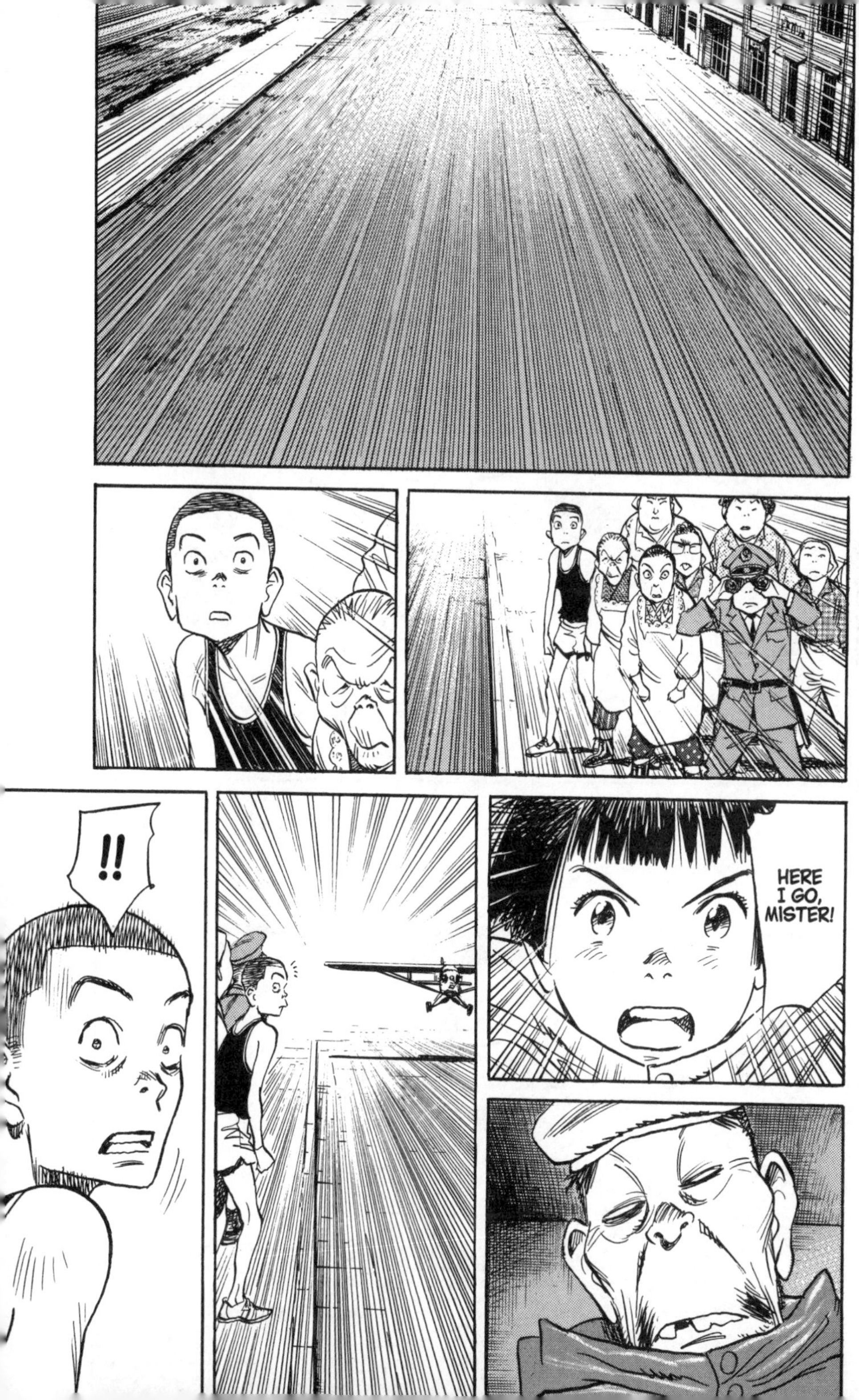
HERE I GO, MISTER!
!!

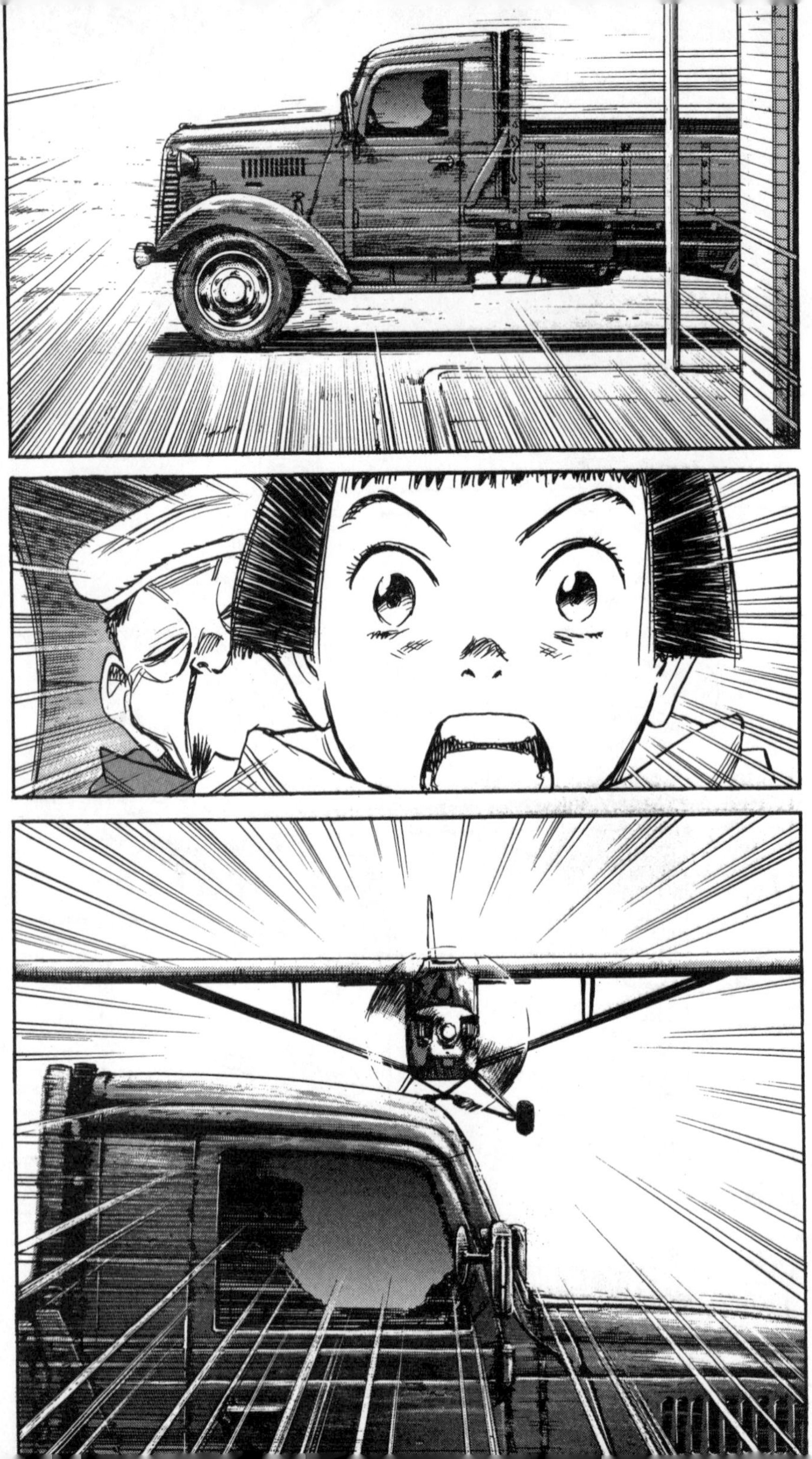

Chapter 13 ● Birthday

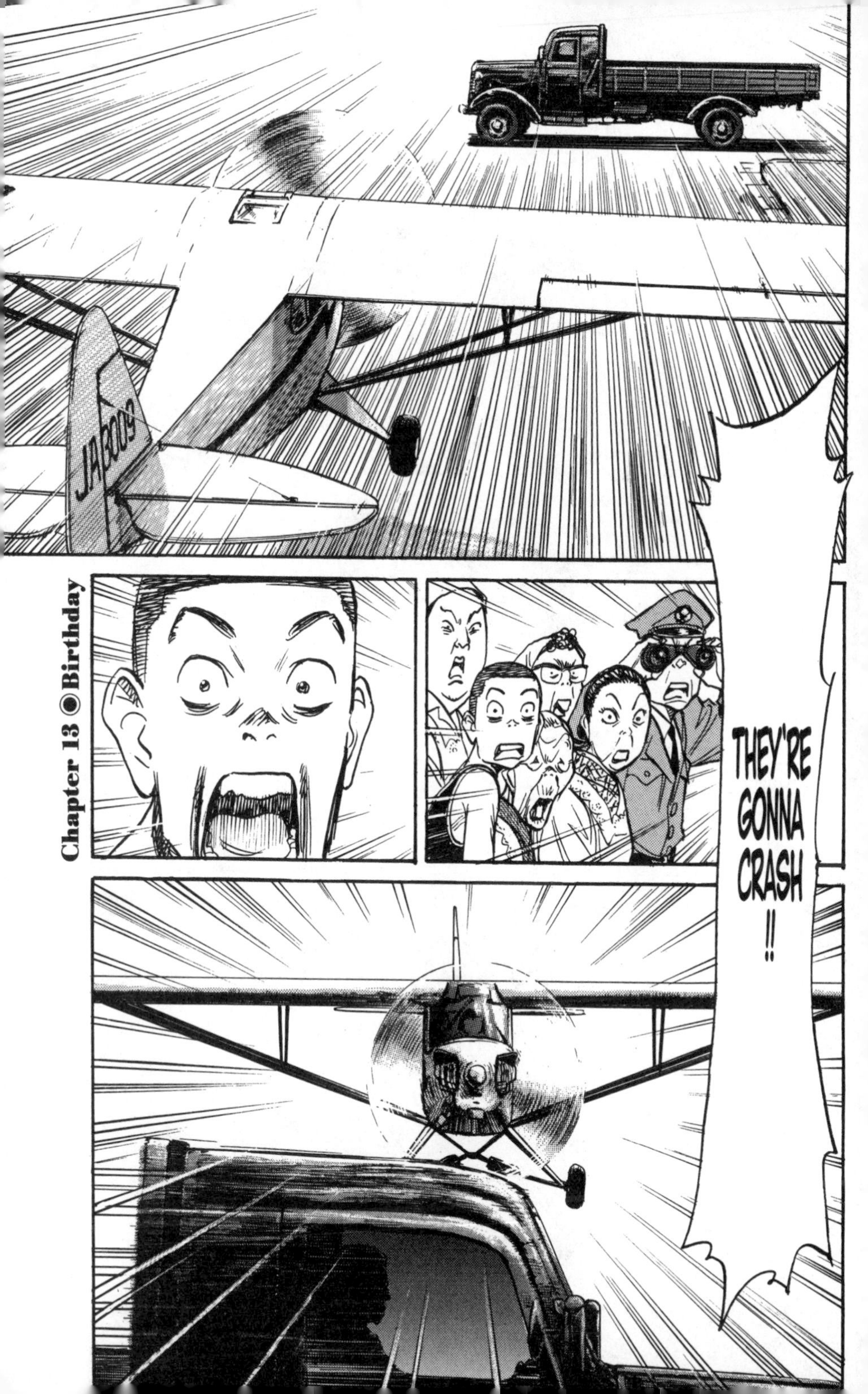
JA3009
THEY'RE GONNA CRASH!!

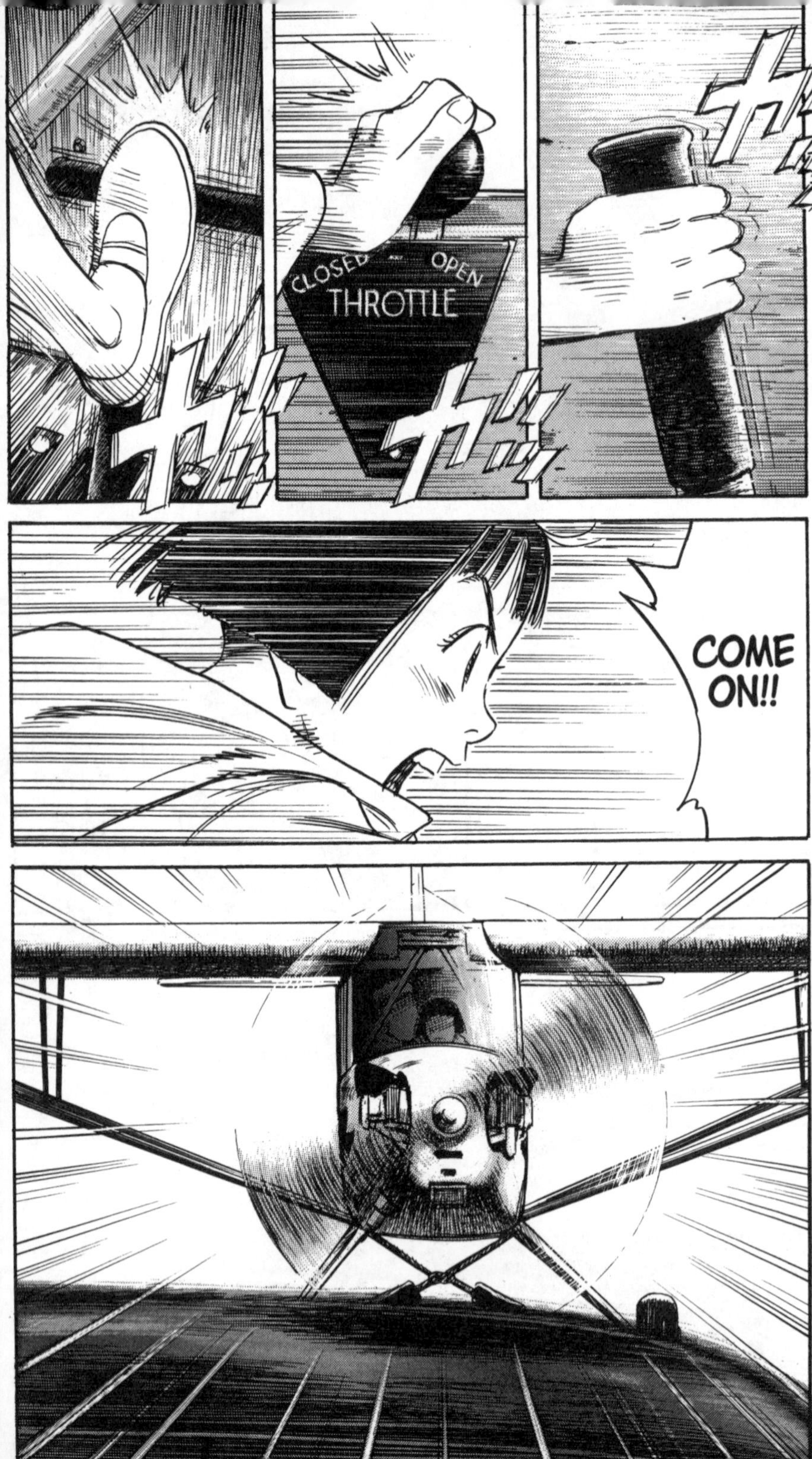
CLOSED
OPEN
THROTTLE
COME ON!!

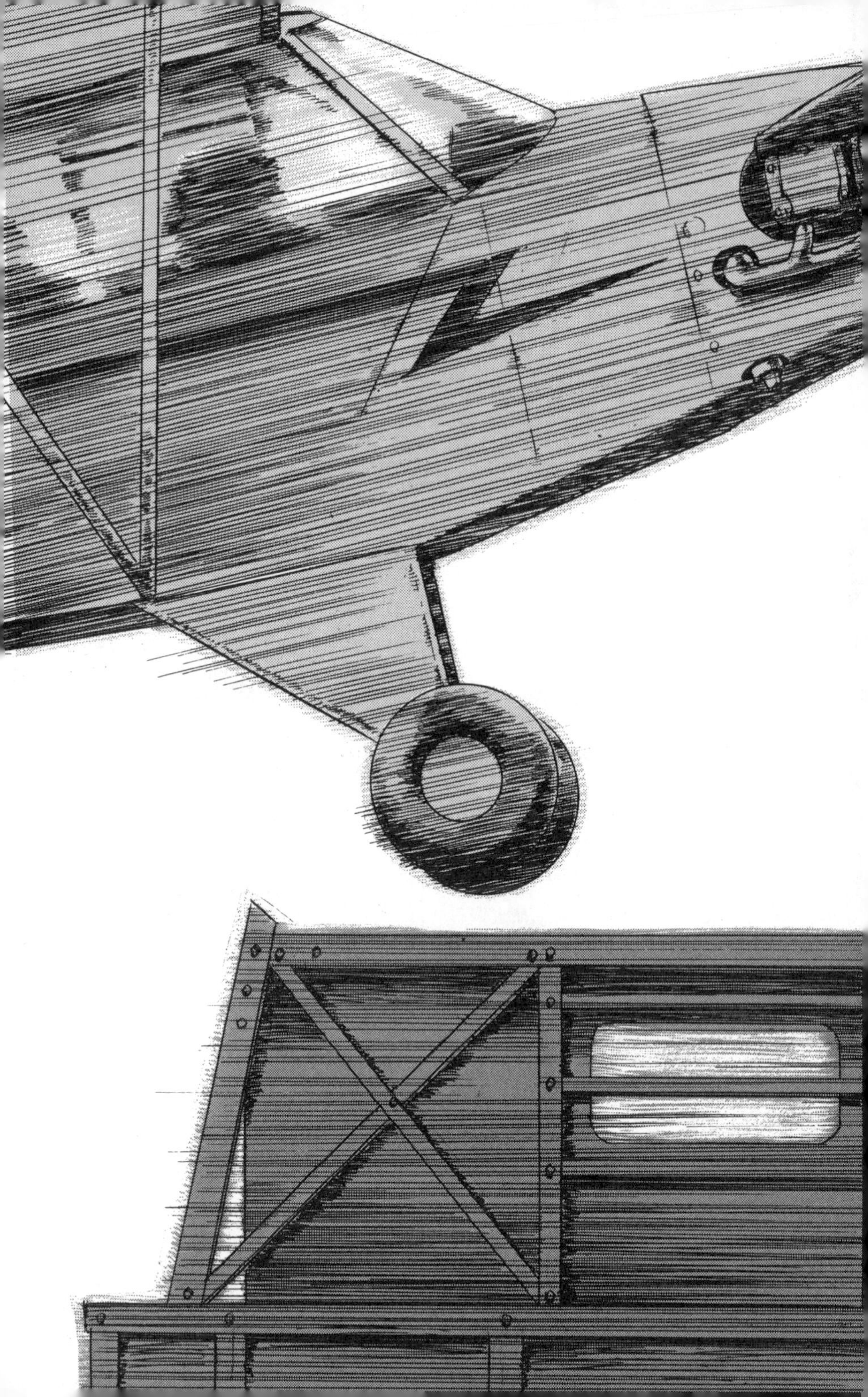

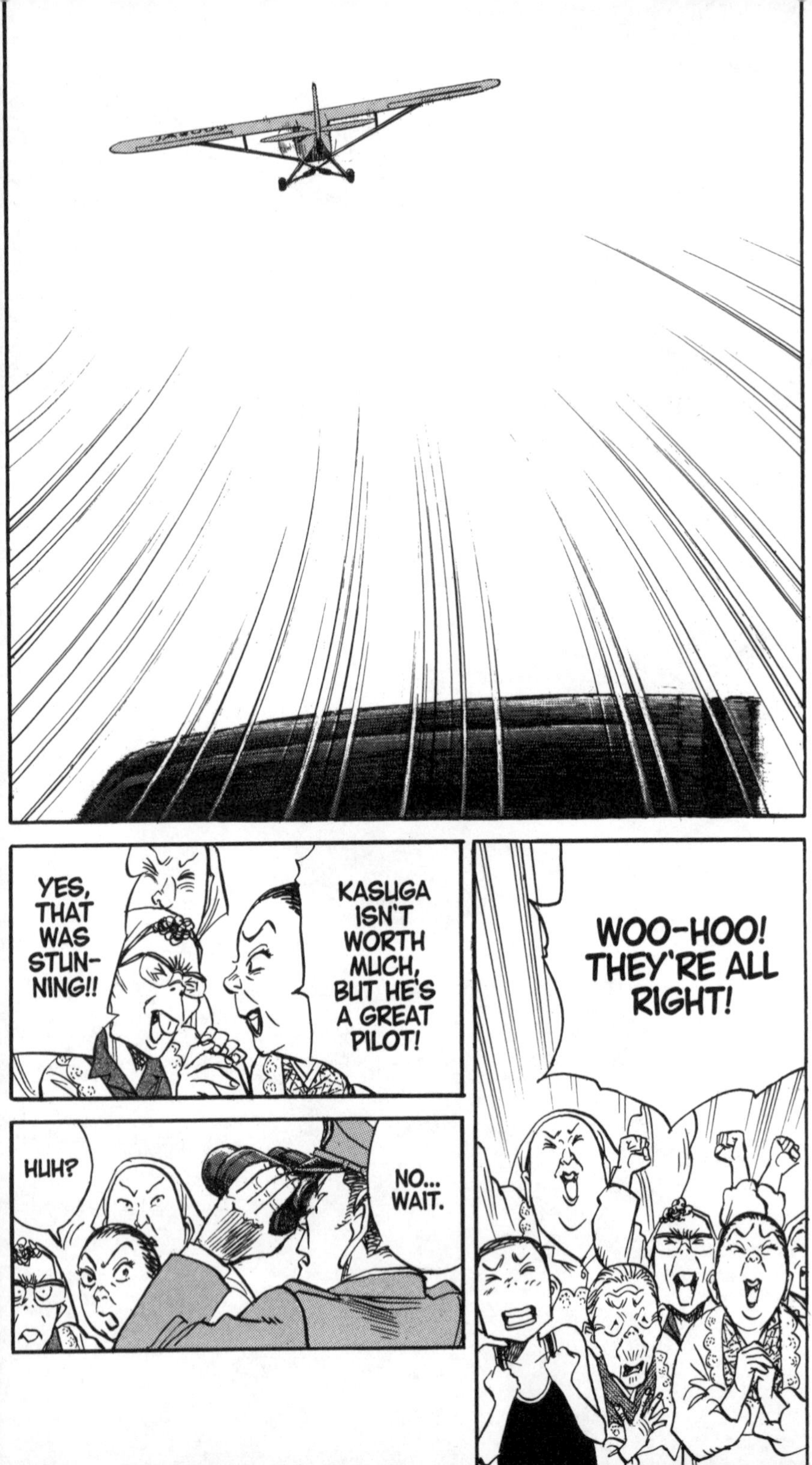
WOO-HOO! THEY'RE ALL RIGHT!
KASUGA ISN'T WORTH MUCH, BUT HE'S A GREAT PILOT!
YES, THAT WAS STUN-NING!!
NO... WAIT.
HUH?

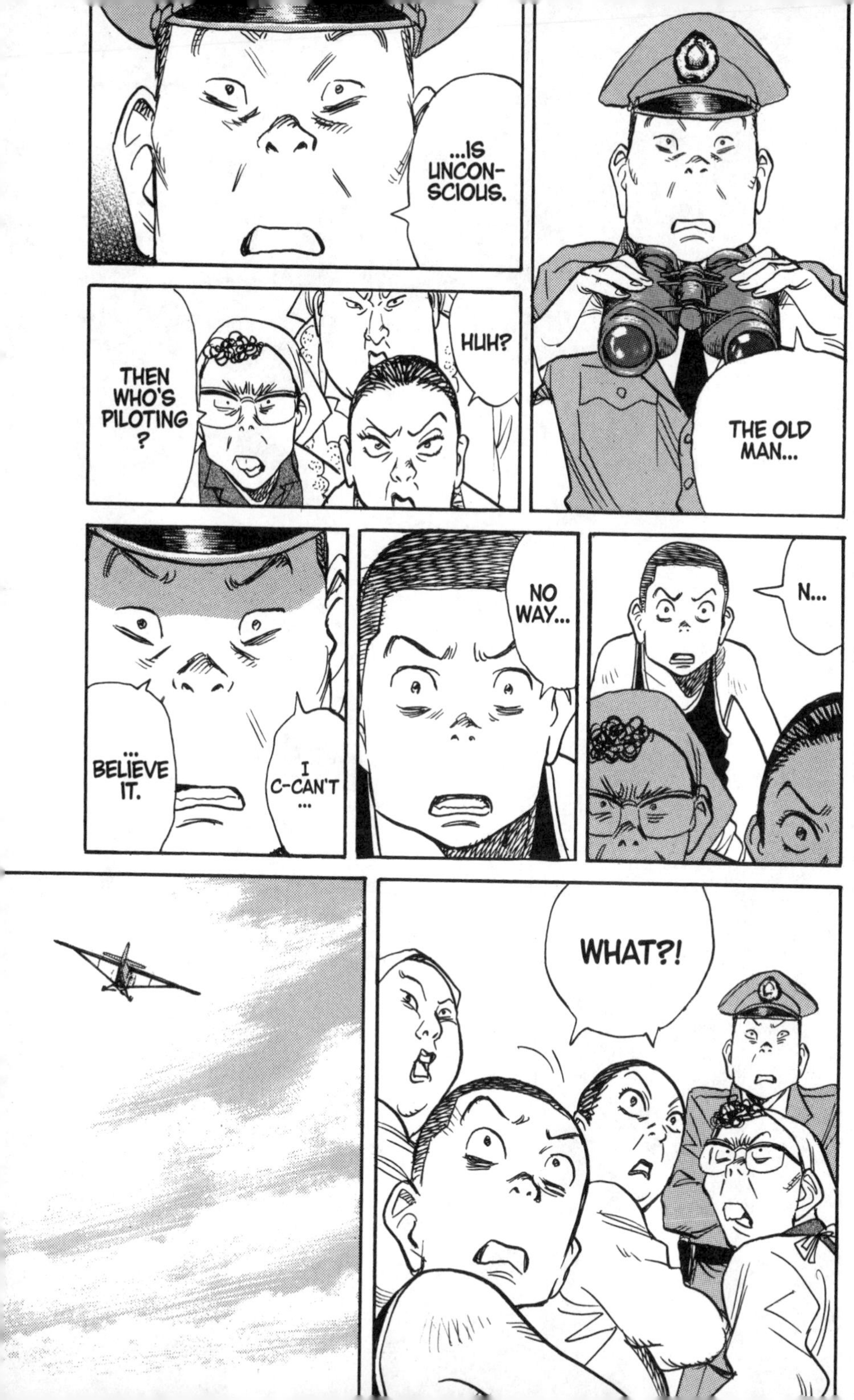
THE OLD MAN...
...IS UNCON-SCIOUS.
HUH?
THEN WHO'S PILOTING?
N...
NO WAY...
I C-CAN'T ...
... BELIEVE IT.
WHAT?!

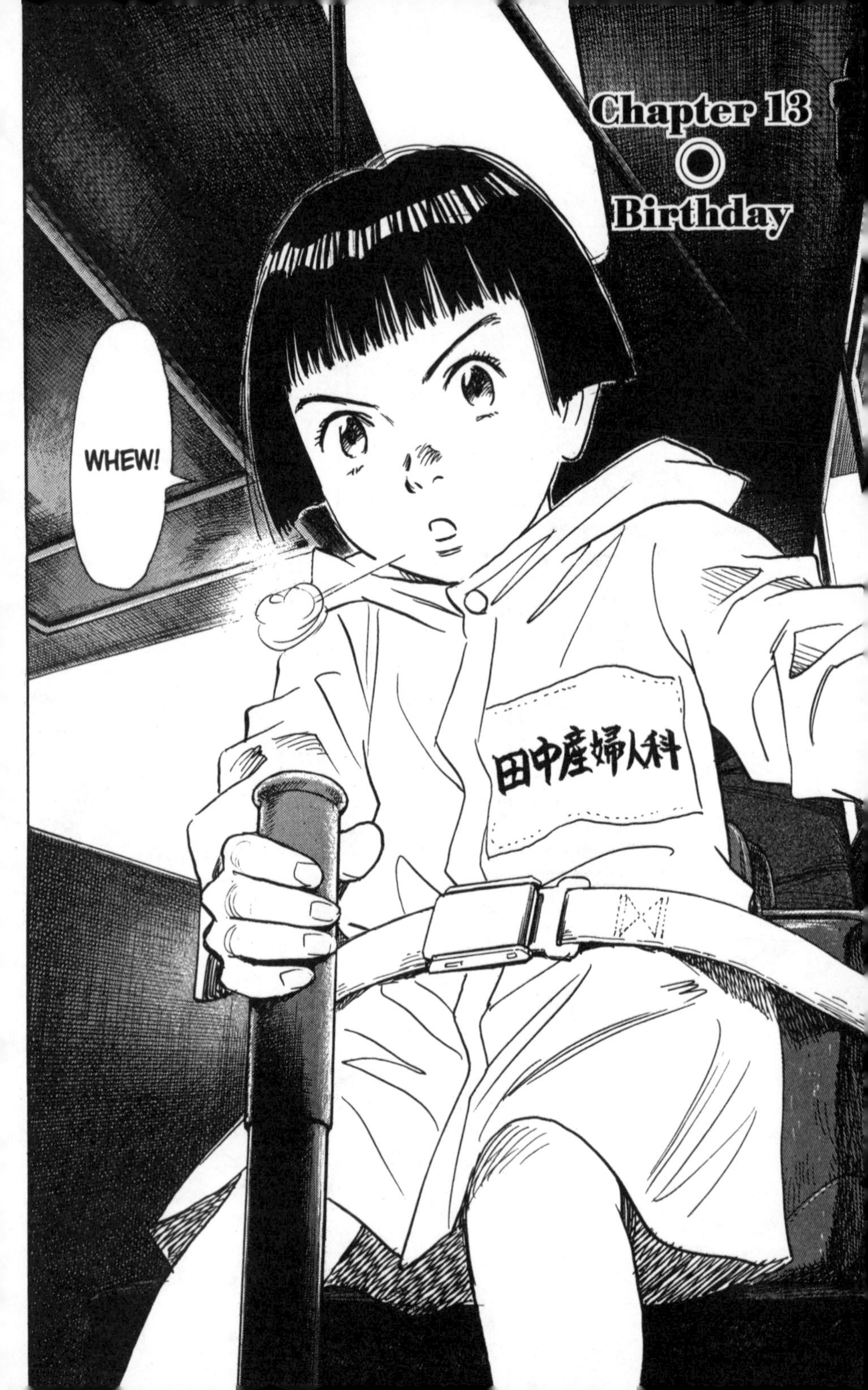
Chapter 13
Birthday
WHEW!
田中産婦人科

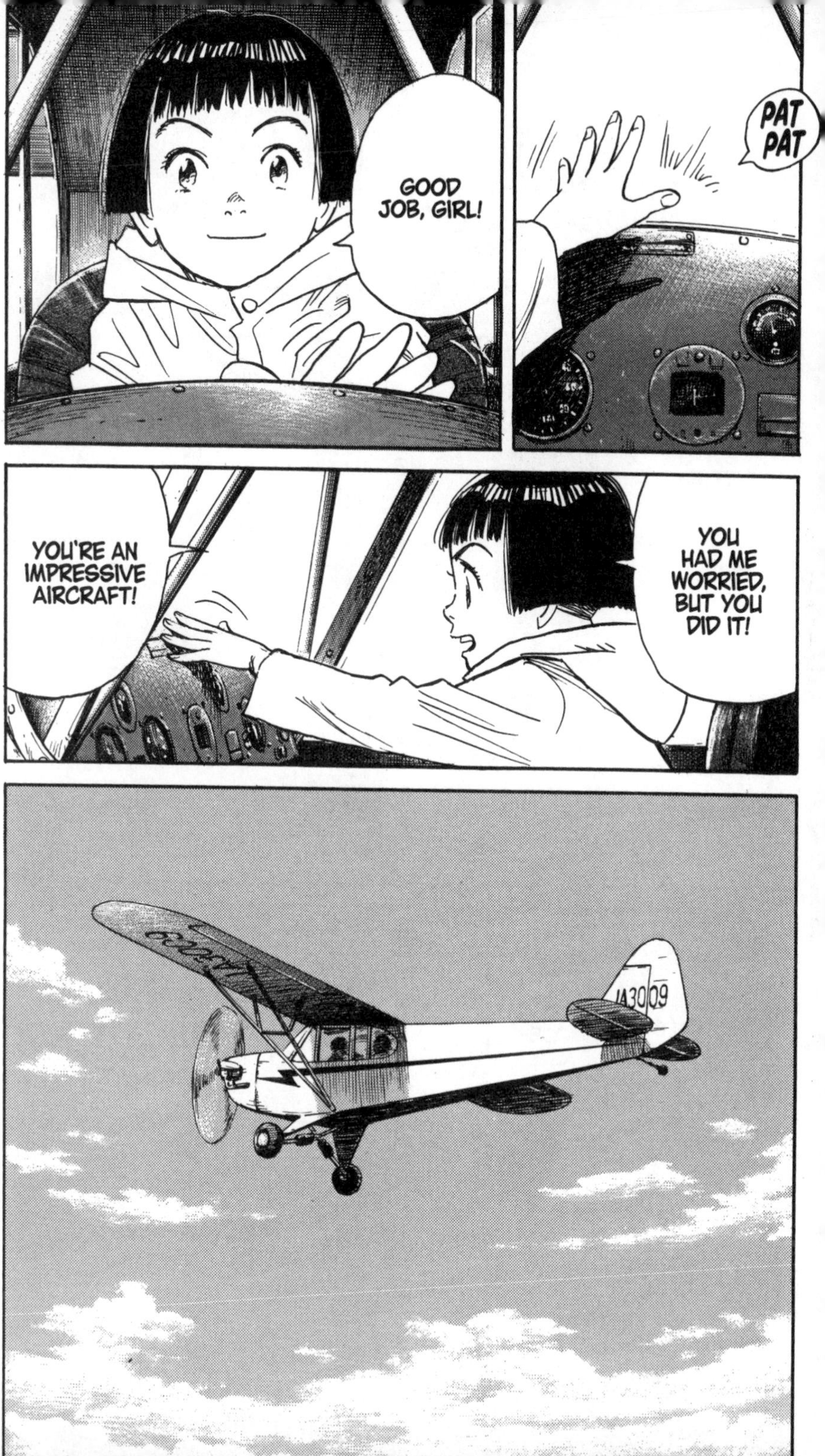
PAT PAT
GOOD JOB, GIRL!
YOU HAD ME WORRIED, BUT YOU DID IT!
YOU'RE AN IMPRESSIVE AIRCRAFT!
JA3009

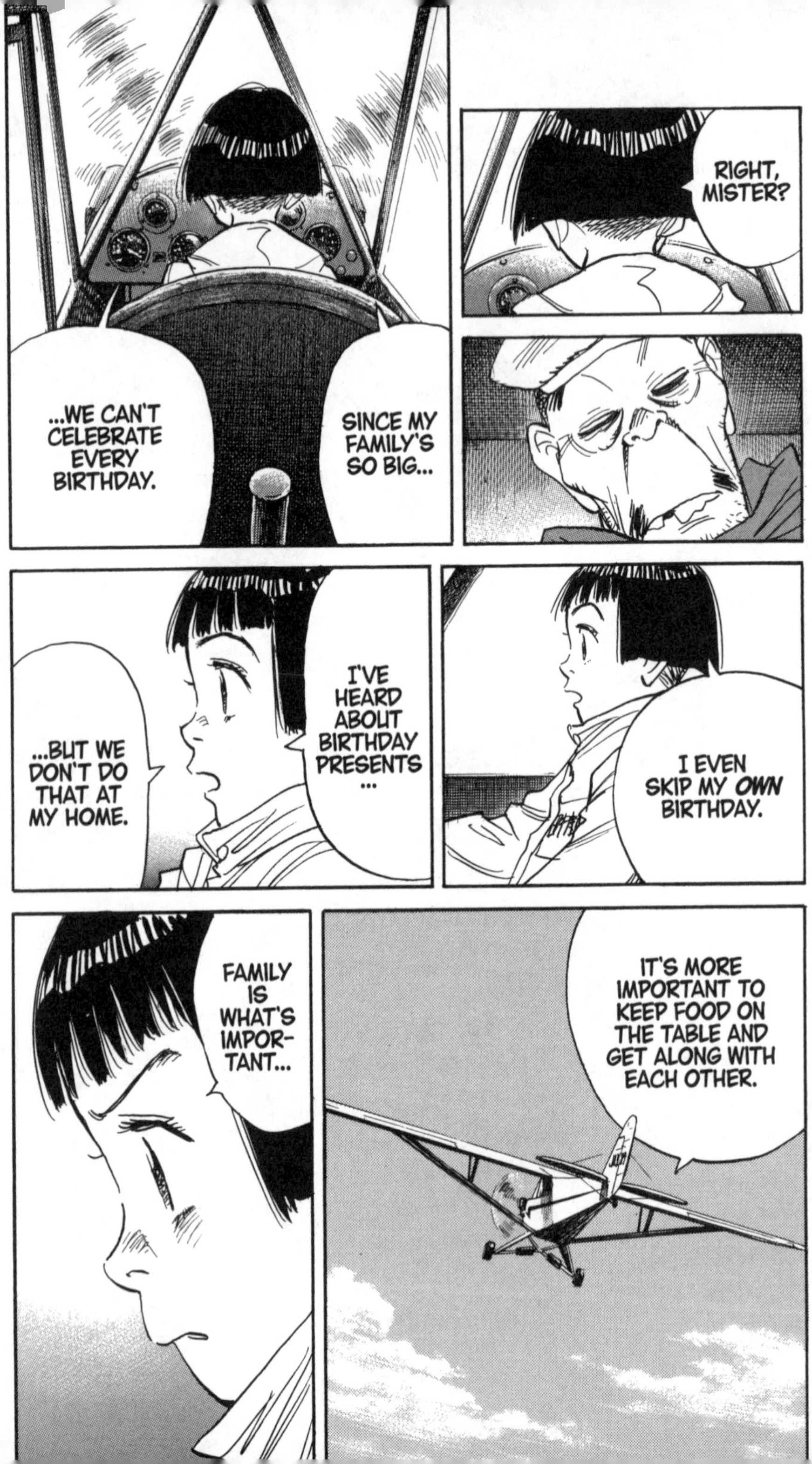
RIGHT, MISTER?
SINCE MY FAMILY'S SO BIG...
...WE CAN'T CELEBRATE EVERY BIRTHDAY.
I EVEN SKIP MY *OWN* BIRTHDAY.
I'VE HEARD ABOUT BIRTHDAY PRESENTS...
...BUT WE DON'T DO THAT AT MY HOME.
IT'S MORE IMPORTANT TO KEEP FOOD ON THE TABLE AND GET ALONG WITH EACH OTHER.
FAMILY IS WHAT'S IMPOR-TANT...

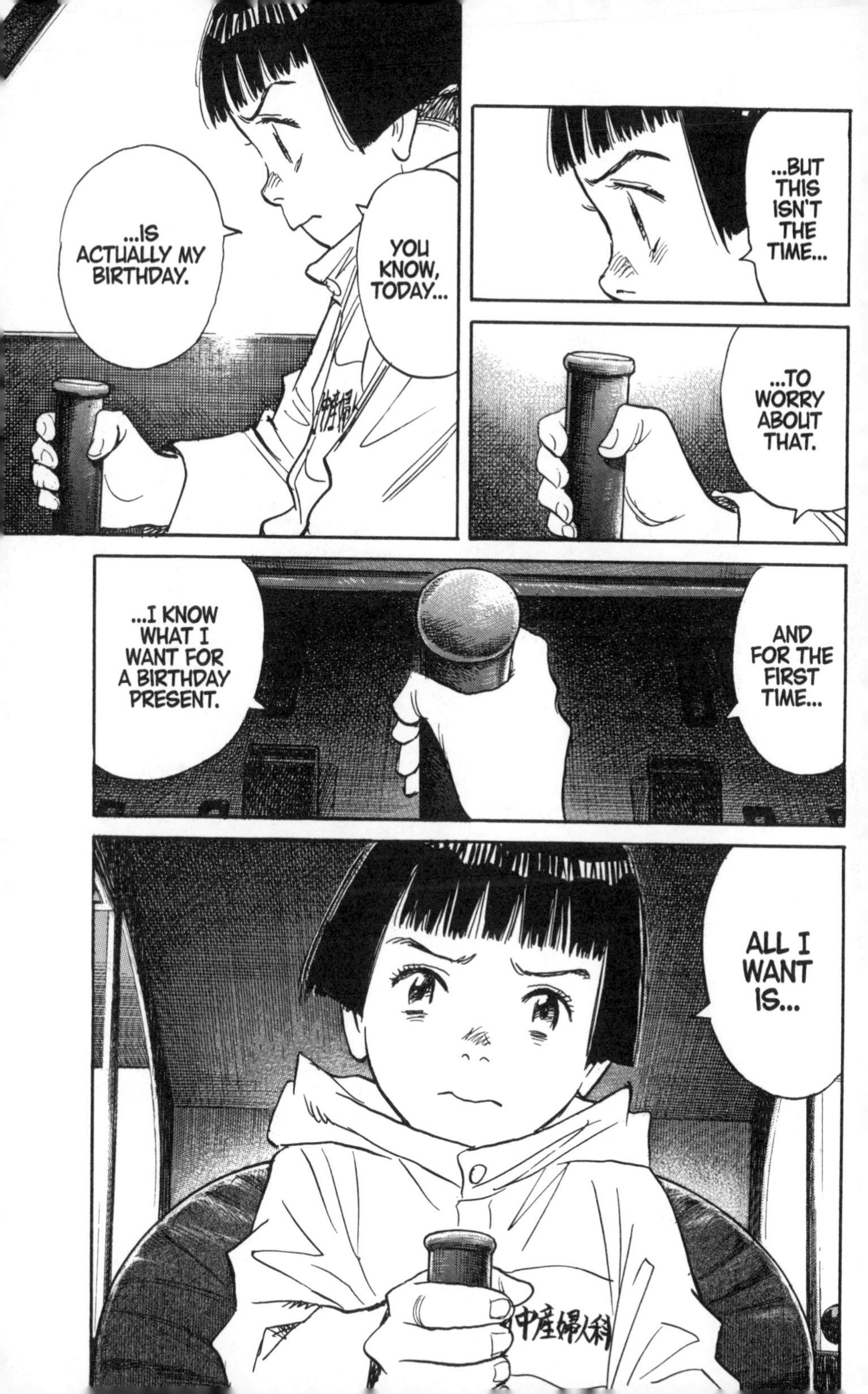
...BUT THIS ISN'T THE TIME...
...TO WORRY ABOUT THAT.
YOU KNOW, TODAY...
...IS ACTUALLY MY BIRTHDAY.
AND FOR THE FIRST TIME...
...I KNOW WHAT I WANT FOR A BIRTHDAY PRESENT.
ALL I WANT IS...
中産婦人科

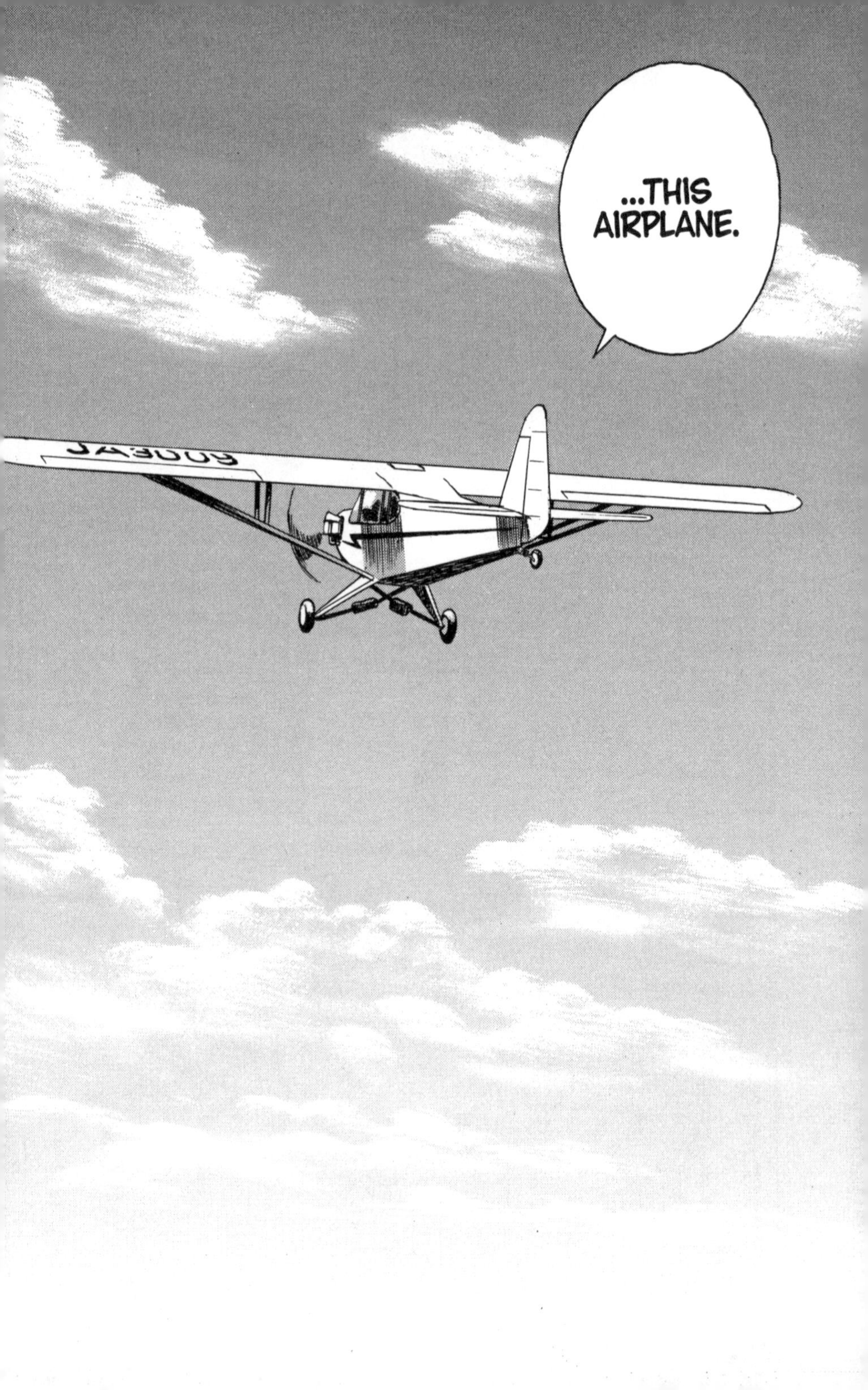
...THIS AIRPLANE.

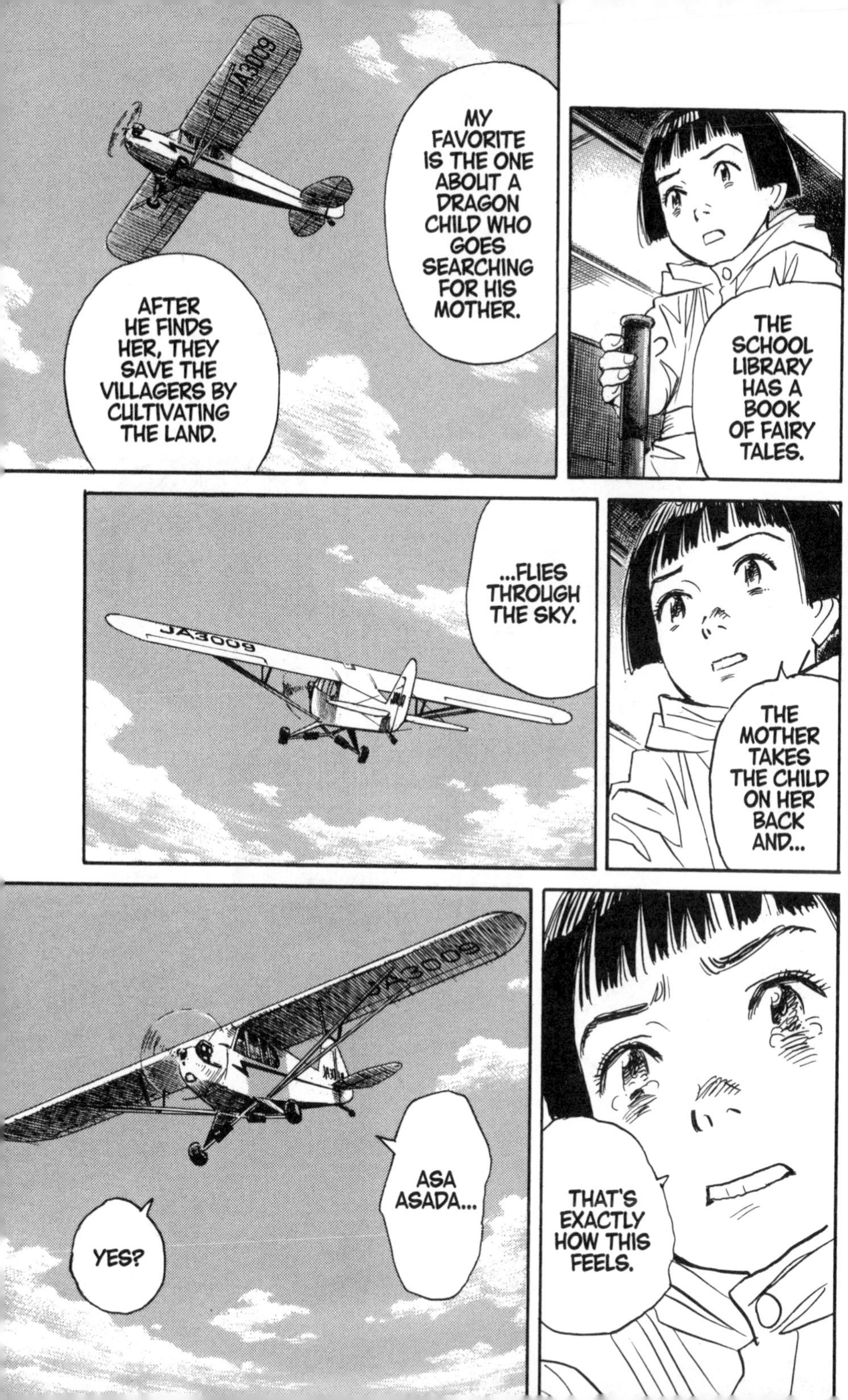
THE SCHOOL LIBRARY HAS A BOOK OF FAIRY TALES.
MY FAVORITE IS THE ONE ABOUT A DRAGON CHILD WHO GOES SEARCHING FOR HIS MOTHER.
AFTER HE FINDS HER, THEY SAVE THE VILLAGERS BY CULTIVATING THE LAND.
THE MOTHER TAKES THE CHILD ON HER BACK AND...
...FLIES THROUGH THE SKY.
THAT'S EXACTLY HOW THIS FEELS.
ASA ASADA...
YES?

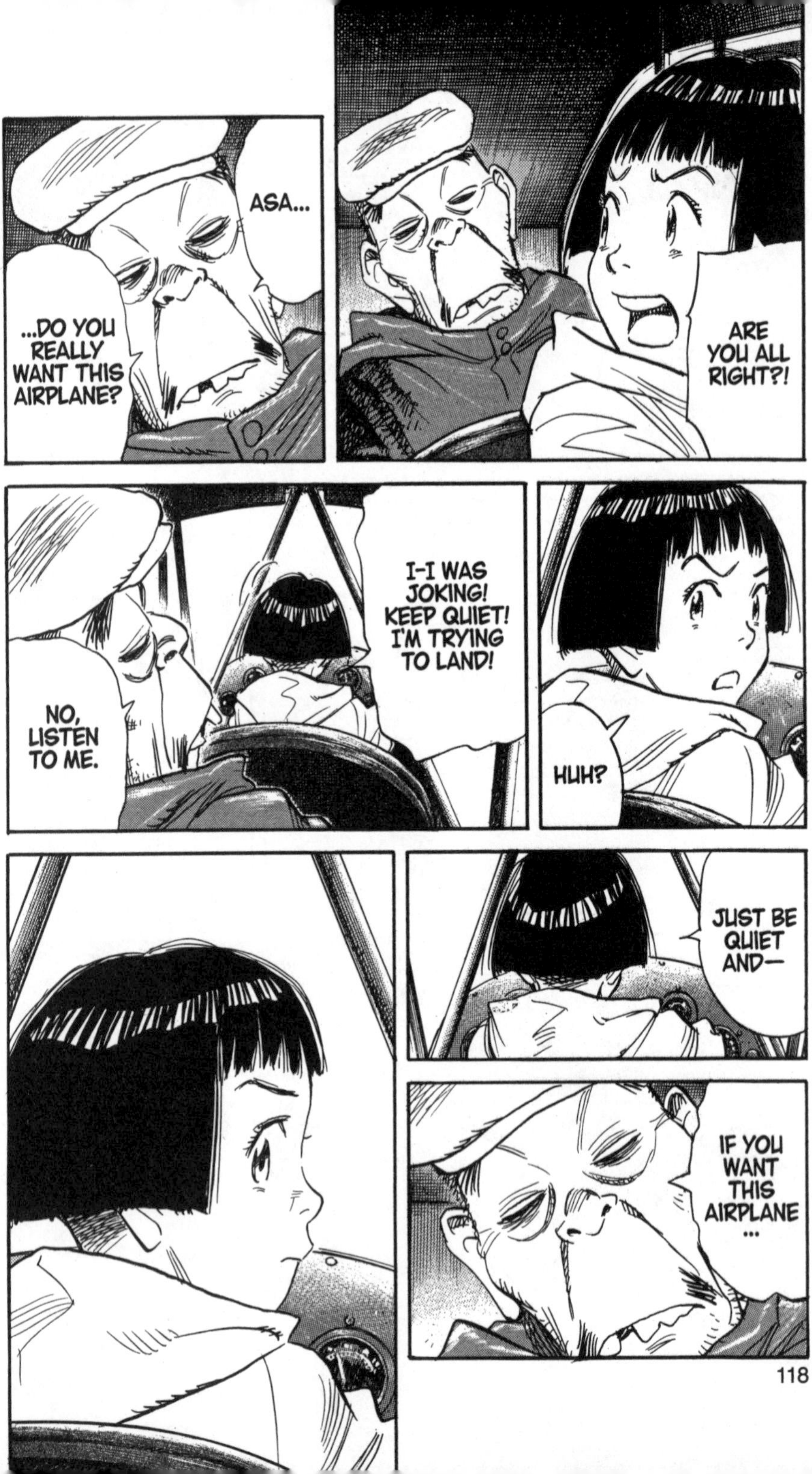
ARE YOU ALL RIGHT?!
ASA...
...DO YOU REALLY WANT THIS AIRPLANE?
HUH?
I-I WAS JOKING! KEEP QUIET! I'M TRYING TO LAND!
NO, LISTEN TO ME.
JUST BE QUIET AND—
IF YOU WANT THIS AIRPLANE ...

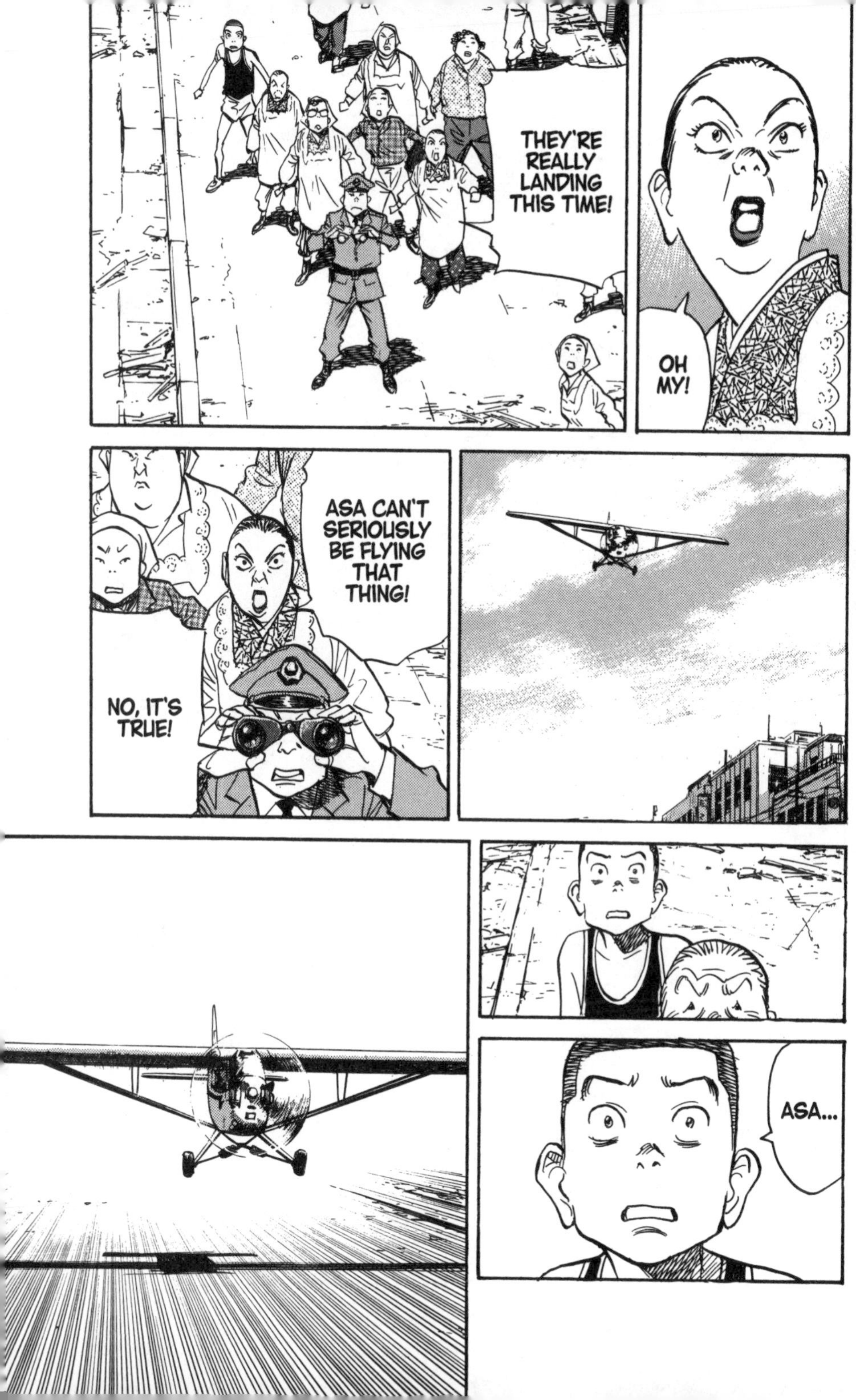
OH MY!
THEY'RE REALLY LANDING THIS TIME!
ASA CAN'T SERIOUSLY BE FLYING THAT THING!
NO, IT'S TRUE!
ASA...

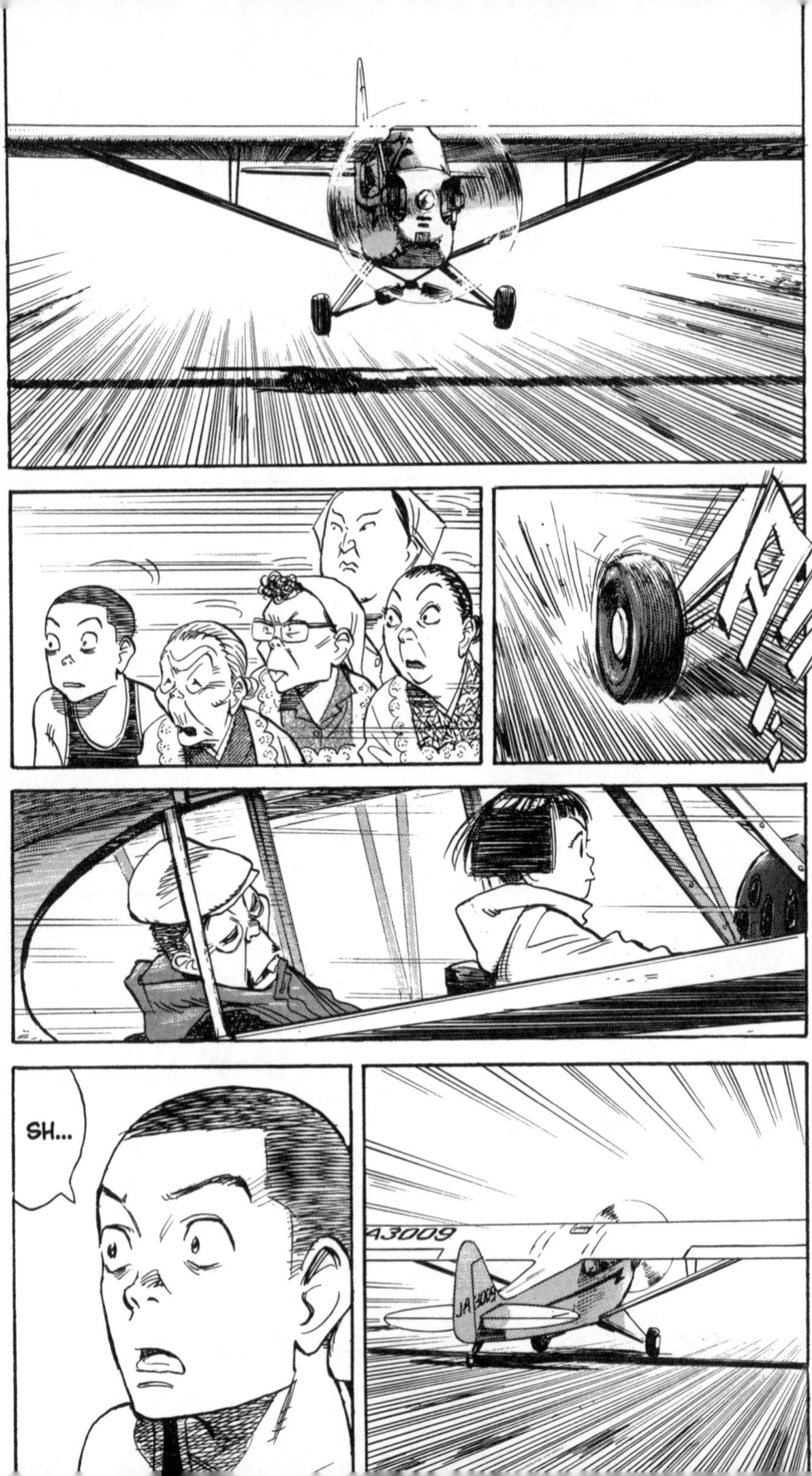

A3009
SH...

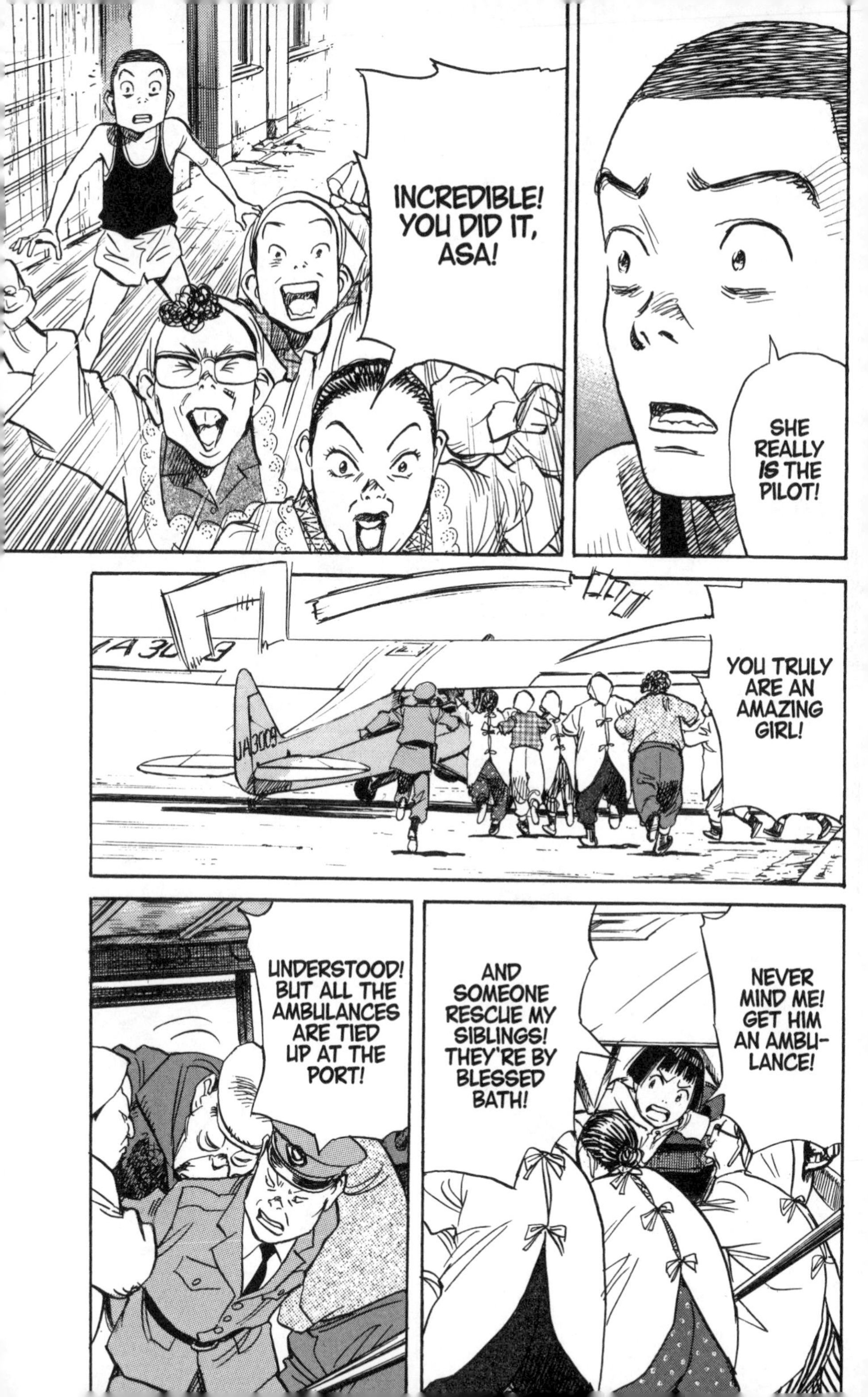
SHE REALLY IS THE PILOT!
INCREDIBLE! YOU DID IT, ASA!
YOU TRULY ARE AN AMAZING GIRL!
NEVER MIND ME! GET HIM AN AMBU-LANCE!
AND SOMEONE RESCUE MY SIBLINGS! THEY'RE BY BLESSED BATH!
UNDERSTOOD! BUT ALL THE AMBULANCES ARE TIED UP AT THE PORT!

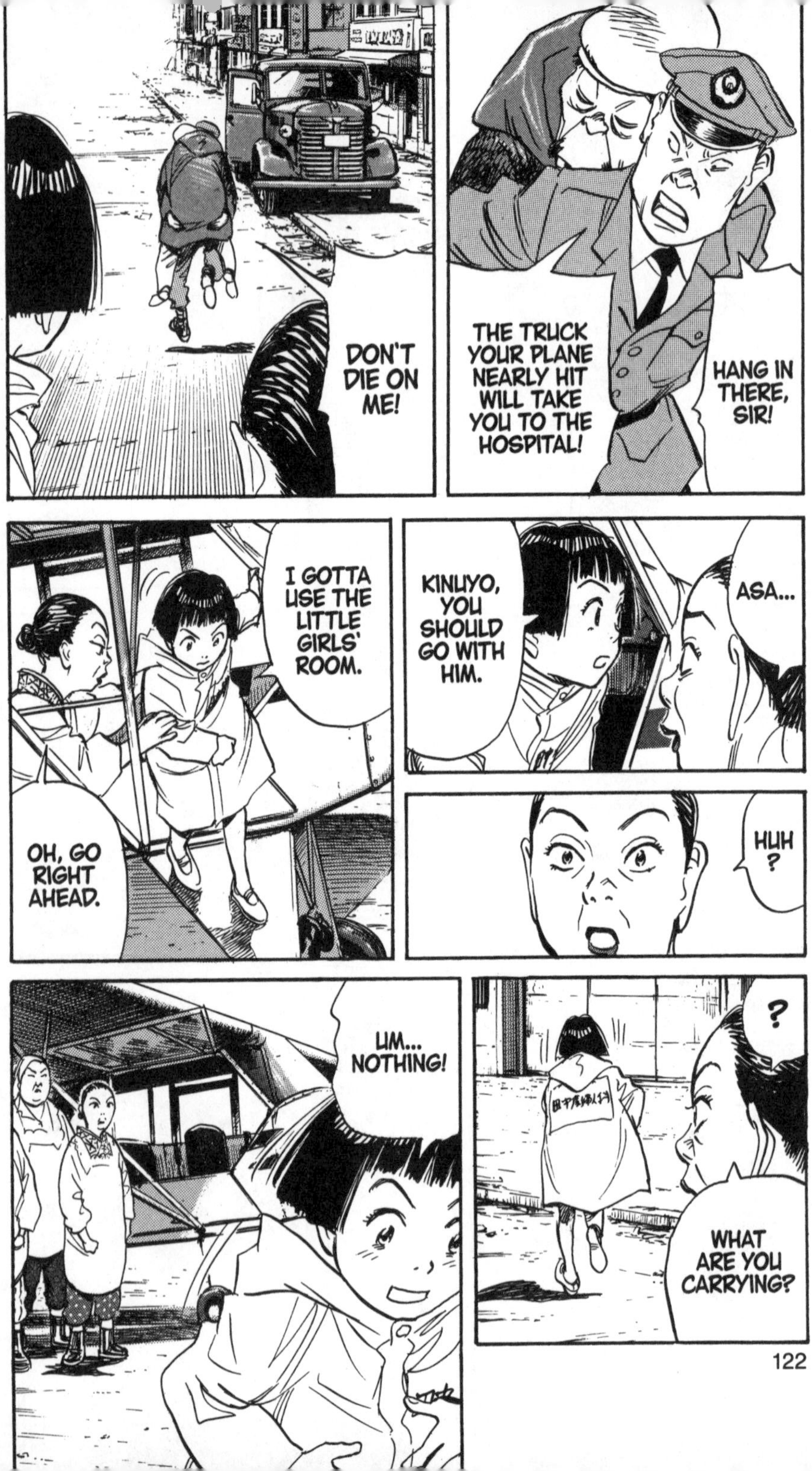
HANG IN THERE, SIR!
THE TRUCK YOUR PLANE NEARLY HIT WILL TAKE YOU TO THE HOSPITAL!
DON'T DIE ON ME!
ASA...
KINUYO, YOU SHOULD GO WITH HIM.
HUH?
I GOTTA USE THE LITTLE GIRLS' ROOM.
OH, GO RIGHT AHEAD.
?
WHAT ARE YOU CARRYING?
UM... NOTHING!

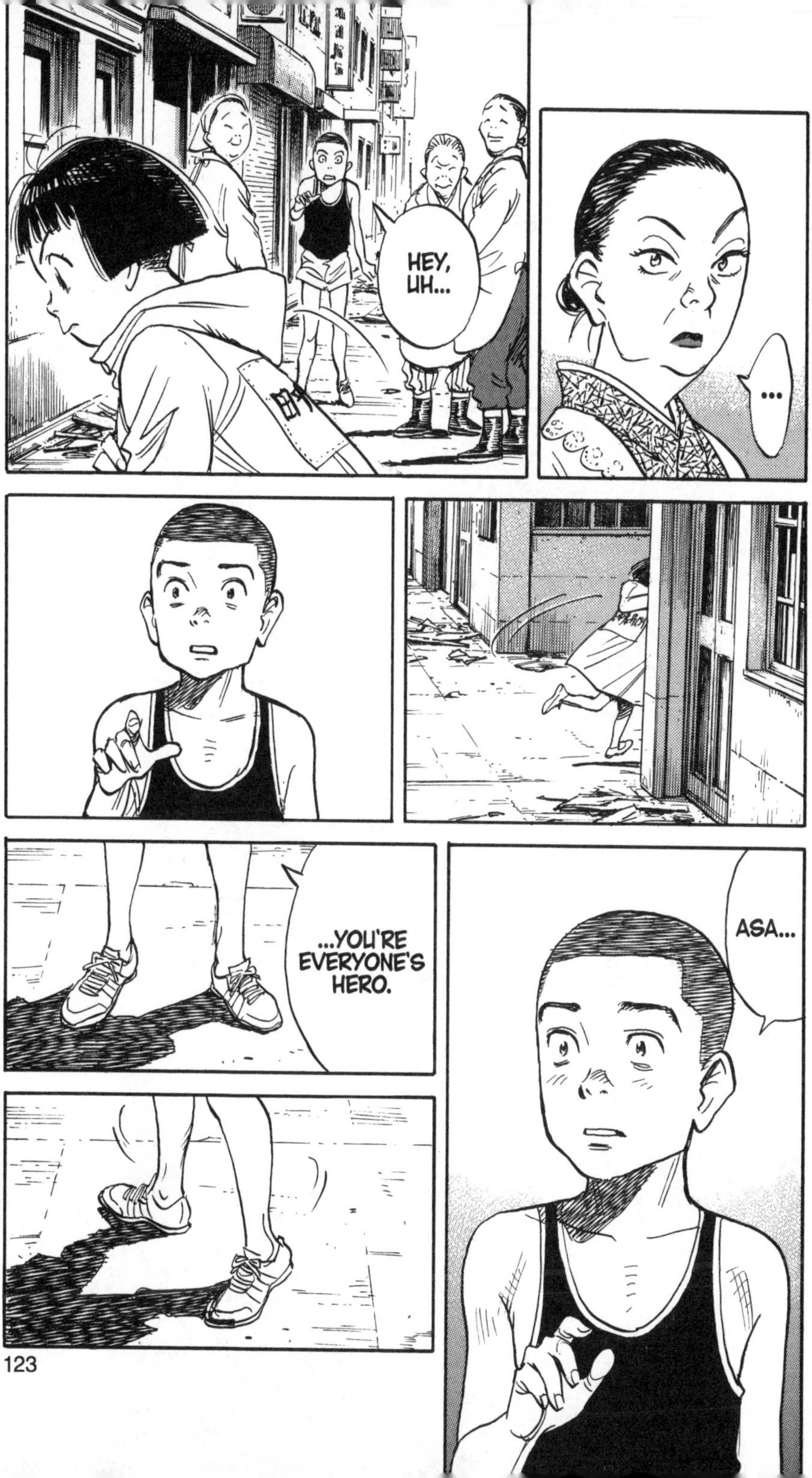
...
HEY, UH...
ASA...
...YOU'RE EVERYONE'S HERO.

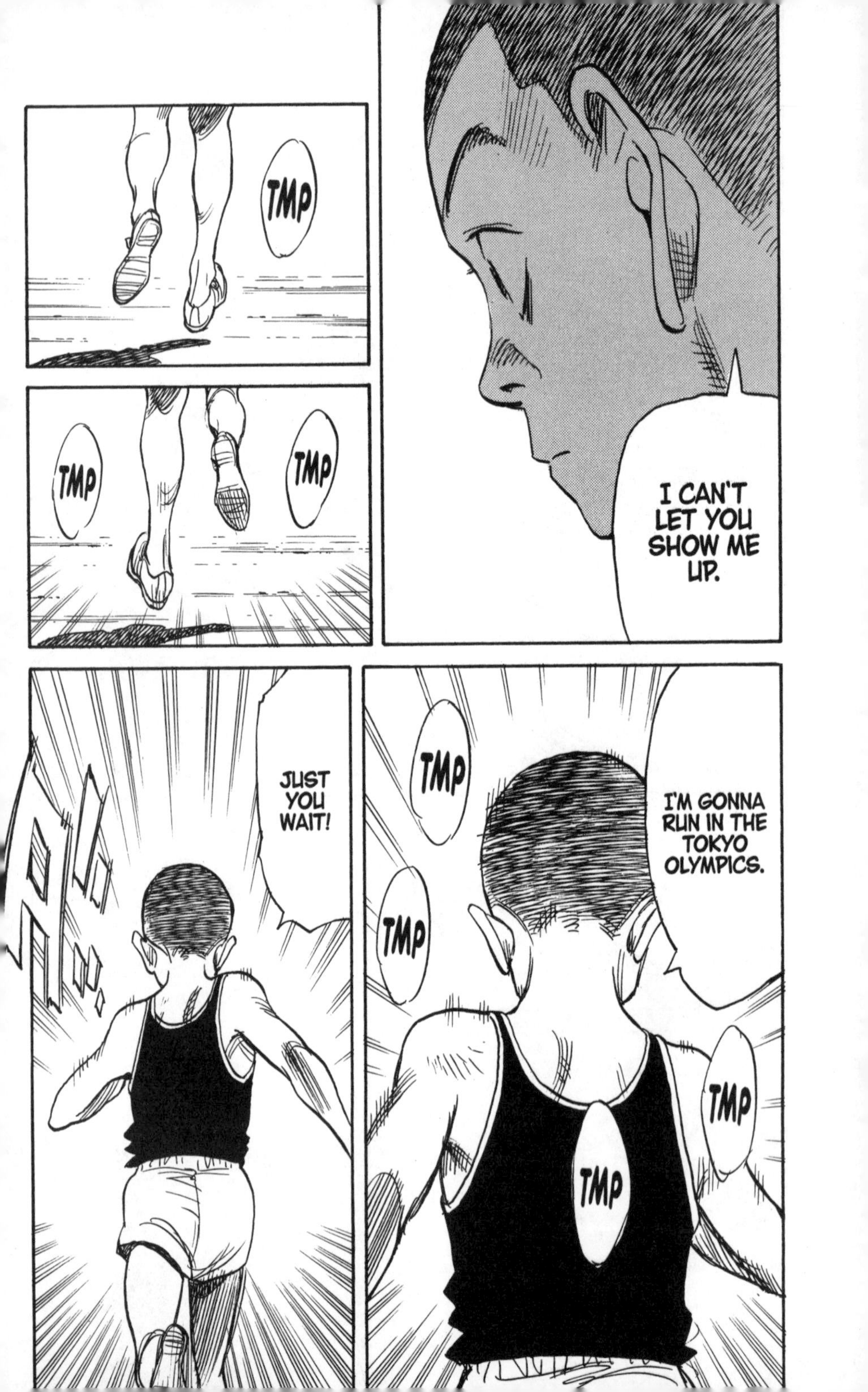
I CAN'T LET YOU SHOW ME UP.
TMP
TMP
TMP
I'M GONNA RUN IN THE TOKYO OLYMPICS.
TMP
TMP
TMP
TMP
JUST YOU WAIT!

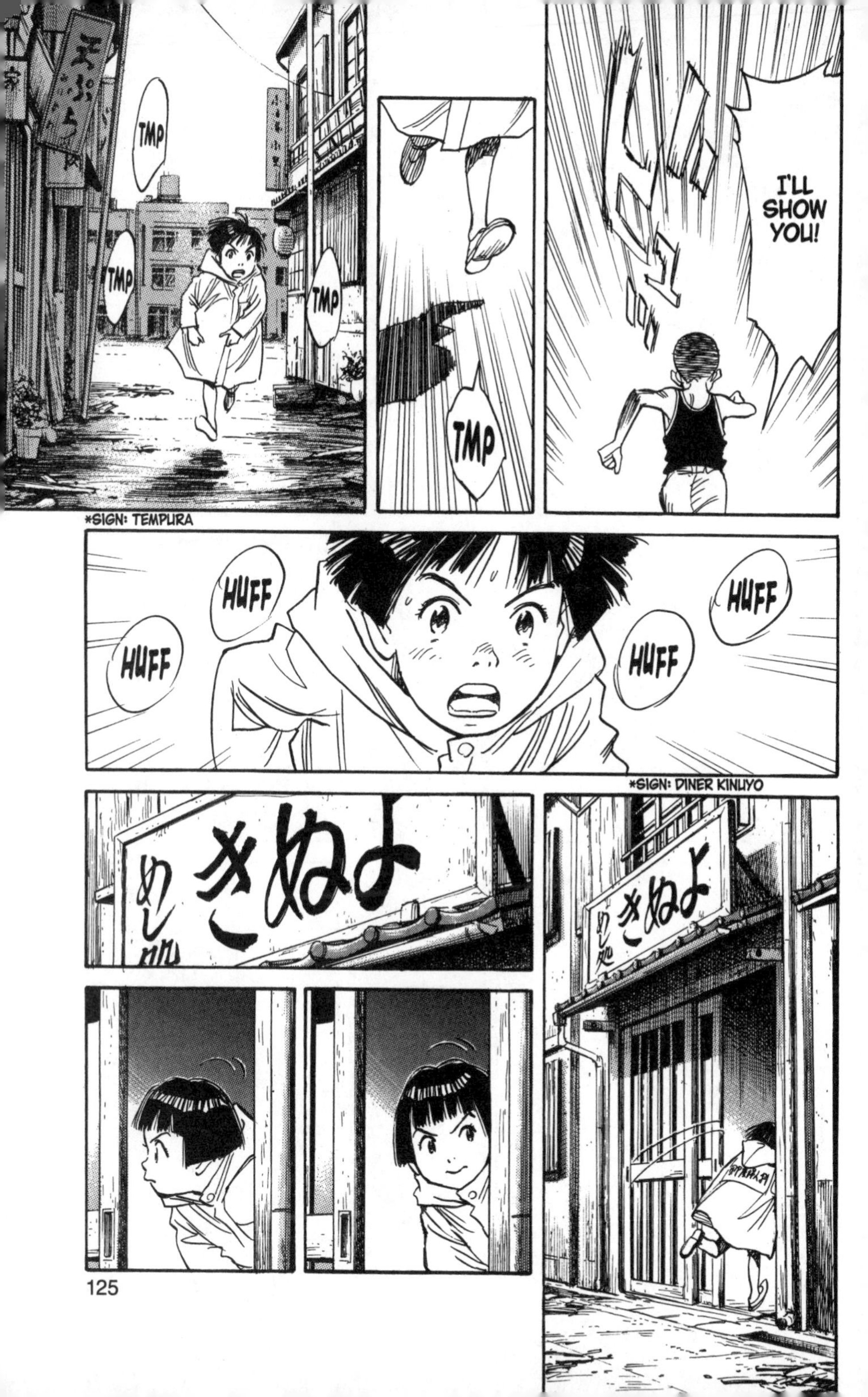
I'LL SHOW YOU!
TMP
TMP
TMP
TMP
*SIGN: TEMPURA
HUFF
HUFF
HUFF
HUFF
*SIGN: DINER KINUYO
めし処 きぬよ
きぬよ

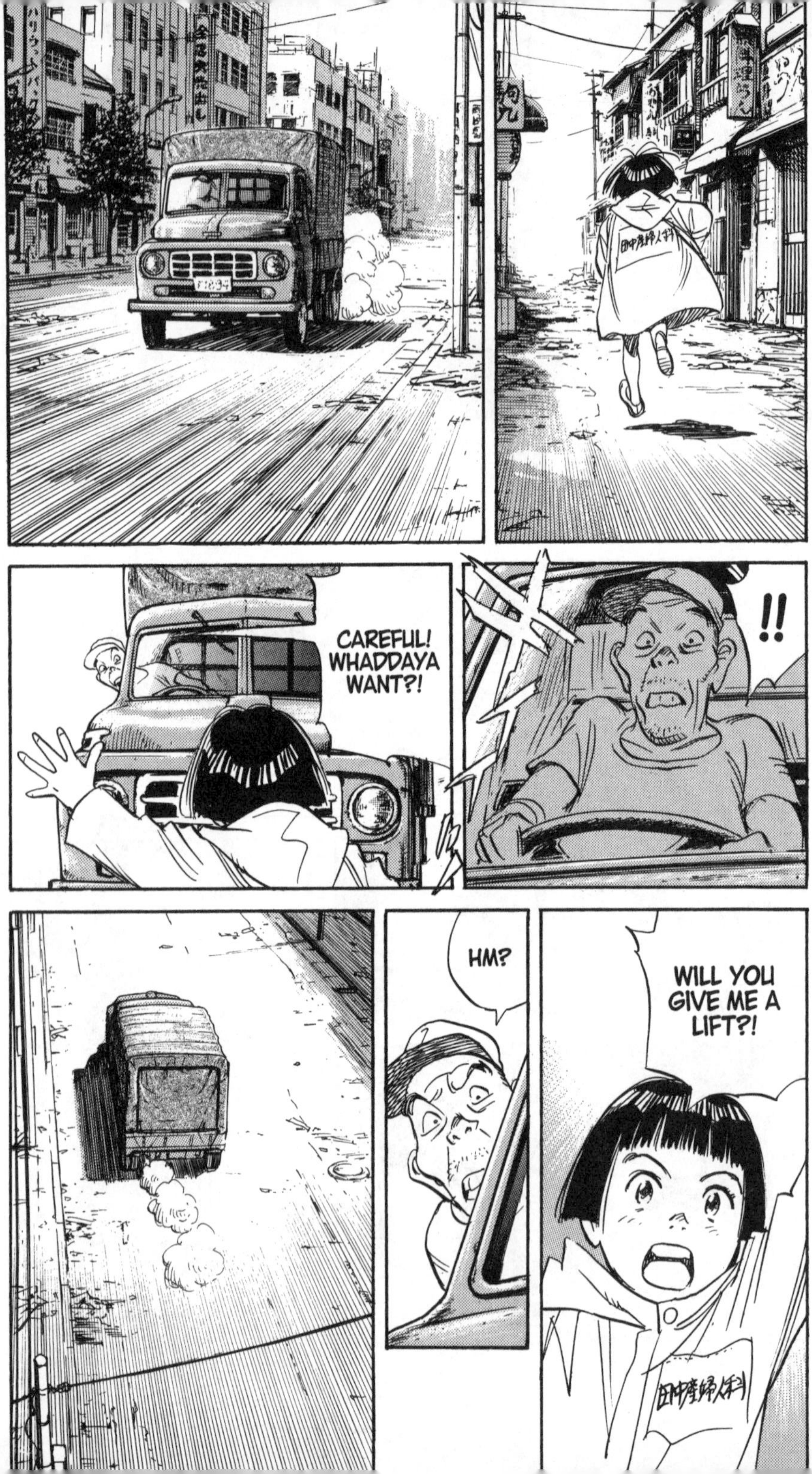
!!
CAREFUL! WHADDAYA WANT?!
WILL YOU GIVE ME A LIFT?!
HM?

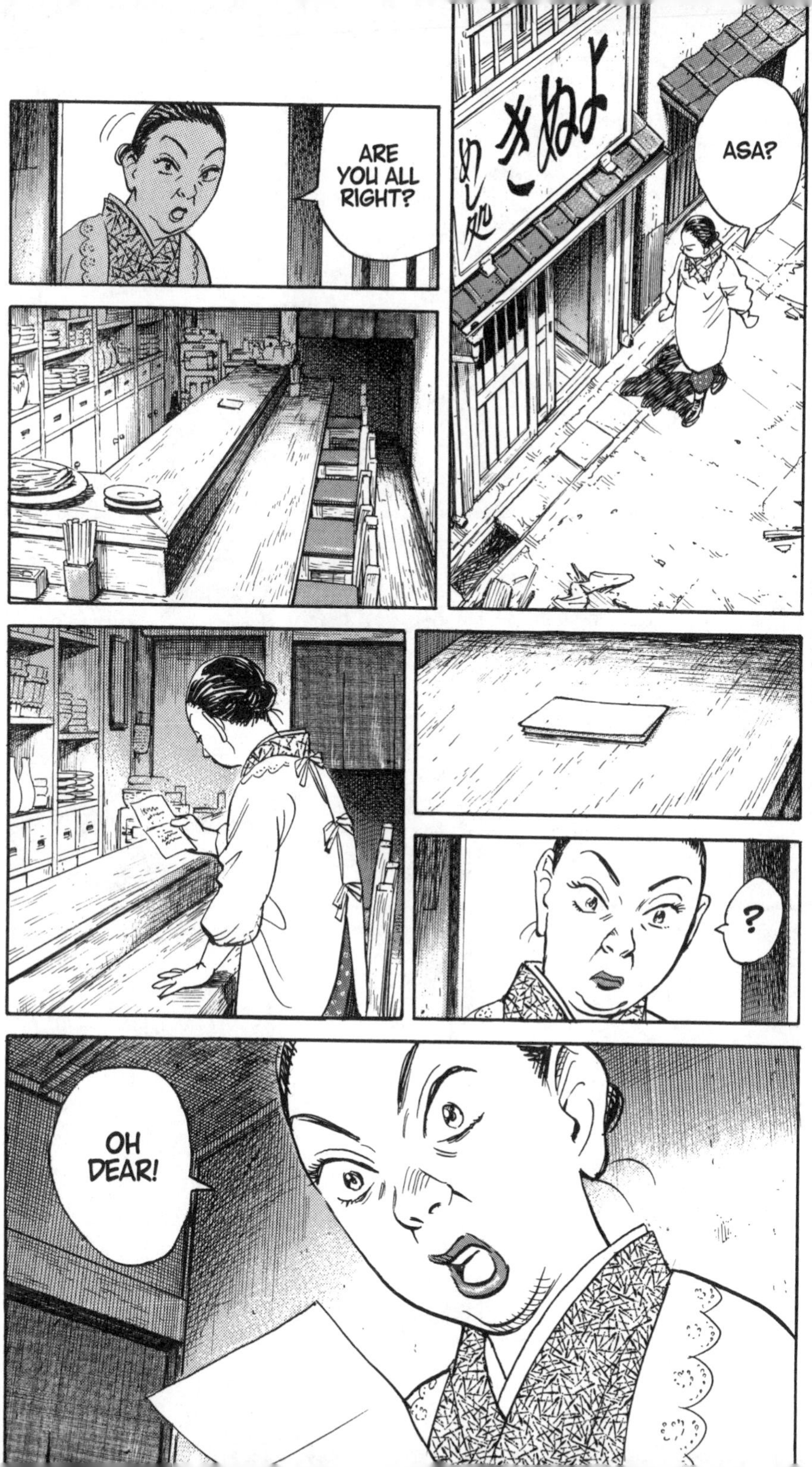
きぬよ
めし処
ASA?
ARE YOU ALL RIGHT?
?
OH DEAR!

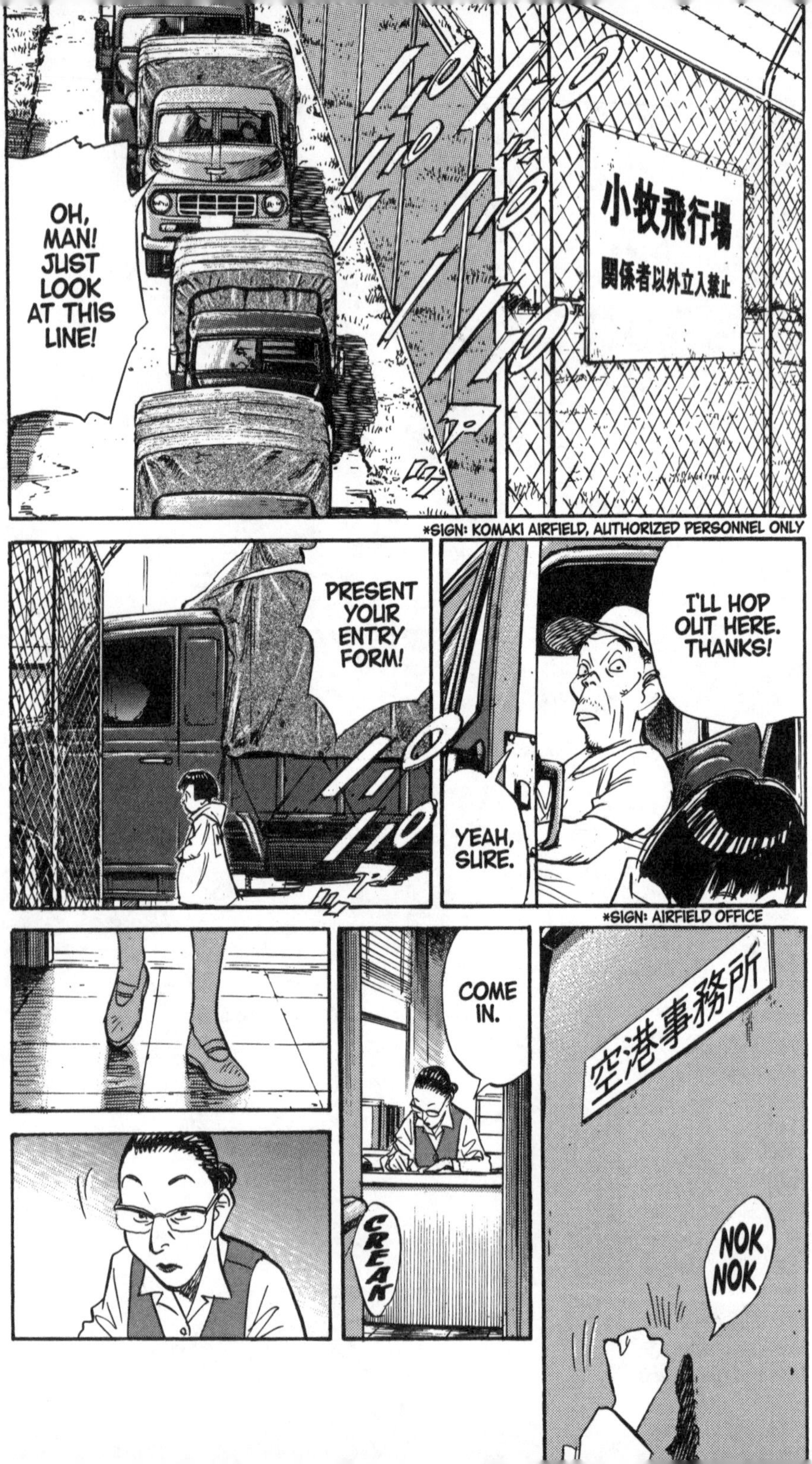
OH, MAN! JUST LOOK AT THIS LINE!
小牧飛行場
関係者以外立入禁止
*SIGN: KOMAKI AIRFIELD, AUTHORIZED PERSONNEL ONLY
I'LL HOP OUT HERE. THANKS!
YEAH, SURE.
PRESENT YOUR ENTRY FORM!
*SIGN: AIRFIELD OFFICE
空港事務所
NOK NOK
CREAK
COME IN.

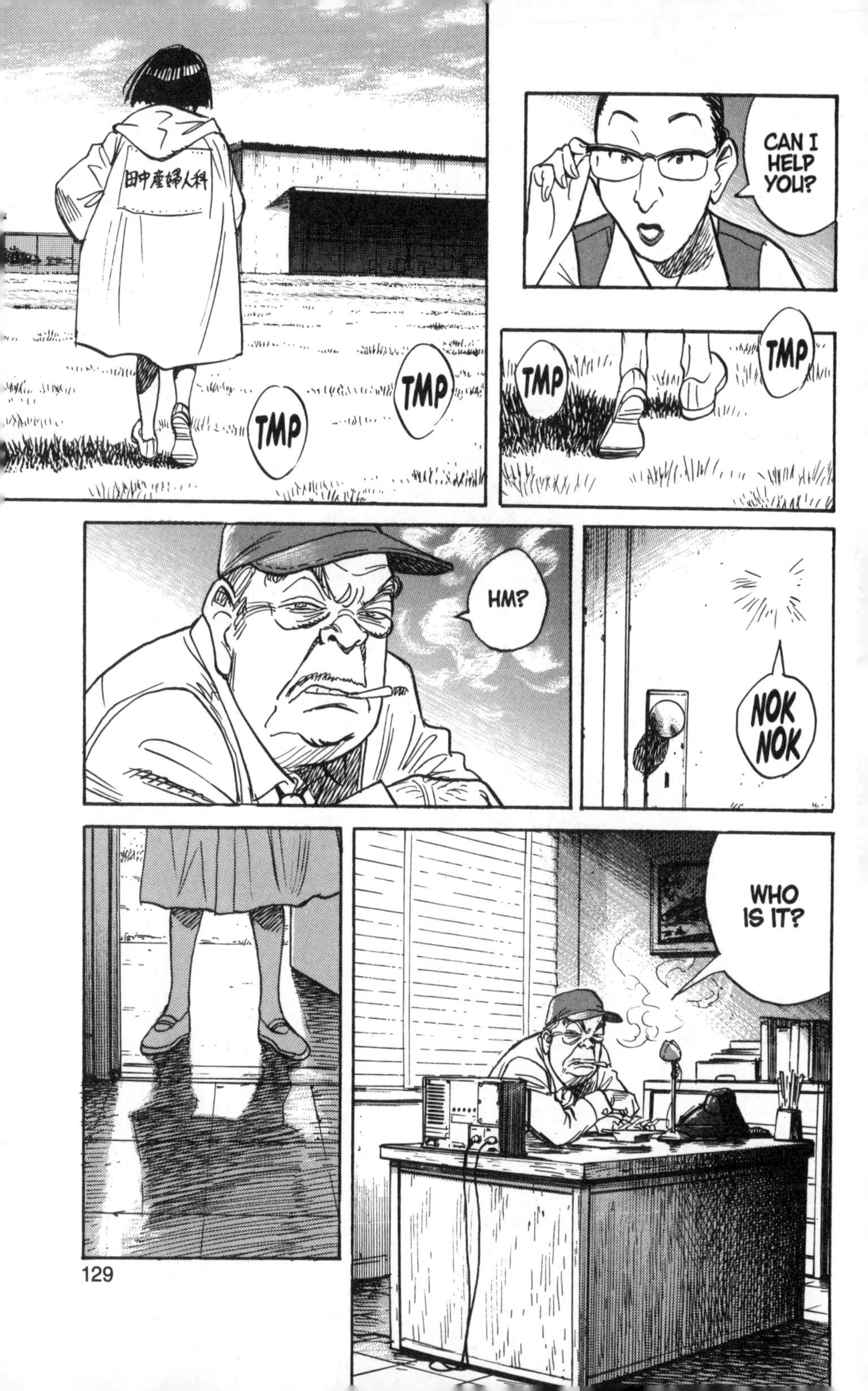
CAN I HELP YOU?
TMP
TMP
田中産婦人科
TMP
TMP
NOK NOK
HM?
WHO IS IT?

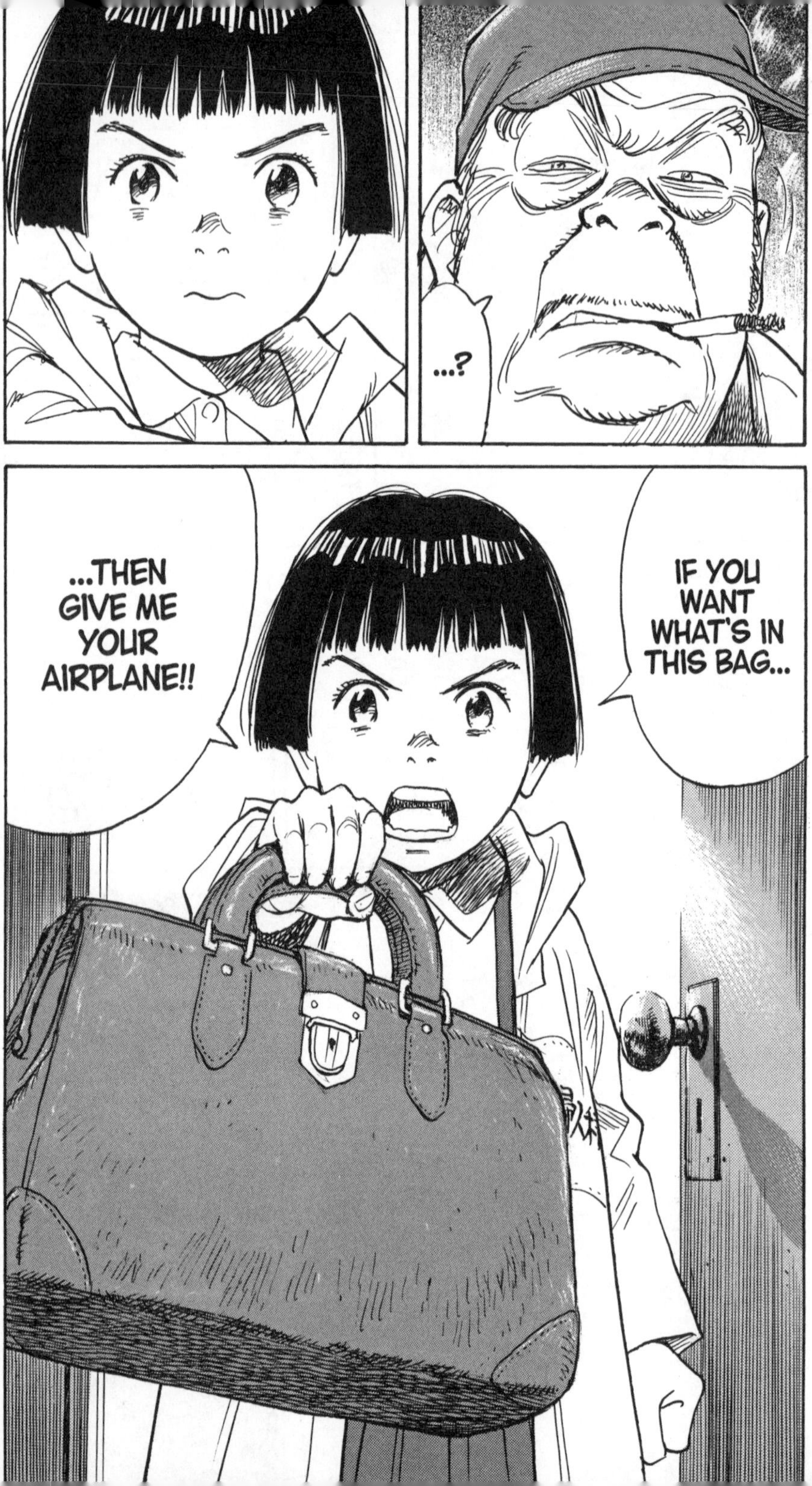
...?
IF YOU WANT WHAT'S IN THIS BAG...
...THEN GIVE ME YOUR AIRPLANE!!

ASADORA!

ASADORA!

Chapter 14 ● That Airplane

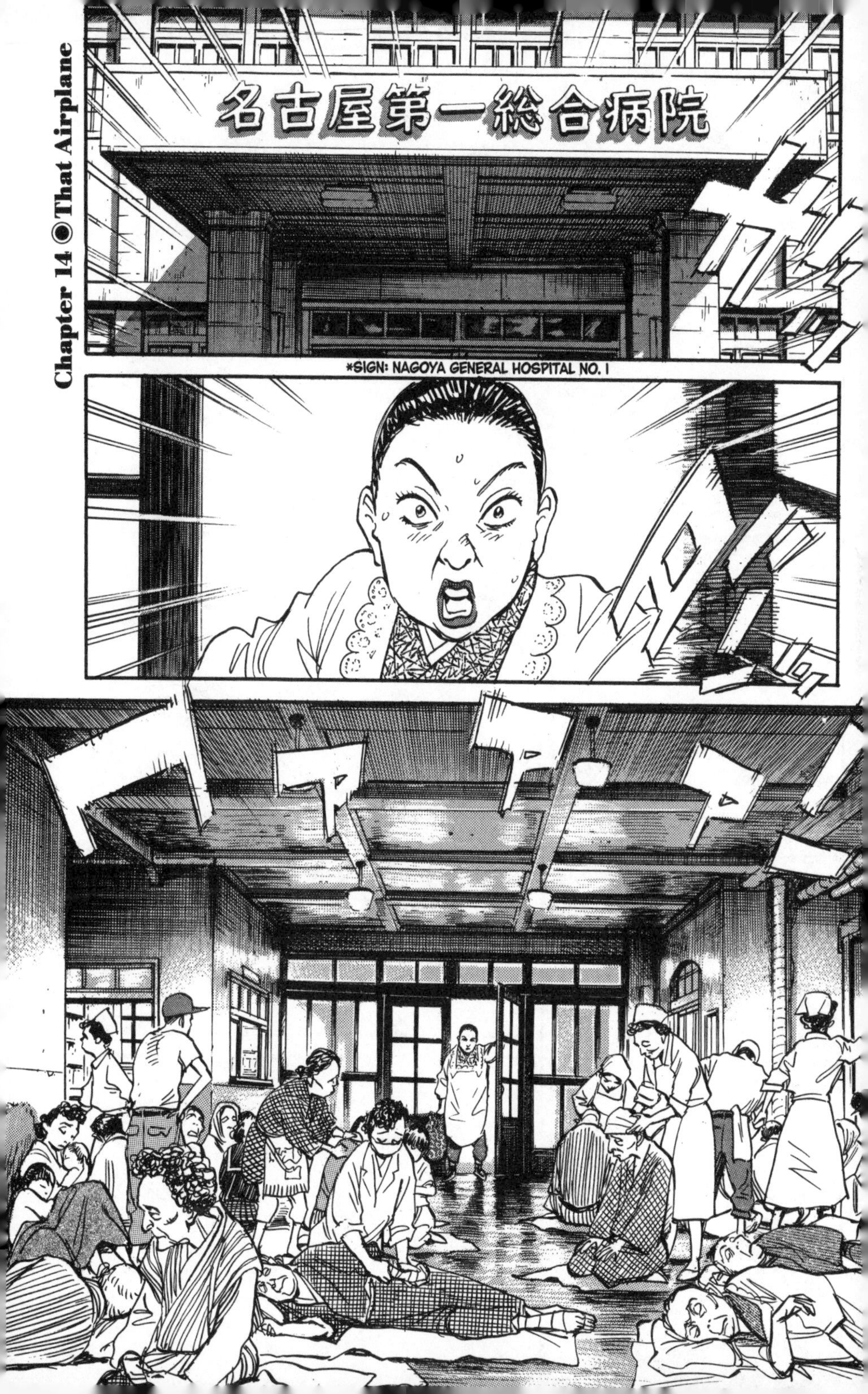
名古屋第一総合病院
*SIGN: NAGOYA GENERAL HOSPITAL NO. 1

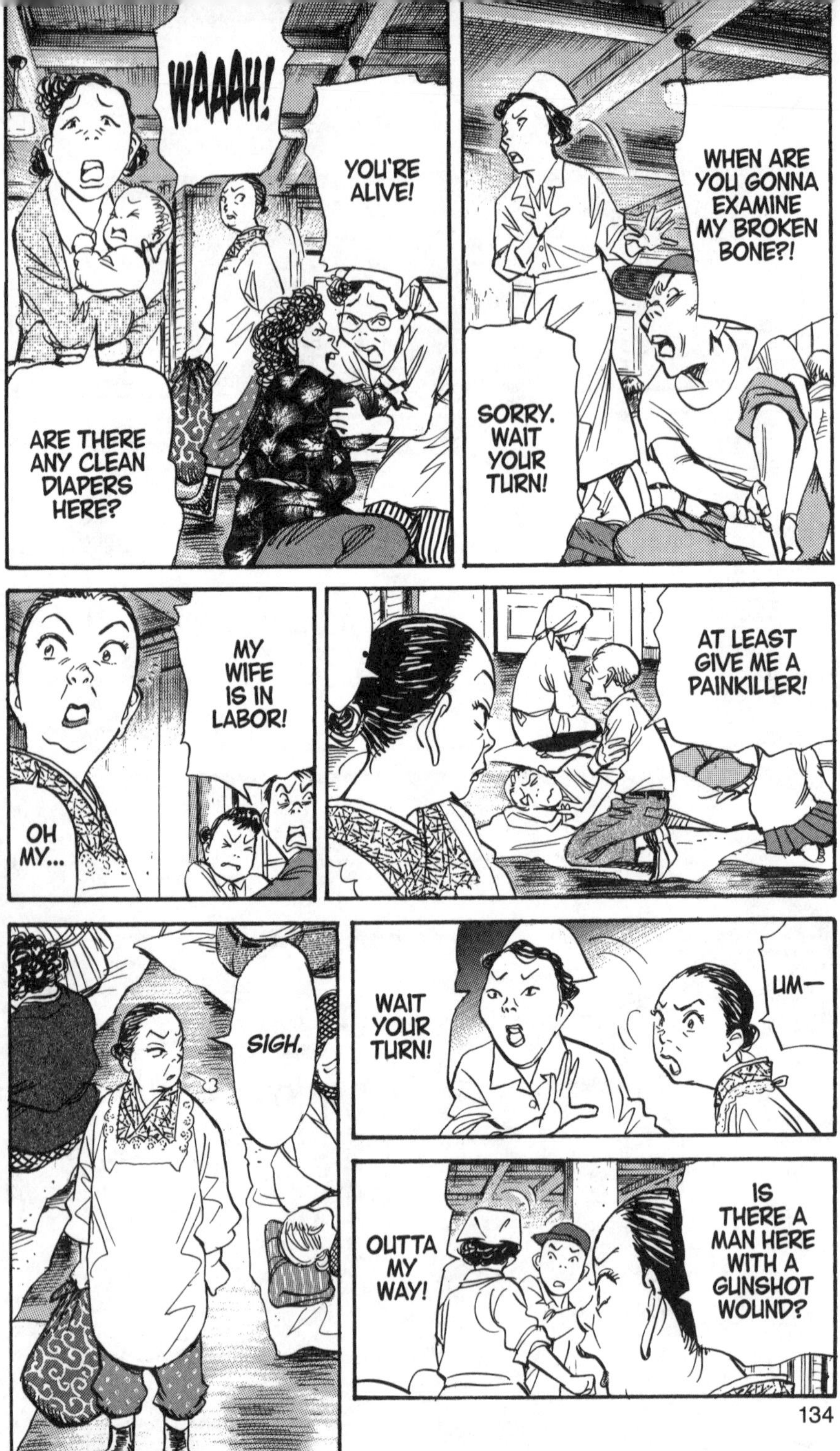

WHEN ARE YOU GONNA EXAMINE MY BROKEN BONE?!
SORRY. WAIT YOUR TURN!
WAAAH!
YOU'RE ALIVE!
ARE THERE ANY CLEAN DIAPERS HERE?
AT LEAST GIVE ME A PAINKILLER!
MY WIFE IS IN LABOR!
OH MY...
UM—
WAIT YOUR TURN!
IS THERE A MAN HERE WITH A GUNSHOT WOUND?
OUTTA MY WAY!
SIGH.

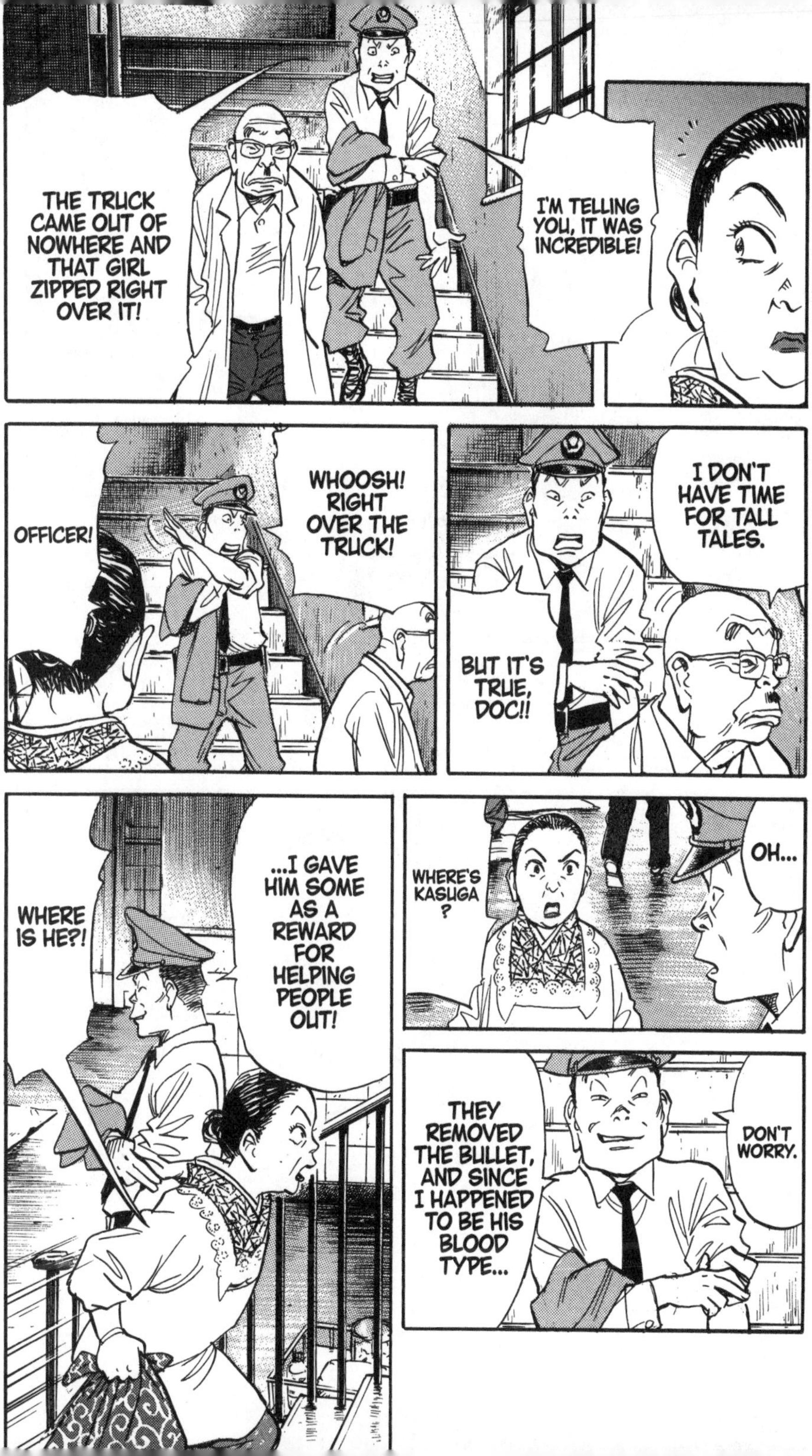
I'M TELLING YOU, IT WAS INCREDIBLE!
THE TRUCK CAME OUT OF NOWHERE AND THAT GIRL ZIPPED RIGHT OVER IT!
I DON'T HAVE TIME FOR TALL TALES.
BUT IT'S TRUE, DOC!!
WHOOSH! RIGHT OVER THE TRUCK!
OFFICER!
OH...
WHERE'S KASUGA?
DON'T WORRY.
THEY REMOVED THE BULLET, AND SINCE I HAPPENED TO BE HIS BLOOD TYPE...
...I GAVE HIM SOME AS A REWARD FOR HELPING PEOPLE OUT!
WHERE IS HE?!

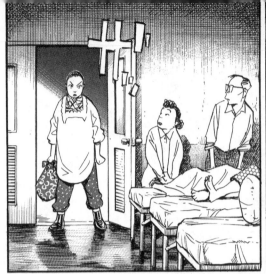

H-HEY! HE'S FINE NOW!

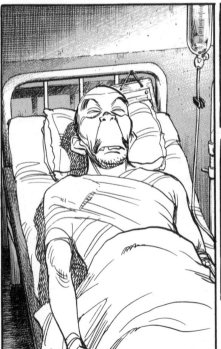

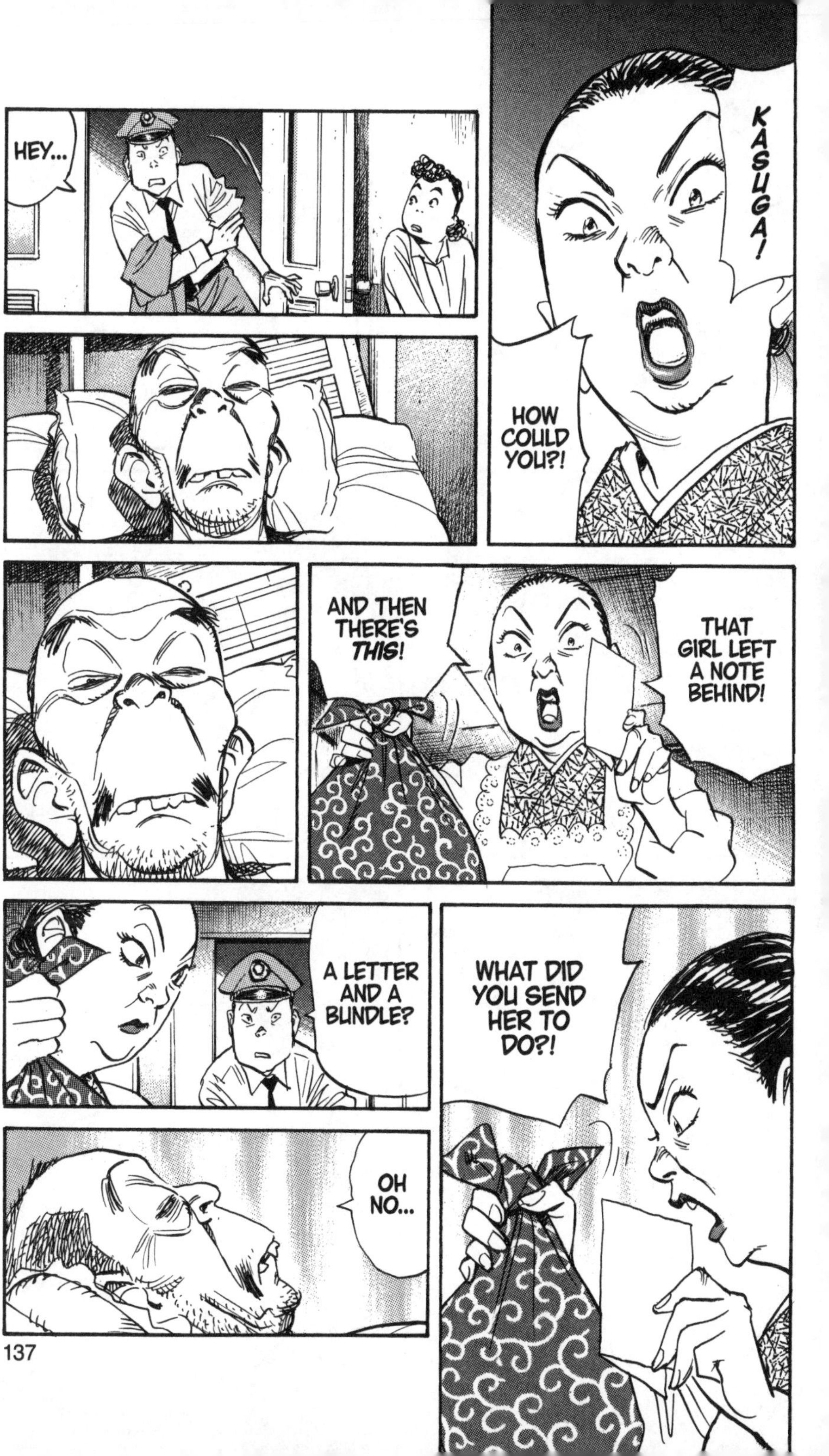
KASUGA!
HOW COULD YOU?!
HEY...
THAT GIRL LEFT A NOTE BEHIND!
AND THEN THERE'S *THIS*!
WHAT DID YOU SEND HER TO DO?!
A LETTER AND A BUNDLE?
OH NO...

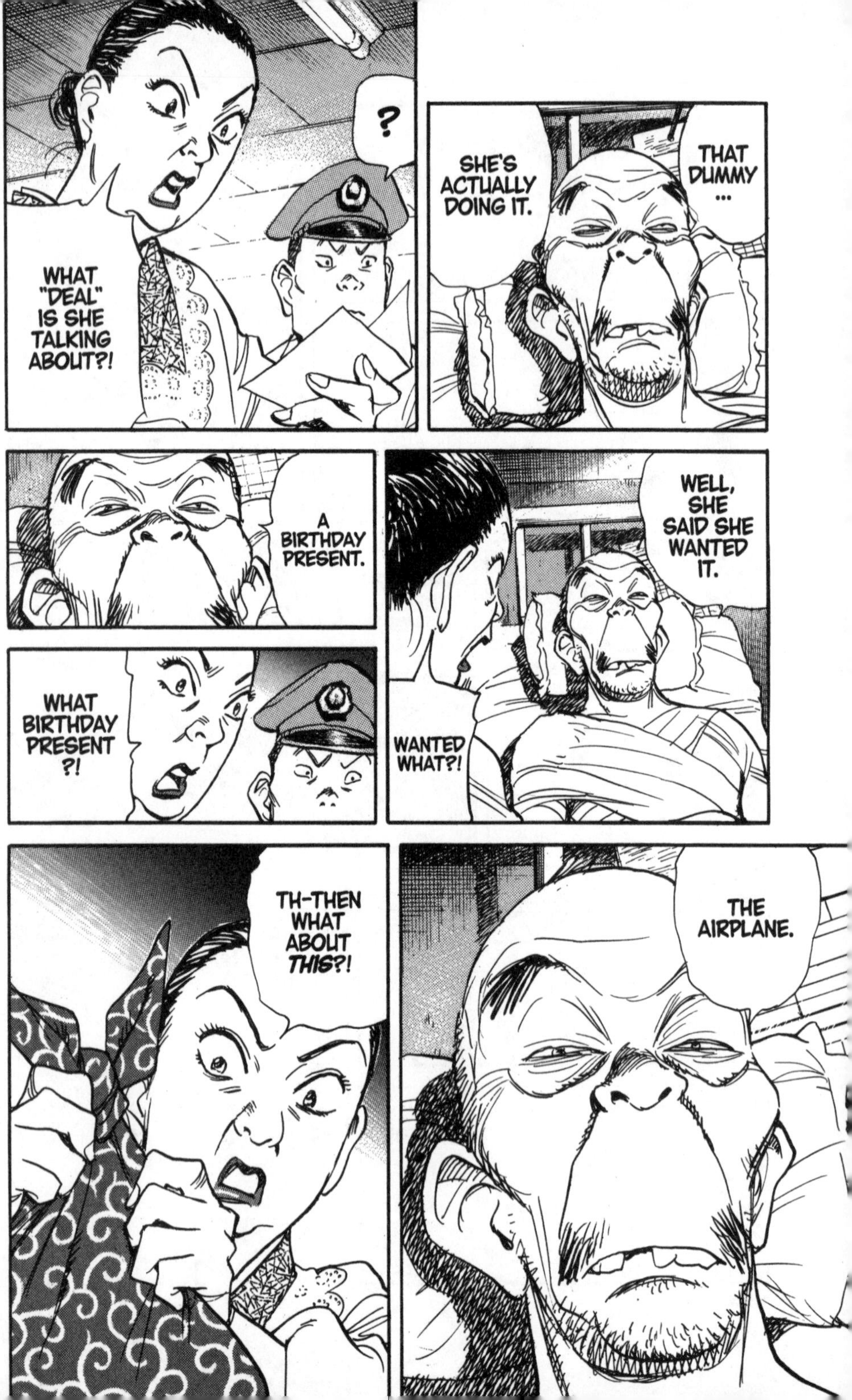
THAT DUMMY ...
SHE'S ACTUALLY DOING IT.
?
WHAT "DEAL" IS SHE TALKING ABOUT?!
WELL, SHE SAID SHE WANTED IT.
WANTED WHAT?!
A BIRTHDAY PRESENT.
WHAT BIRTHDAY PRESENT ?!
THE AIRPLANE.
TH-THEN WHAT ABOUT *THIS*?!

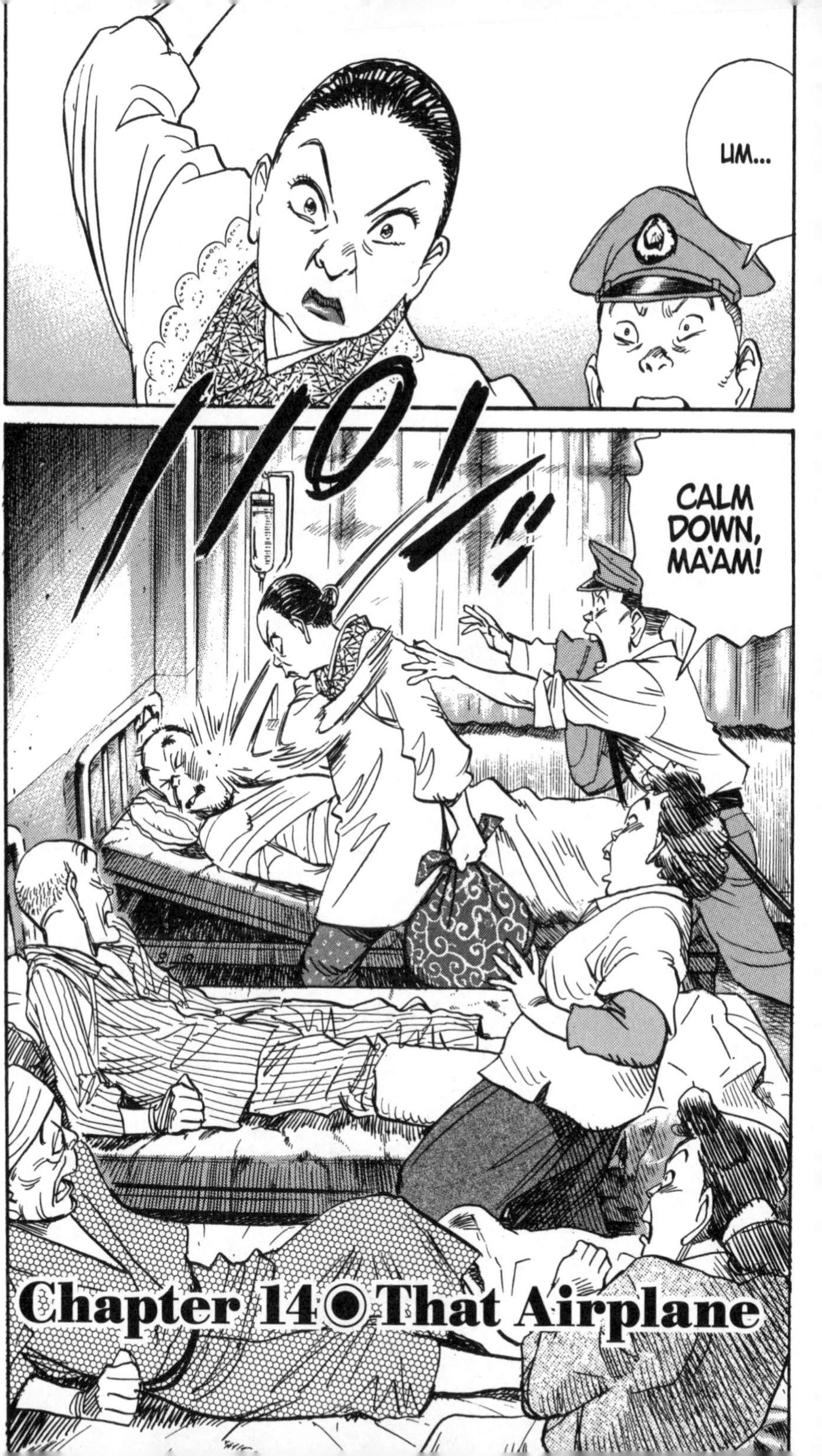
UM...
CALM DOWN, MA'AM!
Chapter 14 ● That Airplane

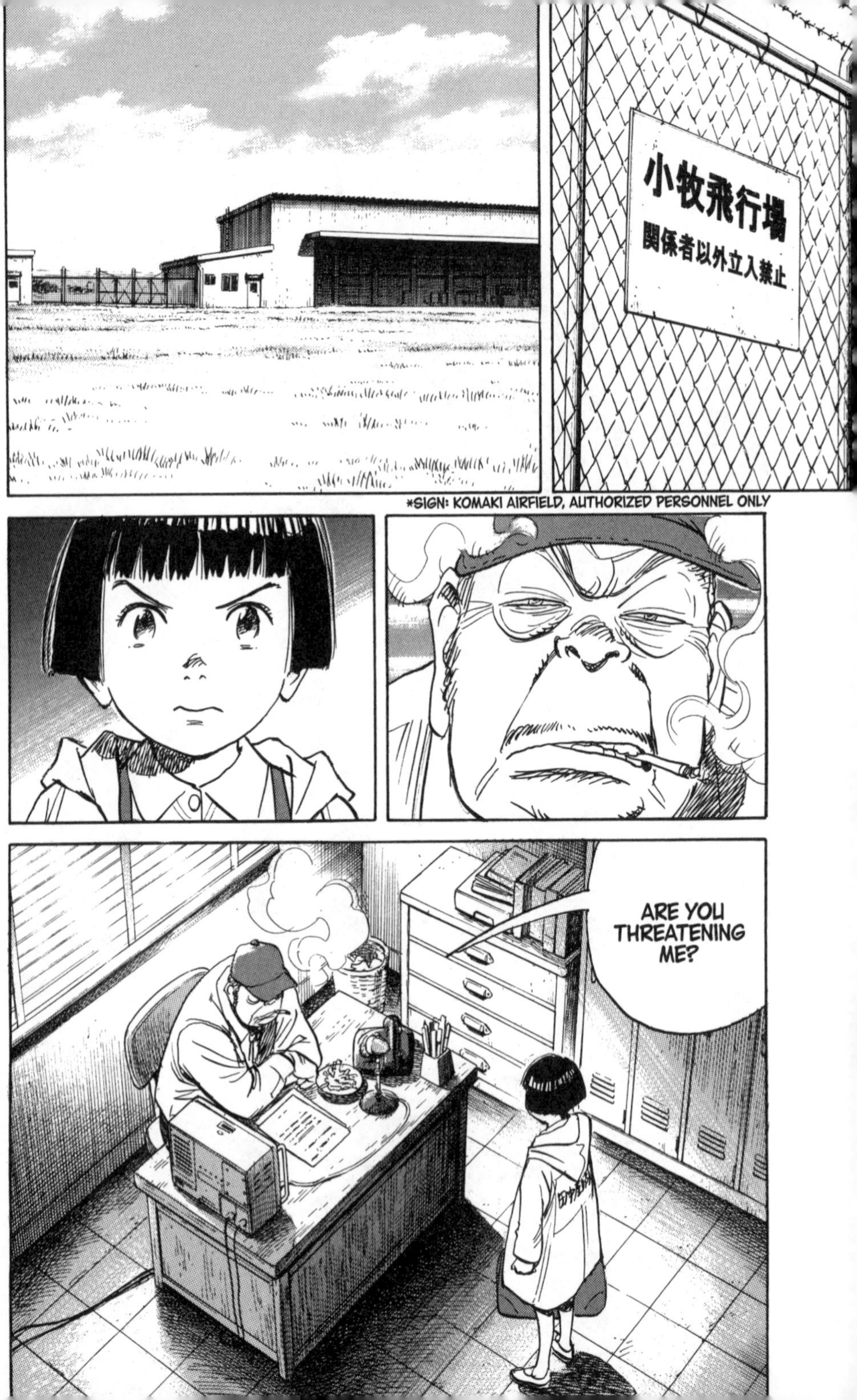
小牧飛行場
関係者以外立入禁止
*SIGN: KOMAKI AIRFIELD, AUTHORIZED PERSONNEL ONLY
ARE YOU THREATENING ME?

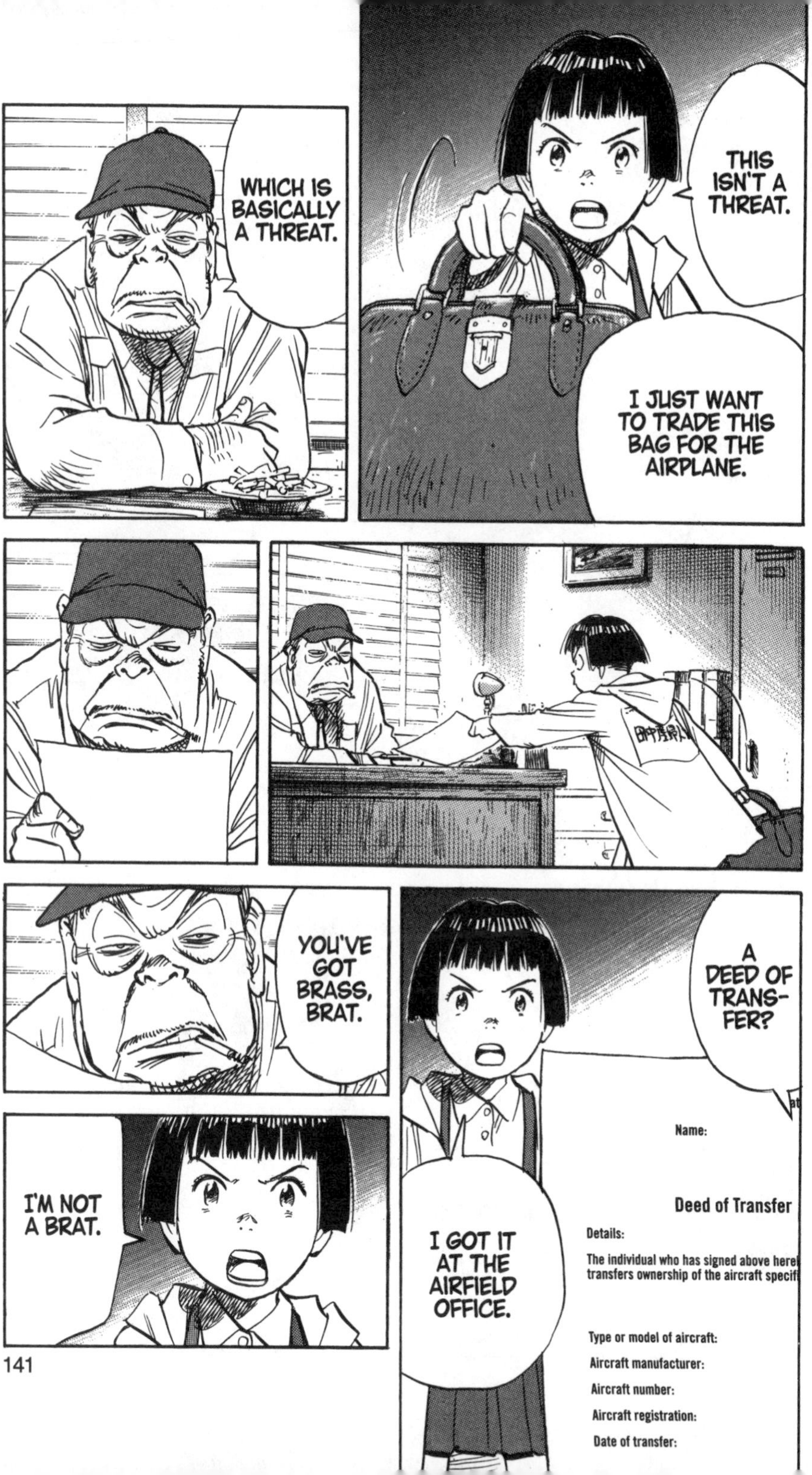
THIS ISN'T A THREAT.
I JUST WANT TO TRADE THIS BAG FOR THE AIRPLANE.
WHICH IS BASICALLY A THREAT.
A DEED OF TRANS-FER?
I GOT IT AT THE AIRFIELD OFFICE.
Name:
Deed of Transfer
Details:
The individual who has signed above here
transfers ownership of the aircraft speci
Type or model of aircraft:
Aircraft manufacturer:
Aircraft number:
Aircraft registration:
Date of transfer:
YOU'VE GOT BRASS, BRAT.
I'M NOT A BRAT.

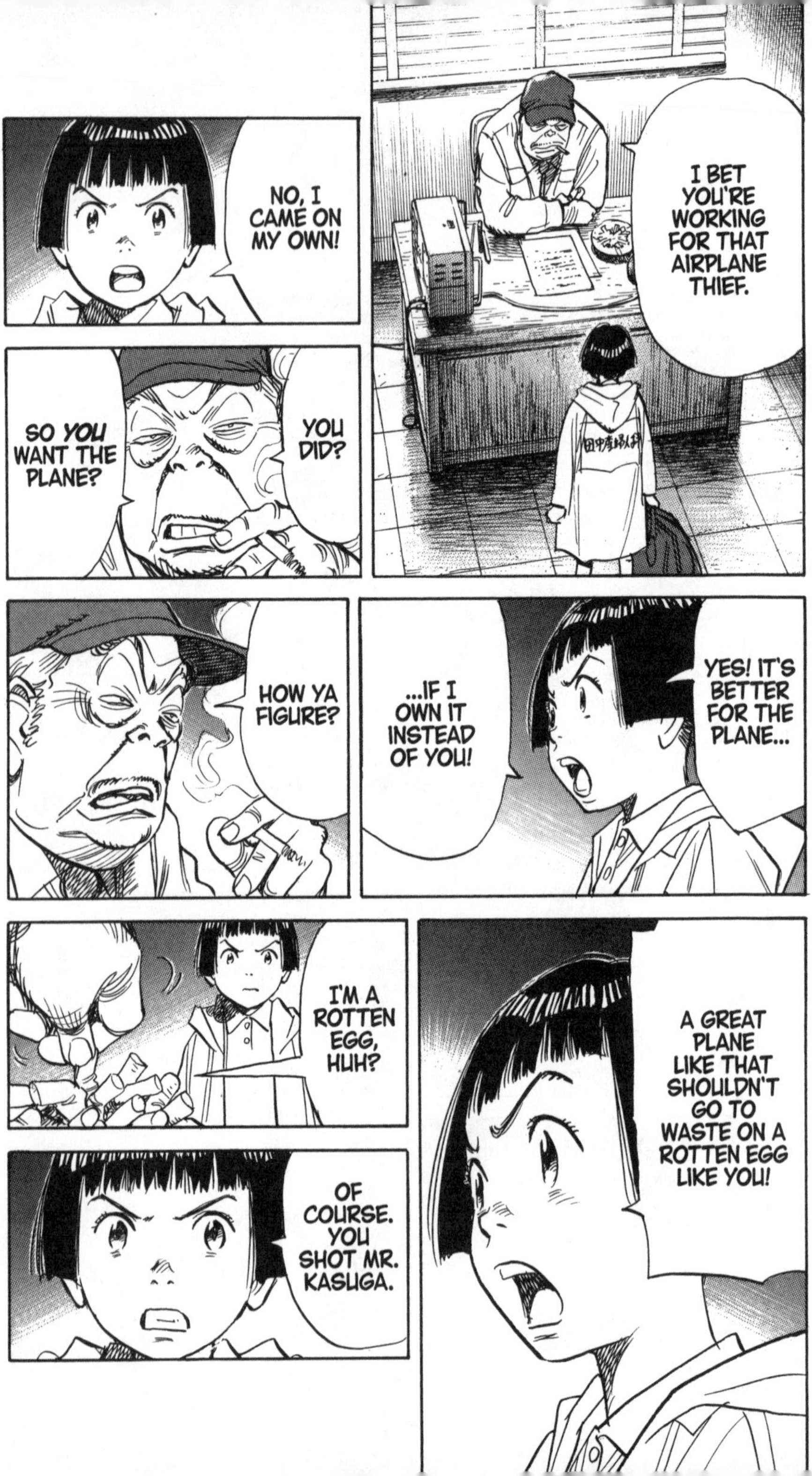
I BET YOU'RE WORKING FOR THAT AIRPLANE THIEF.
NO, I CAME ON MY OWN!
YOU DID?
SO YOU WANT THE PLANE?
YES! IT'S BETTER FOR THE PLANE...
...IF I OWN IT INSTEAD OF YOU!
HOW YA FIGURE?
A GREAT PLANE LIKE THAT SHOULDN'T GO TO WASTE ON A ROTTEN EGG LIKE YOU!
I'M A ROTTEN EGG, HUH?
OF COURSE. YOU SHOT MR. KASUGA.

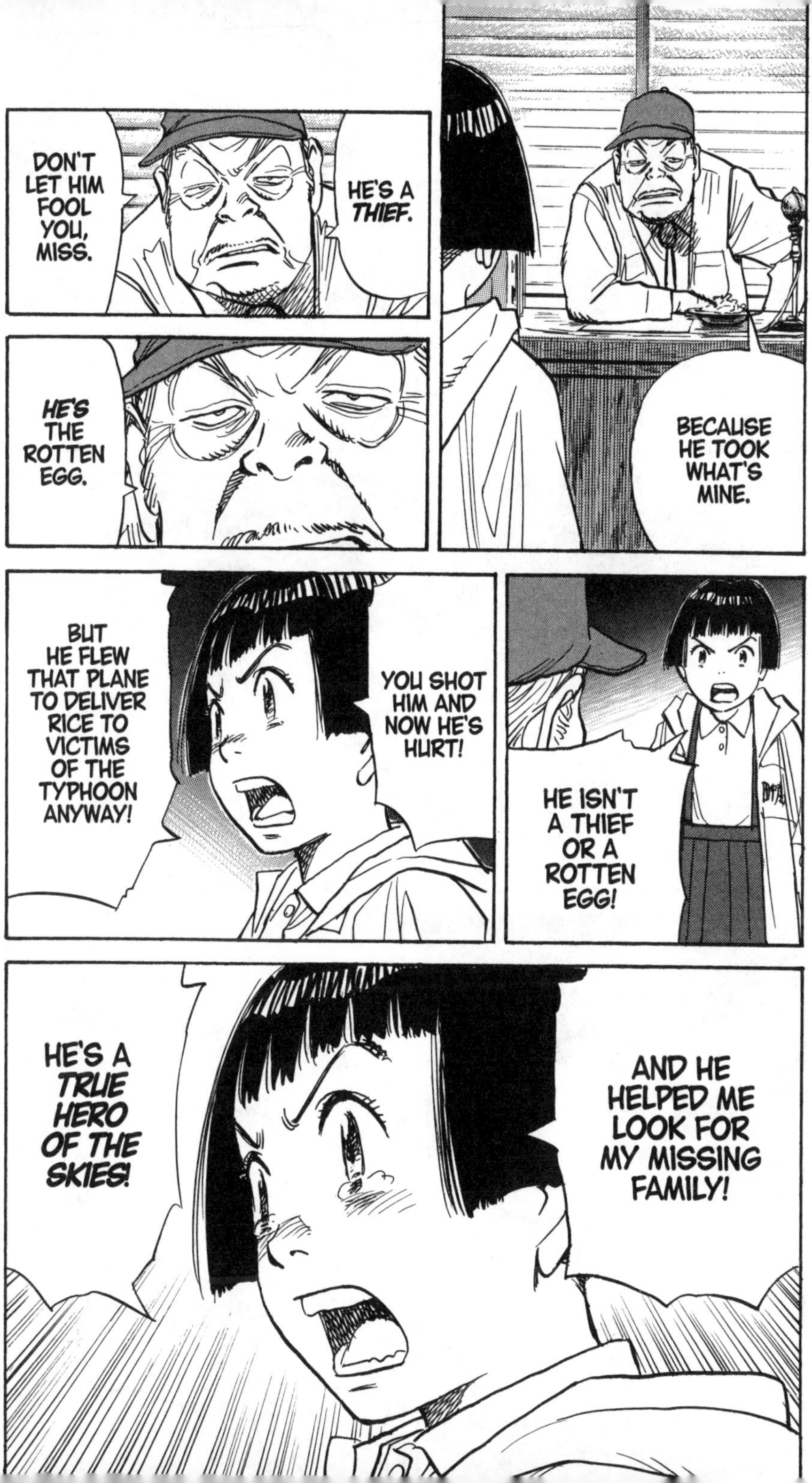
BECAUSE HE TOOK WHAT'S MINE.
HE'S A *THIEF.*
DON'T LET HIM FOOL YOU, MISS.
HE'S THE ROTTEN EGG.
HE ISN'T A THIEF OR A ROTTEN EGG!
YOU SHOT HIM AND NOW HE'S HURT!
BUT HE FLEW THAT PLANE TO DELIVER RICE TO VICTIMS OF THE TYPHOON ANYWAY!
AND HE HELPED ME LOOK FOR MY MISSING FAMILY!
HE'S A *TRUE HERO OF THE SKIES!*

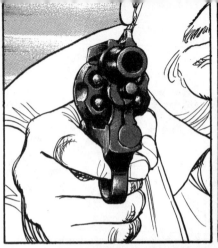

IF HE DIES, I'M BLAMING *YOU*!!

...

...

YOU'RE STARTIN' TO BUG ME.

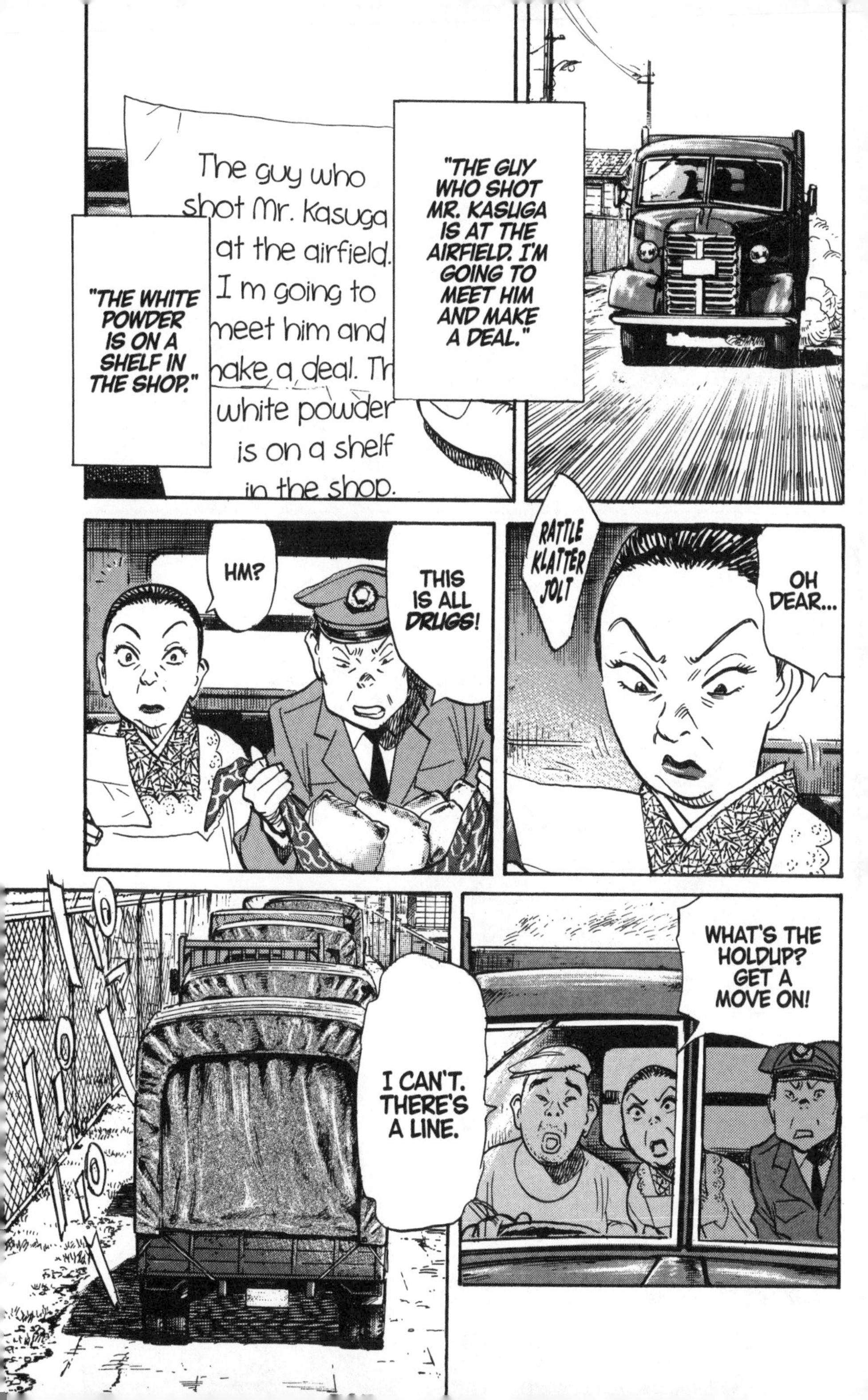
"THE GUY WHO SHOT MR. KASUGA IS AT THE AIRFIELD. I'M GOING TO MEET HIM AND MAKE A DEAL."
The guy who shot Mr. Kasuga at the airfield. I m going to meet him and make a deal. The white powder is on a shelf in the shop.
"THE WHITE POWDER IS ON A SHELF IN THE SHOP."
OH DEAR...
RATTLE KLATTER JOLT
THIS IS ALL DRUGS!
HM?
WHAT'S THE HOLDUP? GET A MOVE ON!
I CAN'T. THERE'S A LINE.

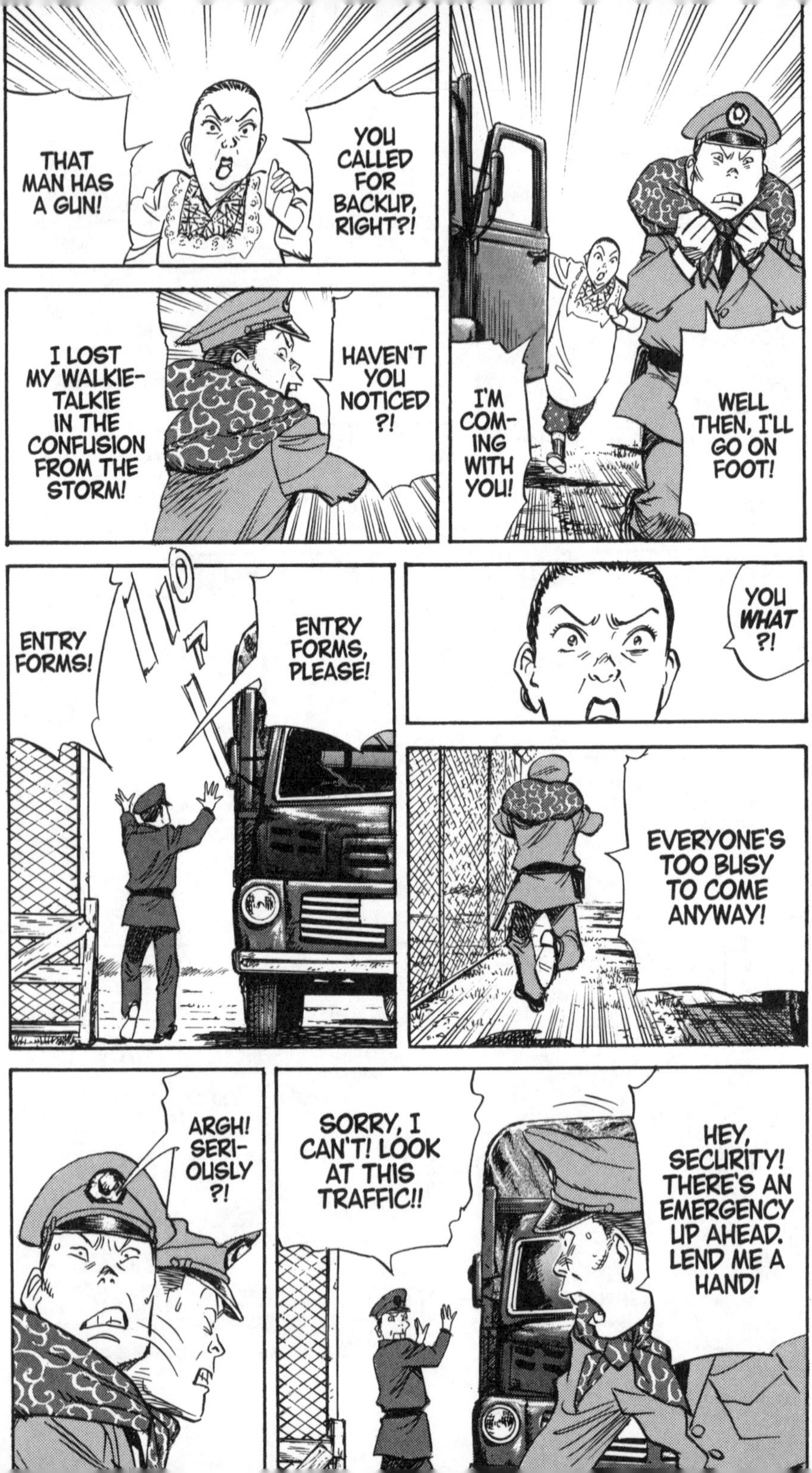
WELL THEN, I'LL GO ON FOOT!
I'M COMING WITH YOU!
YOU CALLED FOR BACKUP, RIGHT?!
THAT MAN HAS A GUN!
HAVEN'T YOU NOTICED?!
I LOST MY WALKIE-TALKIE IN THE CONFUSION FROM THE STORM!
YOU *WHAT*?!
EVERYONE'S TOO BUSY TO COME ANYWAY!
ENTRY FORMS, PLEASE!
ENTRY FORMS!
HEY, SECURITY! THERE'S AN EMERGENCY UP AHEAD. LEND ME A HAND!
SORRY, I CAN'T! LOOK AT THIS TRAFFIC!!
ARGH! SERIOUSLY?!

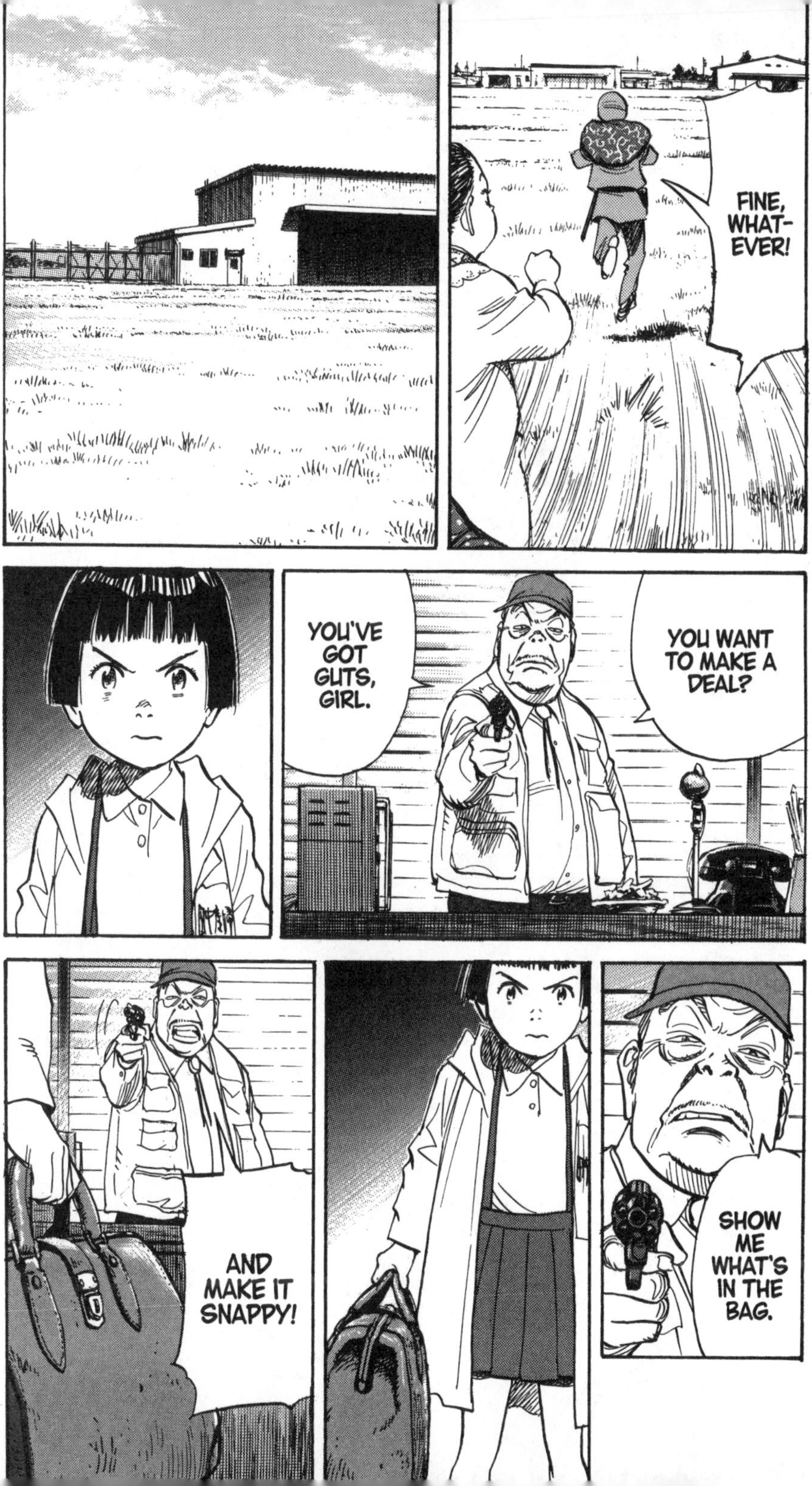
FINE, WHAT-EVER!
YOU WANT TO MAKE A DEAL?
YOU'VE GOT GUTS, GIRL.
SHOW ME WHAT'S IN THE BAG.
AND MAKE IT SNAPPY!

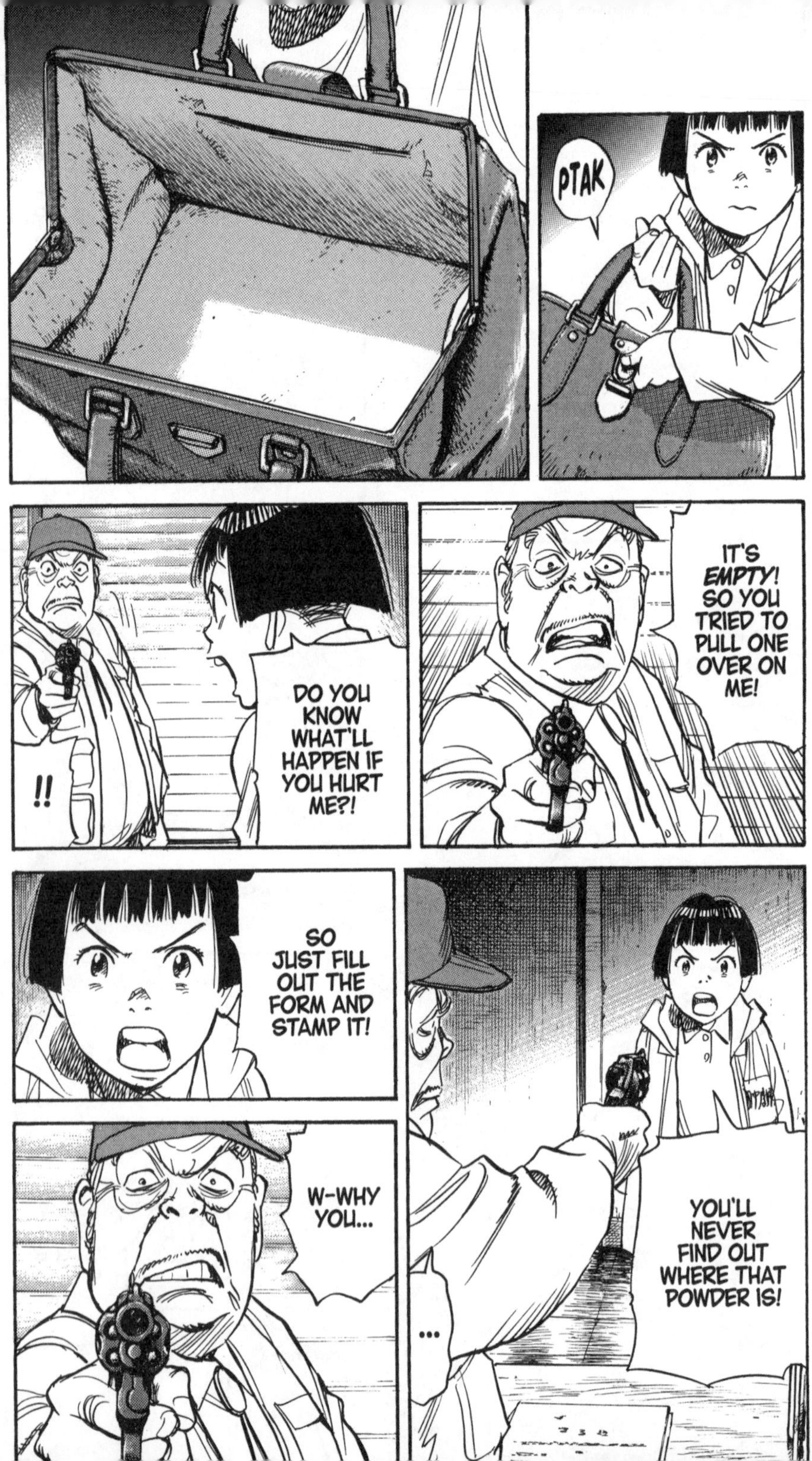
PTAK
IT'S *EMPTY*! SO YOU TRIED TO PULL ONE OVER ON ME!
DO YOU KNOW WHAT'LL HAPPEN IF YOU HURT ME?!
!!
YOU'LL NEVER FIND OUT WHERE THAT POWDER IS!
...
SO JUST FILL OUT THE FORM AND STAMP IT!
W-WHY YOU...

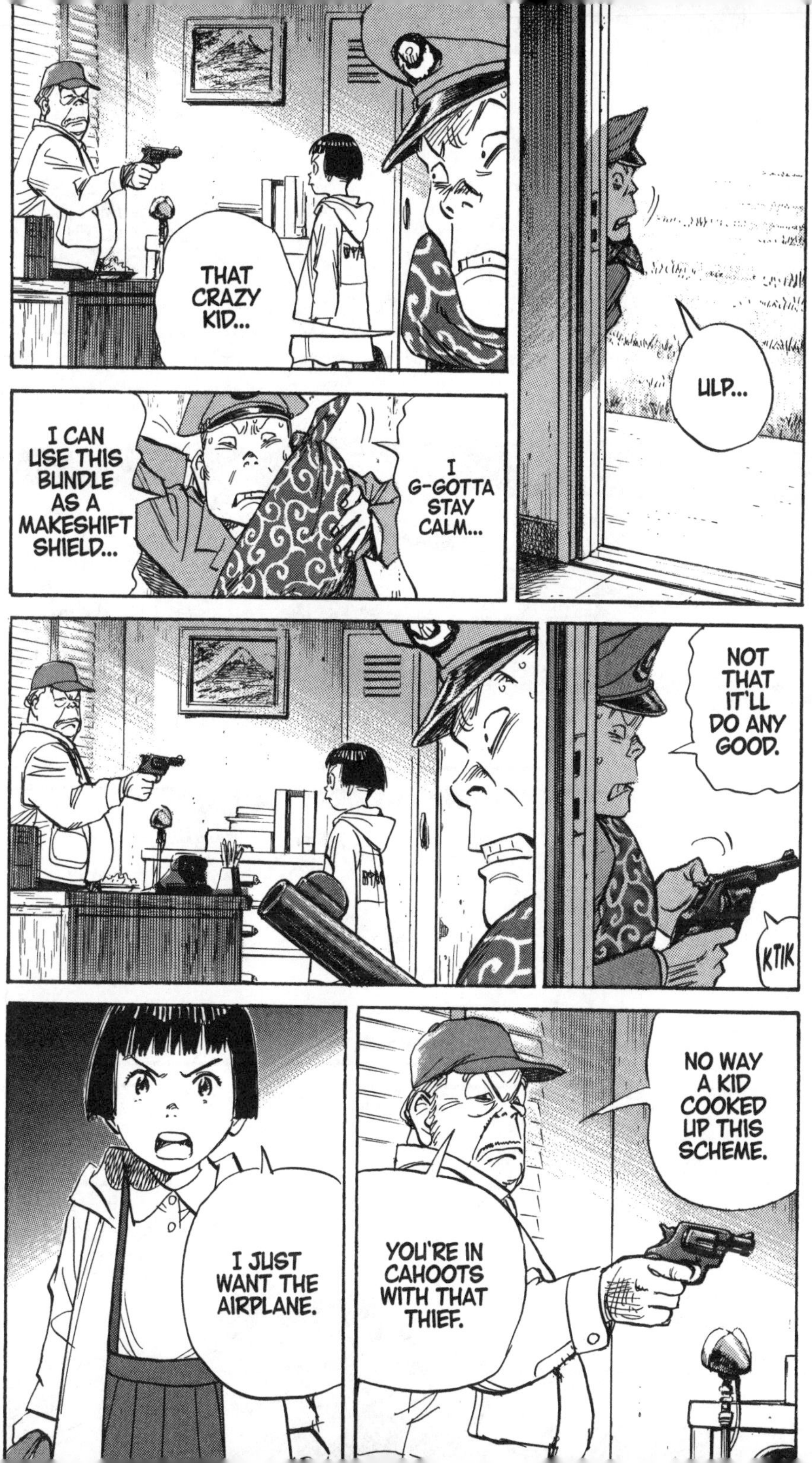
ULP...
THAT CRAZY KID...
I G-GOTTA STAY CALM...
I CAN USE THIS BUNDLE AS A MAKESHIFT SHIELD...
NOT THAT IT'LL DO ANY GOOD.
KTIK
NO WAY A KID COOKED UP THIS SCHEME.
YOU'RE IN CAHOOTS WITH THAT THIEF.
I JUST WANT THE AIRPLANE.

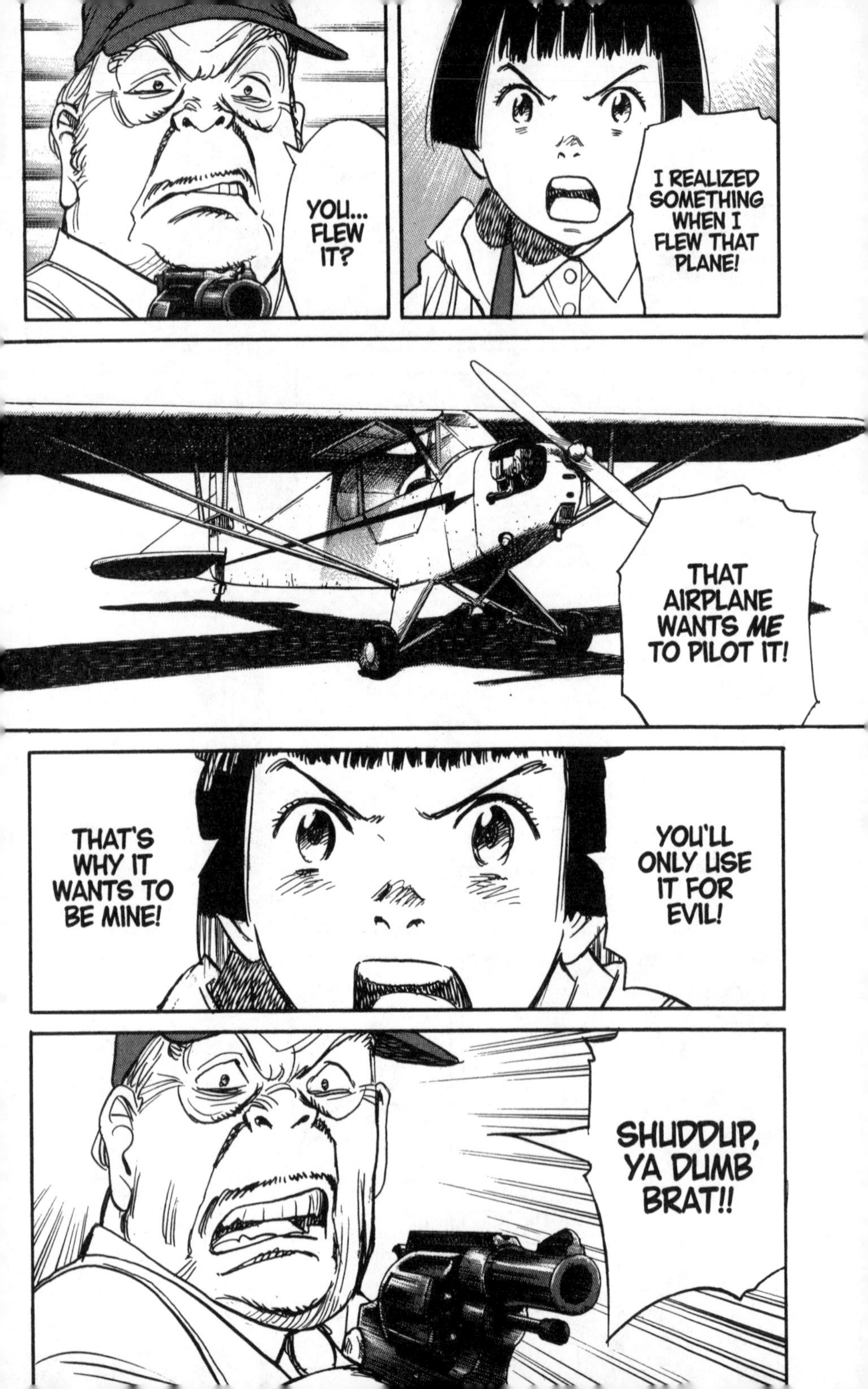
I REALIZED SOMETHING WHEN I FLEW THAT PLANE!
YOU... FLEW IT?
THAT AIRPLANE WANTS *ME* TO PILOT IT!
YOU'LL ONLY USE IT FOR EVIL!
THAT'S WHY IT WANTS TO BE MINE!
SHUDDUP, YA DUMB BRAT!!

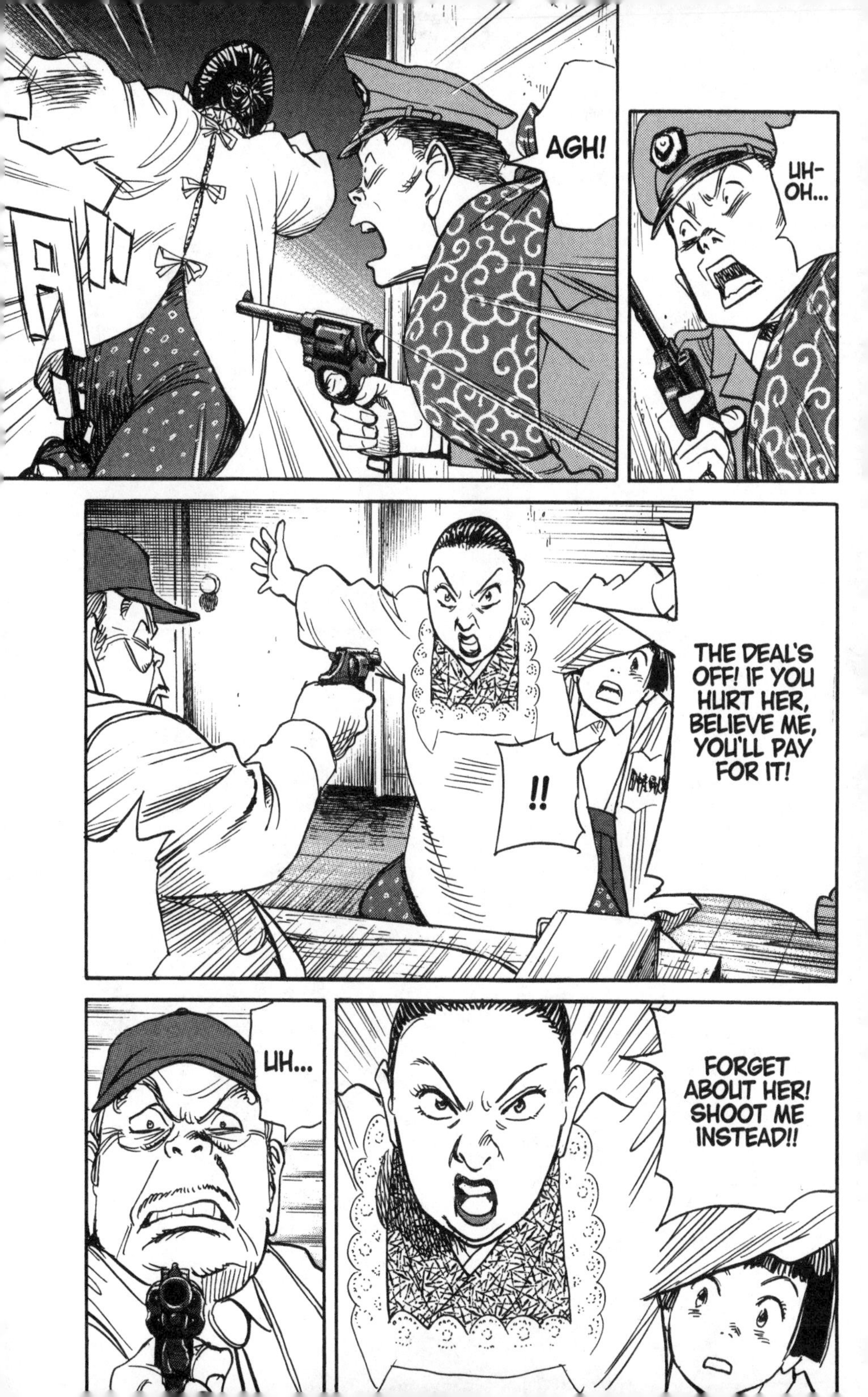
UH-OH...
AGH!
THE DEAL'S OFF! IF YOU HURT HER, BELIEVE ME, YOU'LL PAY FOR IT!
!!
FORGET ABOUT HER! SHOOT ME INSTEAD!!
UH...

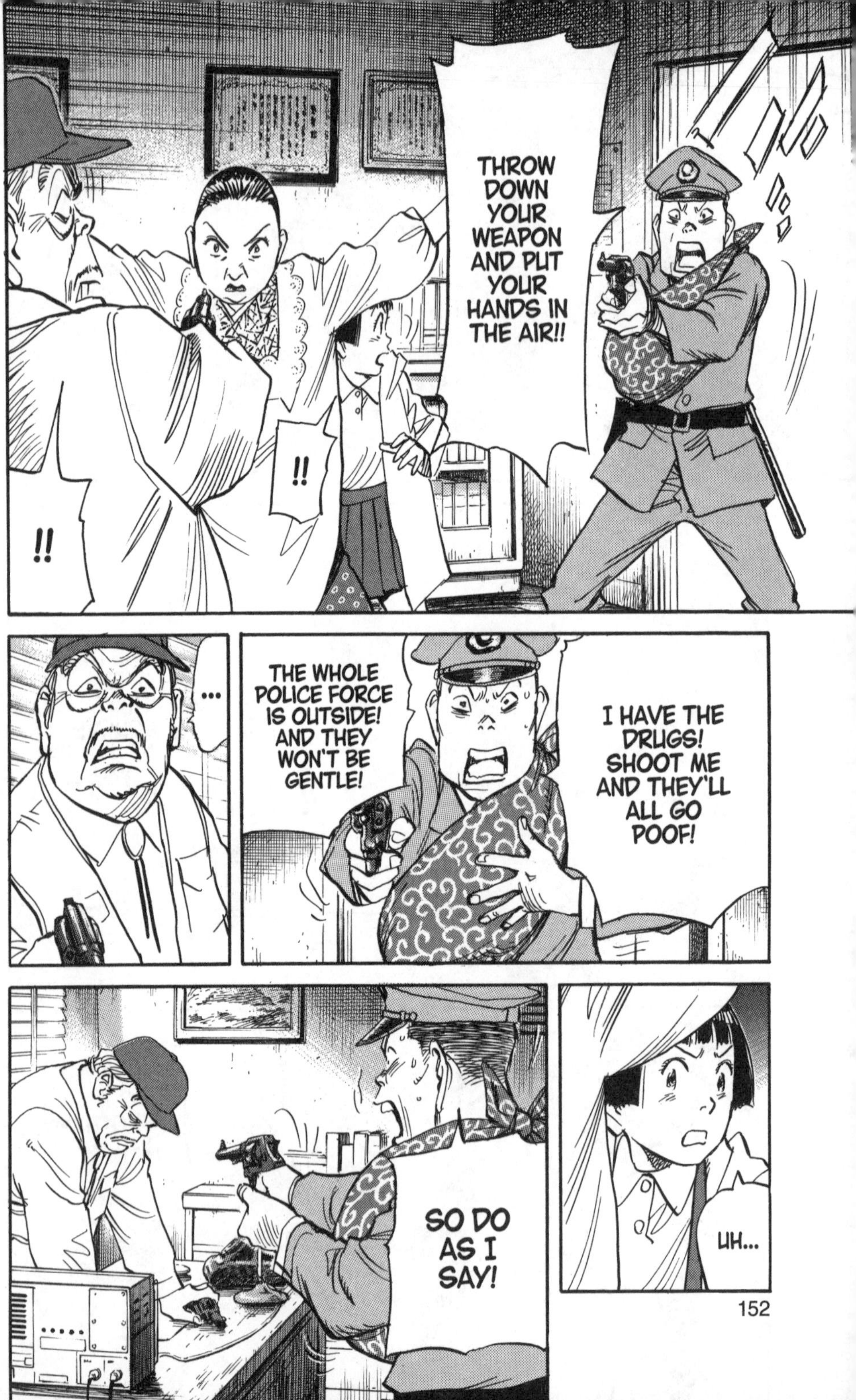
THROW DOWN YOUR WEAPON AND PUT YOUR HANDS IN THE AIR!!
!!
!!
I HAVE THE DRUGS! SHOOT ME AND THEY'LL ALL GO POOF!
THE WHOLE POLICE FORCE IS OUTSIDE! AND THEY WON'T BE GENTLE!
...
UH...
SO DO AS I SAY!

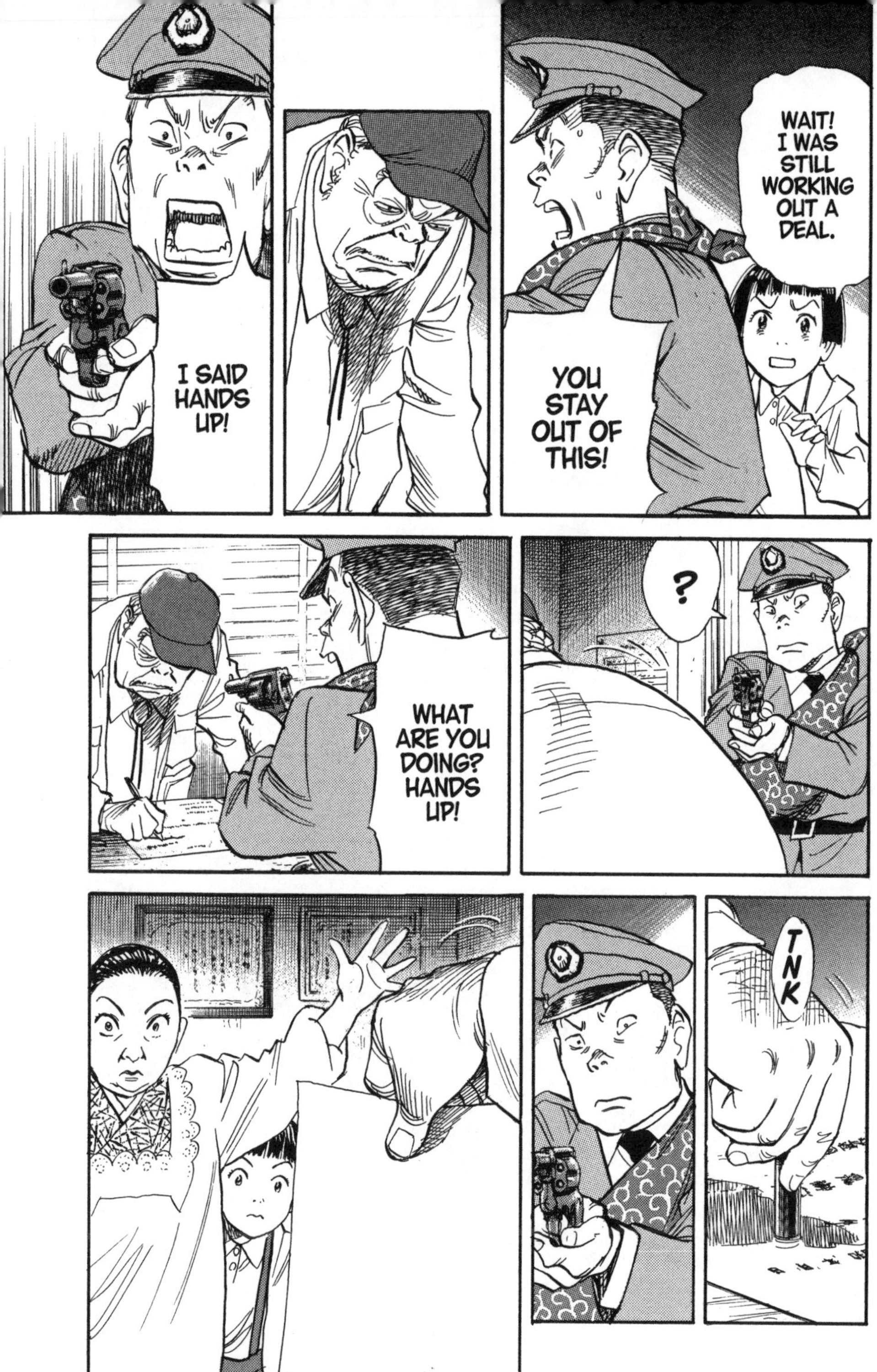
WAIT! I WAS STILL WORKING OUT A DEAL.
YOU STAY OUT OF THIS!
I SAID HANDS UP!
?
WHAT ARE YOU DOING? HANDS UP!
TNK

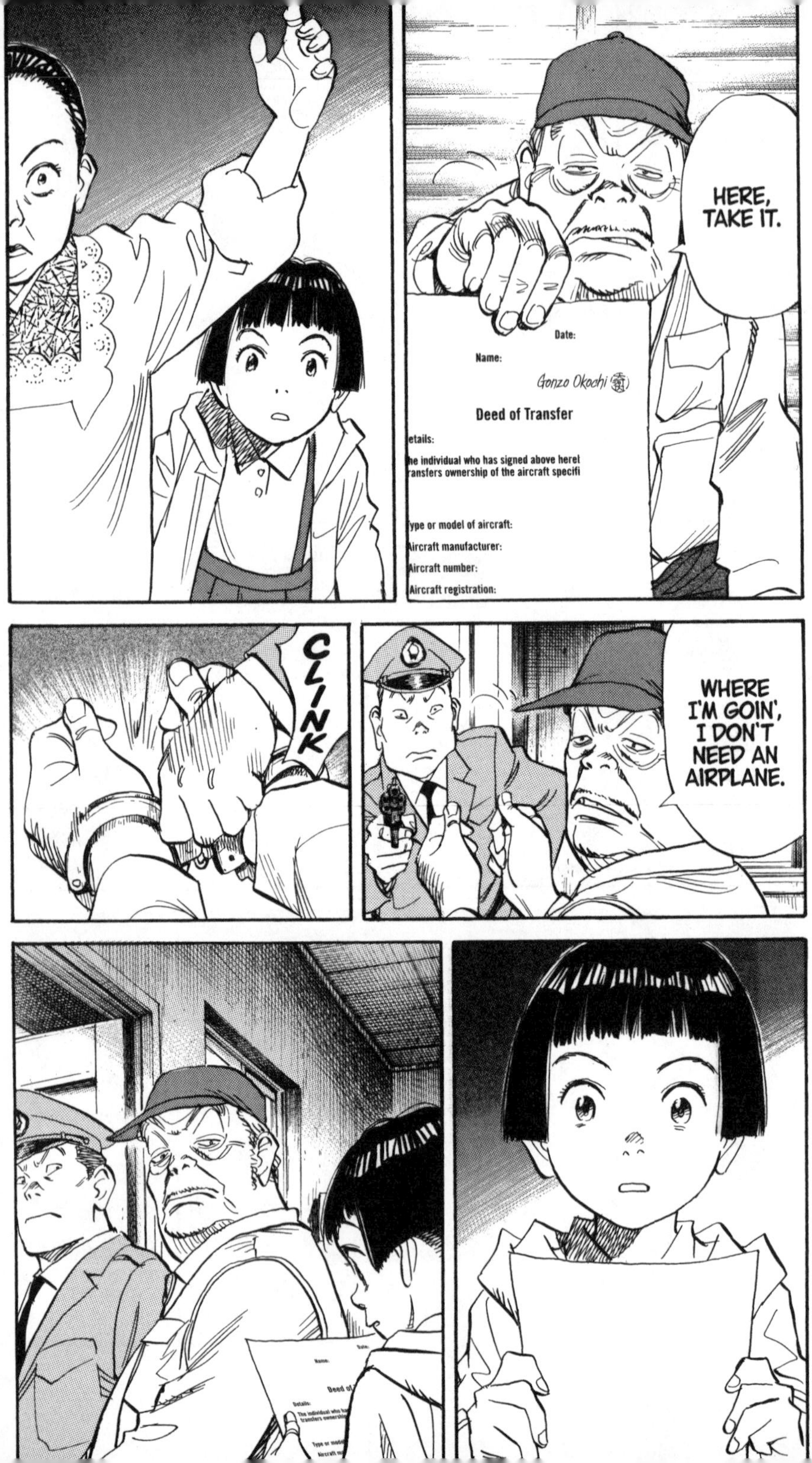
HERE, TAKE IT.
Date:
Name:
Gonzo Okochi
Deed of Transfer
etails:
he individual who has signed above herel
ransfers ownership of the aircraft specifi
ype or model of aircraft:
Aircraft manufacturer:
Aircraft number:
Aircraft registration:
WHERE I'M GOIN', I DON'T NEED AN AIRPLANE.
CLINK

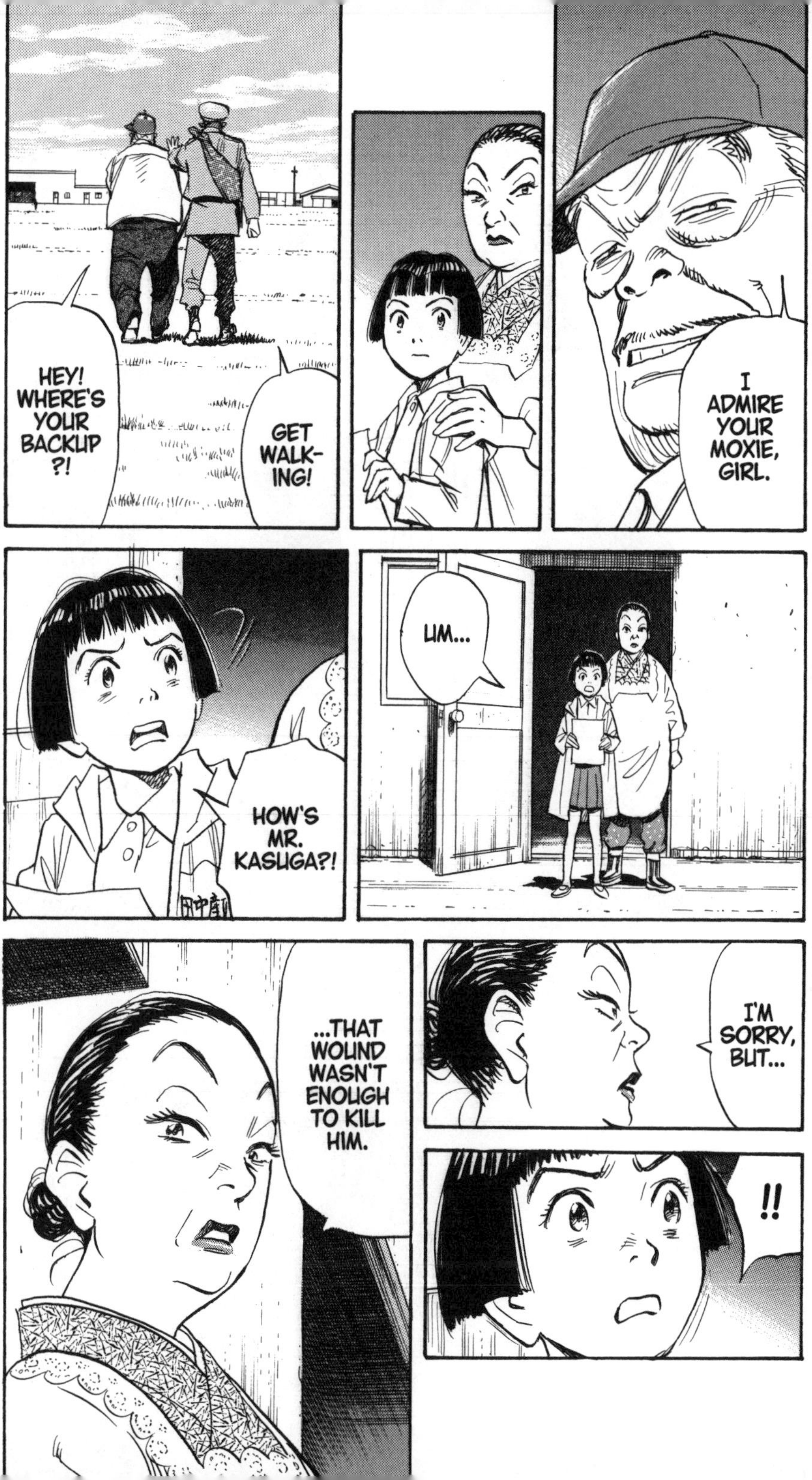
I ADMIRE YOUR MOXIE, GIRL.
GET WALKING!
HEY! WHERE'S YOUR BACKUP?!
UM...
HOW'S MR. KASUGA?!
I'M SORRY, BUT...
!!
...THAT WOUND WASN'T ENOUGH TO KILL HIM.

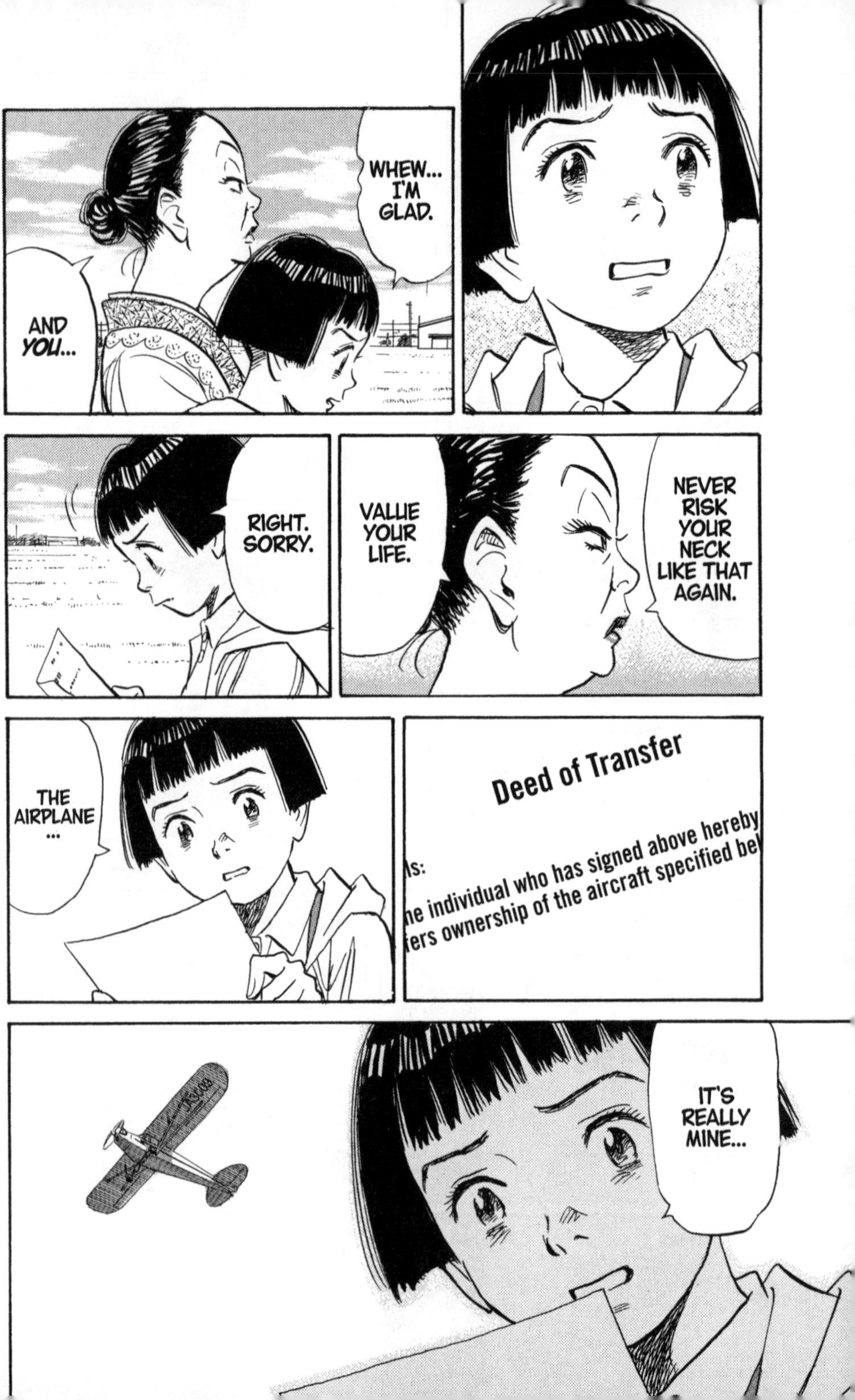
WHEW... I'M GLAD.
AND YOU...
NEVER RISK YOUR NECK LIKE THAT AGAIN.
VALUE YOUR LIFE.
RIGHT. SORRY.
Deed of Transfer
ls:
he individual who has signed above hereby
fers ownership of the aircraft specified bel
THE AIRPLANE ...
IT'S REALLY MINE...

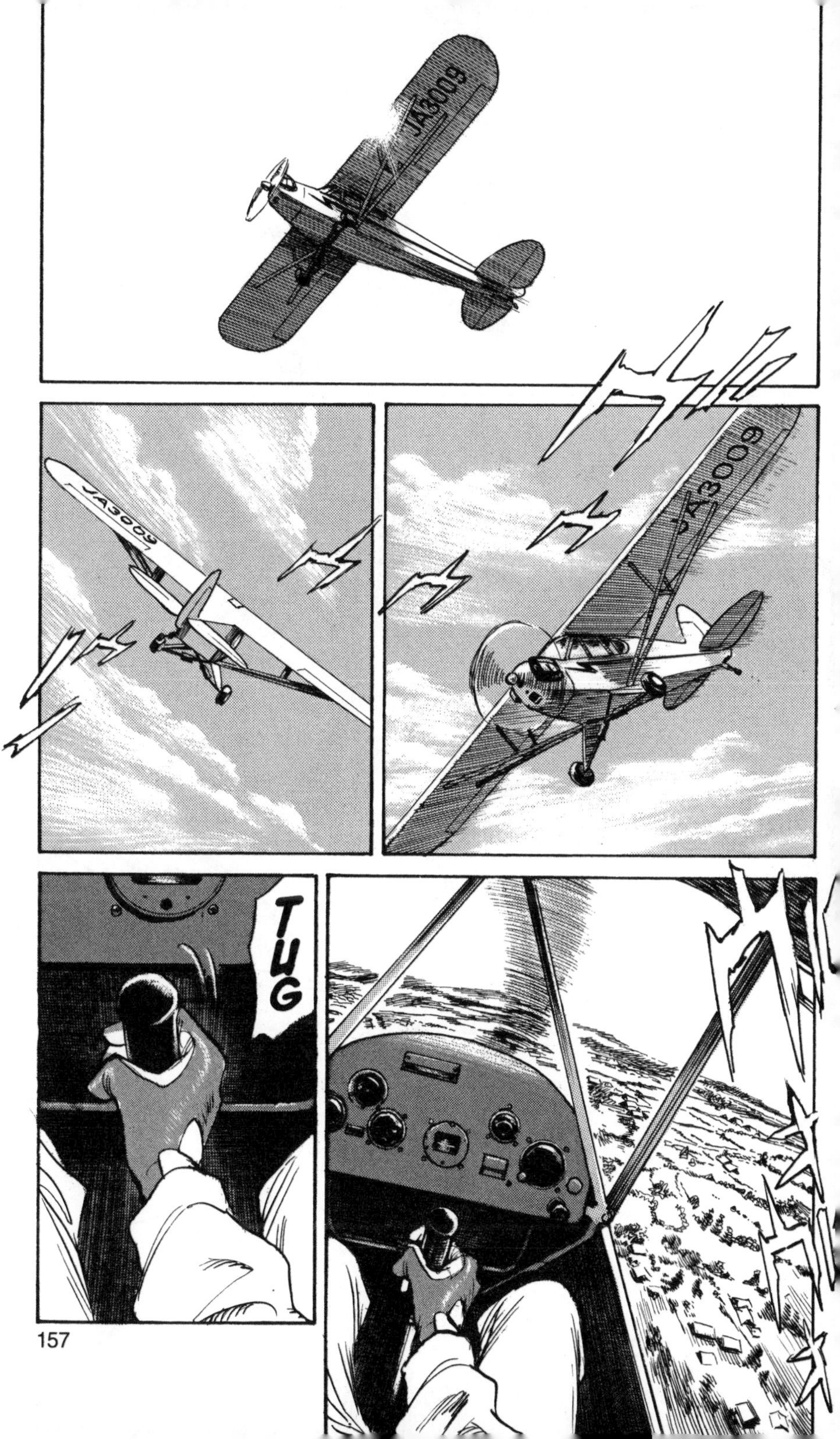
JA3009
JA3009
JA3009
TUG

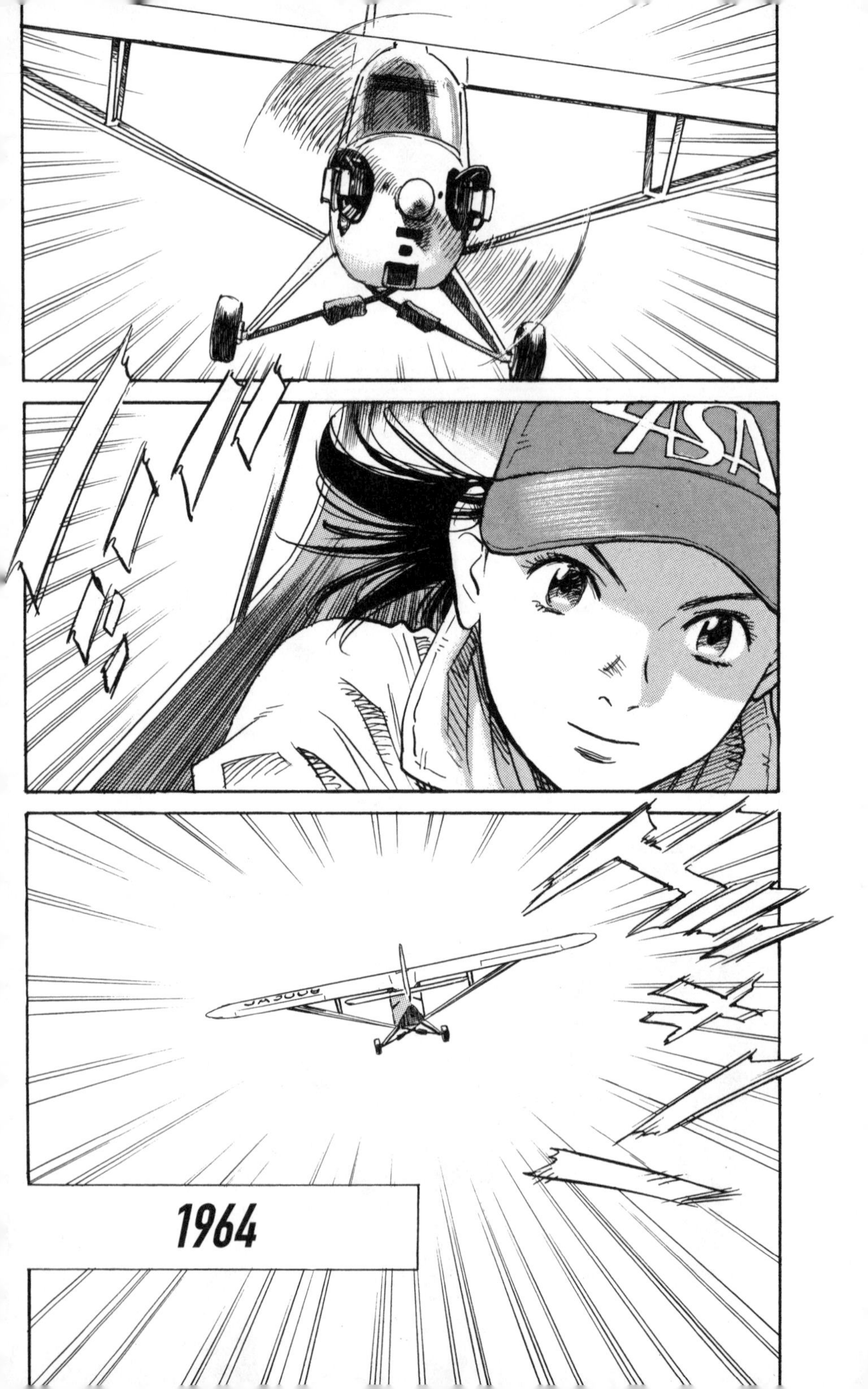
1964

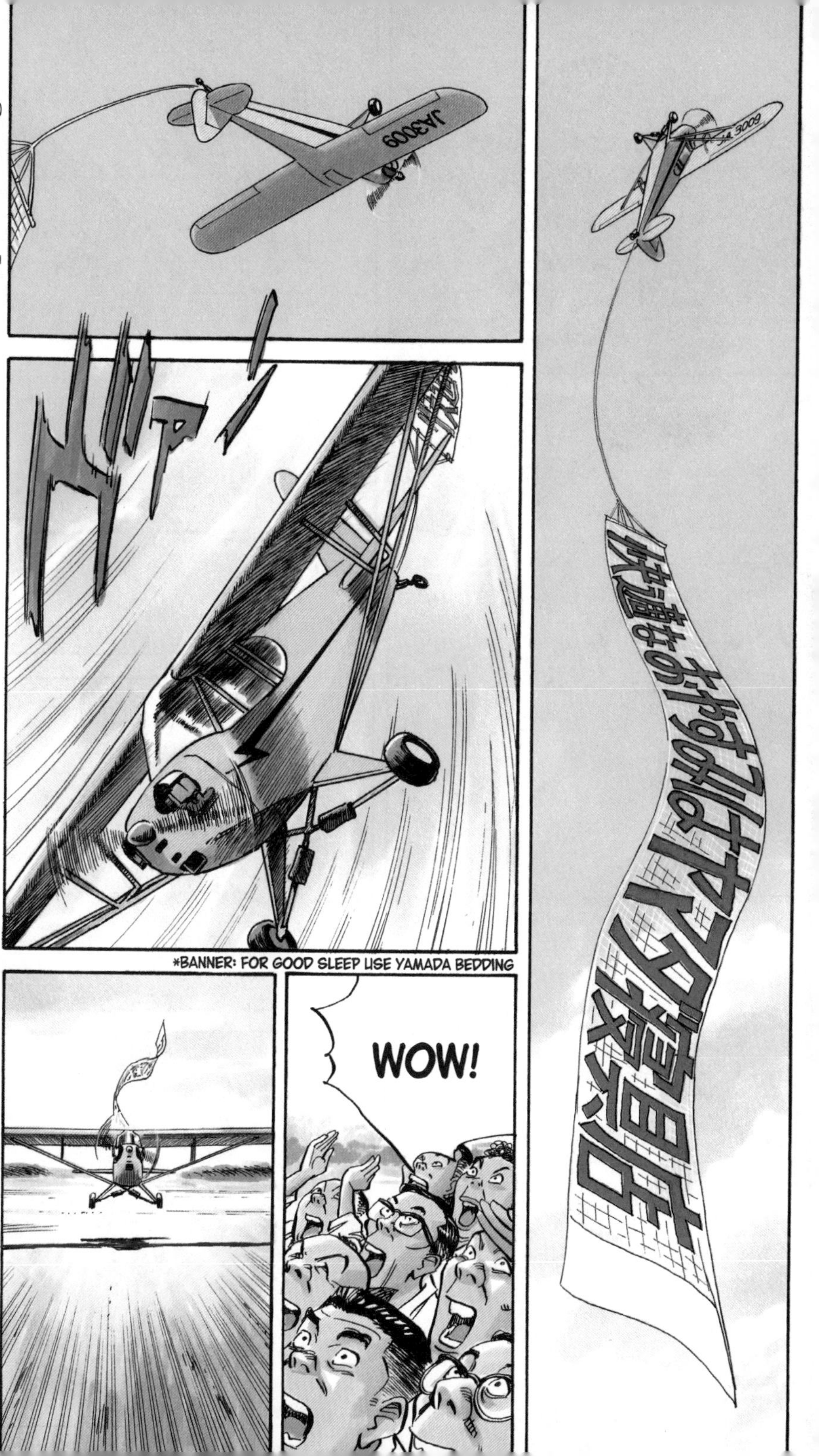
快適なおやすみはヤマダ寝具店
*BANNER: FOR GOOD SLEEP USE YAMADA BEDDING
WOW!

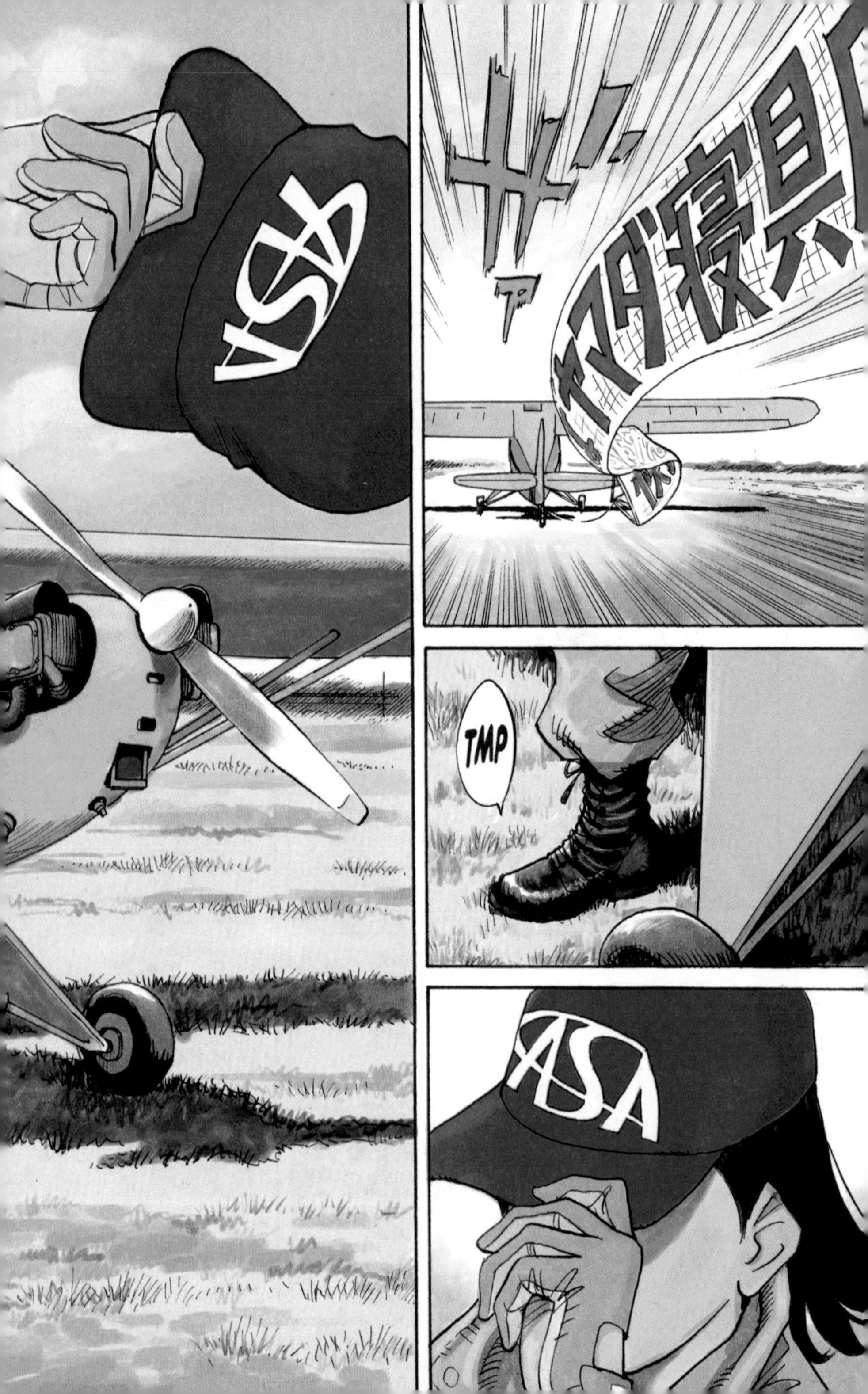
TMP

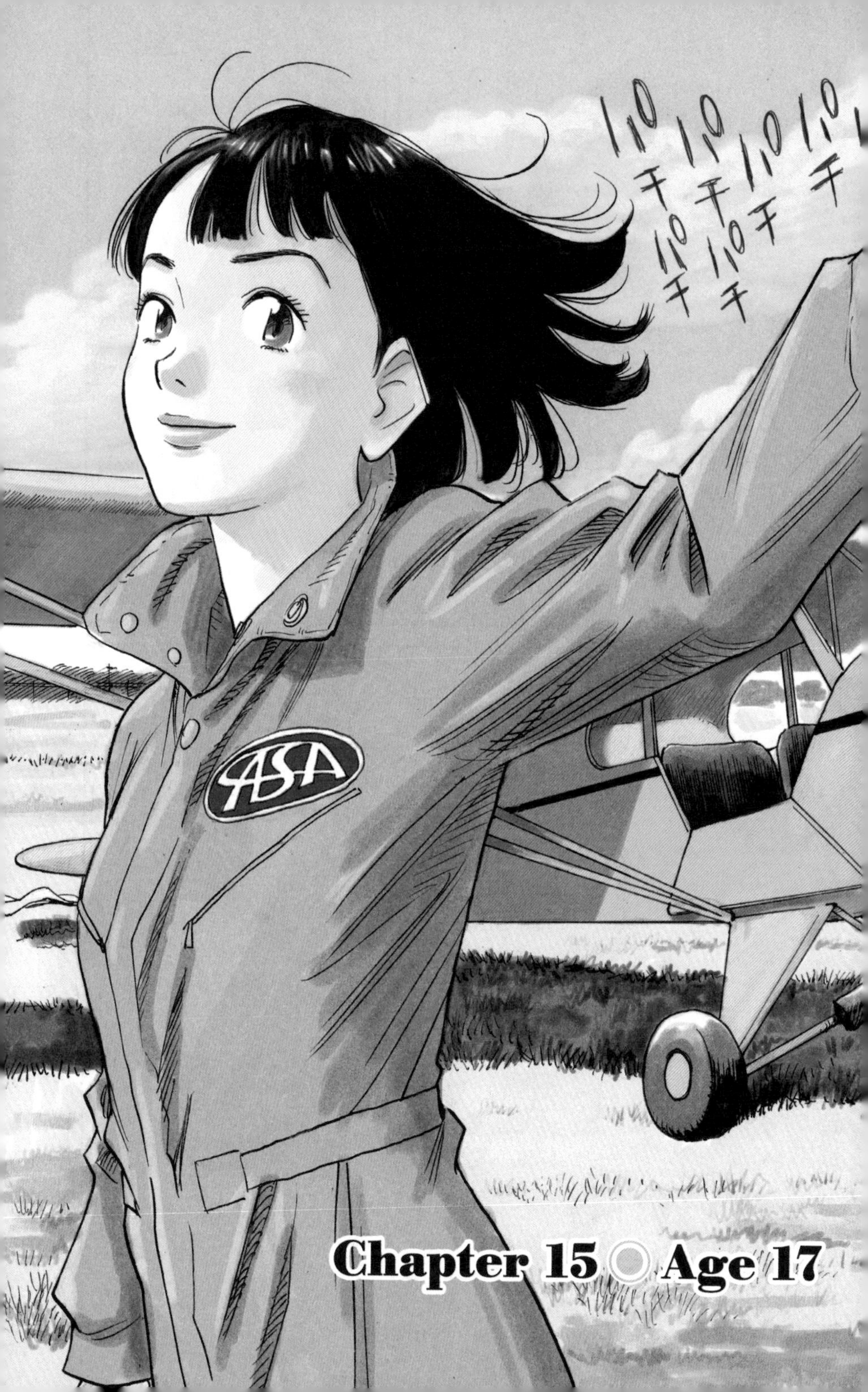
パチ
パチ
パチパチ
パチパチ

Chapter 15 ◯ Age 17

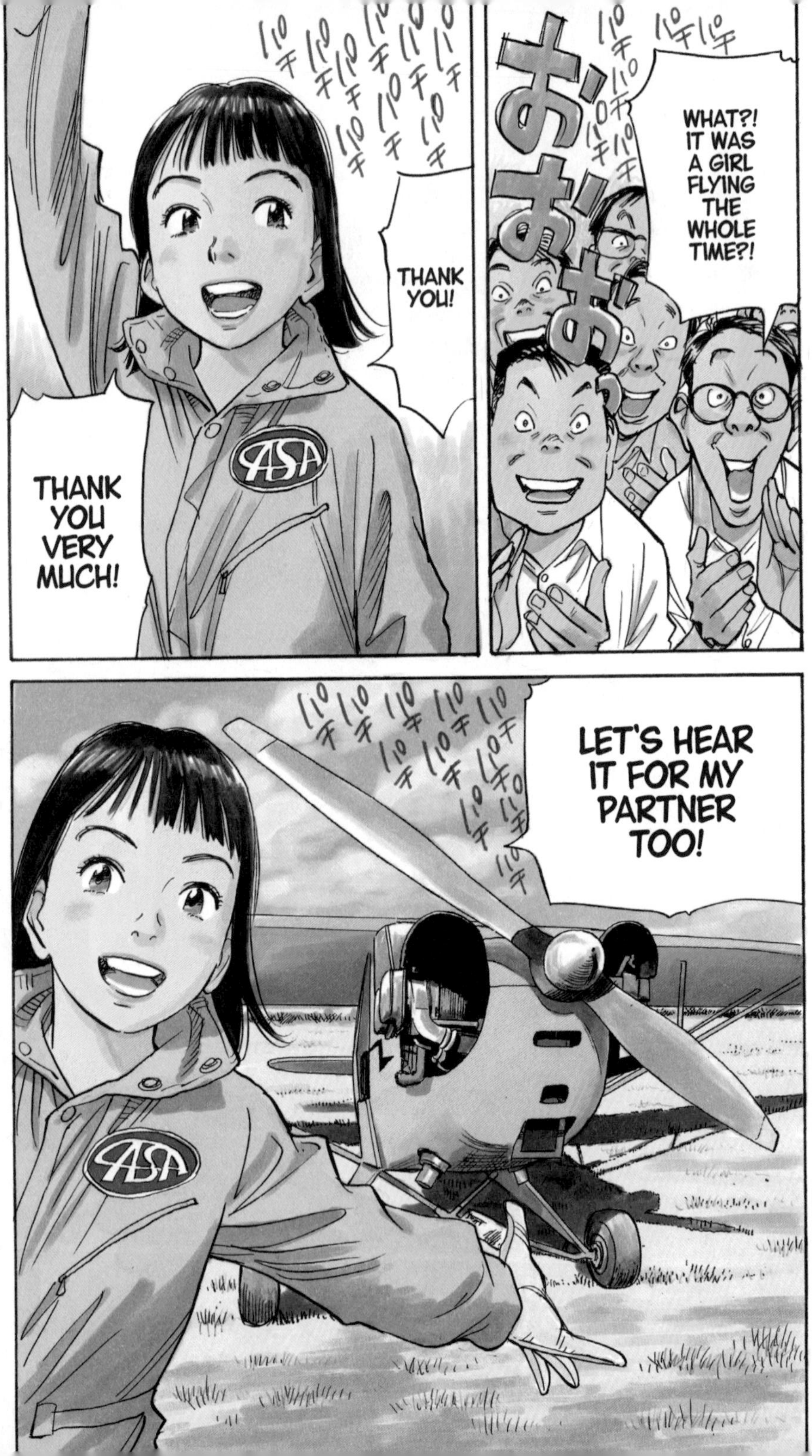
パチパチ
WHAT?! IT WAS A GIRL FLYING THE WHOLE TIME?!
パチパチ
THANK YOU!
THANK YOU VERY MUCH!
パチパチ
LET'S HEAR IT FOR MY PARTNER TOO!

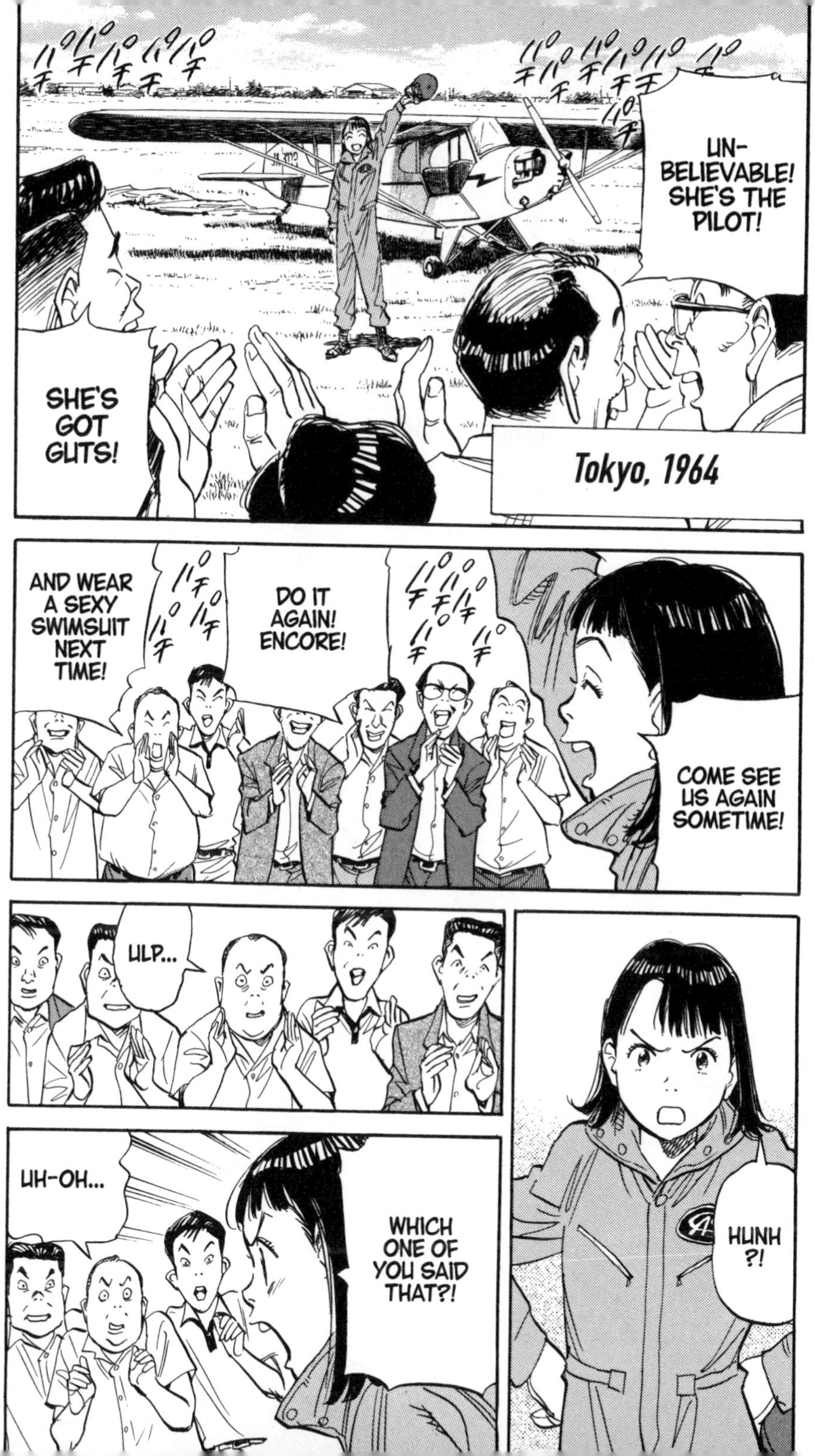
UN-BELIEVABLE! SHE'S THE PILOT!
Tokyo, 1964
SHE'S GOT GUTS!
COME SEE US AGAIN SOMETIME!
DO IT AGAIN! ENCORE!
AND WEAR A SEXY SWIMSUIT NEXT TIME!
HUNH ?!
ULP...
WHICH ONE OF YOU SAID THAT?!
UH-OH...

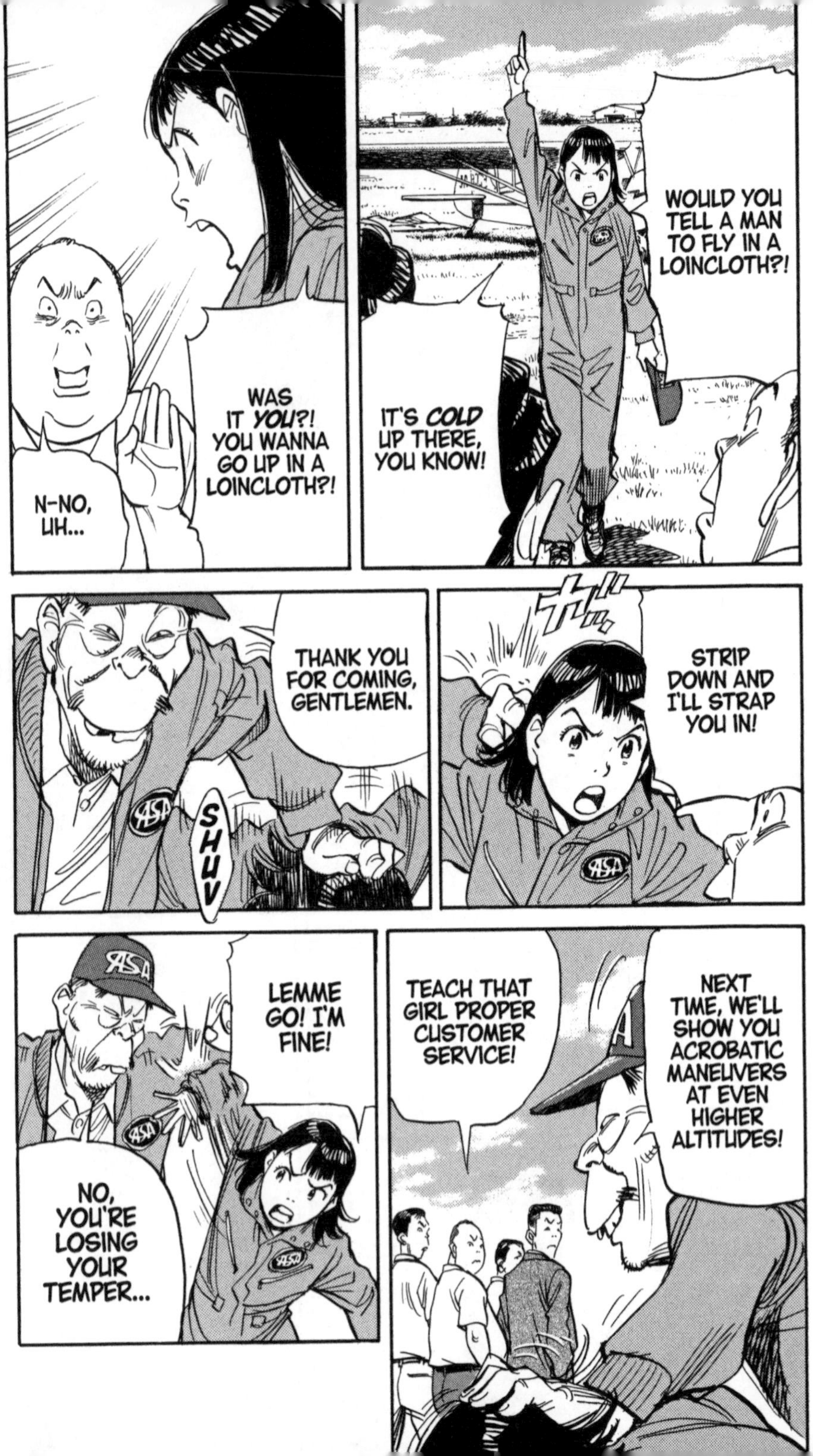
WOULD YOU TELL A MAN TO FLY IN A LOINCLOTH?!
IT'S *COLD* UP THERE, YOU KNOW!
WAS IT *YOU*?! YOU WANNA GO UP IN A LOINCLOTH?!
N-NO, UH...
STRIP DOWN AND I'LL STRAP YOU IN!
THANK YOU FOR COMING, GENTLEMEN.
SHUV
NEXT TIME, WE'LL SHOW YOU ACROBATIC MANEUVERS AT EVEN HIGHER ALTITUDES!
TEACH THAT GIRL PROPER CUSTOMER SERVICE!
LEMME GO! I'M FINE!
NO, YOU'RE LOSING YOUR TEMPER...

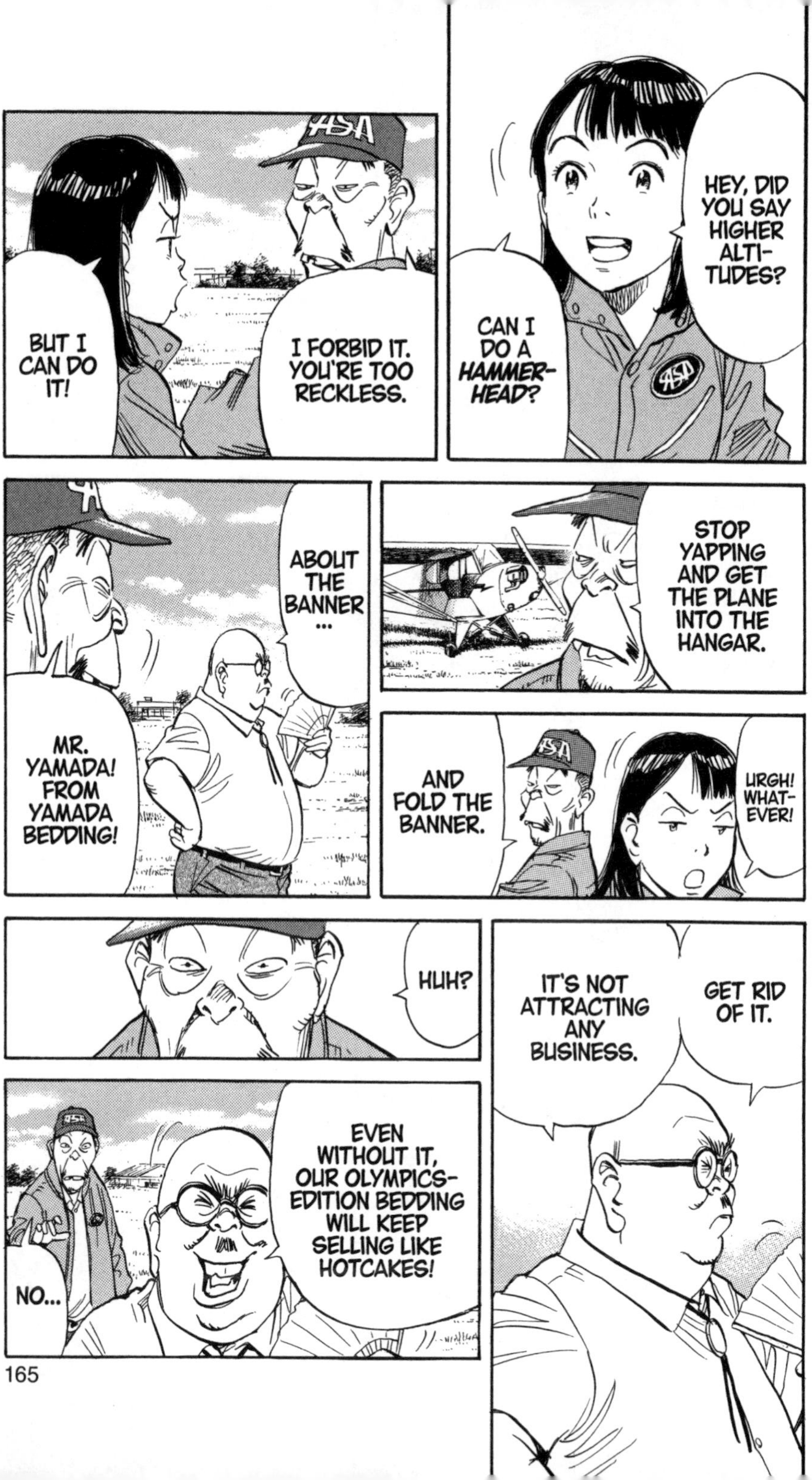
HEY, DID YOU SAY HIGHER ALTI-TUDES?
CAN I DO A *HAMMER-HEAD?*
I FORBID IT. YOU'RE TOO RECKLESS.
BUT I CAN DO IT!
STOP YAPPING AND GET THE PLANE INTO THE HANGAR.
URGH! WHAT-EVER!
AND FOLD THE BANNER.
ABOUT THE BANNER...
MR. YAMADA! FROM YAMADA BEDDING!
GET RID OF IT.
IT'S NOT ATTRACTING ANY BUSINESS.
HUH?
EVEN WITHOUT IT, OUR OLYMPICS-EDITION BEDDING WILL KEEP SELLING LIKE HOTCAKES!
NO...

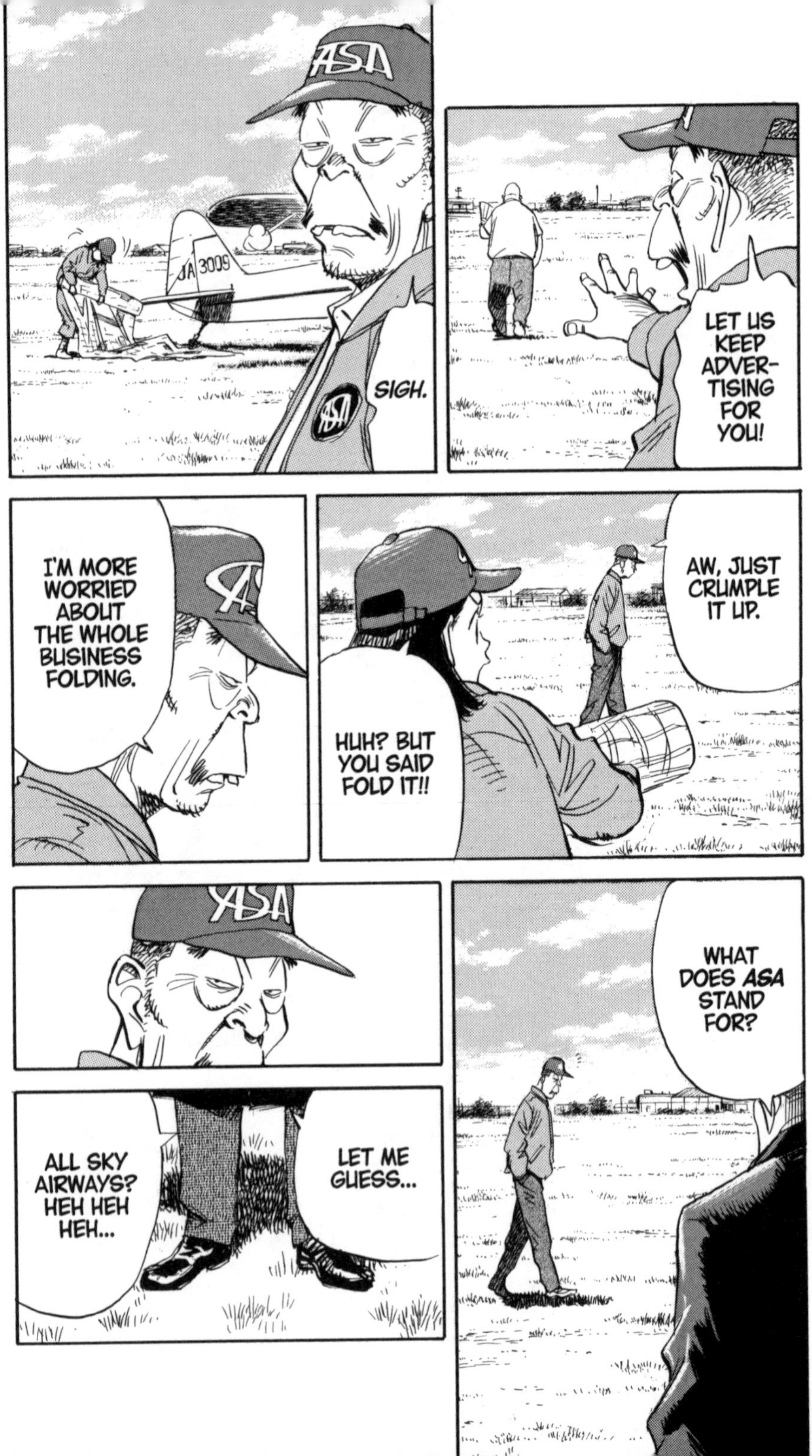
LET US KEEP ADVERTISING FOR YOU!
SIGH.
AW, JUST CRUMPLE IT UP.
HUH? BUT YOU SAID FOLD IT!!
I'M MORE WORRIED ABOUT THE WHOLE BUSINESS FOLDING.
WHAT DOES ASA STAND FOR?
LET ME GUESS...
ALL SKY AIRWAYS? HEH HEH HEH...

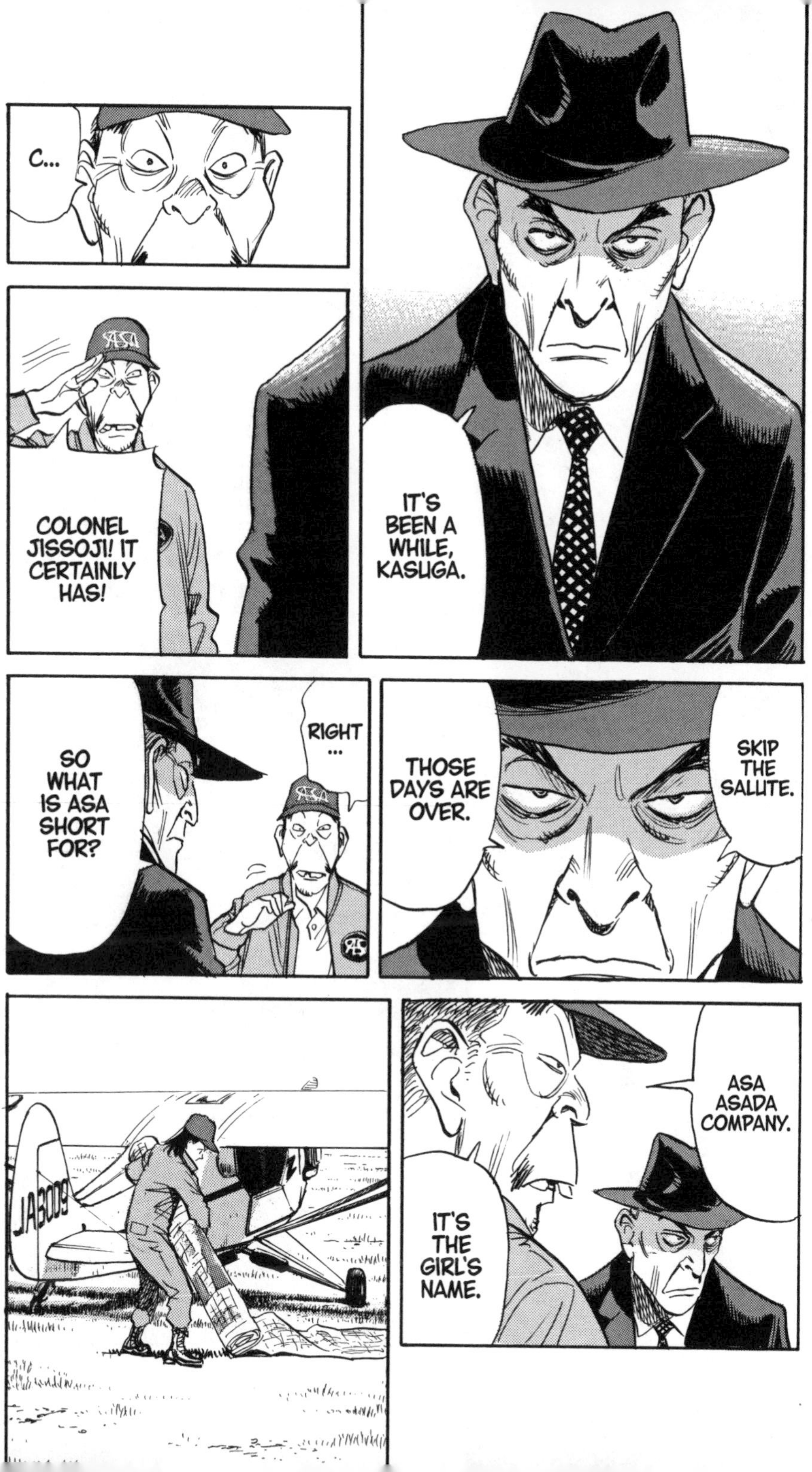
IT'S BEEN A WHILE, KASUGA.
C...
COLONEL JISSOJI! IT CERTAINLY HAS!
SKIP THE SALUTE.
THOSE DAYS ARE OVER.
RIGHT ...
SO WHAT IS ASA SHORT FOR?
ASA ASADA COMPANY.
IT'S THE GIRL'S NAME.

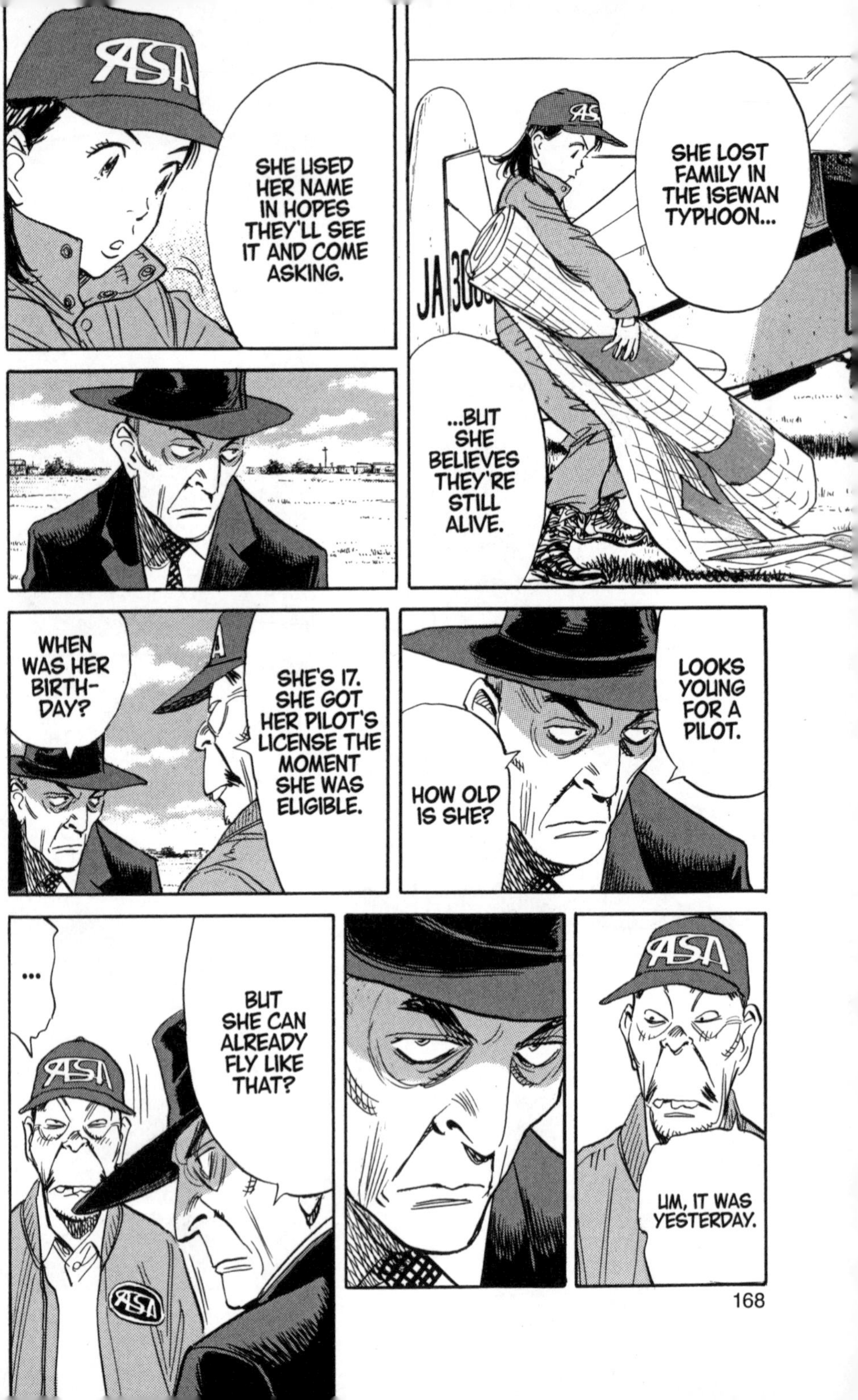
SHE LOST FAMILY IN THE ISEWAN TYPHOON...
...BUT SHE BELIEVES THEY'RE STILL ALIVE.
SHE USED HER NAME IN HOPES THEY'LL SEE IT AND COME ASKING.
LOOKS YOUNG FOR A PILOT.
HOW OLD IS SHE?
SHE'S 17. SHE GOT HER PILOT'S LICENSE THE MOMENT SHE WAS ELIGIBLE.
WHEN WAS HER BIRTHDAY?
UM, IT WAS YESTERDAY.
BUT SHE CAN ALREADY FLY LIKE THAT?
...

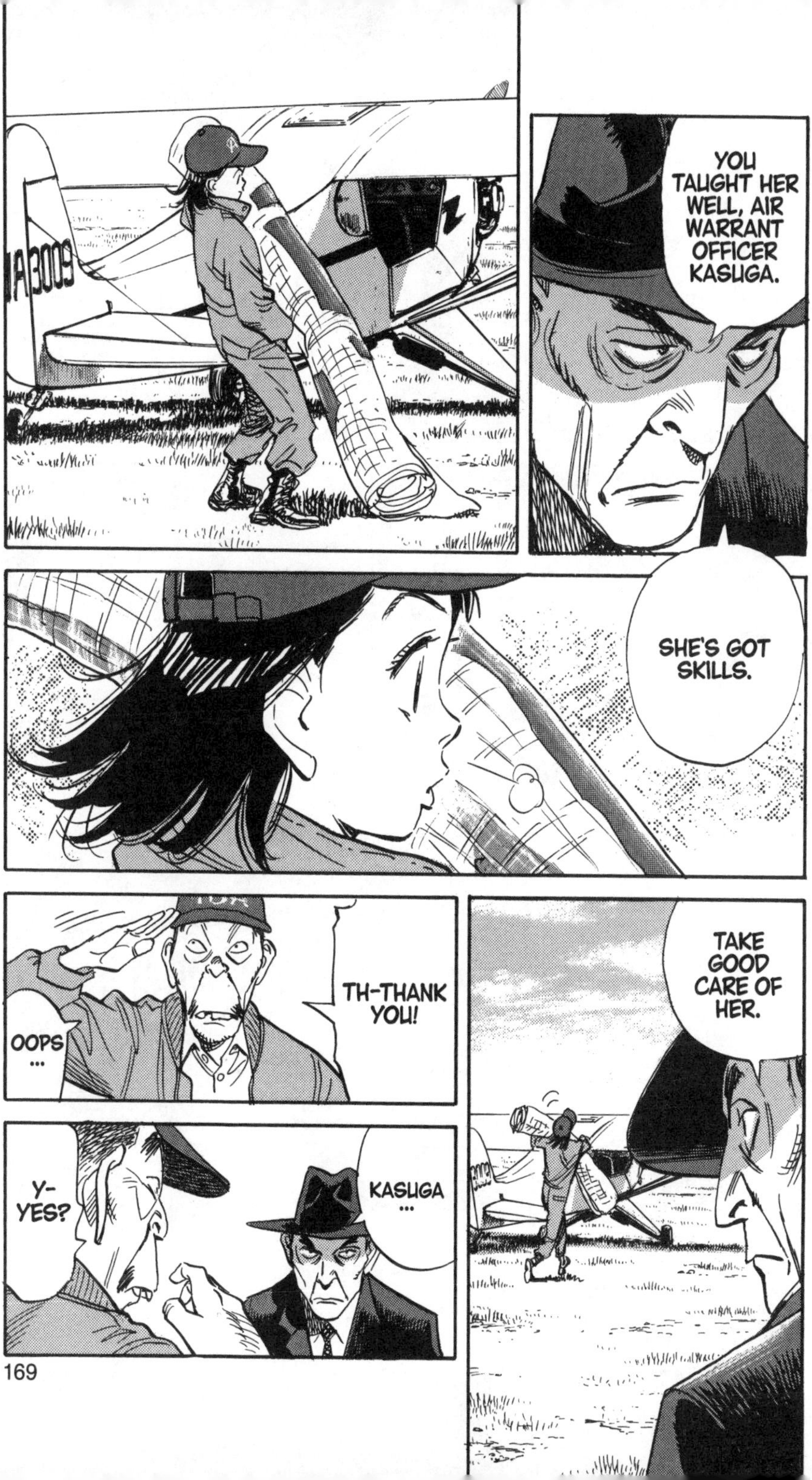
YOU TAUGHT HER WELL, AIR WARRANT OFFICER KASUGA.
SHE'S GOT SKILLS.
TAKE GOOD CARE OF HER.
TH-THANK YOU!
OOPS ...
KASUGA ...
Y-YES?

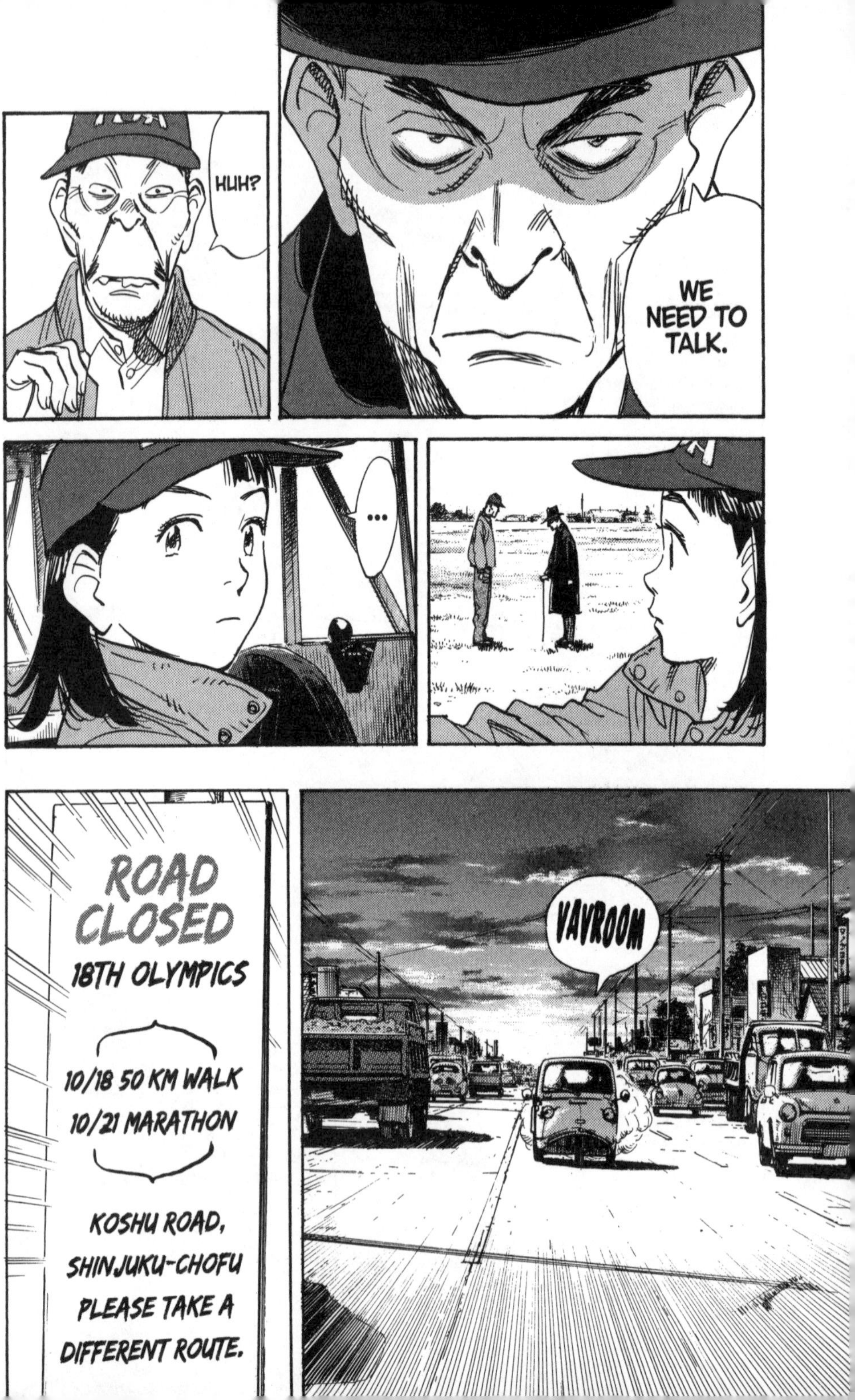
WE NEED TO TALK.
HUH?
...
VAVROOM
ROAD CLOSED
18TH OLYMPICS
10/18 50 KM WALK
10/21 MARATHON
KOSHU ROAD, SHINJUKU-CHOFU
PLEASE TAKE A DIFFERENT ROUTE.

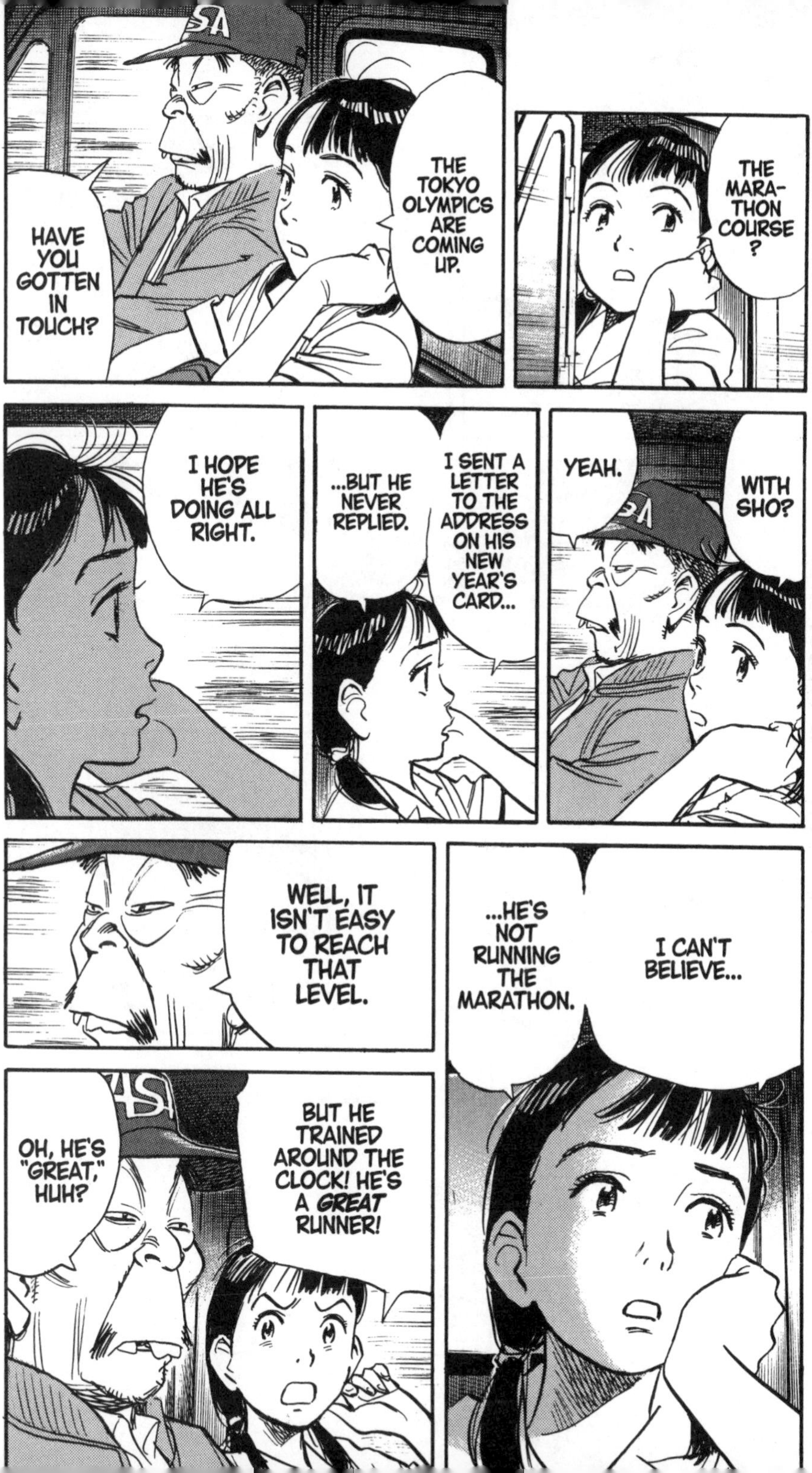
THE MARATHON COURSE?
THE TOKYO OLYMPICS ARE COMING UP.
HAVE YOU GOTTEN IN TOUCH?
WITH SHO?
YEAH.
I SENT A LETTER TO THE ADDRESS ON HIS NEW YEAR'S CARD...
...BUT HE NEVER REPLIED.
I HOPE HE'S DOING ALL RIGHT.
I CAN'T BELIEVE...
...HE'S NOT RUNNING THE MARATHON.
WELL, IT ISN'T EASY TO REACH THAT LEVEL.
BUT HE TRAINED AROUND THE CLOCK! HE'S A *GREAT* RUNNER!
OH, HE'S "GREAT," HUH?

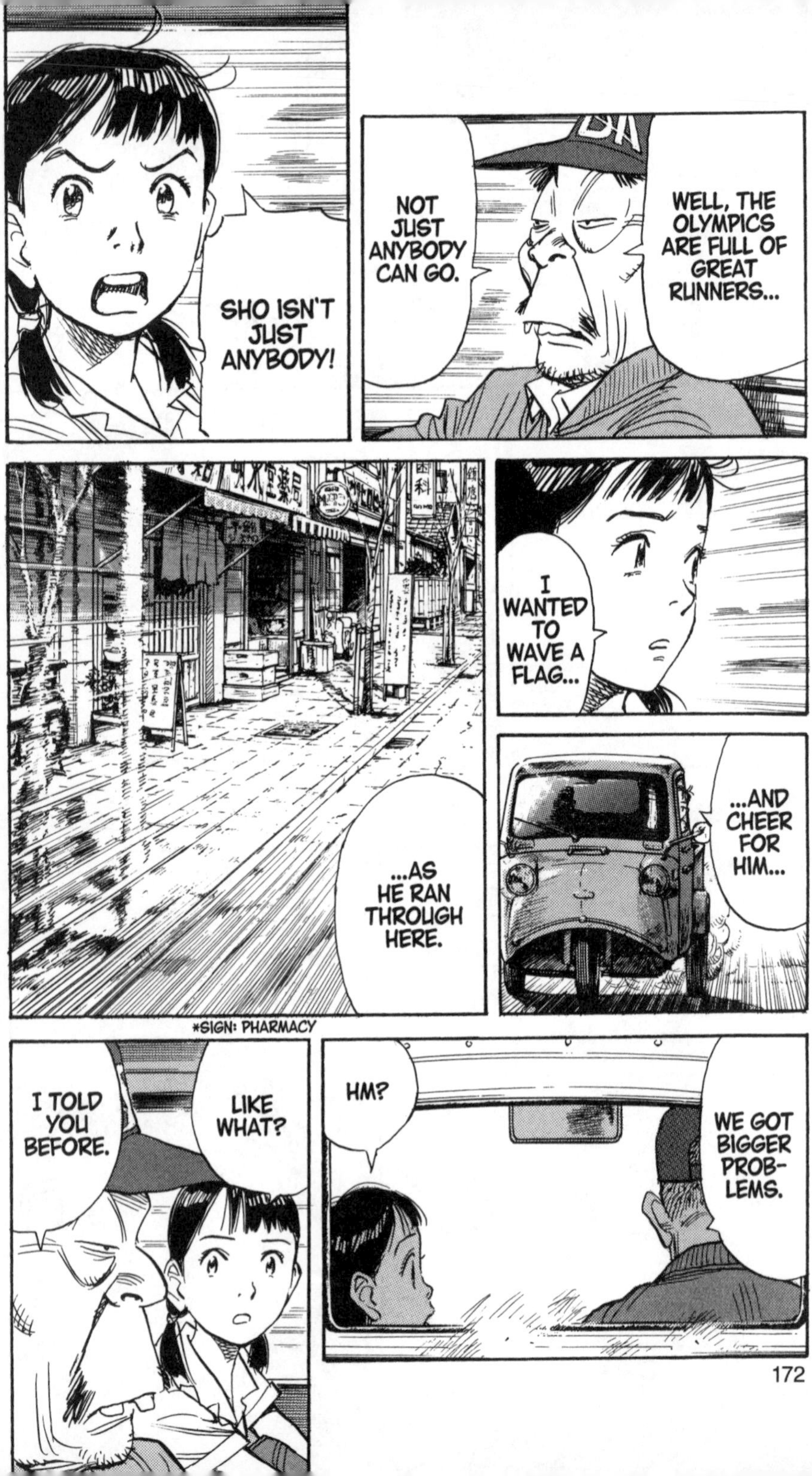
WELL, THE OLYMPICS ARE FULL OF GREAT RUNNERS...
NOT JUST ANYBODY CAN GO.
SHO ISN'T JUST ANYBODY!
I WANTED TO WAVE A FLAG...
...AND CHEER FOR HIM...
...AS HE RAN THROUGH HERE.
*SIGN: PHARMACY
WE GOT BIGGER PROB-LEMS.
HM?
LIKE WHAT?
I TOLD YOU BEFORE.

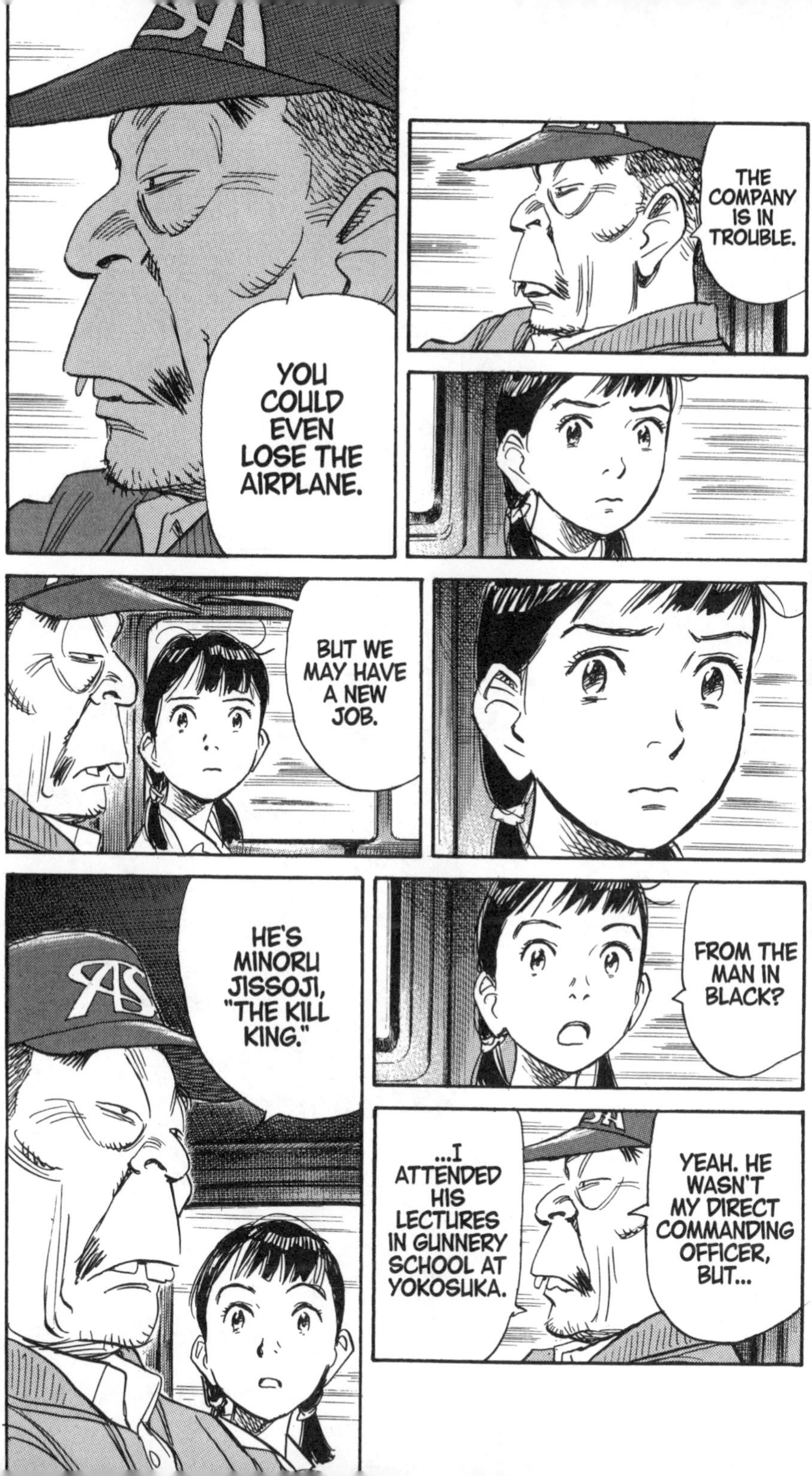
THE COMPANY IS IN TROUBLE.
YOU COULD EVEN LOSE THE AIRPLANE.
BUT WE MAY HAVE A NEW JOB.
FROM THE MAN IN BLACK?
YEAH. HE WASN'T MY DIRECT COMMANDING OFFICER, BUT...
...I ATTENDED HIS LECTURES IN GUNNERY SCHOOL AT YOKOSUKA.
HE'S MINORU JISSOJI, "THE KILL KING."

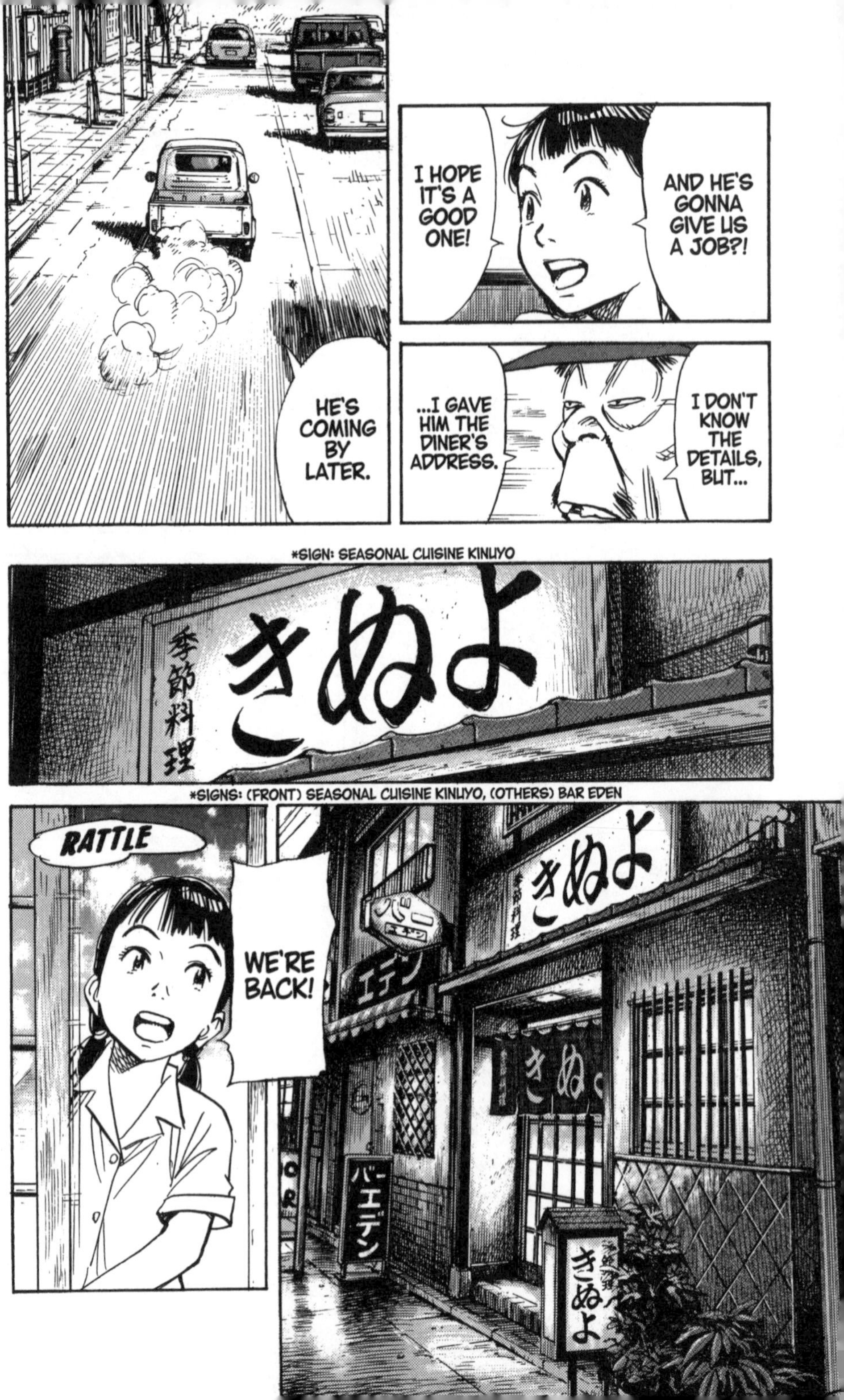
AND HE'S GONNA GIVE US A JOB?!
I HOPE IT'S A GOOD ONE!
I DON'T KNOW THE DETAILS, BUT...
...I GAVE HIM THE DINER'S ADDRESS.
HE'S COMING BY LATER.
*SIGN: SEASONAL CUISINE KINUYO
季節料理
きぬよ
*SIGNS: (FRONT) SEASONAL CUISINE KINUYO, (OTHERS) BAR EDEN
きぬよ
季節料理
バー
エデン
バー
エデン
きぬよ
RATTLE
WE'RE BACK!

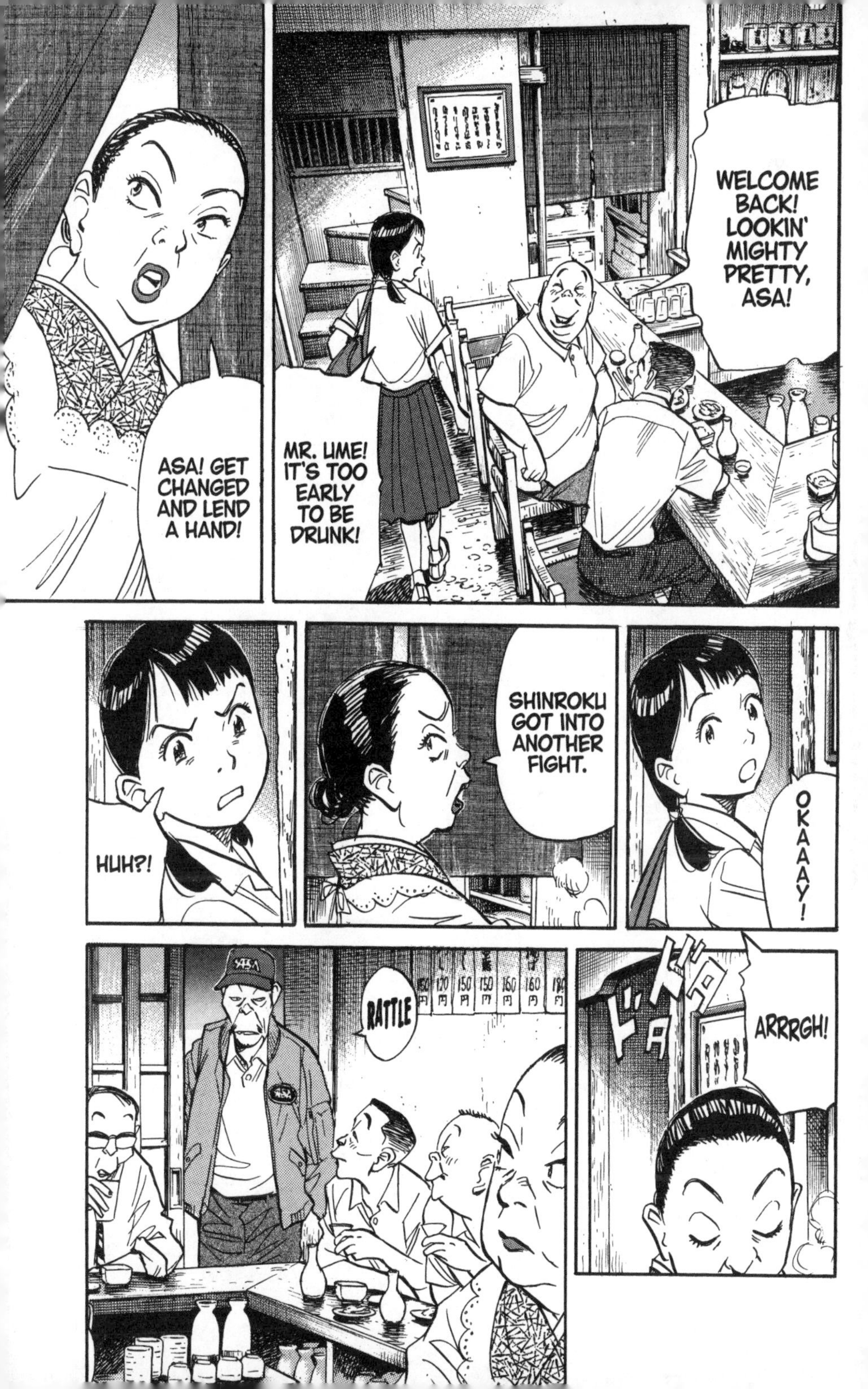
WELCOME BACK! LOOKIN' MIGHTY PRETTY, ASA!
MR. UME! IT'S TOO EARLY TO BE DRUNK!
ASA! GET CHANGED AND LEND A HAND!
OKAAAY!
SHINROKU GOT INTO ANOTHER FIGHT.
HUH?!
ドタドタ
ARRRGH!
RATTLE

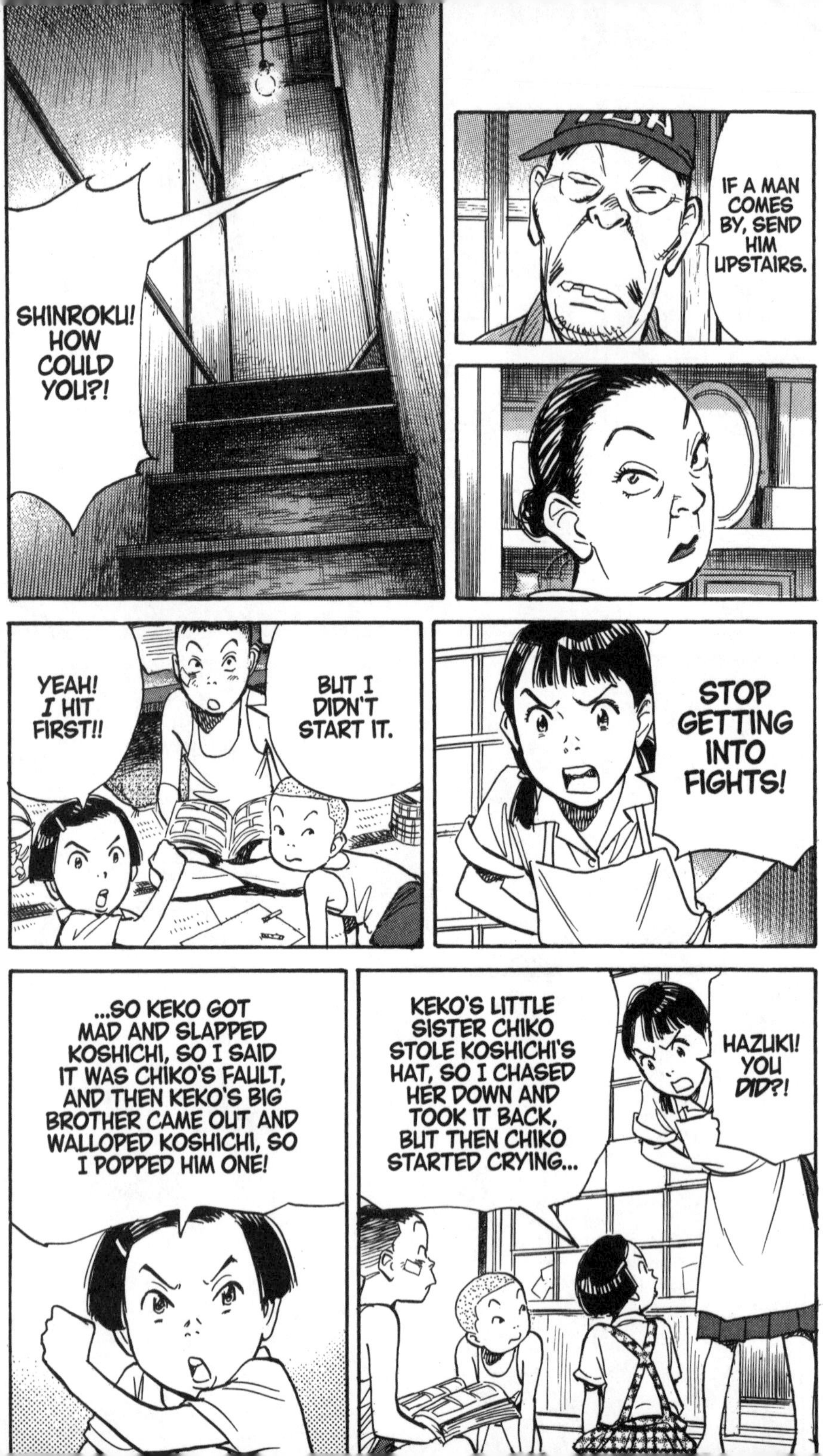
IF A MAN COMES BY, SEND HIM UPSTAIRS.
SHINROKU! HOW COULD YOU?!
STOP GETTING INTO FIGHTS!
BUT I DIDN'T START IT.
YEAH! *I* HIT FIRST!!
HAZUKI! YOU *DID*?!
KEKO'S LITTLE SISTER CHIKO STOLE KOSHICHI'S HAT, SO I CHASED HER DOWN AND TOOK IT BACK, BUT THEN CHIKO STARTED CRYING...
...SO KEKO GOT MAD AND SLAPPED KOSHICHI, SO I SAID IT WAS CHIKO'S FAULT, AND THEN KEKO'S BIG BROTHER CAME OUT AND WALLOPED KOSHICHI, SO I POPPED HIM ONE!

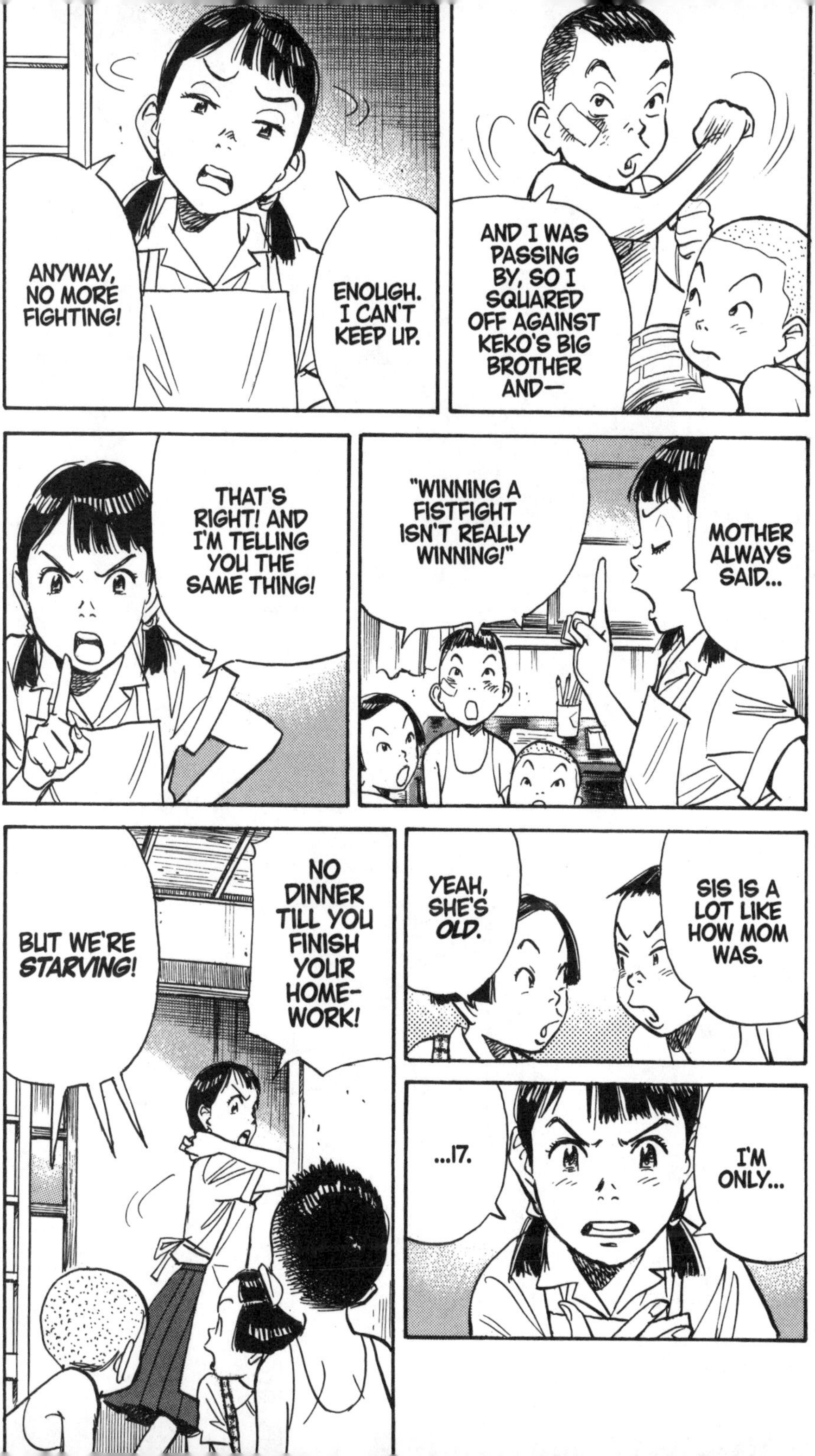
AND I WAS PASSING BY, SO I SQUARED OFF AGAINST KEKO'S BIG BROTHER AND—
ENOUGH. I CAN'T KEEP UP.
ANYWAY, NO MORE FIGHTING!
MOTHER ALWAYS SAID...
"WINNING A FISTFIGHT ISN'T REALLY WINNING!"
THAT'S RIGHT! AND I'M TELLING YOU THE SAME THING!
SIS IS A LOT LIKE HOW MOM WAS.
YEAH, SHE'S *OLD*.
I'M ONLY...
...17.
NO DINNER TILL YOU FINISH YOUR HOME-WORK!
BUT WE'RE *STARVING*!

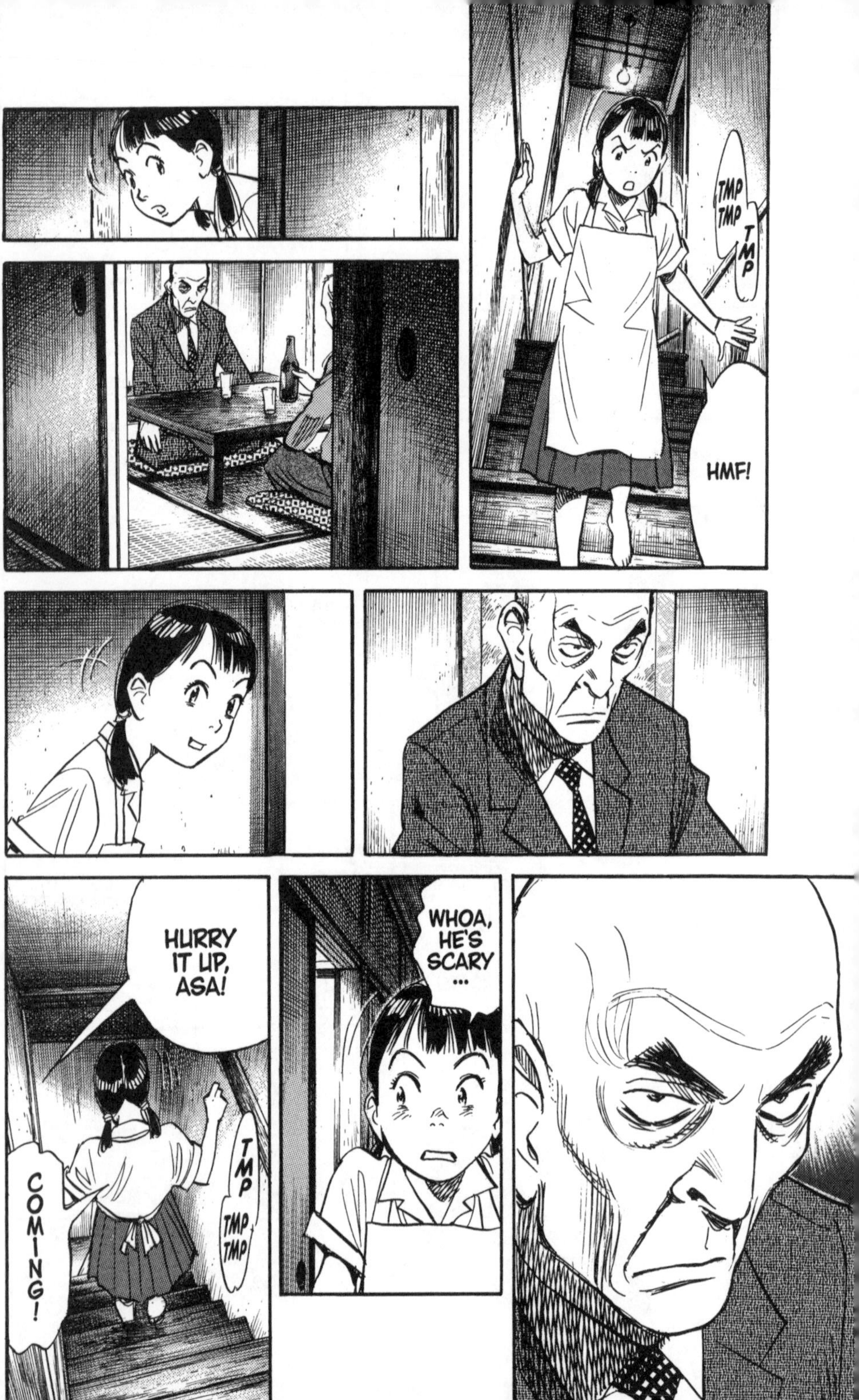
TMP TMP TMP
HMF!
WHOA, HE'S SCARY ...
HURRY IT UP, ASA!
TMP TMP TMP
COMING!

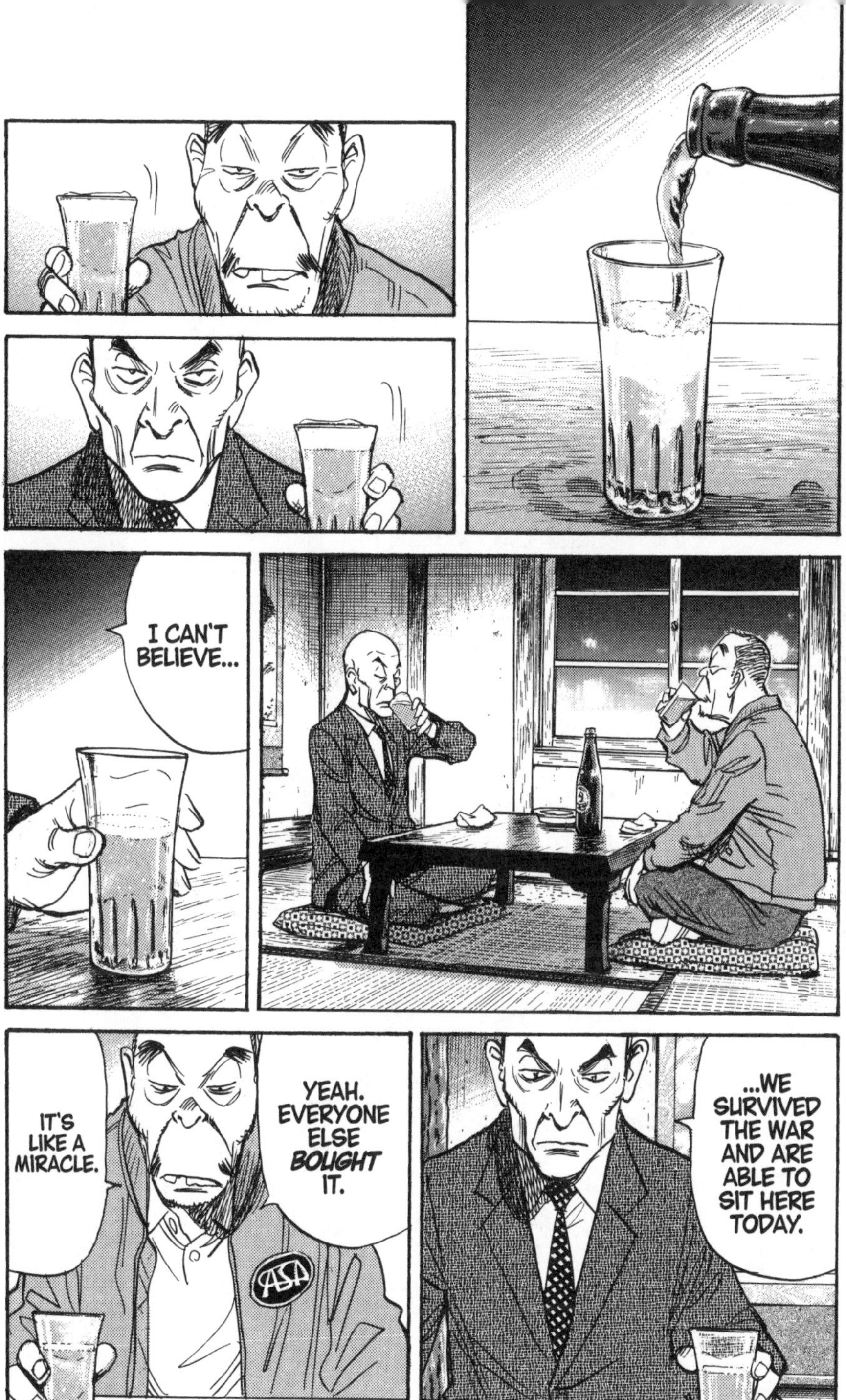
I CAN'T BELIEVE...
...WE SURVIVED THE WAR AND ARE ABLE TO SIT HERE TODAY.
YEAH. EVERYONE ELSE *BOUGHT* IT.
IT'S LIKE A MIRACLE.

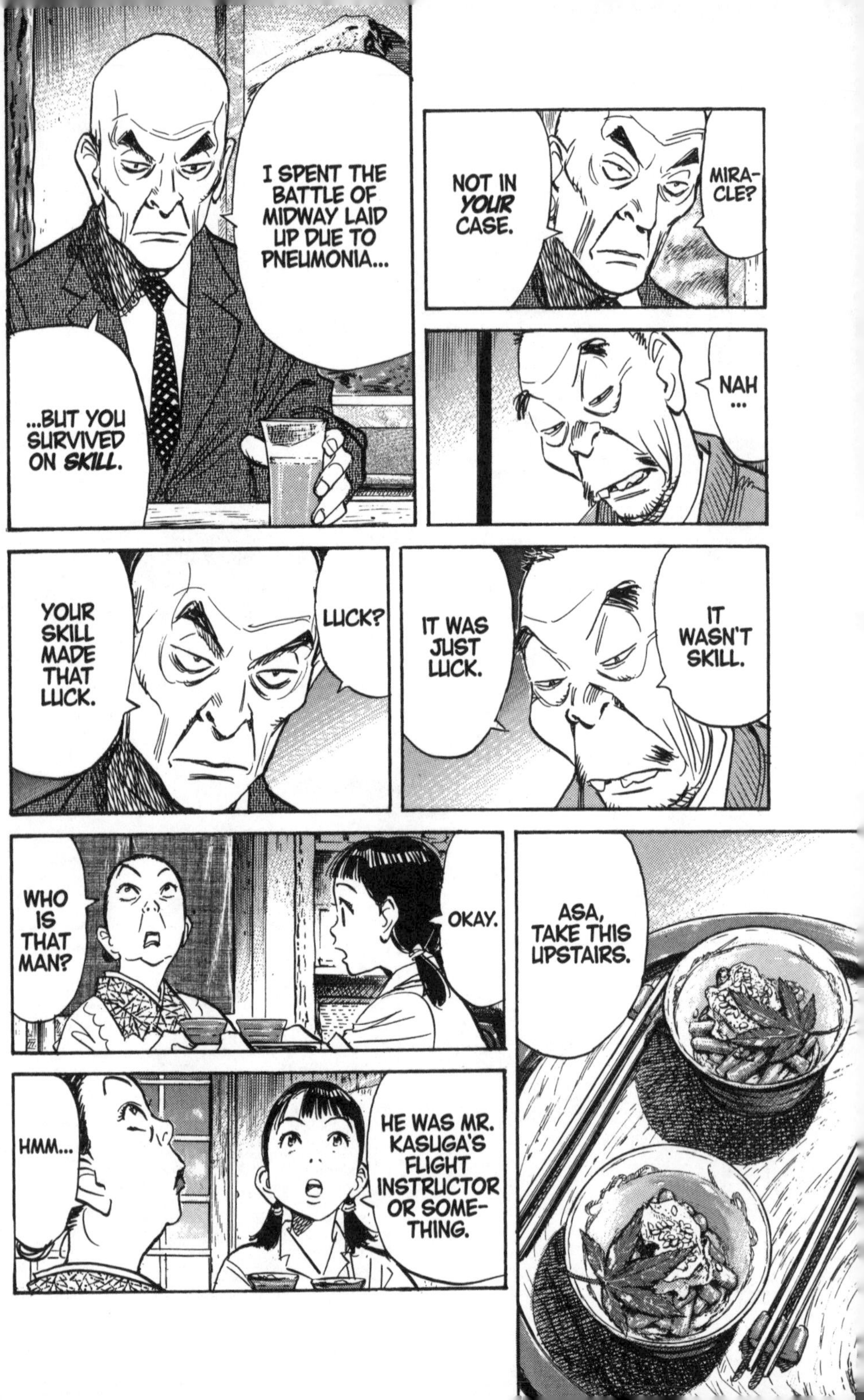
MIRA-CLE?
NOT IN *YOUR* CASE.
NAH ...
I SPENT THE BATTLE OF MIDWAY LAID UP DUE TO PNEUMONIA...
...BUT YOU SURVIVED ON *SKILL*.
IT WASN'T SKILL.
IT WAS JUST LUCK.
LUCK?
YOUR SKILL MADE THAT LUCK.
ASA, TAKE THIS UPSTAIRS.
OKAY.
WHO IS THAT MAN?
HE WAS MR. KASUGA'S FLIGHT INSTRUCTOR OR SOME-THING.
HMM...

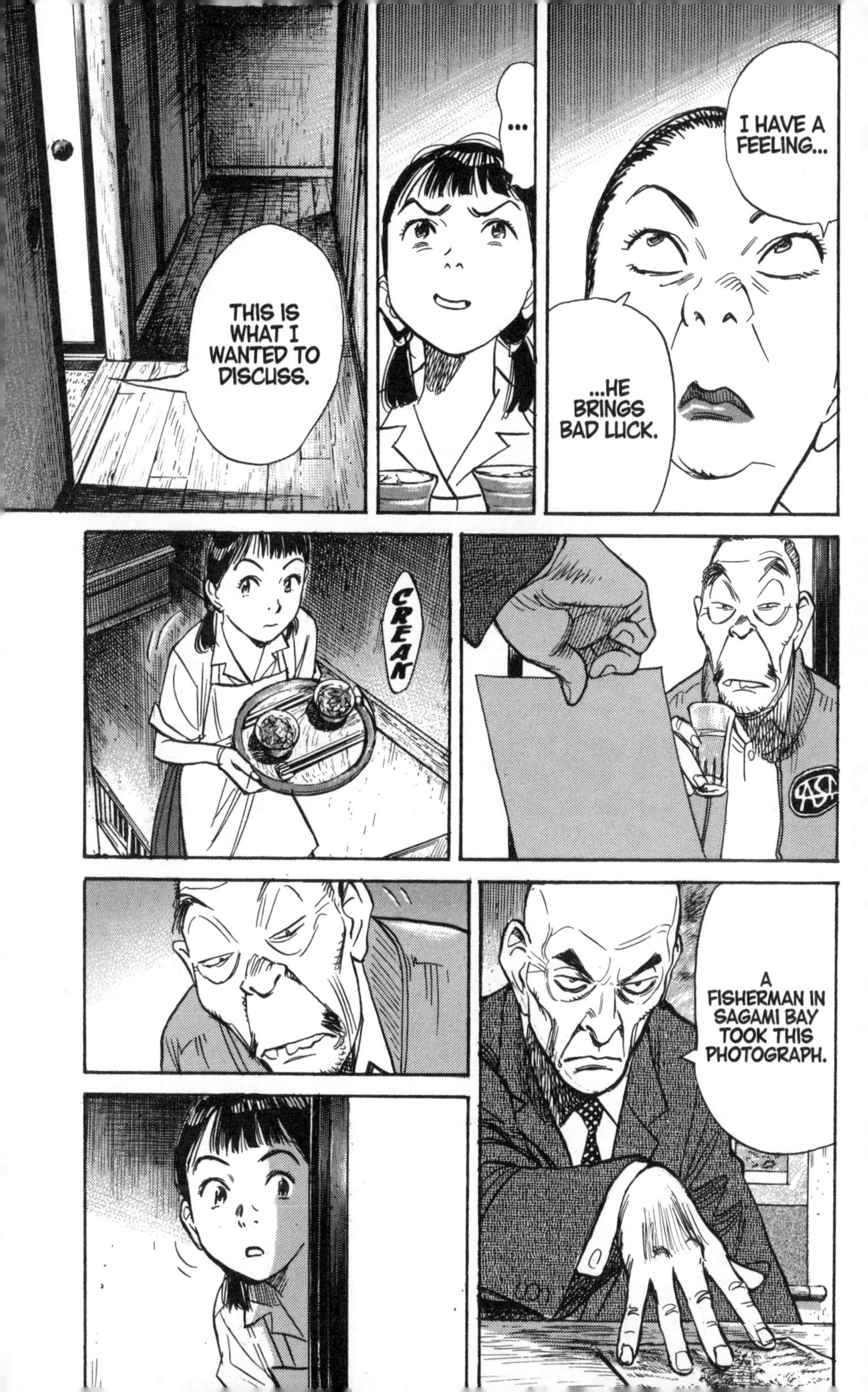
I HAVE A FEELING...
...HE BRINGS BAD LUCK.
...
THIS IS WHAT I WANTED TO DISCUSS.
CREAK
A FISHERMAN IN SAGAMI BAY TOOK THIS PHOTOGRAPH.

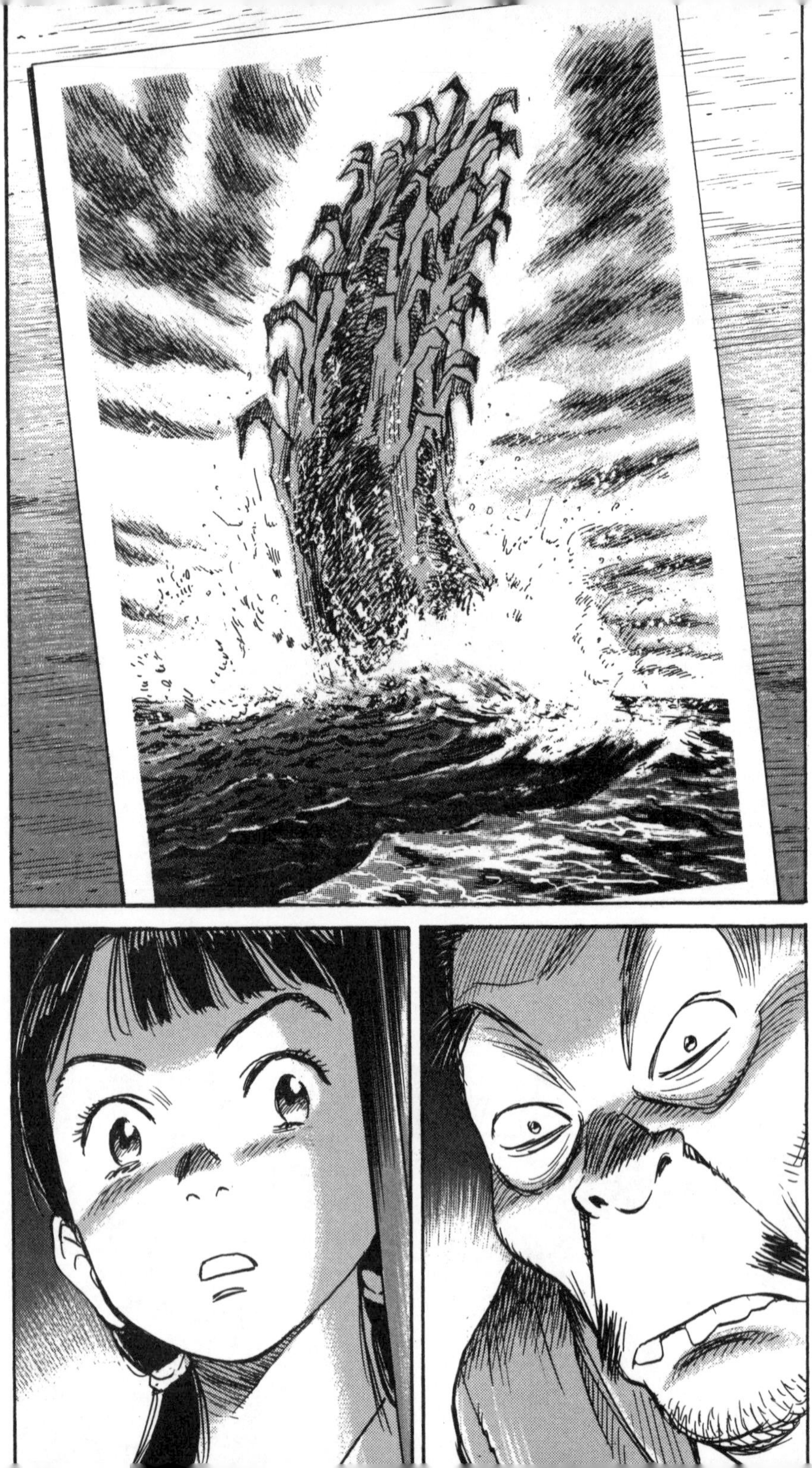

Chapter 16 ◉ Don't Turn Around

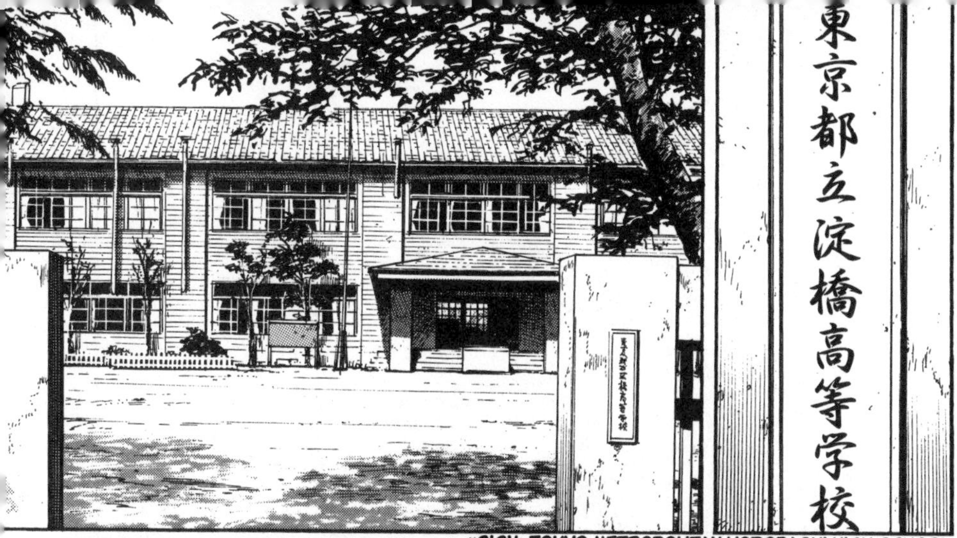
東京都立淀橋高等学校
*SIGN: TOKYO METROPOLITAN YODOBASHI HIGH SCHOOL

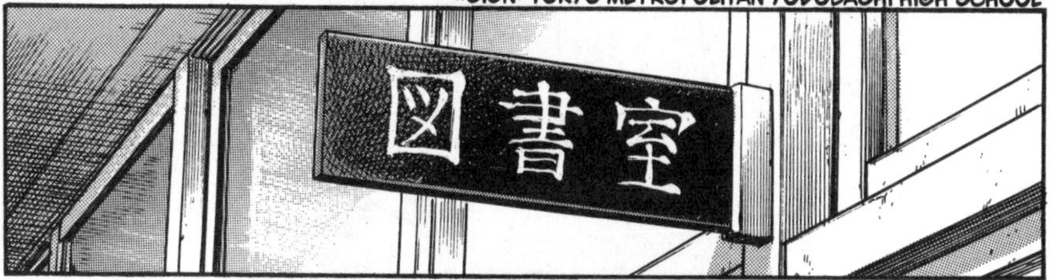
図書室
*SIGN: LIBRARY

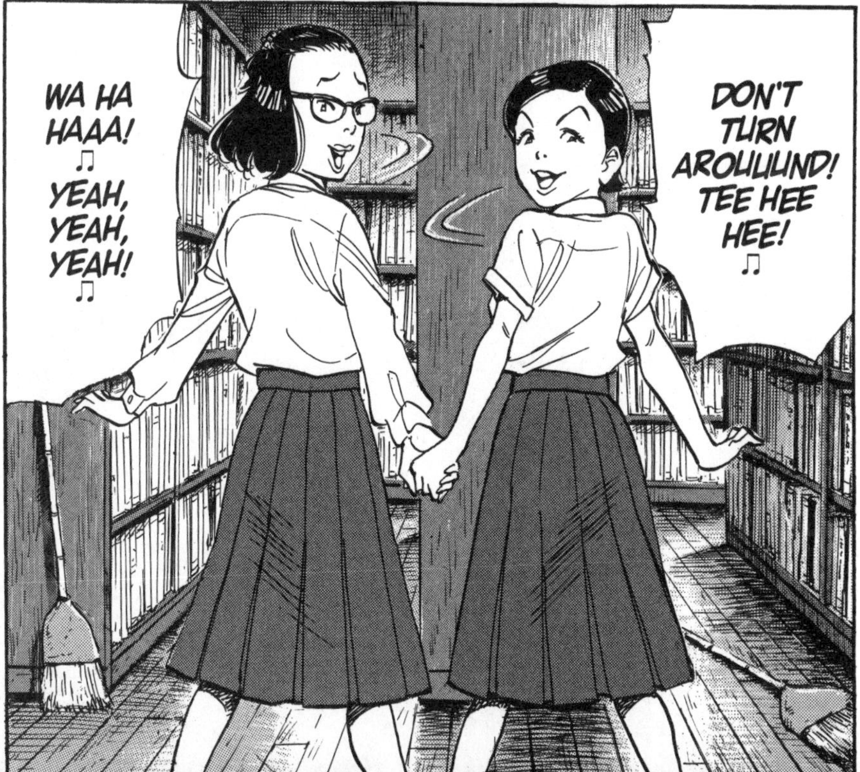
DON'T TURN AROUUUND! TEE HEE HEE! ♫
WA HA HAAA! ♫ YEAH, YEAH, YEAH! ♫

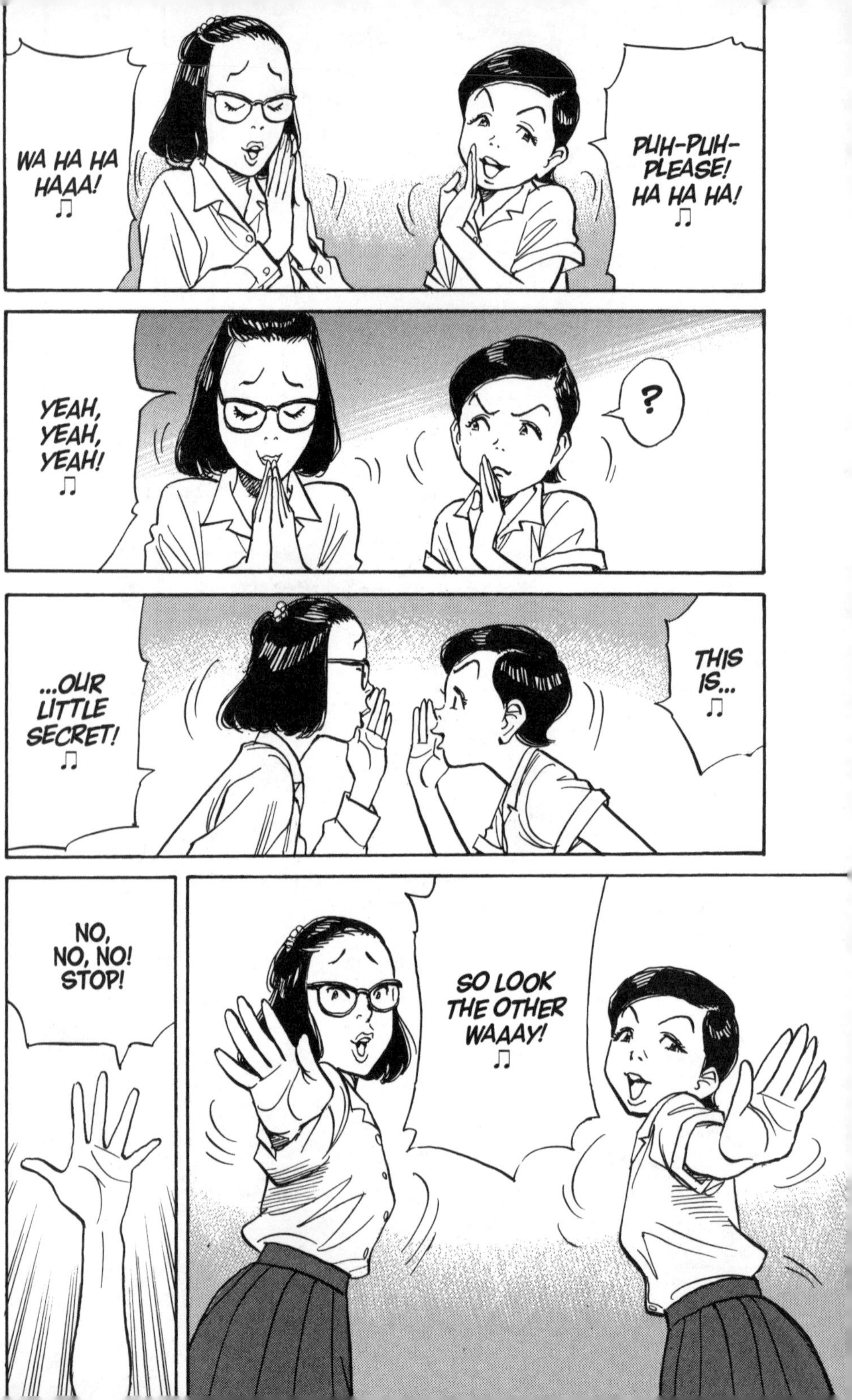
PUH-PUH-PLEASE! HA HA HA! ♫
WA HA HA HAAA! ♫
?
YEAH, YEAH, YEAH! ♫
THIS IS... ♫
...OUR LITTLE SECRET! ♫
SO LOOK THE OTHER WAAAY! ♫
NO, NO, NO! STOP!

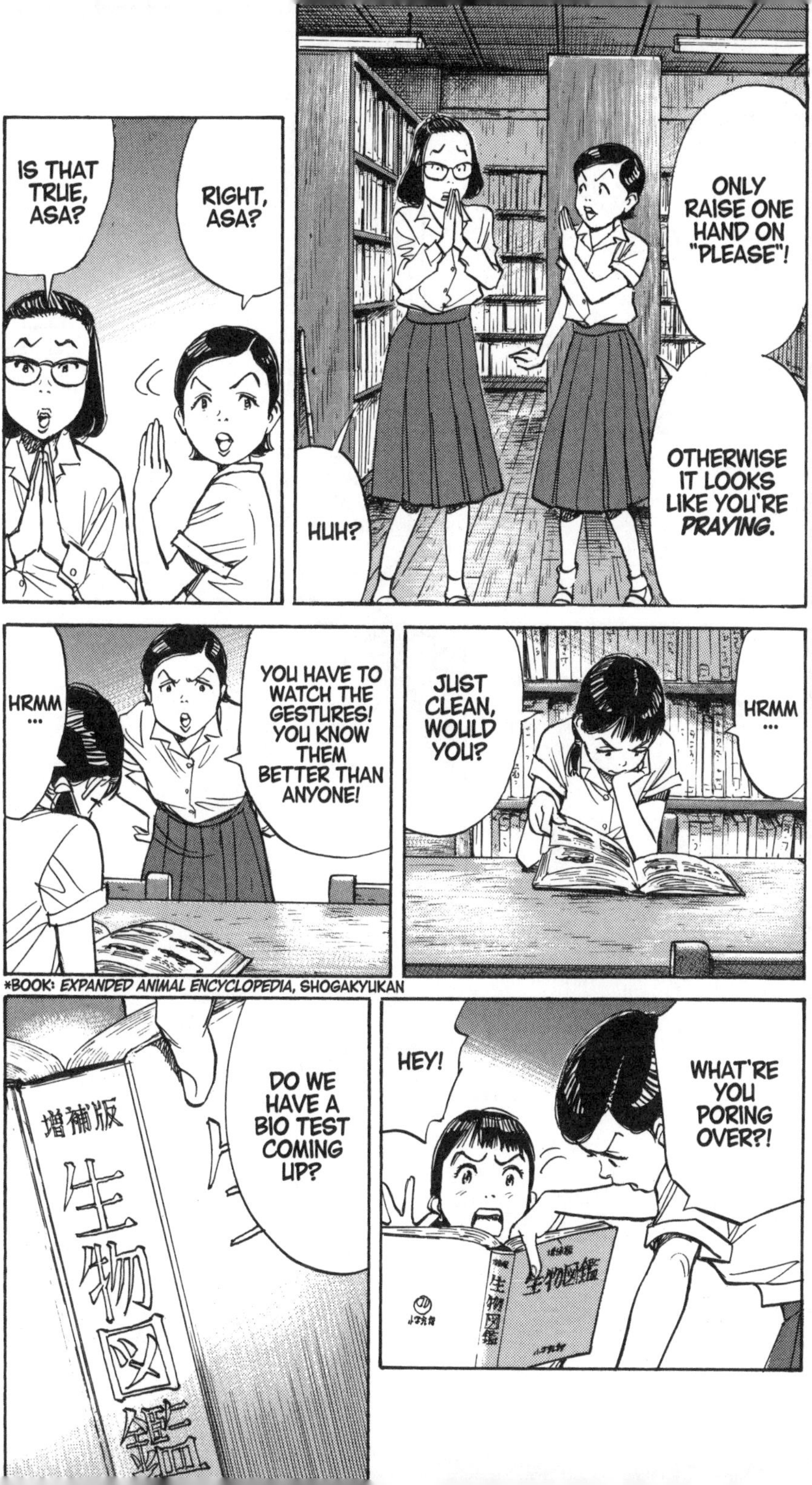
ONLY RAISE ONE HAND ON "PLEASE"!
OTHERWISE IT LOOKS LIKE YOU'RE *PRAYING*.
HUH?
RIGHT, ASA?
IS THAT TRUE, ASA?
HRMM ...
JUST CLEAN, WOULD YOU?
YOU HAVE TO WATCH THE GESTURES! YOU KNOW THEM BETTER THAN ANYONE!
HRMM ...
WHAT'RE YOU PORING OVER?!
HEY!
生物図鑑
DO WE HAVE A BIO TEST COMING UP?
増補版
生物図鑑

*BOOK: *EXPANDED ANIMAL ENCYCLOPEDIA*, SHOGAKUKAN

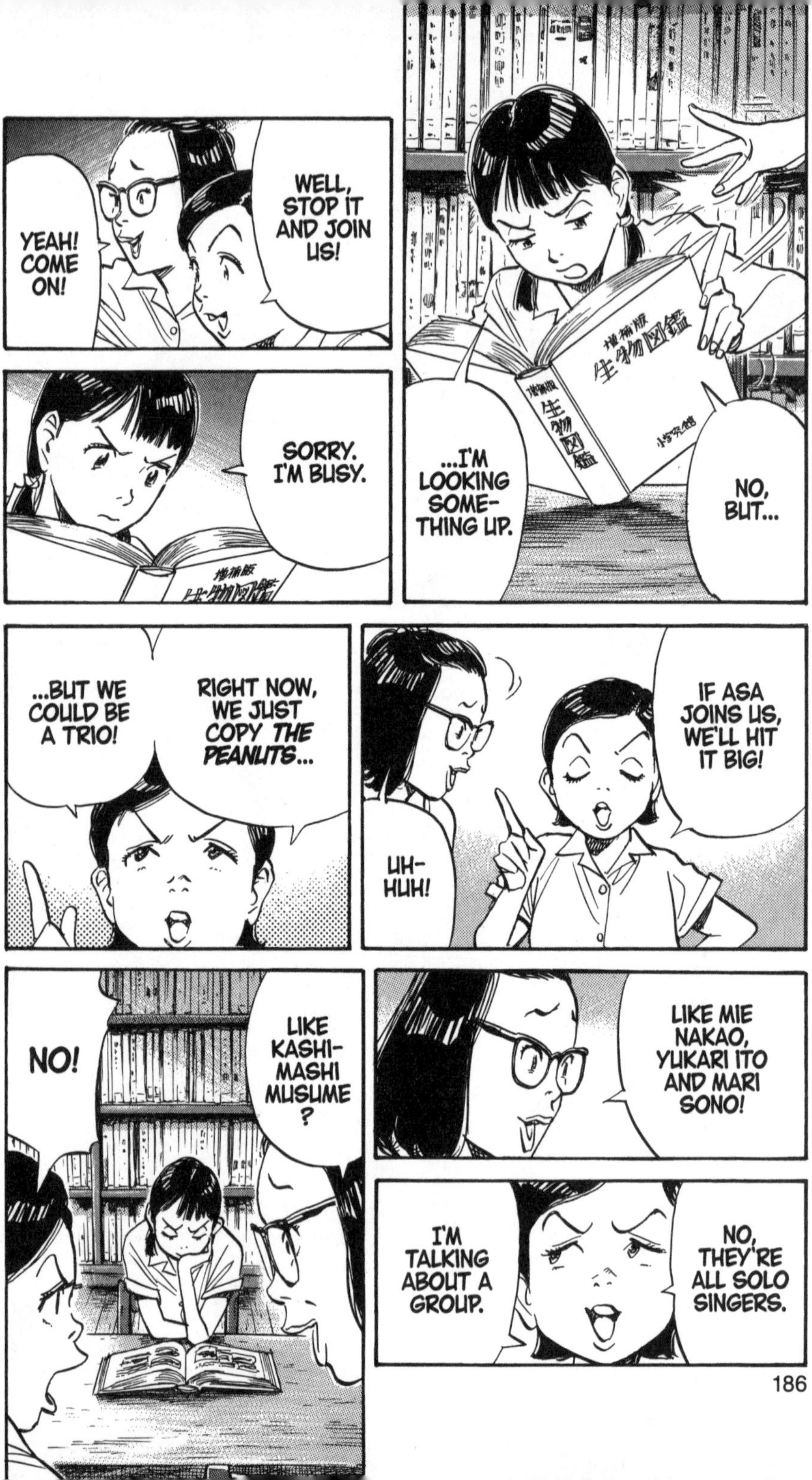
増補版 生物図鑑
小学館
NO, BUT...
...I'M LOOKING SOME-THING UP.
WELL, STOP IT AND JOIN US!
YEAH! COME ON!
SORRY. I'M BUSY.
IF ASA JOINS US, WE'LL HIT IT BIG!
UH-HUH!
RIGHT NOW, WE JUST COPY *THE PEANUTS*...
...BUT WE COULD BE A TRIO!
LIKE MIE NAKAO, YUKARI ITO AND MARI SONO!
NO, THEY'RE ALL SOLO SINGERS.
I'M TALKING ABOUT A GROUP.
LIKE KASHI-MASHI MUSUME?
NO!

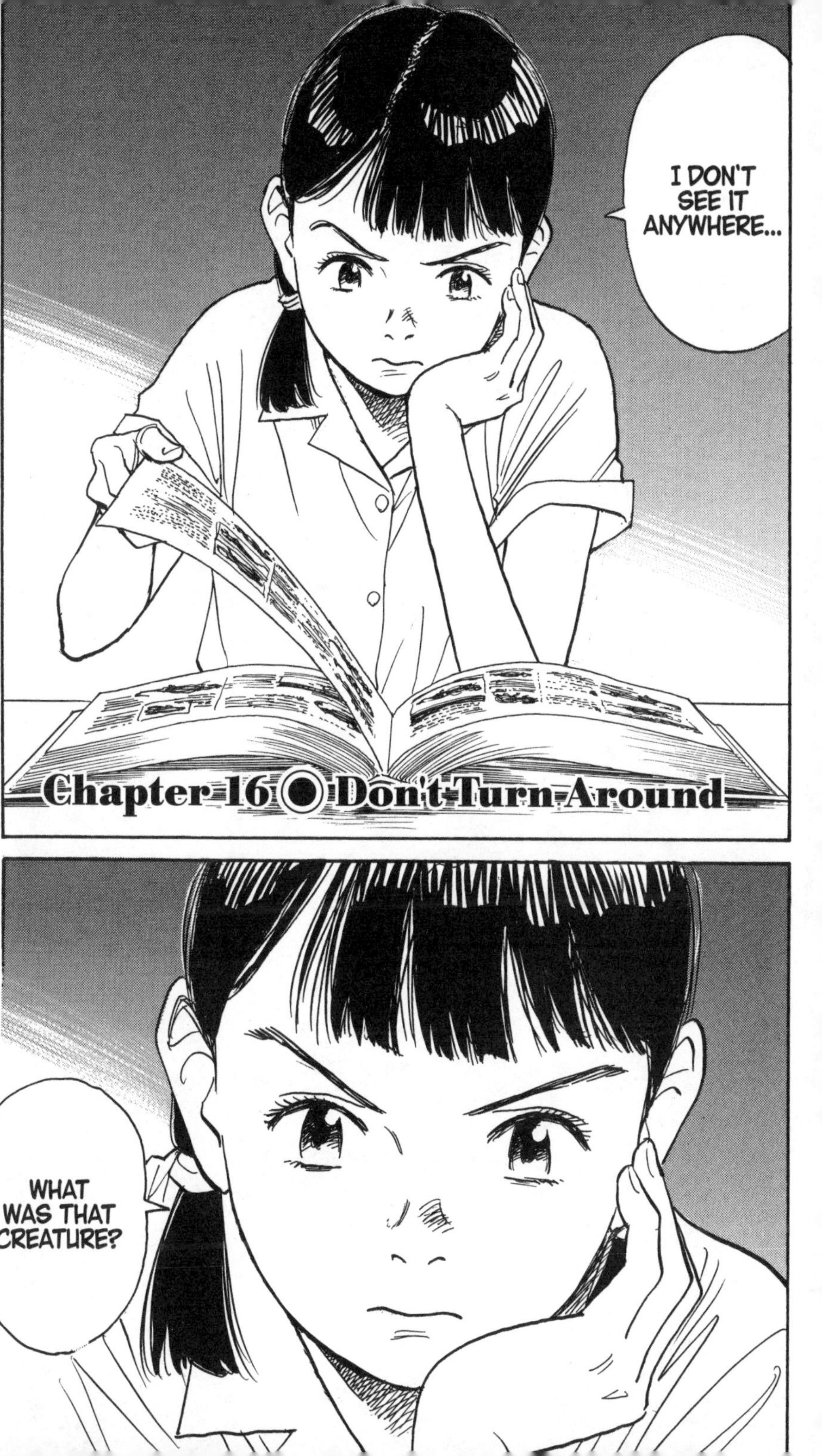
I DON'T SEE IT ANYWHERE...
Chapter 16 ● Don't Turn Around
WHAT WAS THAT CREATURE?

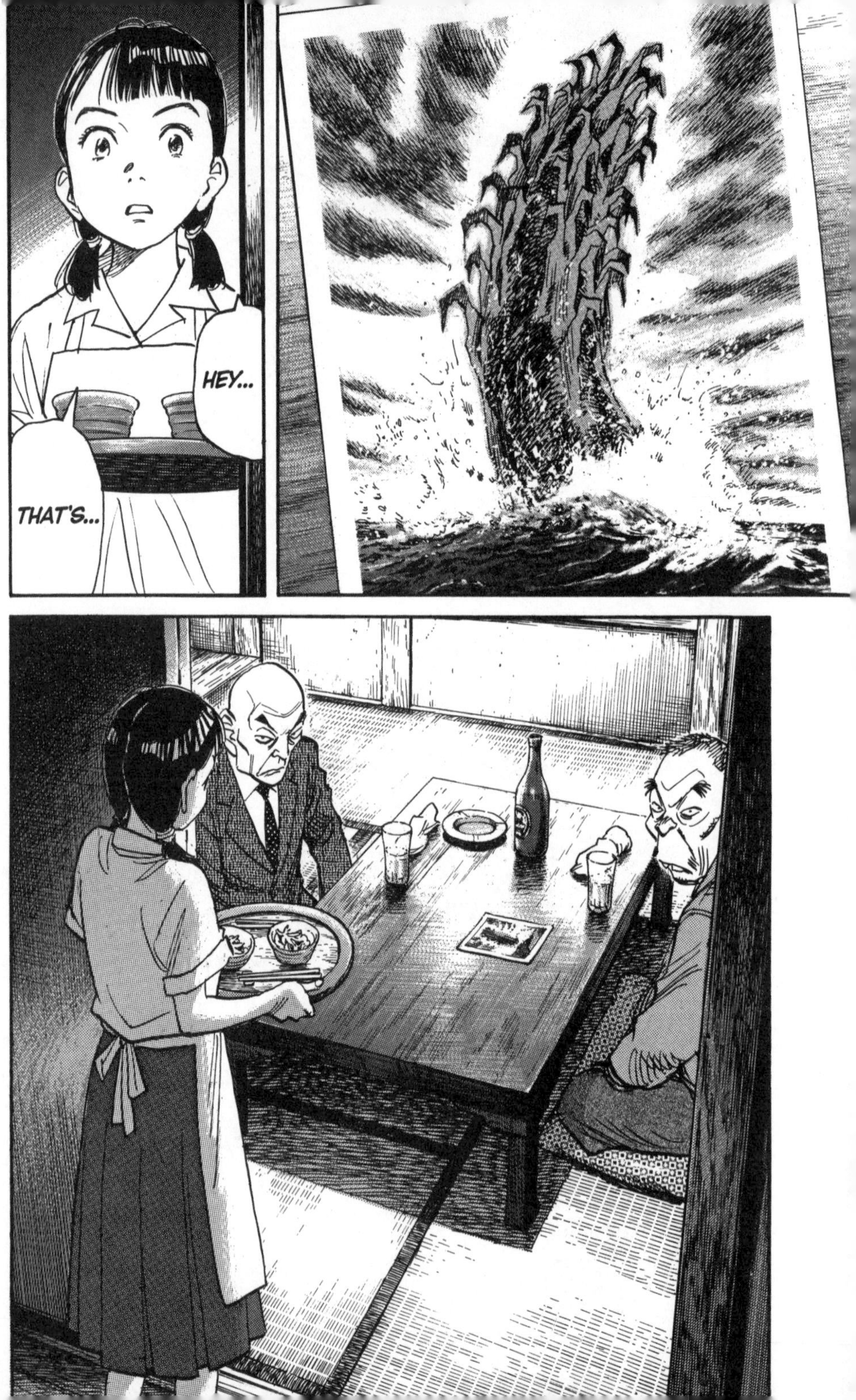
HEY...
THAT'S...

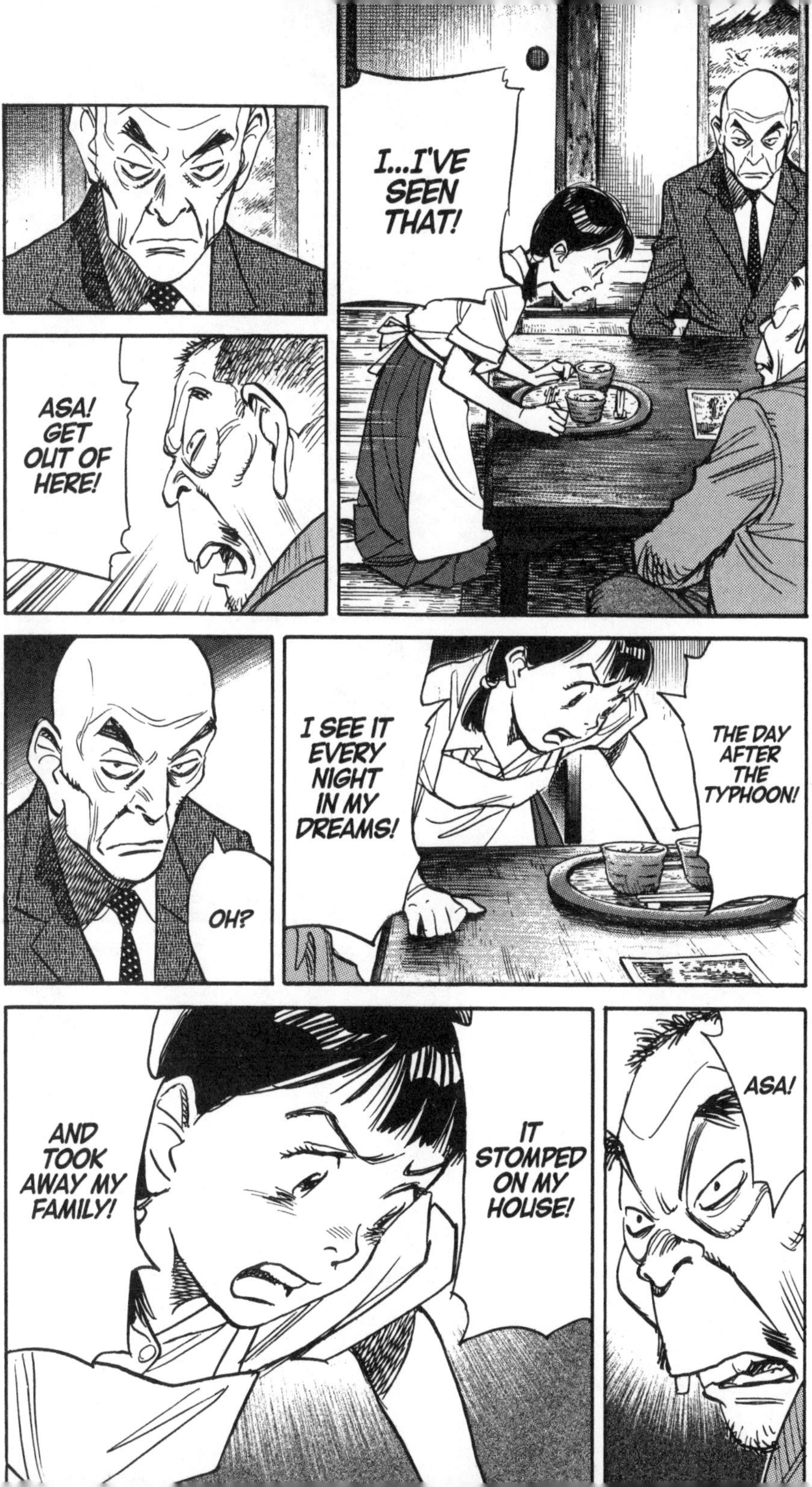

I...I'VE SEEN THAT!
ASA! GET OUT OF HERE!
THE DAY AFTER THE TYPHOON!
I SEE IT EVERY NIGHT IN MY DREAMS!
OH?
ASA!
IT STOMPED ON MY HOUSE!
AND TOOK AWAY MY FAMILY!

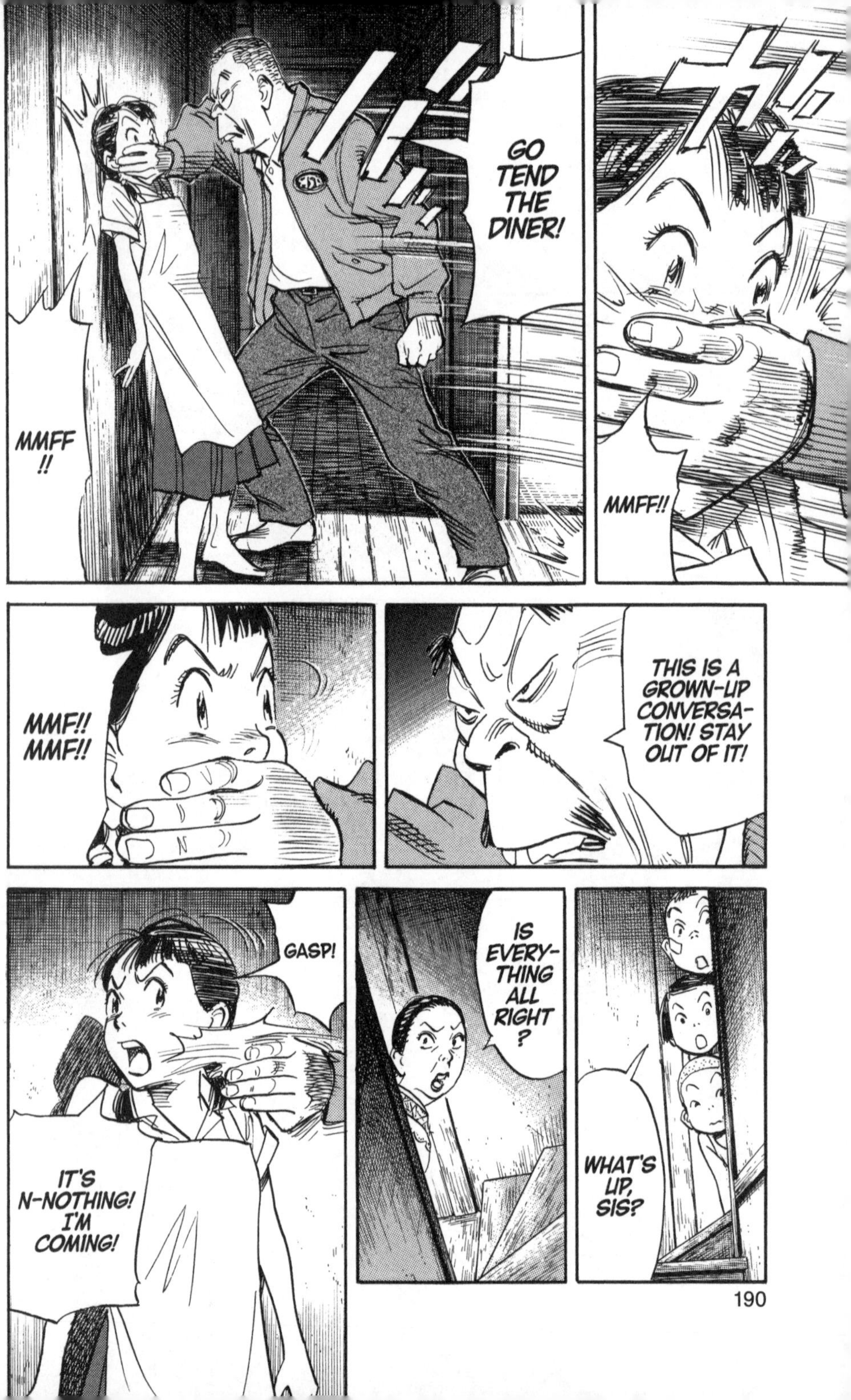
MMFF!!
GO TEND THE DINER!
MMFF !!
THIS IS A GROWN-UP CONVERSA-TION! STAY OUT OF IT!
MMF!! MMF!!
WHAT'S UP, SIS?
IS EVERY-THING ALL RIGHT?
GASP!
IT'S N-NOTHING! I'M COMING!

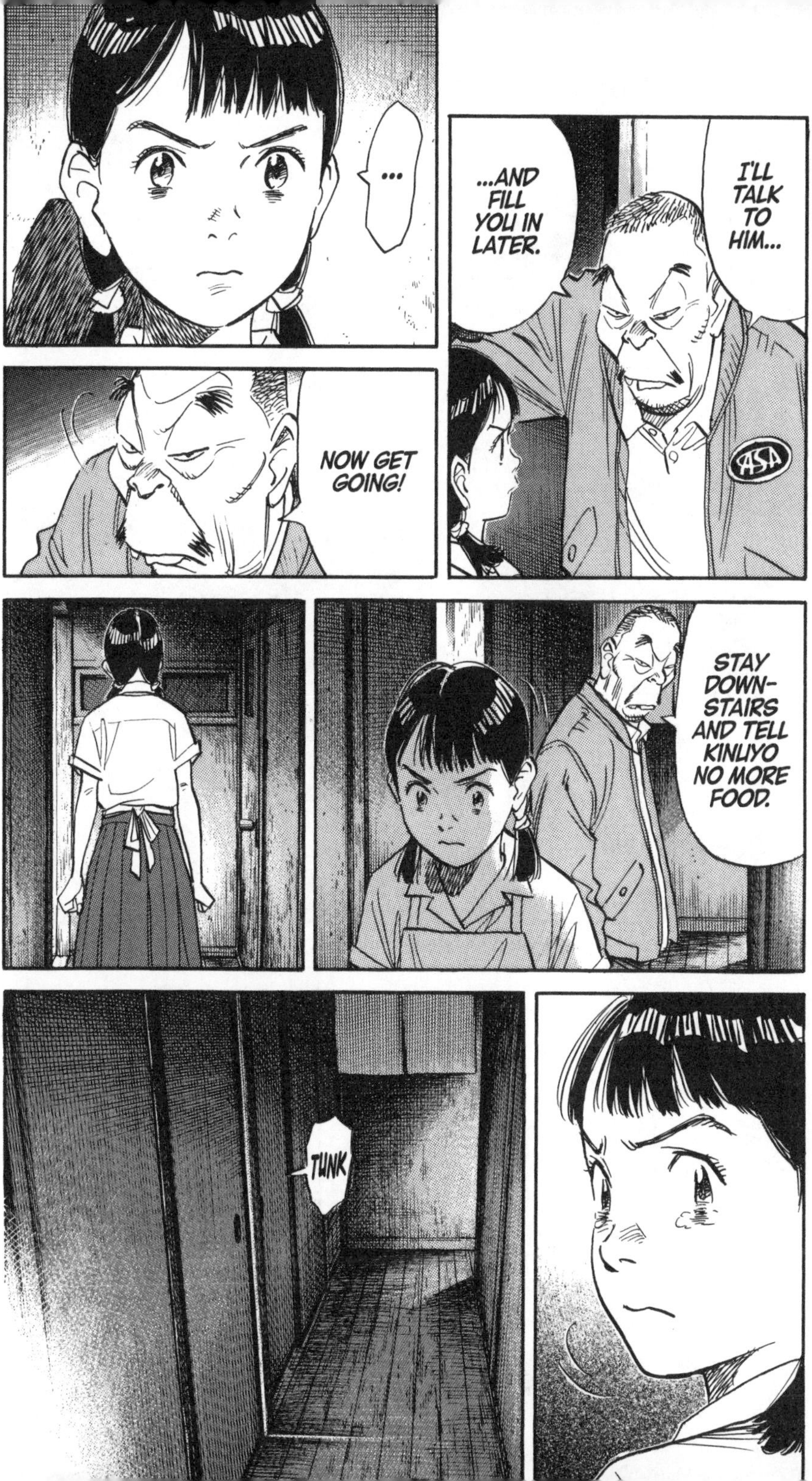
I'LL TALK TO HIM...
...AND FILL YOU IN LATER.
...
NOW GET GOING!
STAY DOWN-STAIRS AND TELL KINUYO NO MORE FOOD.
TUNK

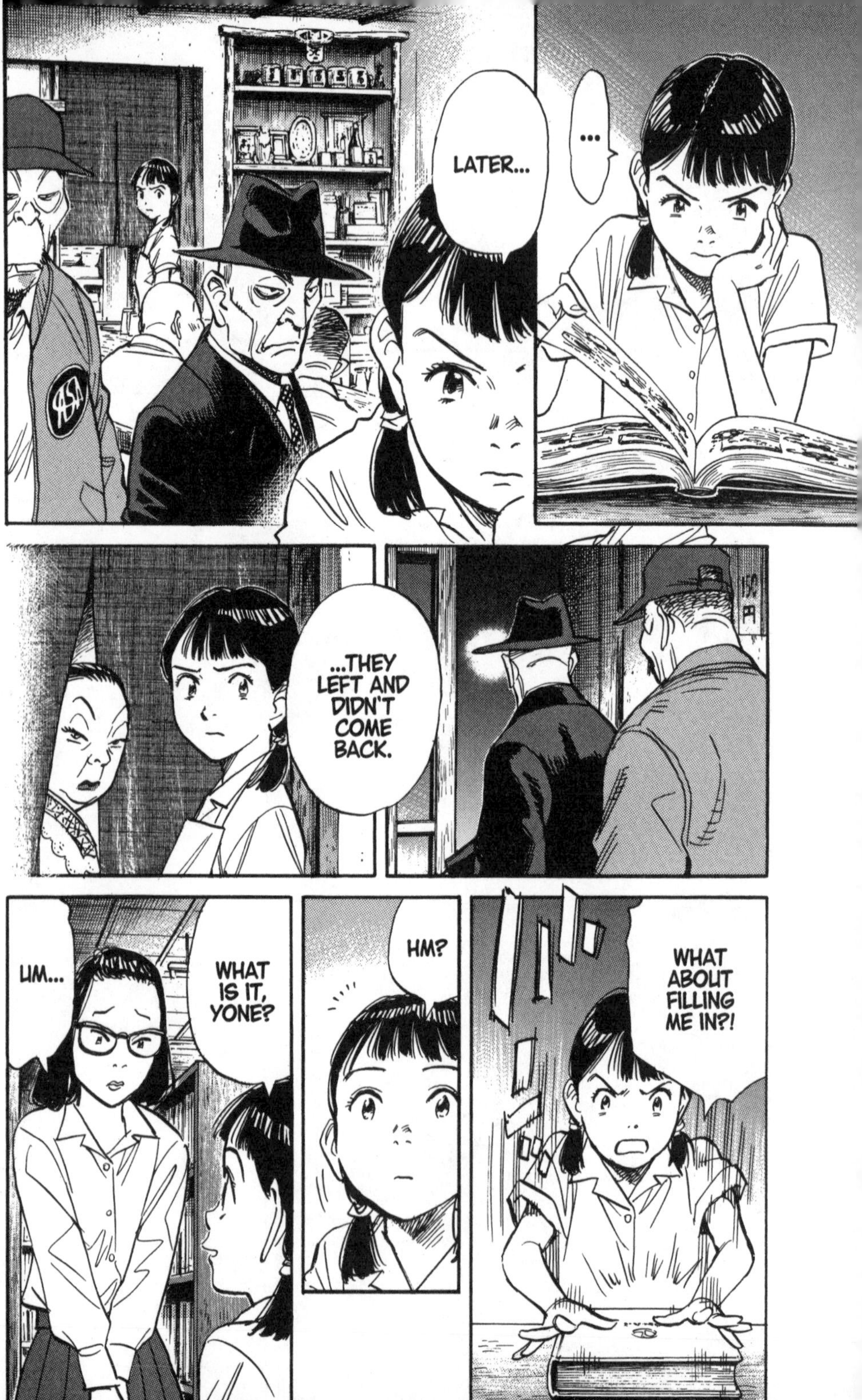
...
LATER...
150円
...THEY LEFT AND DIDN'T COME BACK.
WHAT ABOUT FILLING ME IN?!
HM?
WHAT IS IT, YONE?
UM...

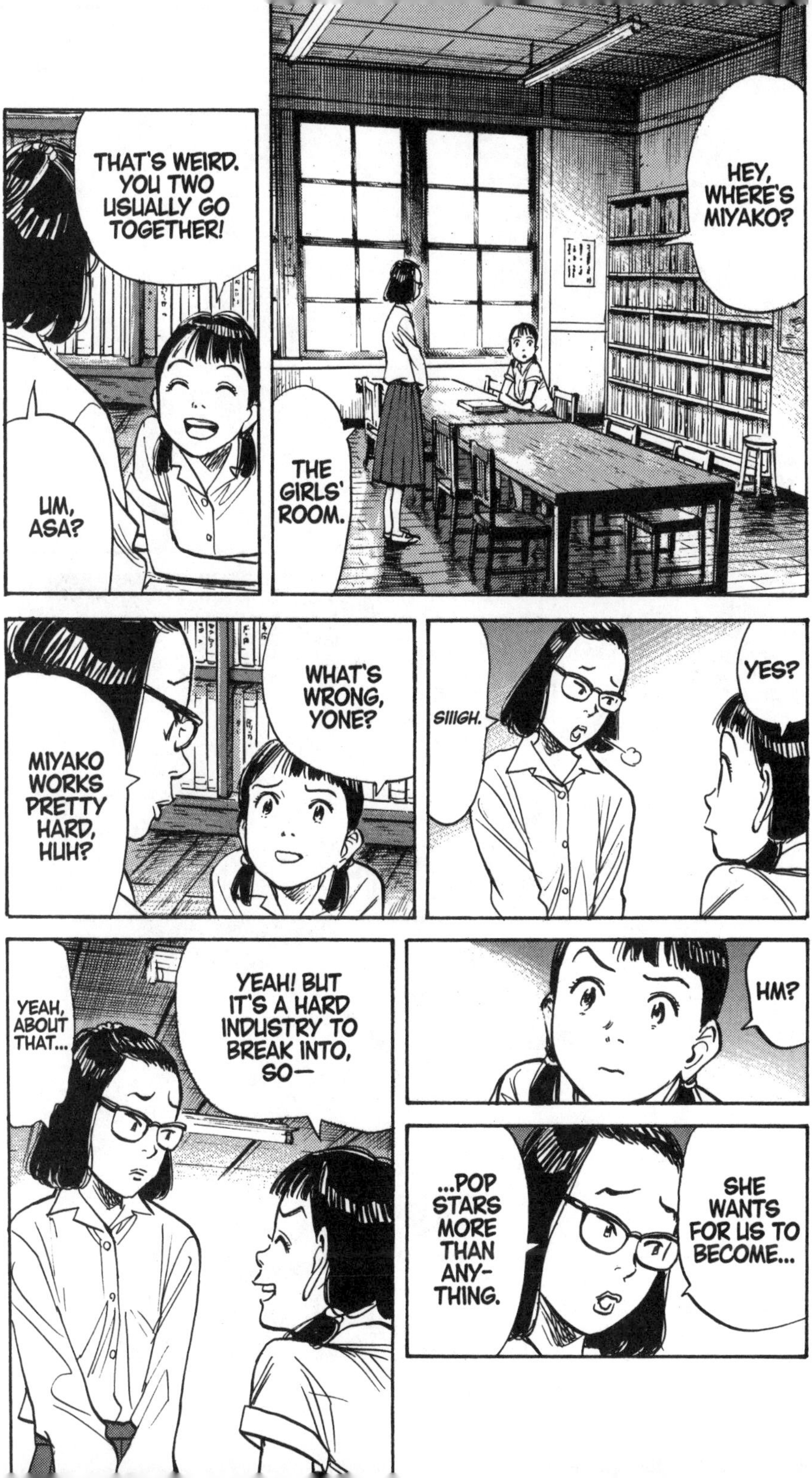
HEY, WHERE'S MIYAKO?
THE GIRLS' ROOM.
THAT'S WEIRD. YOU TWO USUALLY GO TOGETHER!
UM, ASA?
YES?
SIIIGH.
WHAT'S WRONG, YONE?
MIYAKO WORKS PRETTY HARD, HUH?
HM?
SHE WANTS FOR US TO BECOME...
...POP STARS MORE THAN ANY-THING.
YEAH! BUT IT'S A HARD INDUSTRY TO BREAK INTO, SO—
YEAH, ABOUT THAT...

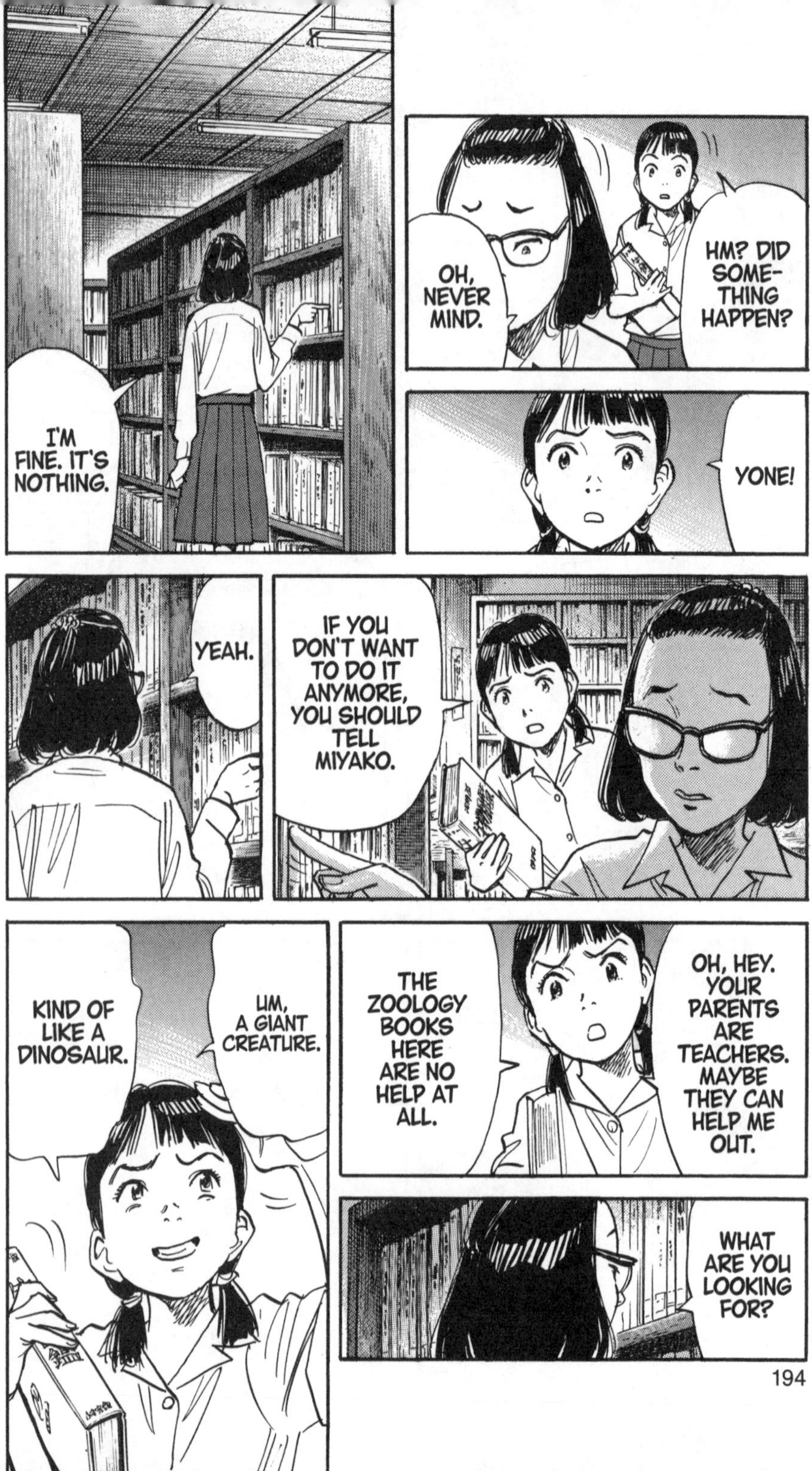
HM? DID SOMETHING HAPPEN?
OH, NEVER MIND.
YONE!
I'M FINE. IT'S NOTHING.
IF YOU DON'T WANT TO DO IT ANYMORE, YOU SHOULD TELL MIYAKO.
YEAH.
OH, HEY. YOUR PARENTS ARE TEACHERS. MAYBE THEY CAN HELP ME OUT.
THE ZOOLOGY BOOKS HERE ARE NO HELP AT ALL.
WHAT ARE YOU LOOKING FOR?
UM, A GIANT CREATURE.
KIND OF LIKE A DINOSAUR.

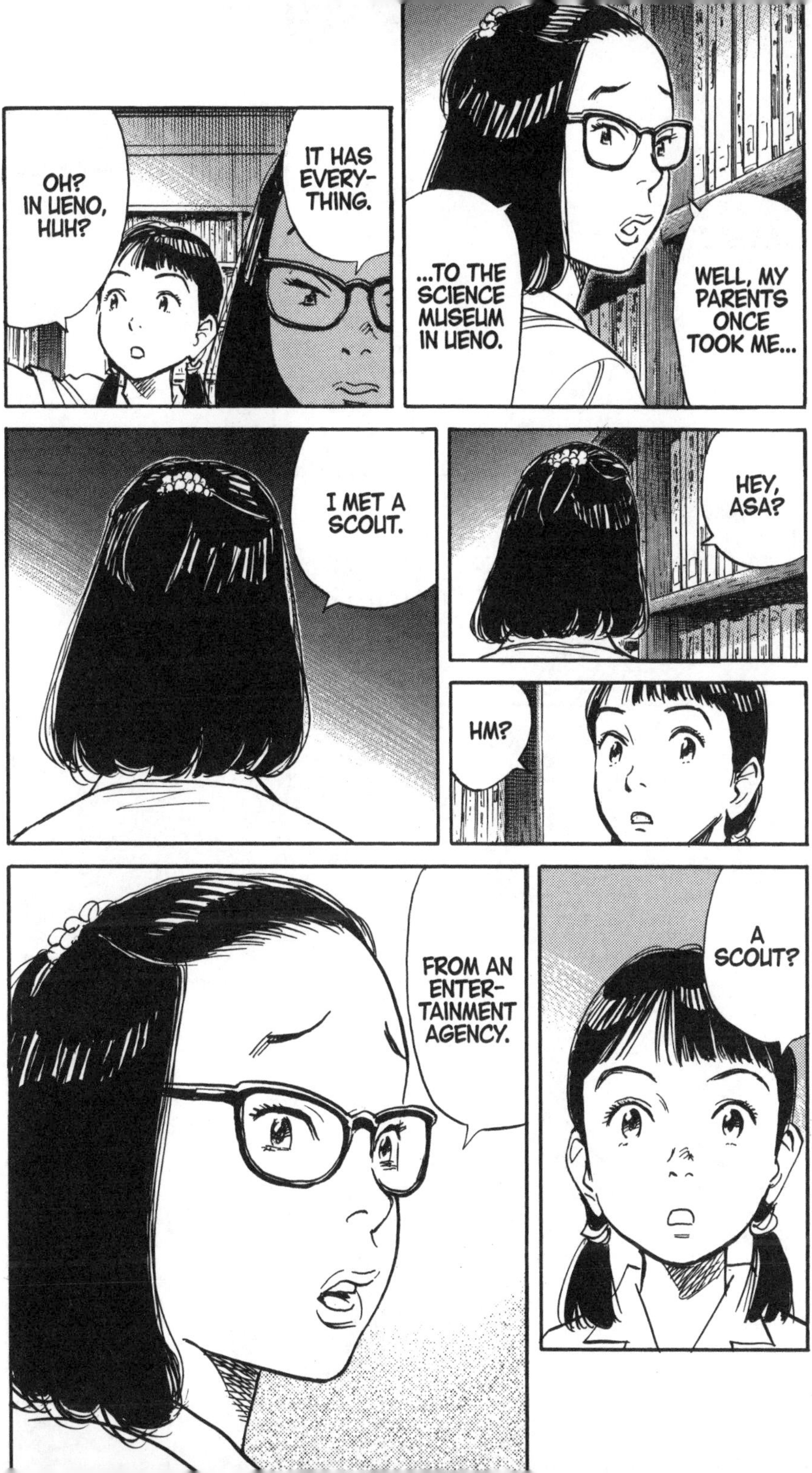
WELL, MY PARENTS ONCE TOOK ME...
...TO THE SCIENCE MUSEUM IN UENO.
IT HAS EVERY-THING.
OH? IN UENO, HUH?
HEY, ASA?
HM?
I MET A SCOUT.
A SCOUT?
FROM AN ENTER-TAINMENT AGENCY.

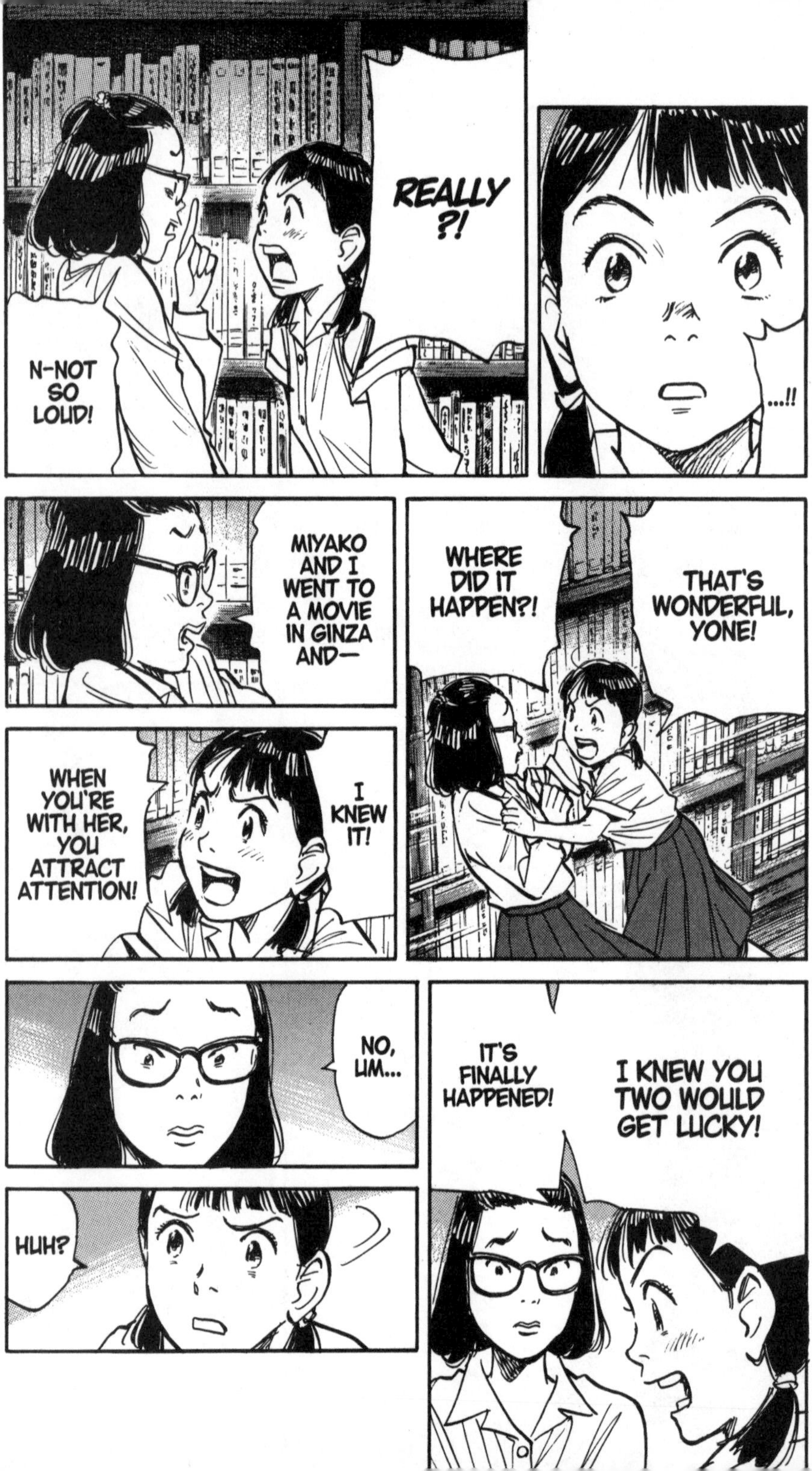
...!!
REALLY ?!
N-NOT SO LOUD!
THAT'S WONDERFUL, YONE!
WHERE DID IT HAPPEN?!
MIYAKO AND I WENT TO A MOVIE IN GINZA AND—
I KNEW IT!
WHEN YOU'RE WITH HER, YOU ATTRACT ATTENTION!
I KNEW YOU TWO WOULD GET LUCKY!
IT'S FINALLY HAPPENED!
NO, UM...
HUH?

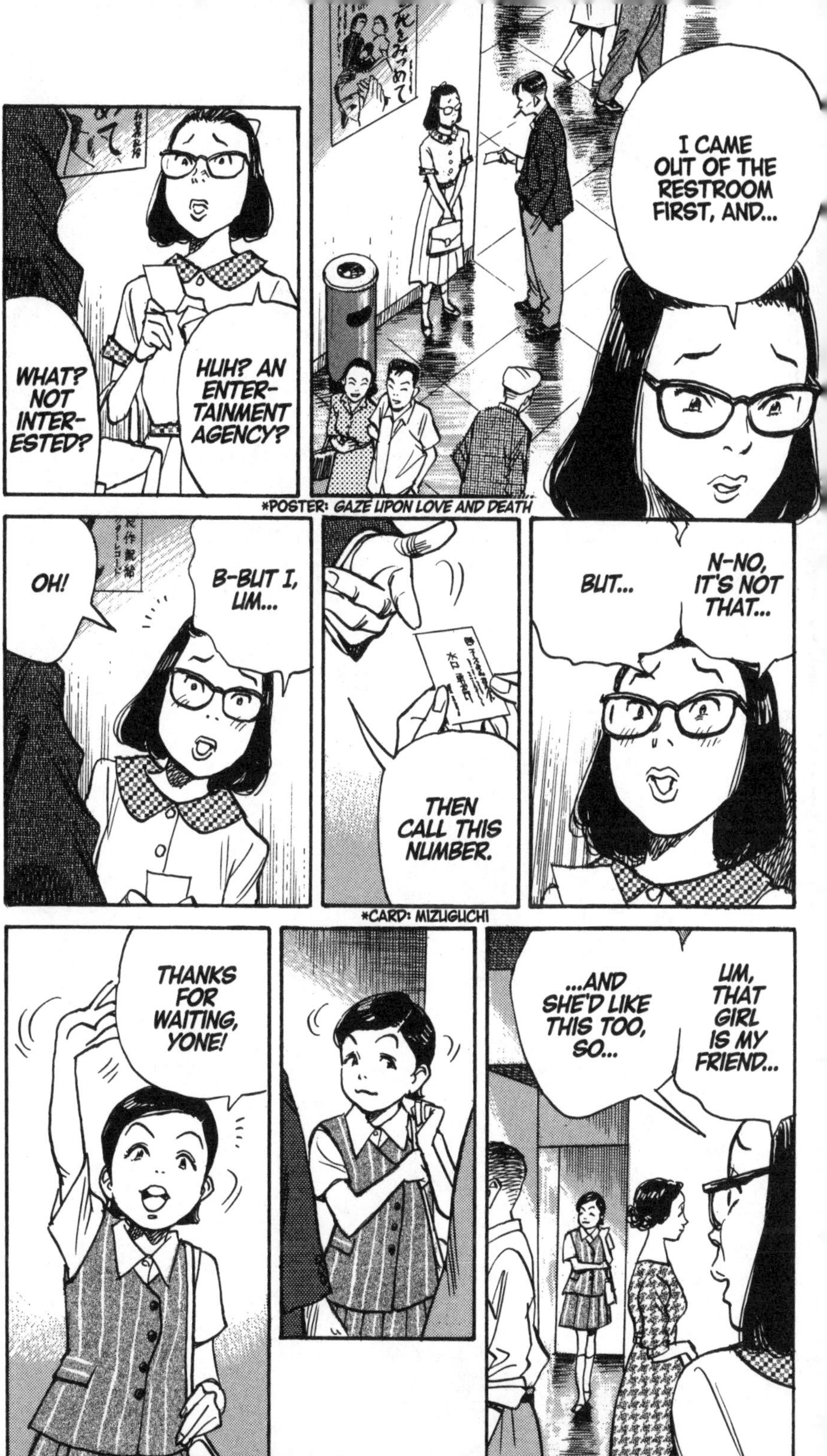
I CAME OUT OF THE RESTROOM FIRST, AND...
HUH? AN ENTERTAINMENT AGENCY?
WHAT? NOT INTERESTED?
*POSTER: GAZE UPON LOVE AND DEATH
N-NO, IT'S NOT THAT...
BUT...
THEN CALL THIS NUMBER.
B-BUT I, UM...
OH!
*CARD: MIZUGUCHI
UM, THAT GIRL IS MY FRIEND...
...AND SHE'D LIKE THIS TOO, SO...
THANKS FOR WAITING, YONE!

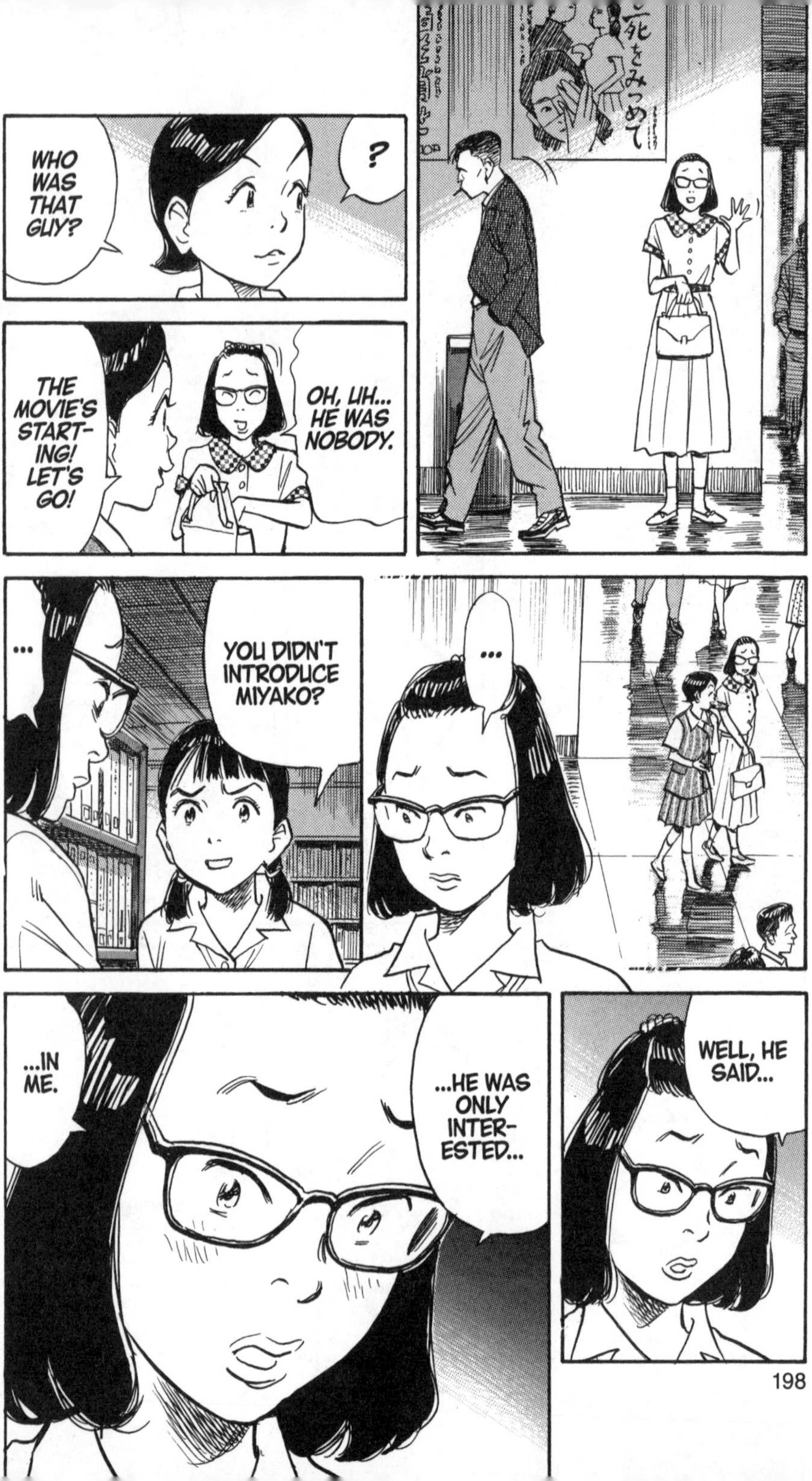
死をみつめて
?
WHO WAS THAT GUY?
OH, UH... HE WAS NOBODY.
THE MOVIE'S START-ING! LET'S GO!
...
YOU DIDN'T INTRODUCE MIYAKO?
...
WELL, HE SAID...
...HE WAS ONLY INTER-ESTED...
...IN ME.

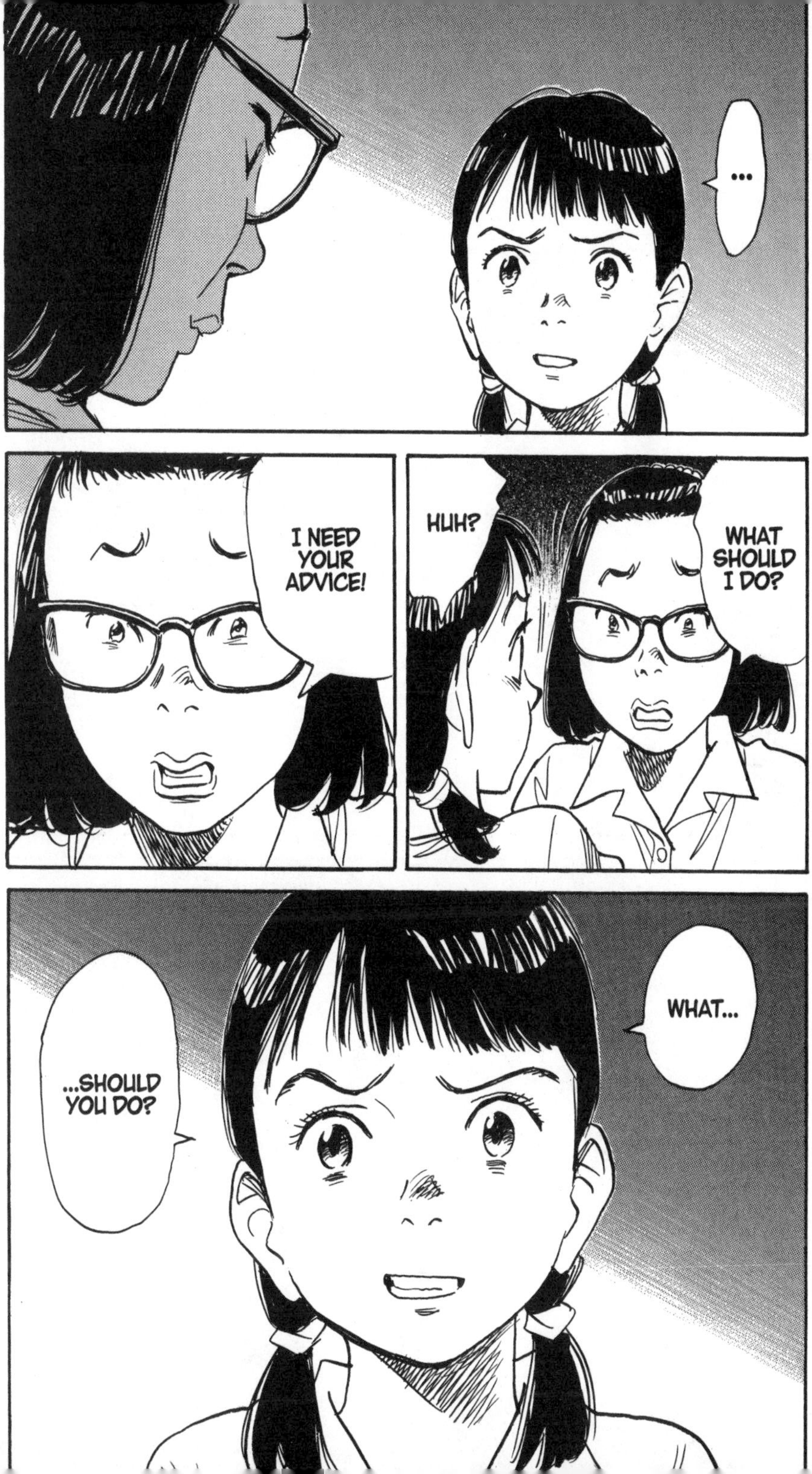
...
WHAT SHOULD I DO?
HUH?
I NEED YOUR ADVICE!
WHAT...
...SHOULD YOU DO?

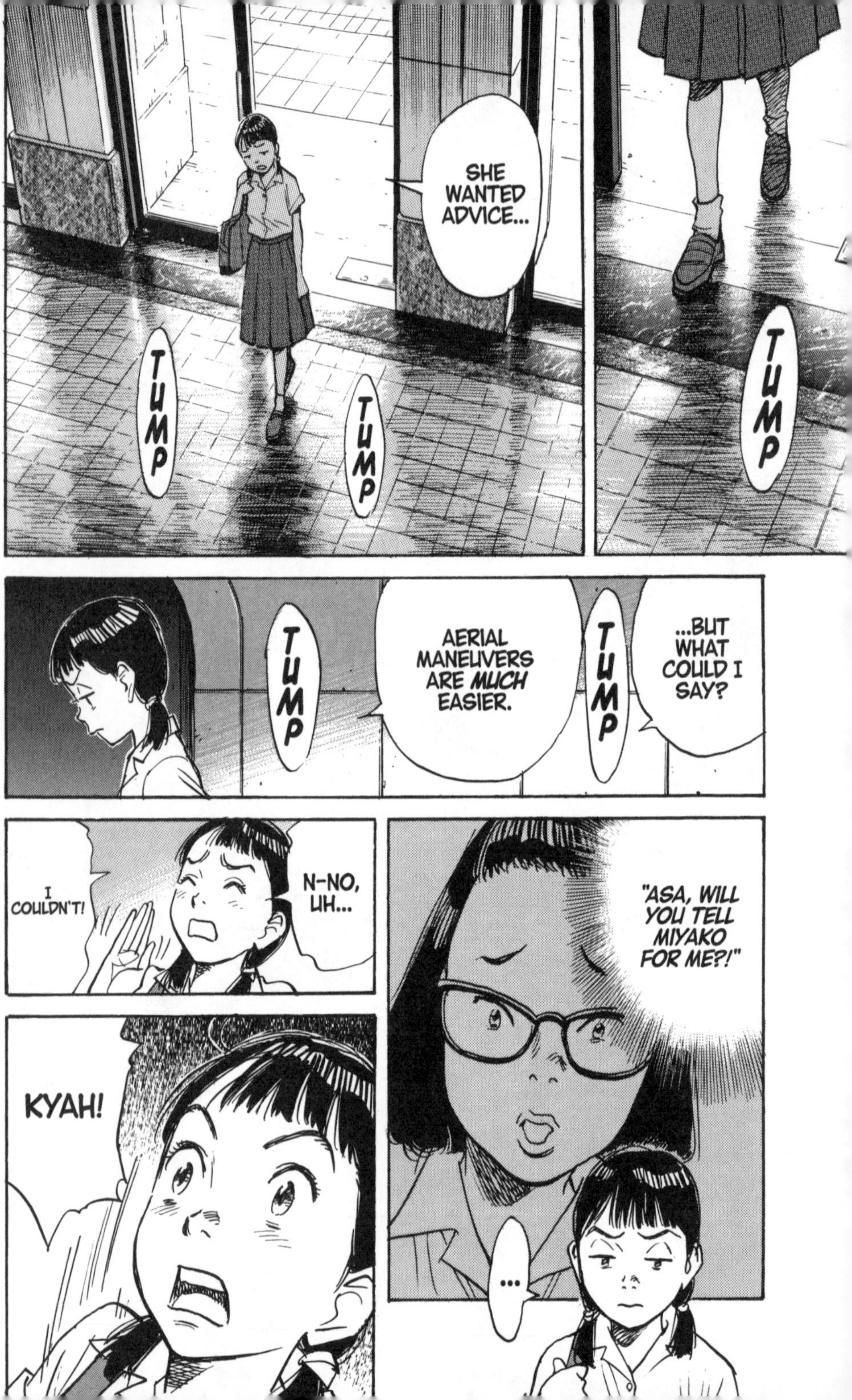
TUMP
SHE WANTED ADVICE...
TUMP
TUMP
...BUT WHAT COULD I SAY?
TUMP
AERIAL MANEUVERS ARE MUCH EASIER.
TUMP
"ASA, WILL YOU TELL MIYAKO FOR ME?!"
...
N-NO, UH...
I COULDN'T!
KYAH!

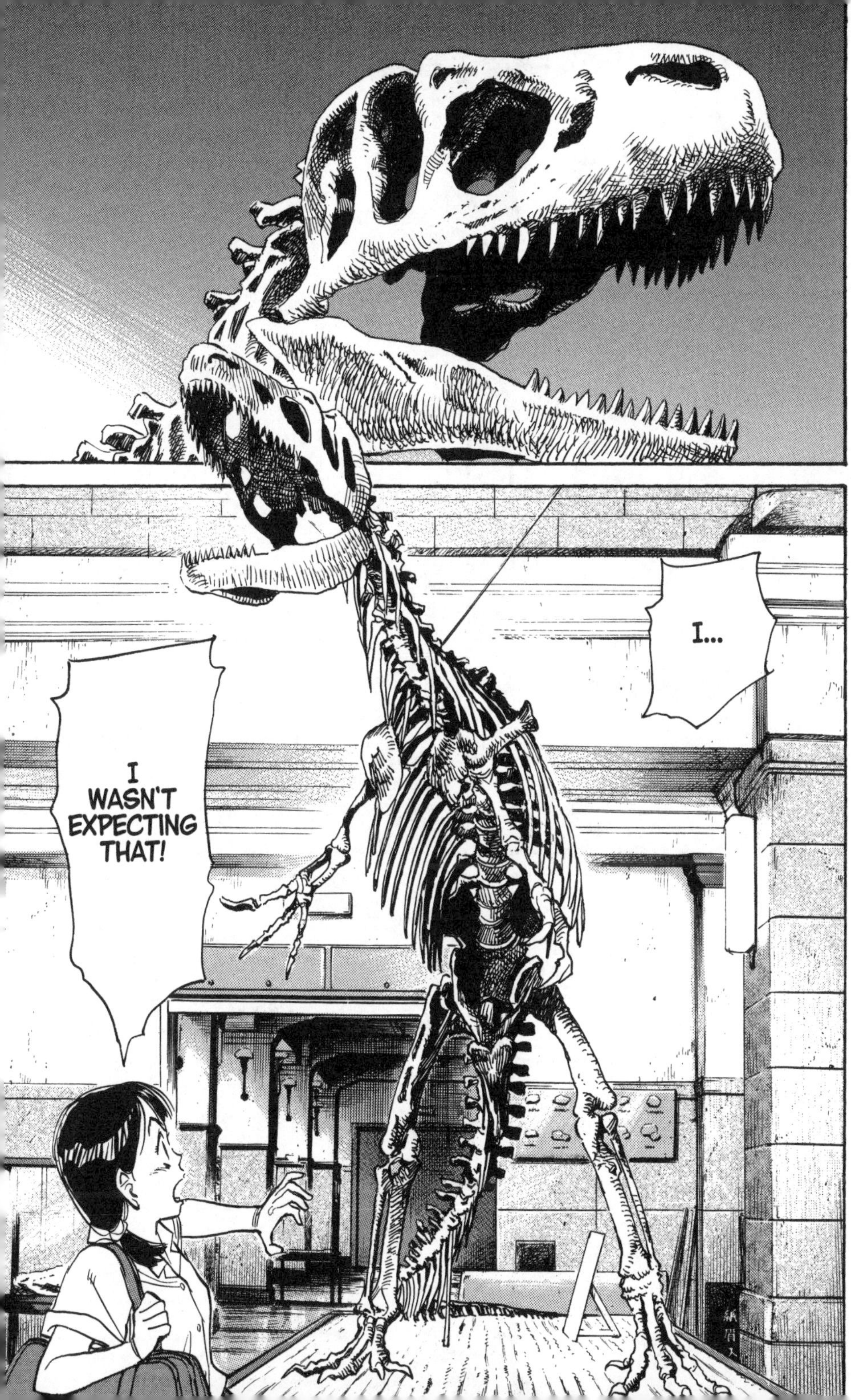
I...
I WASN'T EXPECTING THAT!

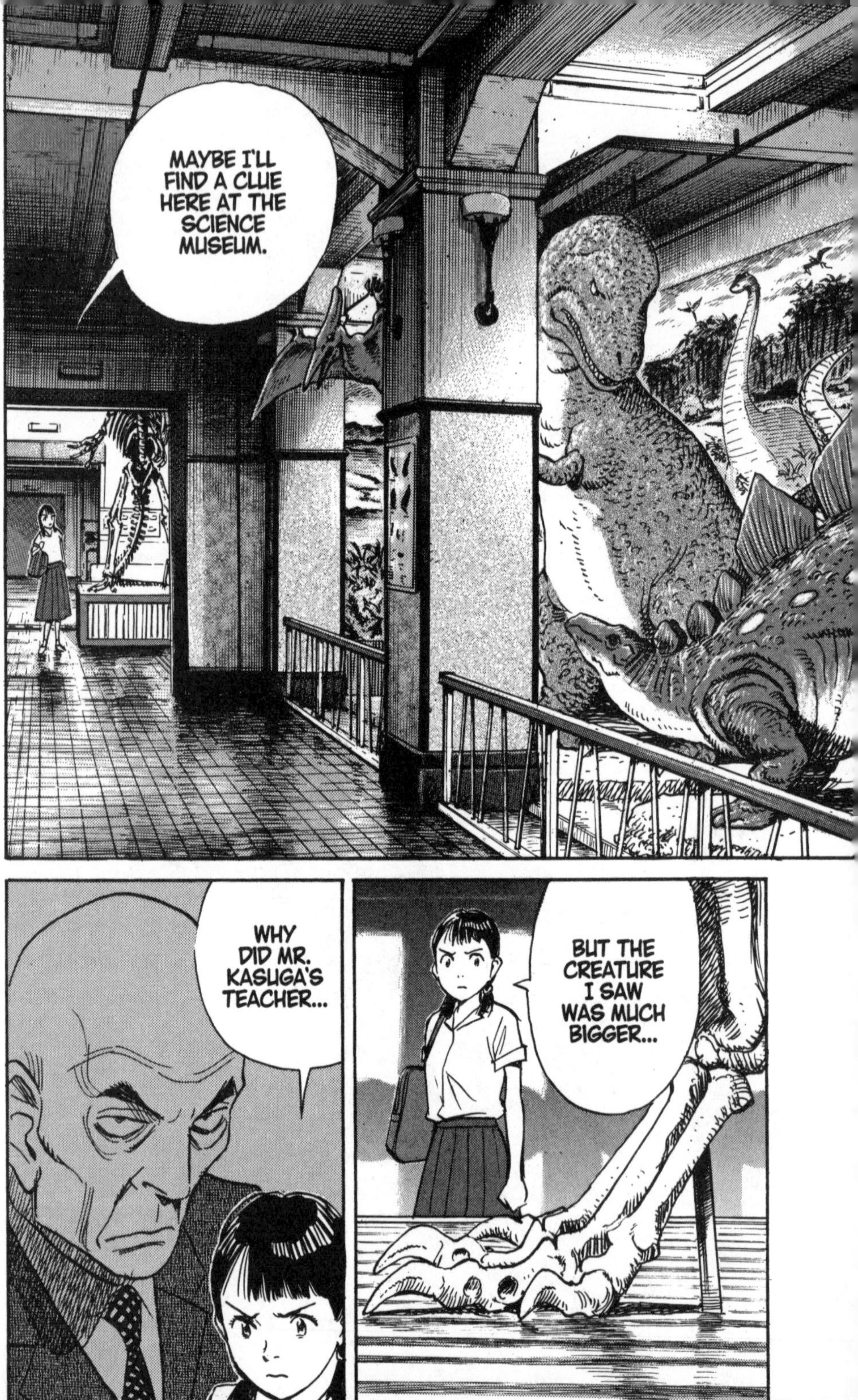
MAYBE I'LL FIND A CLUE HERE AT THE SCIENCE MUSEUM.
BUT THE CREATURE I SAW WAS MUCH BIGGER...
WHY DID MR. KASUGA'S TEACHER...

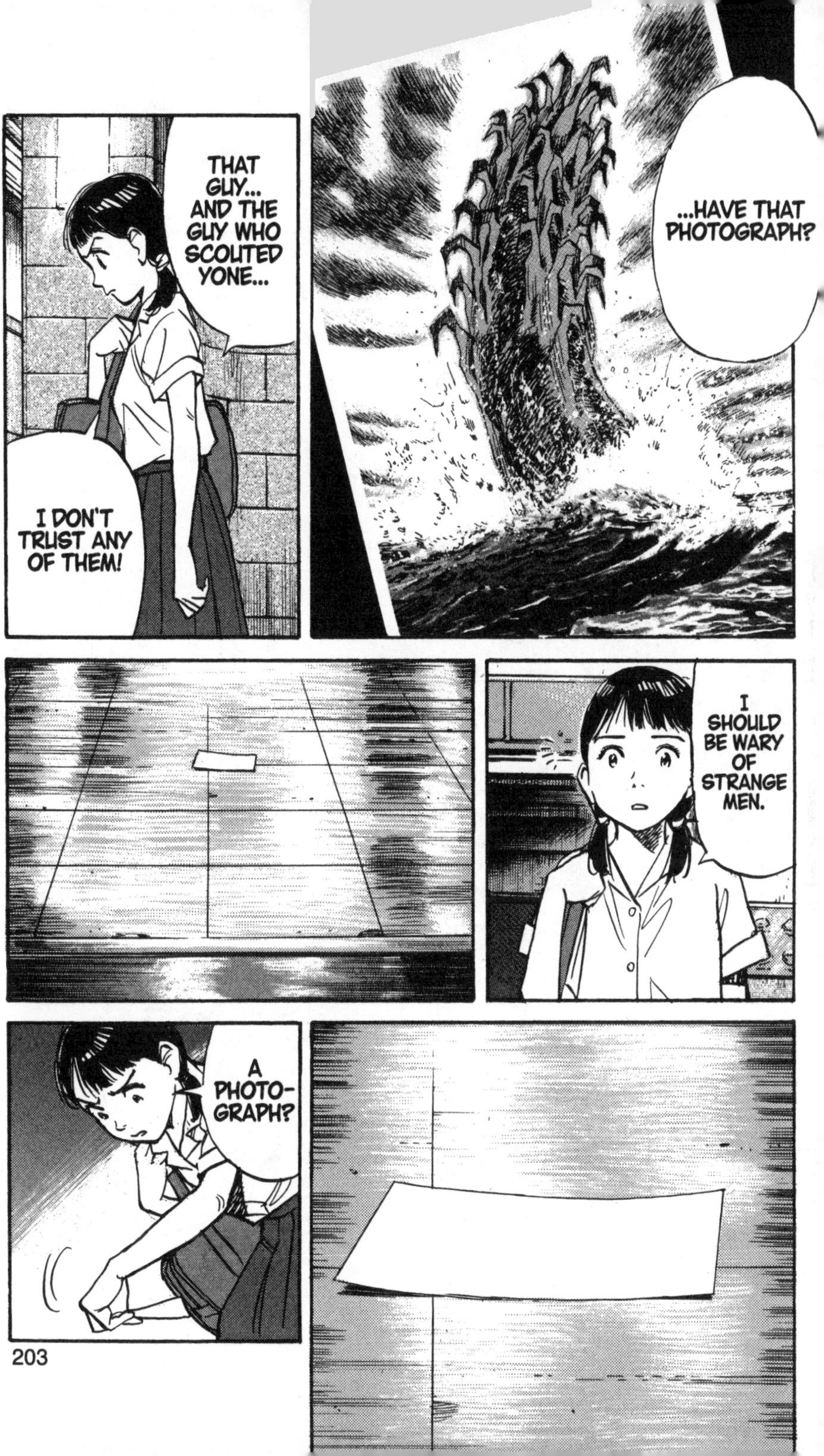
...HAVE THAT PHOTOGRAPH?
THAT GUY... AND THE GUY WHO SCOUTED YONE...
I DON'T TRUST ANY OF THEM!
I SHOULD BE WARY OF STRANGE MEN.
A PHOTO-GRAPH?

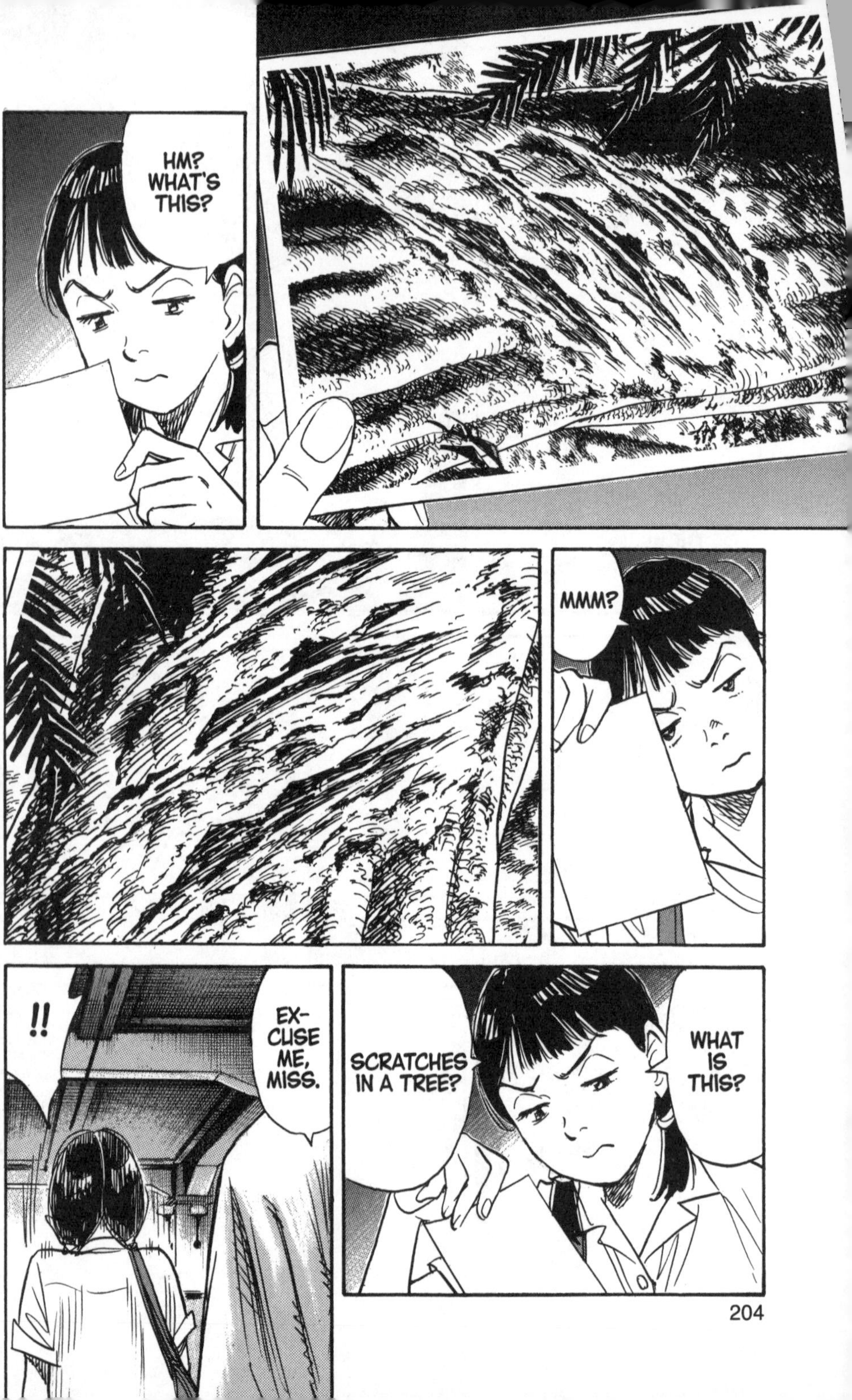
HM? WHAT'S THIS?
MMM?
WHAT IS THIS?
SCRATCHES IN A TREE?
EX-CUSE ME, MISS.
!!

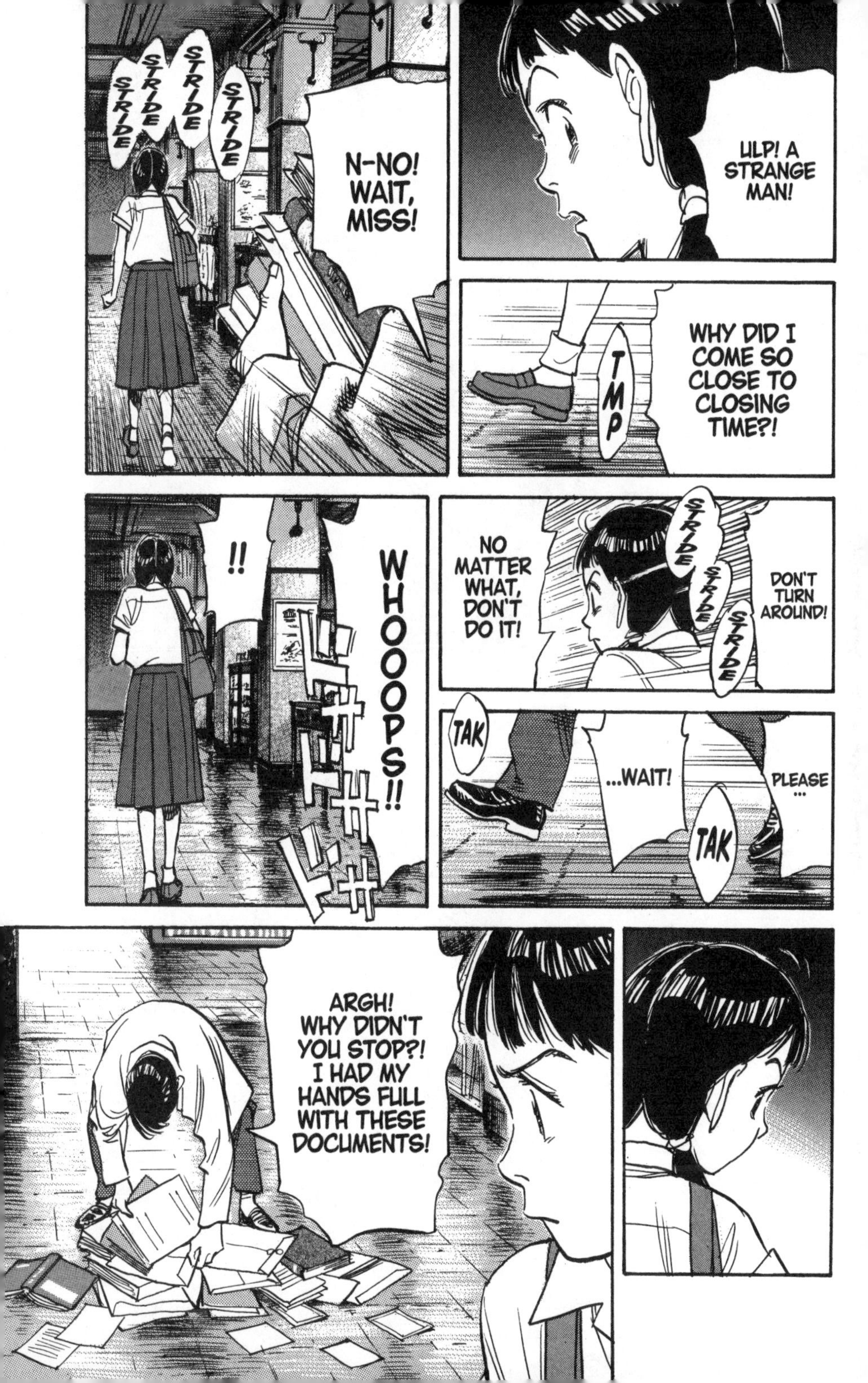
ULP! A STRANGE MAN!
TMP
WHY DID I COME SO CLOSE TO CLOSING TIME?!
STRIDE
STRIDE
STRIDE
STRIDE
N-NO! WAIT, MISS!
STRIDE
STRIDE
STRIDE
DON'T TURN AROUND!
NO MATTER WHAT, DON'T DO IT!
PLEASE ...
TAK
...WAIT!
TAK
WHOOOOPS!!
!!
ARGH! WHY DIDN'T YOU STOP?! I HAD MY HANDS FULL WITH THESE DOCUMENTS!

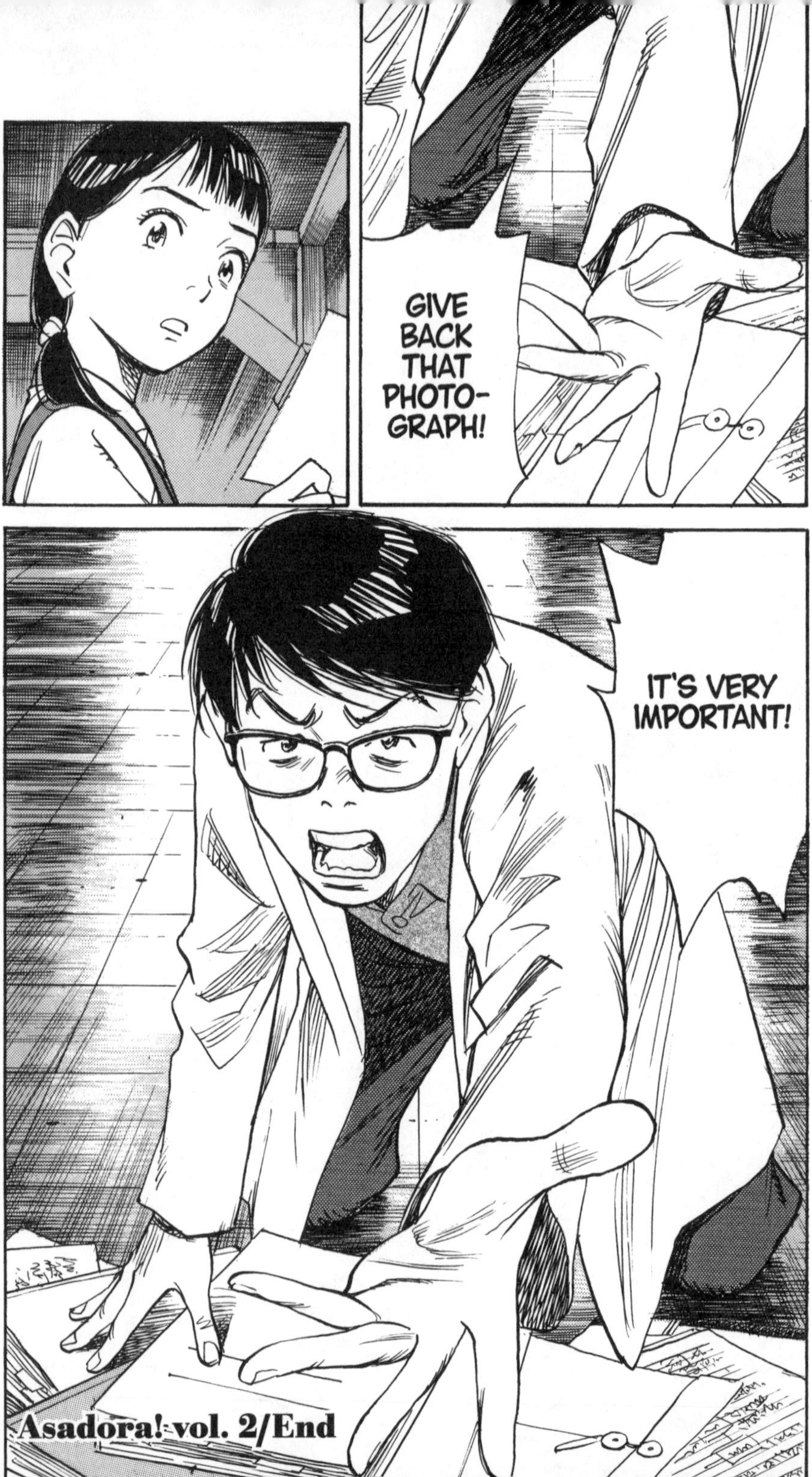
GIVE BACK THAT PHOTO-GRAPH!
IT'S VERY IMPORTANT!
Asadora! vol. 2/End

ASADORA!

To be continued...

Production Staff:
Hideaki Urano
Tohru Sakata

Cooperation:
Satoshi Akatsuka (TAC Photography)
Jun Takahashi
Nagoya Times, Archives Committee
Japan Aeronautic Association, Aviation Library
Hidetaka Shiba
Hajime Matsubara (The University Museum, The University of Tokyo)
National Museum of Nature and Science
Takeshi Ijichi (Ikaros Publications, Ltd.)
Chihiro Katsu
Nobuyuki Kojima
Satomi Danno

Editor:
Haruka Ikegawa

References:
Takahashi, Jun. *Jun-san no Ozora Jinsei, Oreryu* (Jun's Life in the Skies, My Way).
Assisted by Masahiro Kaneda. Ikaros Publications, Ltd.

Thank you to everyone else who offered help.

PAGE 173: Yokosuka, Japan, is known for the naval base United States Fleet Activities Yokosuka. The base is the United States' largest overseas naval installation. Situated south of Tokyo at the entrance to Tokyo Bay, the base is considered to be one of the United States' most strategically important military bases.

PAGE 186: The Peanuts were a vocal duo consisting of twin sisters Emi and Yumi Ito. The pair was discovered at a nightclub while they were still in high school. They went on to record original songs in the *kayokyoku* genre, a Japanese style of music that served as the foundation for modern J-pop.

PAGE 186: Mie Nakao, Yukari Ito and Mari Sono were popular singers during the fifties, sixties and seventies. The three singers starred in the teen movie *Hai, Hai Sannin Musume* (Yes, Yes, the Three Daughters).

PAGE 195: The science museum that Yone's parents took her to is the National Museum of Nature and Science in Ueno Park, Tokyo. Founded in 1877, the museum is one of the oldest in Japan and features comprehensive exhibitions of natural history and the history of science and technology.

Translation Notes

PAGE 117: The fairy tale Asa refers to is "Taro the Dragon Boy," which was originally published by children's author Miyoko Matsutani in 1960. The tale spawned several adaptations—a televised puppet series in Japan (1966), an anime (late 1970s) and an animated film (1979).

PAGE 165: The hammerhead turn, or stall turn, is an aerobatic maneuver in which the pilot flies the plane straight up until the airspeed drops to a certain critical point. Before the upward motion stops, the pilot uses the rudder to yaw the plane through a 180-degree cartwheel until the nose points straight down. The pilot then returns to level flight at the same altitude they started at, exiting the maneuver in the opposite direction.

PAGE 168: The Isewan Typhoon, also known as Typhoon Vera, was a real-life tropical cyclone that hit Japan in 1959. Isewan is estimated to have caused more than 5,000 fatalities, making it the deadliest typhoon to ever strike Japan. The widespread devastation it caused led the Japanese government to make significant improvements to its disaster management and relief systems.

Sound Effects Glossary

The sound effects in this edition of *Asadora!* have been preserved in their original Japanese format. To avoid additional lettering cluttering up the panels, a list of the sound effects is provided here. Each sound effect is listed by page and panel number; for example, "6.3" would mean the effect appears in panel 3 of page 6.

3.3 - fwap fwap (basasa: wings flapping)
19.1 - vrrr (buun: airplane)
35.3 - gwooosh (goooo: fast movement)
36.1 - smash smash (baki bakii: destroying)
36.3 - hwomp (doon: footstep)
41.6 - bdunk (zaa: landing)
45.1 - thrum vwsh (dorun dododo: propeller starting)
45.8 - vrrr (dodododo: airplane)
46.2 - vrr (buun: airplane)
51.8 - fwsh (ba: falling)
54.3 - vwoooo (vuuuuun: plummeting)
57.1-2 - gwooo (gooooo: airplane flying)
58.1 - ping pang (gan kiin: bullets striking)
58.2-3 - brakka brakka (dodododo: gunfire)
58.4 - kthunk (gashan: releasing torpedo)
58.7 - gwoosh (goo: flying)
59.8 - batatoom (dododo: anti-aircraft fire)
59.8 - boom baboom (bon dodon: explosions)
59.8 - bablam (papan: gunfire)
60-61.1 - ratta tatta (totatatatata: gunfire)
60-61.1 - babababablam (papapapapa: gunfire)
60-61.1 - brakka brakka (dodododo: gunfire)
62.1 - spak spakk (gan gagan: bullets striking)
62.3 - spash (bakin: window breaking)
62.3 - zing (kiin: bullet flying)
62.3 - shatter (barin: glass breaking)
62.2/4 - spak (gan: bullet striking)
65.1 - gwup (ga: gripping)
79.1 - thwap (bashii: slapping)
80.3 - hwup (da: leaping away)
80.4 - woosh (da: running)
93.3 - tump tump tump (ta ta ta: footsteps)
97.2 - tromp tromp (dota dota: running)
97.7 - vwoosh (vuun: airplane passing)
98.1 - vroosh (vuuuuun: airplane passing)
98.2 - bam (don: knocking aside)
101.4 - vwoom (vuan: airplane rising)
108.1 - kchunk (ga: moving lever)
108.2 - ktokk (ga: opening throttle)
108.3 - kwunk (ga: stepping on pedal)
120.2 - bwunk (da: landing)
121.3 - yaaay (waaa: shouting)

124.5 - woosh (da: running)
125.1 - hwoosh (byu: running faster)
126.3 - screech (kiii: truck stopping)
128.2 - honk honk honk (paa pappaa papaa: truck horns)
128.4 - honk (papaa: truck horn)
133.1 - whsh (za: approaching hospital)
133.2 - bam (dan: opening door)
133.3 - waaah (waaaan: commotion)
136.2-5 - clomp clomp clomp clomp clomp clomp clomp (za za za za za za za: footsteps)
151.2 - fwoosh (da: running)
152.1 - fwup (ba: entering room)
157.2-3 - vrrrrr (vuuuuun: airplane)
157.4 - vrr vrr (vuo vuo: airplane)
158.2 - whsh (ba: flying fast)
158.3 - vroosh (vuon: flying)
159.3 - vwoosh (vuan: flying)
160.1 - swoosh (zaa: banner)
161.1 - pachi pachi pachi pachi pachi: applause)
162.1 - clap clap clap clap clap clap (pachi pachi pachi pachi pachi pachi: applause)
162.2 - clap clap clap clap clap clap clap clap clap (pachi pachi pachi pachi pachi pachi pachi pachi pachi: applause)
162.3 - clap clap clap clap clap clap clap clap clap clap clap (pachi pachi pachi pachi pachi pachi pachi pachi pachi pachi pachi: applause)
163.1 - clap clap clap clap clap clap clap (pachi pachi pachi pachi pachi pachi pachi: applause)
163.1 - clap clap clap clap clap (pachi pachi pachi pachi pachi: applause)
163.2 - clap clap clap clap clap (pachi pachi pachi pachi pachi: applause)
163.2 - clap clap clap (pachi pachi pachi: applause)
164.3 - gwuf (ga: grabbing)
175.6 - fomp bomp (dota dota: stomping)
190.1 - fwap (ga: covering mouth)
190.2 - hwoosh (ba: fast movement)
192.5 - bamp (ban: closing book)
205.6 - tumble scatter tumble (dosa dosa dosa: dropping documents)

ASADORA!

Volume 2
VIZ Signature Edition

By **Naoki URASAWA/N WOOD STUDIO**

Translation & Adaptation John Werry
Touch-up Art & Lettering Steve Dutro
Design Jimmy Presler
Editor Karla Clark

ASADORA!
by Naoki URASAWA/N WOOD STUDIO
© 2019 Naoki URASAWA/N WOOD STUDIO
All rights reserved.
Original Japanese edition published by SHOGAKUKAN.
English translation rights in the United States of America, Canada,
the United Kingdom, Ireland, Australia and New Zealand arranged with SHOGAKUKAN.

Original Cover Design: Isao YOSHIMURA + Bay Bridge Studios

Printed in Canada

Published by VIZ Media, LLC
P.O. Box 77010
San Francisco, CA 94107

10 9 8 7 6 5 4 3 2 1
First printing, April 2021

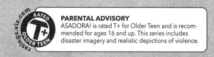

viz.com   vizsignature.com

This is the last page.

Asadora! has been printed in the original Japanese format
to preserve the orientation of the artwork.